# The
# Art of
# Aeschylus

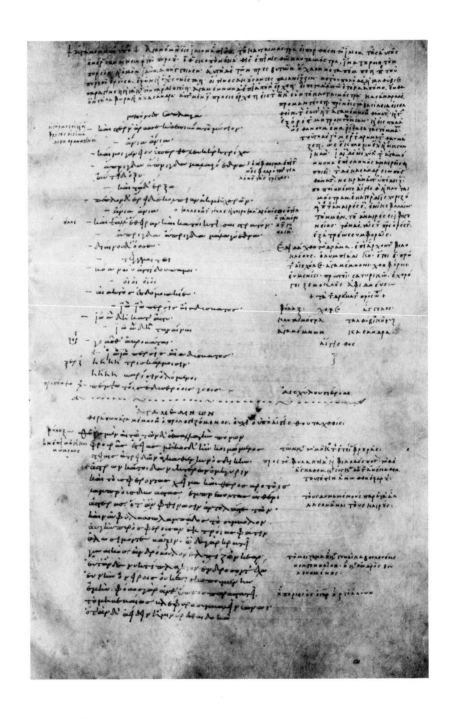

*Persians* 1070–77 and *Agamemnon* 1–16, from ms. Florentinus Laur. 32.9, of ca. 1000 A.D., courtesy of the Biblioteca Medicea Laurenziana in Florence. Photo by G. B. Pineider.

# The
# Art of
# Aeschylus

Thomas G. Rosenmeyer

UNIVERSITY OF CALIFORNIA PRESS

BERKELEY     LOS ANGELES     LONDON

University of California Press
Berkeley and Los Angeles, California

University of California Press, Ltd.
London, England

Library of Congress Cataloging in Publication Data

Rosenmeyer, Thomas G.
The art of Aeschylus.

Bibliography: p.
Includes indexes.
1. Aeschylus—Criticism and interpretation.
I. Title.
PA3829.R63      882'.01      81-1289
ISBN 0-520-04440-1

Printed in the United States of America


1  2  3  4  5  6  7  8  9

*For August Frugé*

Aeschylus's high-thinking, his old-style,
the unconventionality of his ideas and
of his diction, seemed proper to tragedy
and the ancient heroic manner. It had
no share in guile or prattle or vulgarity.
Dio of Prusa (*Oration* 52.4)


The tragic style of Aeschylus is still
imperfect. Now and then its constituents,
epic and lyric, are not properly fused.
He is often abrupt, immoderate, hard.
To succeed him with a more artful tragedy
was easy; in his almost superhuman
greatness he is likely to remain unexcelled. . . .
A. W. Schlegel

# CONTENTS

# ACKNOWLEDGMENTS

In the course of the many years during which this book has been moving toward its present shape, I have incurred more debts than I could possibly name. I am grateful to the National Endowment for the Humanities, to the University of California at Berkeley, and to Princeton University, whose support permitted me to take time out from teaching. Among the colleagues and friends who read part or all of the manuscript and lent me their counsel, let me mention Stephen Greenblatt, Robert Kinsman, Donald Mastronarde, Norman Rabkin, Raphael Sealey, Ronald Stroud, Florence Verducci, and three anonymous readers. Their kindness and their advice, even where it was not fully taken, have meant more than they can know. Among the members of the University of California Press who assisted me with the preparation of the book I am especially indebted to Doris Kretschmer, Marilyn Schwartz, and Mary Lamprech; and to Peter Dreyer, whose sure sense of style greatly improved a difficult text. Victoria Stafford eased the burden by helping with the references, the proofs, and the indexes. Finally, I am deeply grateful to two friends who encouraged me with detailed comments on all parts of the developing manuscript, at great cost to their time and patience: Mark Griffith, the Compleat Aeschylean; and the vigilant naturalist whose name appears in the dedication.

# ABBREVIATIONS
## USED IN THE NOTES

AJP   *American Journal of Philology*
CQ   *Classical Quarterly*
GRBS   *Greek, Roman and Byzantine Studies*
JHS   *Journal of Hellenic Studies*
TAPA   *Transactions of the American Philological Association*

NOTE: The fragments of Aeschylus are cited from H. W. Smyth, ed. and tr., *Aeschylus* (Cambridge, Mass., 1922, 1926; 2nd volume rev. H. Lloyd-Jones, 1957); or from H. J. Mette, ed., *Die Fragmente der Tragödien des Aischylos* (Berlin, 1959). Other tragic fragments are cited from A. Nauck, ed., *Tragicorum graecorum fragmenta* [2] (Leipzig, 1889). The fragments of lyric poety are cited from E. Diehl, *Anthologia lyrica* (Leipzig, 1936–54). The fragments of the Presocratics are cited from H. Diels and W. Kranz, eds. and trs., *Die Fragmente der Vorsokratiker* [6] (Berlin, 1952–56).

# Introduction

Aeschylus has always defied criticism. Most of the great dramatists have written plays which are, in a sense, replicas and modifications of others before them. They can be read against a model. Their effect in the theater can be measured by means of standards furnished by a living tradition. That is as true of Sophocles as it is of Racine or Kleist. It is not true of Aeschylus. To him, especially, applies that sense of loss which Hofmannsthal made the elegiac theme of his own career as a literary archaeologist: "How difficult, in our confusion, to hear a song that is pure and light. . . . of many things we have barely the name, like the name of an alien flower."[1] The distance and the foreignness of the roots of Western drama have seemed irrecoverable.

There is no dearth of specialized investigations of Aeschylean drama. Studies of Aeschylus's style, of the textual tradition, of the early stage, of his political thought, and much more, are published with increasing frequency. But general books on Aeschylean drama have, in English at least, always been a rarity. Comprehensive studies of Sophocles and of Euripides are readily available. But the last full treatment of Aeschylus is now more than a generation old.[2] The neglect of Aeschylus has a respectable history. Dryden, in his *Essay on Dramatic Poesy*, has his Crites talk admiringly of the ancient dramatists without even so much as mentioning Aeschylus, while in Eugenius's counterattack Aeschylus is referred to only once, in passing. Nor is the situation much different elsewhere. Stendhal, in the third chapter of the 1823 version of his *Racine et Shakespeare*, calls Sophocles and Euripides romantics, but has nothing to say about Aeschylus, an omission doubly curious in the light of Fontenelle's finding that "Aeschylus was a kind of madman, with an imagination too lively and not sufficiently controlled."[3] Fontenelle's gibe goes back ultimately to the deceptively harmless evaluation of Aeschylus in Aristophanes's *Frogs*. One wonders whether Victor Hugo had a clear idea of what he meant when he said that "anyone who does not understand Aeschylus is irremediably mediocre," for else-

---

1. H. von Hoffmannsthal, "Aufzeichnungen 1890–1895," *Corona* 9 (1939–40):681.

2. G. Murray, *Aeschylus* (Oxford, 1940). G. D. Thomson, *Aeschylus and Athens* (London, 1941) is idiosyncratic rather than general; E. T. Owen, *The Harmony of Aeschylus* (Toronto, 1952) is largely about the *Oresteia*; J. H. Finley, Jr., *Pindar and Aeschylus* (Cambridge, Mass., 1966) divides its attention between the two authors.

3. Bernard Le Bovier de Fontenelle, *Oeuvres complètes* (Paris, 1818), vol. 3, p. 235.

where his comments are clearly indebted to the Aristophanic perspective. [4] Throughout the nineteenth century, Aeschylean criticism, both pro and con, appears to have been scarcely more substantial than the silence that was usually his lot.

Now, however, it might be thought that the time for a general book on Aeschylus is long past. When the great classical scholars and critics Croiset, Murray, Smyth, and Reinhardt wrote their works, they intended to convey an impression of what Aeschylus meant to them, intellectually, politically, philosophically. [5] We are no longer quite so confident that such a meaning can be uncovered, or indeed that it needs uncovering. The study of dramatic forms has made tremendous progress in the past generation, with various typologies and countless historical data asserting their claims. The study of the authorial voice, of the function of the theater in society, of the scenic versus the topical has enriched and complicated our understanding (and our ignorance) and has made our task more difficult.

If in what follows I attempt, in spite of all the warning signals, to write a book that aspires to summarize what I consider significant in Aeschylus, my hope is that those who do not read Aeschylus in the original and who have little access to specialized studies may welcome the attempt. At the very least the book may assist some readers in avoiding some of the more common errors of perspective that tend to put the modern public at a disadvantage. An ancient dramatist can be read in a number of ways. It is possible to read him and thus to infer a dramatic experience in translation, any translation, as if the author were writing today and meant to speak to the issues that we see all about us. This is a valid approach, but it has certain shortcomings, and it may not give all the pleasure that Aeschylus is capable of giving. Conversely, it is possible to read the ancient author, either in the original or in a faithful translation, as if he spoke only to his contemporaries and therefore to no one today. That is assigning him to the basement of the museum.

My own reading of Aeschylus is calculated to move somewhere between these extremes. My hope is to recreate the author, or his shadow, in his setting, at his distance, while also showing that for all his remoteness and his time-bound concerns, Aeschylus should interest and move us. Between the extremes, my preferences and obligations put me closer to the footing of the historian. One cannot, to be sure, stage Aeschylus *à l'antique*. But a book about Aeschylus cannot do the job of the modern director who takes the ancient text as a point of departure. It must try to recover, with some degree of approximation, the ancient conditions and the ancient objectives,

4. Quoted by W. H. Matheson, *Claudel and Aeschylus* (Ann Arbor, Mich., 1965), p. 16.

5. M. Croiset, *Éschyle* (Paris, 1928); H. W. Smyth, *Aeschylean Tragedy* (Berkeley and Los Angeles, 1924); K. Reinhardt, *Aischylos als Regisseur und Theologe* (Bern, 1949).

and show that an appreciation of the distance is not incompatible with a realization of the power.[6] The book does not contain a chapter on Aeschylus's philosophy or on Aeschylus as a poet of ideas. The topic is at once too easy and too difficult. Incidental remarks on this head, especially in chapters 10 through 12, may be considered a token contribution. The principal goal of this study is to furnish various sets of information, ask some difficult questions, and, especially in the latter half of the book, suggest a number of readings, all of them designed to help the reader formulate his own view of where Aeschylus stands in the history of literate thought. George Steiner has recently revived a notion that goes back to Lukács and Voltaire and beyond, that Aeschylus was a "strong *Tendenzpoet*," but with the qualification "that the thesis must spring from the situation and action itself, without being explicitly displayed. . . . there is no compulsion for the writer to put into the reader's hands the future historical resolution of the social conflicts which he is depicting."[7] For Aeschylus we may wish to add that where we find him saying things that lend themselves to exploitation by systematic, especially Marxist, critics, they should be regarded as occasions, not for teaching, but for reminding. They tend to evoke insights the audience in the theater would readily acknowledge. Ideas, if that is not too pale a term for a drama that proceeds lyrically as much as discursively, represent assent no less than invention. As we shall see, they can also mislead.

Some of the key terms that have loomed large in discussions indebted to Renaissance criticism, such as *hero, hamartia, pathos,* and *catastrophe,* are rarely found in this book. Nor, on the other hand, does the discussion take its cue from the recently powerful stimulus regarding tragedy as a subspecies of religion. Such critics as Otto, Spira, and Burnett, reacting salutarily against the skepticism of the nineteenth century, see in the ancient dramatic texts a vindication and celebration of the works of the gods among men.[8] My discussion will show where I part company with them. On a related issue, I am not going to say anything about the possible roots of Greek tragedy. The current controversy, ably carried out between the ritualists and those who prefer to derive drama from earlier literary sources, will

6. I hope I will be forgiven if for the present purpose I disregard the hermeneutic quandary associated with the names of Heidegger and Gadamer and the *Nouvelle Critique.*
7. The words are those of Engels writing to Minna Kautsky in 1885. They are cited by G. Steiner in E. and T. Burns, eds., *Sociology of Literature and Drama* (Harmondsworth, 1973), p. 159. Lukács, in his pre-Marxist days, was less circumspect: "The Greek knows only answers, no questions; only solutions (albeit enigmatic ones), no enigmas" (*Die Theorie des Romans* [Berlin, 1920], p. 10).
8. W. F. Otto, *Die Götter Griechenlands* (Bonn, 1929); A. Spira, *Untersuchungen zum Deus ex Machina bei Sophokles und Euripides* (Kallmünz, 1960); A. Burnett, *Catastrophe Survived* (Oxford, 1971).

be left to one side.[9] We shall take Aeschylus as we have him, and only now and then will we take note of the possibility that this or that feature of the text may be the echo of a conjectured antecedent.

I am aware of not having imposed full interpretive consistency on the material. That there are deeper identities in Aeschylus's art is evident to anyone who has grappled with it, but we can hardly fathom them by clamping a system on its exuberance. Perhaps the post-structuralist insight is correct, and "the force, the power of any text, even the most unabashedly mimetic, lies in those moments which exceed our ability to categorize, which collide with our interpretive codes but nevertheless seem right." The same writer goes on to say that "the criticism which encounters the greatest success is one which attends to its strangeness, awakening in it a drama whose actors are all those assumptions and operations which make the text the work of another period." [10] The imagery from drama is of interest here. It is as if the writer felt that a play, the most popular and hence the most time-conditioned of literary artifacts, lends itself to critical analysis only to the degree that it is strange and virtually (and appealingly) incomprehensible. Aeschylus might well be the model text for this approach.

Modern literary and dramatic criticism cannot do without some perception of social and sociological insights. Not only for *Danton's Death* but also for *Miss Julie* and *The Flies* and *Rhinoceros* we need some understanding of the dislocations and disenchantments in the spiritual and material environment of the author and his public. What can we do in the case of ancient tragedy? The concept of class, chimerical enough for twentieth-century America, is quite empty for the fifth century B.C. Our knowledge of how the average theatergoer felt about his society and his place in it is defective. To what extent can a play by Aeschylus be said to reflect experiences, or hopes, or frustrations known to the audience? We do know that Greek drama was a political reality. It was performed under the supervision of the magistrates. Its setting is analogous to that of a jury court. Only men participate as actors, because only men are citizens. The contest between the playwrights is arranged along the lines of the rivalry among boroughs. Perhaps *civic* is a better term than *political*; the *palio* at Siena is a surviving analogue. In my discussion I have paid little attention to these civic conditions of performance. The farcical comments of Aristophanes and other comedians suggest that the plays were appreciated as "play," perhaps the more easily because political and judicial oratory was also enjoyed in relative abstraction from the tangible issues to which it was directed. Other scholars have succeeded

9. For a recent ritualist treatment, see F. R. Adrados, *Festival, Comedy, and Tragedy: The Greek Origins of Theatre* (Leiden, 1975). The classic statement of the anti-ritualist position is by G. F. Else, *The Origin and Early Form of Greek Tragedy* (Cambridge, Mass., 1965).

10. J. Culler, *Structuralist Poetics* (Ithaca, N.Y., 1975), pp. 261–62.

in situating Aeschylean drama in the contemporary field of specific ambitions, rivalries, and commitments.[11] The danger of subjective guesswork and willful combination dogs nearly every step in this important endeavor of the historical imagination. My own talents do not lie in that direction, and I have thought it better to avoid it altogether.

I have tried to let all the plays and some of the fragments speak. That the *Oresteia* receives the lion's share of attention will, I hope, be excused, especially in the last chapter, where talk about any other trilogy would have been, given the state of our knowledge, pure speculation. More disappointingly, perhaps, there will be no interpretation of individual plays. My purpose has been to assemble and analyze some of the techniques, concerns, and choices that seem to me to be present in most of the plays. It would be priggish to pretend that this information is not itself shaped by my own responses, hidden as well as conscious, to the plays. In this sense my observations may be regarded as a substitute for more systematic readings. I would be the first to acknowledge that there are grave disadvantages to tearing the plays apart and writing across them. Each play has its special quality which will go unnoticed (except in passing) as I explore the features that are true of Aeschylus's work in general and that are bound to undergo subtle or even extensive modification from play to play.

My way of dealing with the material rules out the possibility of tracing Aeschylus's development as a dramatist. Is not *Agamemnon* a more mature play than *Persians?* Possibly. But the developmental approach has on occasion done less than justice to the earlier plays—and it should be remembered that the earliest we have, *Persians*, was produced when Aeschylus was already in his fifties. More important, the constants in Aeschylus's art seem to me to outweigh the mutations. Even *Agamemnon*, I suggest, contains features whose elucidation makes an understanding of *Persians* richer. I would not wish to go as far as Bradley, who asks about the "substance of a Shakespearean tragedy, taken in abstraction both from its form and from the differences in point of substance between one tragedy and another."[12] Bradley himself, happily, proceeds to pay ample attention to form and differentiae. There is, as far as I can imagine it, no such thing as the substance of an Aeschylean play in Bradley's sense. And in any case, each of the plays will receive at least a partial coverage on the occasion that appears to demand it. Thus *Persians* will loom large in the chapter on plot, *Agamemnon* in the chapter on the chorus, *Eumenides* in the chapter on the trilogy. As for *Prometheus*, for the purposes of the discussion I shall assume that its Aeschylean authorship is firm, though in my private thoughts I am by no means

11. See, e.g., A. J. Podlecki, *The Political Background of Aeschylean Tragedy* (Ann Arbor, Mich., 1966).

12. A. C. Bradley, *Shakespearian Tragedy* (London, 1905), p. 5.

convinced.[13] It is a curious play, characterized by formal and structural features which set it apart from the rest. I shall not refer to it as frequently as to the other plays. But it would not for these many years have been accepted as Aeschylean if it did not share with the other plays some important identities. The method of discussion I have chosen will make it possible to do some limited justice to its peculiarities as well as to its conformities.

Each of the topics taken up in the several chapters involves some intelligence concerning others. We cannot talk about the use of animal imagery unless we also talk about characters; we cannot talk about pity as a choral sentiment unless we also address ourselves to the issues of justice and its tempering. It thus became impossible to organize the material in the shape of a logically advancing plot. Things that belong together had to be separated, with minimal advertisement of the significant connections. Occasionally, as between chapters 9 and 10, a substantial overlap made for a certain amount of duplication. I hope the results will still be digestible.

The first few chapters, especially chapters 1 and 2, are of a rather technical nature. I felt that in talking about an ancient dramatist it was important that some of the fundamental conditions of the transmission of the text, of the formal conventions of his art, and of the ancient staging, be presented at the outset, so that the more rarefied critical discussion to follow would emerge from, and be judged against, the background of the stubborn—and sometimes deplorably unstubborn—facts. If the caveats in chapter 1 concerning the state of the Aeschylean text are found distressing, the gains for a more vigilant stance on the part of the critic will, I hope, make up for them. I have tried to present the information as simply and untechnically as I could, using English terms (with the Greek term on its first occurrence in parentheses) where this promised to lighten the reader's load. Barring the risk of a loss in historical exactitude, my principal goal was not to permit needless jargon to interpose itself between the material and its appreciation by an interested non-classicist.

Aeschylean scholarship and criticism have produced a formidable body of exegesis. I have tried to read as much of it as I could. Many of my formulations and responses were shaped by earlier commentators. Of them I give a selection; to indicate the principles of selection would only serve to give needless offense to those who might justly have expected to be cited. Oliver Taplin's two admirable studies (see Bibliography) appeared after my manuscript was complete; I could do little more than add a few references to them. I did not come across Hugh Parry's valuable *The Lyric Poems of Greek Tragedy* until after my book had gone to the printer. Because of the kind of reader for whom the book is intended, sparingness of documentation was

---

13. See M. Griffith, *The Authenticity of "Prometheus Bound"* (Cambridge, 1977).

imperative. Aeschylus's text is cited from the standard editions of Page, Murray, Fraenkel, and Groeneboom.[14] Though there is much room for questioning details of the text (see also chapter 1), large-scale philological discussion had to be avoided. For controverted passages I accept the reading of the text on which most modern editors agree, or which seems to me the most commendable. Only on rare occasions will the choice of a reading be argued.

I take it for granted that the reader knows the rough outlines of what happens in the plays, and does not need the kind of summary plot information which, in the case of Aeschylus, is even less of an aid than for most dramatists. Line references are to the Greek text of Page; their match with the line numbering of the Chicago corpus of *The Complete Greek Tragedies* is not always exact.[15] The translations are my own, except where credited to their authors.

14. G. Murray, ed., *Aeschyli Tragoediae*[2] (Oxford, 1955); D. Page, ed., *Aeschyli Tragoediae* (Oxford, 1972); see also J. D. Denniston and D. Page, eds. and comms., *Aeschylus: Agamemnon* (Oxford, 1957); E. Fraenkel, ed., tr., and comm., *Aeschylus: Agamemnon* (Oxford, 1950). P. Groeneboom's annotated editions of individual plays (Groningen, 1928–) are still useful.

15. D. Grene and R. Lattimore, eds., *Aeschylus* (Chicago, 1959).

# Hard Data

# 1

# Text and Transmission

It is only by the narrowest escape route that Fortune has given us the few plays by Aeschylus that we have. In the second half of the fifth century B.C., when Aeschylus's fame was great and his memory was honored by a special charter of re-performance, it seemed as if his works would live forever. Master copies used in the productions were deposited in the Sanctuary of the Mother, the public archives. Additional copies made from these standard versions or pirated at the time of the original performances found their way into private homes. There is some evidence that private performances, or at least readings, were not unknown. The spoofing of Aeschylus in Aristophanes's *Frogs* and other comedies of the time demonstrates that the old plays, of which there seem to have been more than eighty, continued to be the property of stage-struck men—which is to say, of most Athenians. But the comic quotations also show something else: the fact that there could be a doubt about the reading of this or that passage. In the second half of the fourth century, if we can trust the evidence of Aristotle and the orators, Aeschylus lost some of his popularity, yielding pride of place to Sophocles and especially to Euripides, who even then appeared to be more immediately assimilable. But in the third century, after the establishment of the kingdoms of Alexander's successors, the archaizing preferences of the court literati brought about a moderate renaissance of interest in Aeschylus.[1]

It was only natural that when Ptolemy Euergetes, ruler of Egypt, a little after 240 B.C. authorized his principal minister of culture, the chief librarian of the Library of Alexandria, to acquire a reliable set of Aeschylus for his shelves, he would send to Athens for a loan of the copy in the city archives. To what degree that copy furnished a text that was incontestably Aeschylean is now impossible to tell, as it was then. Some classical scholars suspect that, beginning with the premiere performance of a piece, successful actors would recommend modifications in the author's text. The Shakespearean model is obvious. One of the reasons that early editors adulterated

---

1. The evidence for the statements in the first paragraph, as in those to follow, is now most conveniently assembled in A. Wartelle, *Histoire du texte d'Éschyle dans l'antiquité* (Paris, 1971). See also R. Pfeiffer, *History of Classical Scholarship* (Oxford, 1968), pp. 192 ff., passim. For the number of plays written by Aeschylus, see Appendix below. Most scholars, including Wartelle, are doubtful about the deposition of master copies in the Metroon as early as the fifth century B.C. But without some such recognition of an official text, parallel to the recognition Pisistratus accorded to an official text of Homer, the transmission of the Aeschylean text would be difficult to account for.

Shakespeare's text was the thought that some of the original lines did not give the great actors the scope they felt they needed. We know that in the two centuries after Aeschylus's death the actor's status was similarly enhanced at the expense of the prestige of the playwright. A leading actor may well have insisted on certain liberties with a text that did not seem to him to give him the opportunities he craved. Such actors' interpolations have been detected in some of the plays of Euripides, notably *Iphigenia in Aulis*.[2] It should be remembered, however, that Euripides chose not to act in his plays, while Aeschylus did act in his and was in a position to protect his text against the idiosyncrasies of his fellow actors and to record modifications accepted by him in the production copy.

We cannot, on the other hand, reject the possibility that, on the occasion of re-performances of Aeschylus's works, when the archival text would be dusted off to serve as the principal document of reference, changes and inventions prompted by the taste of a new generation were embodied in the master copy. We simply do not know whether the officials in charge of the archives saw a need to distinguish between a book text and a stage text, between an original version and what might be called a functioning version. For the fourth century B.C., such a distinction is by no means certain. Unlike an author like Plato, whose writings were cherished and protected by disciples who venerated his utterance as that of a god (the divine Plato, as he was soon to be called), Aeschylus had no worshippers save producers and actors who regarded his text as directors and actors have always regarded secular dramatic texts: as documents to be brought to life, respectfully, but not slavishly—that means, with some changes required by the circumstances of the performance.[3]

The Athenian copy of Aeschylus which became the property of the great Library of Alexandria, and from which all later standard editions of Aeschylus are thought to be derived, may not have contained an authoritative text, going back in every detail to Aeschylus's own finished versions of the plays. Fortunately, two considerations permit us to be more hopeful. First, the very difficulty of the text that has come down is its own guarantee. I shall have something to say about the special difficulties of Aeschylus's style, and about corruptions in the text, caused by Medieval scribes not knowing what to make of a passage and transcribing it without understanding. Undue actors' interference would have smoothed out the difficulties—perhaps this

2. D. L. Page, *Actors' Interpolations in Greek Tragedy* (Oxford, 1934). Recent scholarship has tended to doubt that the ancient dramatic texts contain a significant number of actors' interpolations. See, e.g., D. J. Mastronarde, "Are Euripides *Phoinissai* 1104–1140 Interpolated?" *Phoenix* 32 (1978): 105–28.

3. Mark Griffith reminds me that Aeschylus may have been the object of a cult in Sicily. But if this was the case, the veneration did not extend to regarding the Aeschylean text as holy writ.

did happen in the case of *Prometheus*—and substituted language that would have presented no obvious problems to the copyists. It appears, then, that the Alexandrian version or versions continued to exhibit at least some of the peculiarities of Aeschylus's diction which Aristophanes lampooned.

The other consideration that furnishes grounds for optimism is the quality of Alexandrian scholarship. The men in charge of the library had access to secondary copies as well as to the principal records. They did some limited collating of texts for the purpose of putting out their own editions of and commentaries on the classical authors. While the Aeschylean corpus originated roughly three hundred years before this effort was well under way, we have reason to believe that the Alexandrian scholars were able to eliminate the worst accretions to the text, if such existed. One instructive exception is the ending of *Seven*—that is, roughly, lines 861–74 and 1005–78. Though effective voices continue to be heard in defense of the authenticity of these lines, most scholars today condemn them as unworthy of Aeschylus.[4] Chances are that they were added to the play on the occasion of a later performance, when Sophocles's *Antigone* had predisposed the spectators to dissatisfaction with Aeschylus's ending. There are difficulties with this conjecture, but the alternative, accepting the lines as part of the original dramatic plan, fails to meet some very damaging objections. The lines in question introduce a herald, who announces that the corpse of Polynices will be cast out without burial; and Antigone, who affirms her decision to oppose the new order and to bury her brother and who then engages the herald in heated debate. Some of the arguments against authenticity, quite apart from linguistic and stylistic considerations, run as follows. In the body of the play, Eteocles is the ruler of the city; in the ending, the constitution of the city appears to be democratic. Before the messenger arrives, all of the action tends to suggest that the two brothers will be buried together. Ismene, who is said to have entered with Antigone, is given nothing to say. Most important, however, the new development disturbs the settlement that is expected at the conclusion of the final play of a trilogy, a pacification which is most appropriately accomplished by the choral sequences that terminate with line 1004. The case for spuriousness seems to me compelling. Antigone and Ismene may or may not have appeared on stage, but all the singing of the last 169 lines (822–60, 875–1004), forming a massive multiple lament, was probably done by the chorus.

The exception must put us on our guard. Still, let us assume that the Alexandrian texts of Aeschylus were, for the most part, a tolerably reliable

---

4. See now R. D. Dawe, "The End of the *Seven Against Thebes* Yet Again," *Dionysiaca by Former Pupils of Denys Page* (Cambridge, 1978), pp. 87–103. Dawe rejects a larger portion of the text than others would. For a defense of the contested ending, see H. Lloyd-Jones, "The End of the Seven Against Thebes," *CQ* 9 (1959): 80–115.

replica, even if not in every instance a precise duplicate, of what the author had intended. They contained most, if not all, of his plays, or at least the plays then known to have been written by him.[5] Just about the time that the text came to be assured in this manner, the performance of Aeschylus ceased. During the last two centuries before our era, only scholars and grammarians interested themselves in his work. Nor was Aeschylus popular among the Romans. The Roman declamatory tradition preferred the easily adaptable morality tales and intrigues of Euripides to the stiffer constructions of the older tragedian. The plays continued to be read and discussed and excerpted. The entries concerning Aeschylus in Horace, Quintilian, and other critics imply a firsthand acquaintance with the material. There came a time, however, when the full corpus appeared to be a luxury that could no longer be afforded.

Probably in the third century of our era, someone made a selection of seven plays, the seven which we now have, and produced an edition of the text, with separate commentaries, in the tradition started by the Alexandrians. Later, during the early Byzantine period, a further selection of three plays—the so-called Byzantine triad, consisting of *Prometheus*, *Seven Against Thebes*, and *Persians*—was made, and, a somewhat earlier innovation, material from the existing commentaries was entered in the margins and between the lines of the text. Thus the students for whose benefit the select editions were made no longer had to consult separate volumes, but could find on the same page as the text the aids they needed to understand unusual words or difficult verse forms or historical or topographical data. Finally, some time after this, two of the remaining four plays, *Agamemnon* and *Eumenides*, were combined with the triad for a definitive edition of five. Thus Alexandrian and Byzantine learning and conservatism combined to assure us of the continuous transmission of five plays, but at a terrible cost. Just as surely as bad coin drives out good, so select editions lead to the loss of the material not accepted into the more manageable canon. It was, therefore, a very unusual stroke of good fortune which saw, ca. 1423 A.D., at the threshold of the age of printing, the arrival in Italy of an older manuscript, dating from about 1000 A.D. and containing the Roman selection of seven plays rather than the Byzantine selection of three or five. This was the famous Codex Laurentianus, called *M* for "Mediceus" after the Medici who founded the collection of which it is a part. It is a sumptuous parchment volume, containing also the works of Sophocles and Apollonius Rhodius and richly equipped with annotations and comments. If it had not reached the Italian humanists when it did, we would not now have the remaining two plays, *Libation-Bearers* and *Suppliants*.

The manuscripts in which the text of the plays has come to us are of

5. See Appendix below.

varying value, and modern scholars are not always agreed on their relative usefulness.[6] Some of them reflect the triadic edition, others the edition of five; there are also manuscripts which owe their inclusion of *Libation-Bearers* and of *Suppliants* to M. In many cases the manuscripts represent a mixed tradition. That is, even a manuscript that appears to transmit, say, the triadic line may, in its constitution of the text, draw upon authorities closer to the edition of five, or even the older edition of seven. The age of a manuscript is not a guarantee of its value. A more recent book may, through the sources from which it derives, incorporate older and better readings. The chief bone of contention among scholars today is the extent to which certain Byzantine manuscripts are rendered useless by the very fact that their scribes were excellent students of ancient Greek rather than slavish copyists, and were therefore tempted to replace difficult or unintelligible readings with their own emendations. The issue is more acute in the plays of the triad than in the others; least so in *Libation-Bearers* and *Suppliants*. *Prometheus* has come to us with a great welter of textual variants, and with voluminous notes to assist the understanding. *Suppliants*, on the other hand, is furnished with very few notes and offers much less choice in textual matters. We assume that because the text of *Suppliants* is relatively untouched by Byzantine learning, we can be more certain of it closely resembling the text that was available in the third century A.D.

Though modern scholarship is rarely inclined to regard one manuscript as vastly superior to others, there is agreement that M is very much the best of our authorities, less distorted by emendations or by simple copying errors than the rest. It is, therefore, a matter of great regret that it is defective. It lacks most of *Agamemnon* (lines 311–1066 and 1160–1673) and the beginning of *Libation-Bearers*. For *Agamemnon* we have to rely on manuscripts of the thirteenth to the fifteenth centuries, all of them potentially affected by Byzantine zeal. For the missing beginning of *Libation-Bearers* we have, alas, no substitute at all. The loss of most of *Agamemnon*, or rather our forced reliance on a more questionable tradition for the bulk of the lines, is especially awkward in view of the lexical difficulty of the play. Once again, however, it looks as if the Byzantine scholars checked their touch-up pens and permitted the Aeschylean wording to remain largely intact. Still, to gain an appreciation of the superiority of M over its rivals, it may be useful to cite some pertinent passages.

At *Eum.* 111, the ghost of Clytemnestra says of Orestes that he has escaped the hunting nets of the Furies, in the manner of ————. At this point, the later Byzantine tradition has "a dead man," *nekrou*, which is obviously nonsense. M has the right reading: "a fawn," *nebrou*. (In line 246

---

6. The principal treatment of the question is now that of R. D. Dawe, *The Collation and Investigation of Manuscripts of Aeschylus* (Cambridge, 1964).

the dead man has, alas, found his way even into *M*, which is, of course, not infallible.) At *Eum*. 450 and 452, Orestes talks about his purification, which was effected with water and the blood of animals. For "animals," *botou* and *botoisi*, read by *M*, other manuscripts offer "mortals," *brotou* and *brotoisi*, as if Orestes could hope to be purified, within the civilizing expectations of *Eumenides*, by human sacrifice. At *Eum*. 526, the Furies counsel a golden mean between enslavement to a ruler and a life of anarchy. For the latter, *anarkton*, read by *M*, the later tradition substitutes "a life of inadequacy," *anarketon*. Now it looks as if *nekrou* were a plain mistake, which could have happened anywhere along the line of the centuries-old transmission. But *brotou* and *anarketon* are such peculiar readings that the notion of a deliberate change on the basis of specific assumptions or theories concerning culture, language, metrics, or the like cannot be ruled out.[7]

There are times when *M* has the inferior reading. At *Eum*. 697, where Athena, in imitation of the counsel of the Furies, recommends a life half way between despotism and anarchy, *M* has a meaningless "you," *sethen*, in the place of the correct "cherish," *sebein*, read elsewhere. In this case, however, *M* records the correct reading in a marginal note. In any event, the frequency with which *M* is right against other manuscripts is far in excess of the reverse. The few samples listed here for just one play can be duplicated many times for all seven plays, including the portion of *Agamemnon* contained in *M*.

I have already spoken of the notes incorporated in the texts of most of the important manuscripts. They are often disappointing; the commentators were interested chiefly in matters of linguistic usage and of mythology. But some of these notes, called *scholia* (miniature lectures), are very old, and ultimately derive from the commentaries of the first Alexandrian critics. On occasion they can help us to restore a reading or an understanding that had become obscured. At *Seven* 212–13, for instance, all the manuscripts, including *M*, read roughly: "When there was the thunder of snow / snowing at the gates," a phrase whose ambitiousness appears to exceed even Aeschylean standards. Fortunately the scholiast in *M* comments, "the crashing of stones," and this prompted a nineteenth-century scholar to substitute a poetic word for "stones," *lithados*, in the place of "snow," *niphados*. Whether the thunder of rocks snowing at the gates is more acceptable than the more daring phrase in the manuscripts will remain uncertain.[8]

Other notes, especially those that must be associated with the later learn-

7. In fact, the variant readings are found in a manuscript written by Demetrius Triclinius of the early fourteenth century, no slavish copier but a scholar of erudition and independent judgment.

8. See T. G. Rosenmeyer, "On Snow and Stones," *California Studies in Classical Antiquity* 11 (1978): 209–25.

ing, but also some of the older scholia, can be misleading. At *Agam.* 257, the "sole protector and bulwark of this ancient land" is said to be a reference not to Clytemnestra but to the chorus itself, as if the chorus could logically reinforce its prayer by instancing its own desires and as if the old men were already convinced that Clytemnestra was an enemy. This will not do, though some critics have followed the suggestion. At any event, fairness demands that we pay our respects to the ancient and medieval commentators. Throughout the various periods in which the Aeschylean corpus was studied and copied there was much genuine concern for a proper understanding of the text. We owe some fine insights to the late Byzantine humanists who helped to secure the texts so that their Italian successors had them when the invention of printing rescued them for good.

In addition to the scholia, *M* and some of its peers contain three other types of information that were thought to be useful to those who wanted to study the plays: (1) a catalogue of the tragedies and satyr plays by Aeschylus; (2) a description of his life; and (3) the so-called *hypotheseis,* summaries of the action of each play, with additional data about the circumstances of performance. All three present great difficulties to modern research. The catalogue appears in two versions, which cannot be made to agree fully with one another or with the production lists that have been excerpted from other sources, such as incidental references in other ancient writers. The life may go back to a life written by one of Aristotle's students. It is full of valuable information, but needs to be supplemented and corrected with data from other ancient authorities. Finally, the *hypotheseis* or *argumenta* vary from play to play. In some cases they are relatively complete (*Persians, Prometheus, Agamemnon*), in others less so. For *Suppliants* and *Libation-Bearers,* where we are in greatest need of them, they are missing entirely. Furthermore, the evidence suggests that the *hypotheseis* were not, as a rule, copied with as much care as was devoted to the dramatic texts.[9]

This is not the place to talk at length about the printed editions that have appeared since the Renaissance. Again and again some of the greatest men in the history of classical scholarship have been attracted to the study and improvement of the Aeschylean text. High points in this history are the editions of Turnebus (1552), Robortello (1552), Vettori (1557), and Canter (1580) in the sixteenth century; Stanley (1663) in the seventeenth; Schuetz (1821) and Hermann (posthumous, 1852) in the nineteenth; and Wilamowitz (1914) in the twentieth.[10] Of these, the most impressive editions were

9. For a full discussion, in Latin, of these and related issues see W. Steffen, *Studia Aeschylea* (Wroclaw, 1958), chap. 1.

10. E. Fraenkel, ed., tr., and comm., *Aeschylus: Agamemnon* (Oxford, 1950), vol. 1, pp. 34 ff., offers an informative discussion of "Some Editions and Commentaries," limited only

those by the sixteenth-century scholars. Turnebus and Robortello, key figures in the French and Italian revivals of learning, issued their editions at a time when *M*'s version of *Agamemnon* and *Libation-Bearers* was still thought to constitute one play. Their knowledge of Greek and of both ancient literatures and their use of other manuscripts and of the scholia made their editions pioneering feats. But it was Vettori's achievement to recognize that *M* had fourteen leaves missing and needed to be supplemented from another source.[11] Vettori was that rare Renaissance man, a humanist who practiced humility. In his preface he says that since he has had no opportunity for bringing out books, he is glad to let the young Henri Etienne publish it for him. He proudly announces the separation of *Libation-Bearers* from *Agamemnon*, describes the confusion and the lacunae in *M*, and details how he found another manuscript that contained the whole of *Agamemnon*. All along he gives generous credit to various collaborators, and insists that he does not wish his edition to dim the glory of earlier editors, of whom he says, somewhat overstating the case, that there had been many. Etienne himself contributed some sections to the work, which is, in addition to being a historic work of scholarship, a magnificent piece of bookmaking.

Later editors had fewer opportunities. Canter's work is the first to supply the designation of metrical divisions and types, though it must be added that his understanding of metrics was inferior to Robortello's and Vettori's; in fact, Vettori's expertise in this area was unequalled until the early days of the nineteenth century. Stanley's is a variorum edition incorporating the work of many others, both acknowledged and unacknowledged. It contains the text with Latin translation, scholia, fragments of lost plays, notes, commentary, and much else; it is also the first edition with line numbering. Schuetz continued the work on the text which his predecessors had pursued, and provided a tactful commentary on the plays. Hermann contributed his magisterial knowledge of Greek and of poetic meters. Finally, Wilamowitz, the giant of Greek studies of the past century, reexamined the relation of the manuscripts, of which by now a very large number had been assembled, and established the broad outlines of the textual transmission which are still recognized today. What is more, his feeling for the poetry and the dramatic skill of Aeschylus was such that the 1914 companion volume to his edition, entitled *Aischylos—Interpretationen*, remains the primer to which all critics of Aeschylus must turn.

Altogether, Aeschylus has been fortunate in his editors. From Robortello

by the primary focus upon *Agamemnon*. U. von Wilamowitz-Moellendorff, ed., *Aeschyli Tragoediae* (Berlin, 1914) has a fine appreciation of the achievement of Turnebus, the first royal reader of Greek in Paris.

11. P. Victorius, ed., *Aeschyli Tragoediae vii* (Paris, 1557).

and Vettori to Wilamowitz and his more recent successors, many of the men who have busied themselves with the text have been more than narrow philologists or editorial technicians. They have been men of letters, often leading personalities of their time, whose scholarship was fuelled by the challenge of trying to bring order into what remains of the work of a great dramatic poet who was also a prominent public personality. The task remains stupendous, in spite of the progress made. Some two generations ago it looked for a while as if help were on the way. The sands of Egypt began to render up scraps of papyrus, and occasionally almost complete rolls, the earliest dating to the fourth century B.C., prior to the beginnings of Alexandrian scholarship. On the whole, it must be admitted, the help has not been as substantial as had at first been hoped. Above all, in the centuries from which most of our papyri date—from the second century B.C. to the fifth century A.D.—Aeschylus was read less often than Euripides or Sophocles, and even less performed. Hence the total number of Aeschylus papyri has been disappointing. Again, because such scraps usually come from the books of private libraries indebted to what was available in Alexandria, the readings are not greatly different from the standard tradition, except for a few cases in which the readings are so wildly different as to suggest that the book was a makeshift handiwork. The greatest help of the papyri has been in a totally unexpected way. We know from ancient notices that Aeschylus was highly regarded not only for his tragedies but also for his satyr plays, a genre in which he was actually regarded as the undisputed master. Until the papyri started making their appearance, we had only a few miserable quotations from these satyr plays, and in many cases the quotations were not substantial enough to permit us to decide whether the play was a satyr play or not. Now, however, we have sizable chunks of these amusing productions, and we are in a better position to appreciate the justice of the ancient judgment.[12]

With all the information available, from the manuscripts themselves, from the papyri, from citations in other ancient authors, what can be said about the appearance of that original document, or rather series of documents, which Euergetes acquired for his library? The first thing that needs to be said is that the columns of text were written as alternating portions of verse and prose. The iambic passages of speech and dialogue, corresponding roughly to the blank verse of Elizabethan drama, were always arranged in lines of verse. But the lyric portions (see below, chapter 2), representing primarily the contribution of the chorus as singers and dancers, were in the first copies written out as if they were prose, without regard for the struc-

12. R. G. Ussher, "The Other Aeschylus," *Phoenix* 31 (1977): 287–99.

ture of the verse. It was probably only in the second century B.C. that an Alexandrian scholar, Aristophanes of Byzantium, introduced the fashion of writing the text of the lyrics more or less as they are printed today, the line lengths varying in accord with the natural confines of the metrical units employed.[13] The first time that this new arrangement is traceable for us in a dramatic text is in a papyrus of the first century B.C., *P. Oxy. 2336,* containing a portion from the recognition duet of Euripides's *Helen,* lines 630–74.

The text provided the words spoken or sung, but little else. Stage directions not internal to what is said may be counted on the fingers of one hand.[14] Where they do occur, as at *Seven* 84 and 89—"a shouting," or *Eum.* 117 ff.—"a barking," "a baying," they refer to sounds, and add little to what is already implied in the dramatic utterance. Even so, some scholars have been sufficiently embarrassed by their presence to attempt to exorcise them. More typically, stage directions can be extrapolated from what the actors say. At *Eum.* 566 ff, Athena's call upon the herald to make an announcement, and her words about the Tyrrenian trumpet

> So let the trumpet, filled with human breath,
> Sound forth its arching flourish to the host,

give us what we need to know about the stage action accompanying and completing her words. The same goes for Orestes's command to the servants at *Libation-Bearers* 983 ff. to hold up and spread the fatal cloak. At *Prometheus* 272, Prometheus's invitation to the daughters of Ocean to

> Step down and listen to my imminent fate

supplies the cue for the action, much as it still leaves us in the air about precisely what it is they descend from. There are just enough such internal directions to enable us to draw some inferences about the setting of the plays and about the scenario, but also to tantalize us with many reminders of our ignorance. In this respect, the text of Aeschylus treats us about as generously, or as charily, as the text of Shakespeare. We assume that there is no fainting on the Aeschylean stage, but can we be sure? In the Shakespearean folio text there is no provision for Lady Macbeth's swoon; Rowe's "Lady Macbeth is carried out" is not yet there.[15] There is much that has to be filled in by the modern editor on the strength of his understanding of the play and of the generic clues gathered from a variety of sources.

13. W. S. Barrett, ed. and comm., *Euripides: Hippolytus* (Oxford, 1964), Appendix on colometry.

14. O. Taplin, "Did Greek Dramatists Write Stage Instructions?" *Proceedings of the Cambridge Philological Society* 203 (1977): 121–32.

15. A. C. Bradley, "Did Lady Macbeth Really Faint?" in *Shakespearian Tragedy* (London, 1905), pp. 484 ff.

The same need for interpretation and supplementation exists, even more pressingly, on other fronts. We cannot, in every instance, be sure of the names attached to the characters. The name of the Empress Mother in *Persians*, for example, is known only from the scholia and from the list of characters appended to the text; it does not occur in the body of the play as we have it. How did the ancient editor come by his knowledge? Did his text contain a line, no longer extant, in which the name Atossa was indeed used? For our purposes it is better not to fall in with the scholiast, and to identify the Empress Mother simply by her role. The same is true of the herald of *Agamemnon*, who in the list of characters is called Talthybius. These lists of names are notoriously unreliable; that for *Prometheus* includes both Earth and Heracles, neither of whom appears in our version of the play or, presumably, in the original.

This is not all. The identities of the characters who speak or sing any one line are usually not marked.[16] For a rudimentary assignment of the lines we are almost entirely dependent on indications of a change of speaker which are sometimes, but by no means always, supplied in the form of a dash to the left of or under the new line. It seems evident that the ancient and the Medieval critics were often as much at a loss as we are today, and had to fall back on their knowledge of the myths and their general appreciation of the play to supply the missing names. In all likelihood, the indications of change of speaker do not go back to Aeschylus's own copy but were contributed by the Alexandrian scholars. Modern editors have on occasion chosen to differ from their ancient predecessors, or from their modern peers. At *Eum*. 574–75, the manuscripts have a rare marginal *cho*, meaning that the lines are thought to be delivered by the chorus, or rather the chorus leader. Some modern editors accept the notice; others, more plausibly it seems, believe that there ought to be no change of speaker and that the lines belong to Athena. Somewhat later in the same play, lines 676–77 are in the manuscripts assigned to the chorus, but this can hardly be right, for the conventions of choral action do not permit a chorus or its leader to stipulate a time at which they will vacate the stage. In any case, the words are more appropriate in the mouth of Apollo. These are but two of the many cases, most of them not similarly furnished with a reference to the identity of the speaker, in which legitimate dissent is in order.

16. J. C. B. Lowe, "The Manuscript Evidence for Changes of Speaker in Aristophanes," *Bulletin of the Institute of Classical Studies* 9 (London, 1962): 27–39, esp. 35–37 discusses the few cases in the papyri where speakers are identified at first appearance or even elsewhere. According to N. G. Wilson, "Indications of Speaker in Greek Dialogue Texts," *CQ* 20 (1970): 305, who is concerned with prose dialogue, our present systematic procedure of indicating changes of speakers by name in the margin was instituted by the fifth-century church father Theodoret (J. P. Migne, ed., *Patrologiae Cursus Completus, Series Graeca* [Paris, 1857–99], vol. 83, p. 29b).

With the doors of discretion opened wide, false steps are inevitable. One modern critic, unhappy with the meagerness of the role assigned to Pylades in *Libation-Bearers*, has proposed that Pylades be the speaker of Orestes's dissembling speech in lines 674 ff.[17] Until recently, an interesting theory provided for the doubling and tripling of singing roles in *Suppliants*. We have no list of characters for the play, little as that would help us. So we do not know whether, in addition to the chorus of the daughters of Danaus, who are, as it were, the protagonists of the drama, there were also a chorus of Egyptians and a chorus of retainers of Pelasgus. On top of this, it was proposed that the final choral ode, beginning with line 1018, be split between the Danaids and their serving women, the latter warning their mistresses, from their own vantage point of a more plebeian religious commitment, of the risks attending a slighting of the power of Aphrodite. Another critic has argued that the warnings are issued by Argive soldiers. Chances are, however, that the final song is the Danaids' own, arguing with themselves and pondering their next move, thus introducing some of the issues of the play that followed next in the trilogy.[18]

Again, the great question-and-answer session between King Pelasgus and the newly arrived Danaids at *Suppliants* 291 ff. is subject to two different arrangements. On one interpretation, the king does the questioning, and the chorus leader the answering. On another, it is the chorus leader who does most of the questioning—a kind of Socratic questioning, in fact, which induces the king, step by step, to admit the veracity of a tale which he had at first been inclined to doubt. The former reading is, at first glance, the more natural, but it is less likely to be right because it cannot be gotten from the text without the stipulation that a number of lines have been lost in the course of transmission.[19] This is a particularly awkward dilemma. There are just enough cases of this sort to put a considerable strain on our judgment of what is Aeschylean dramaturgy and what is not. Yet the difficulties should not be exaggerated. On the whole, critics and scholars have achieved far-reaching consensus in their assignment of parts. The consensus is pieced together from a great variety of sources and motives, none of them in itself definitive, but together warranting a fair degree of conviction. Concerning this or that attribution—are the lines at *Prometheus* 347 ff. spoken by Prometheus, as *M* has it, or by Ocean, as other manuscripts have

17. H. J. Rose, *A Commentary on the Surviving Plays of Aeschylus (Verh. Nederl. Akad. Wetensch., Afd. Letterk.*, n.s. 64. 1–2; Amsterdam, 1957), ad loc.

18. See M. McCall, "The Secondary Choruses in Aeschylus' *Supplices*," *California Studies in Classical Antiquity* 9 (1976): 117–31.

19. Note what this reading does to the printed page of D. Page, ed., *Aeschyli Tragoediae* (Oxford, 1972), pp. 102–3.

it?—doubts will remain. But a general appreciation of Aeschylus's dramatic art is not significantly affected by the issues that are unresolved. Even in the great lyrical encounter of *Libation-Bearers* 306–465, where who is singing what is at times in doubt, the doubt is less fatal than it would be in a play depending more on the precise distinction among characters through their speech than on the communal lyric rehearsal of the motives of action which this exchange offers.

The beginning of the prologue of *Libation-Bearers* has not survived. What appears in our editions as lines 1–5 has been recaptured from Aristophanes's parody of the passage in *The Frogs*. Other bits and pieces come from ancient commentaries on Pindar and Euripides. The lines lost number at least a dozen, and probably more. What we have of the speech of Orestes suggests that he gave a rather full explanation of his background and his purposes in a greeting addressed not only to Hermes but also to Agamemnon in his tomb. The fullness of the explanation was needed in view of the intrigue that follows later in the play. Fortunately our good luck in having *Agamemnon* and *Eumenides* makes the loss of the lines less painful than if it had occurred in the introductory segment of a play whose companion pieces we do not have.

This is the only loss of which we are certain. Scholarship has posited many other lacunae, of varying length, where the grammar or the sense appears to be defective in a way that argues a loss of words or lines. The first interpretation of *Suppliants* 291 ff. mentioned above is a case in point. The nineteenth century was especially given to assuming such omissions. Today scholars are more willing to believe that the grammar or the sense of a disputed passage can be explained without conjecturing a loss. Here is an example. At *Eum.* 1027, in a speech of Athena regulating processional worship, there is mention of children, women, and old women, but not of men or old men. Further, a spectator or reader might expect a reference to the new name of the Furies, the *Eumenides*, or "Gracious Ones," which occurs nowhere in the play but should, one presumes, have been introduced somewhere to give the play its name. The passage in question might well appear to be an appropriate place for the missing designation. Finally, the imperative at the beginning of line 1029, "honor," carries no object, and does not seem to be functionally related to anything that precedes or follows. This is the kind of cumulative argument which soothes the critical mind into readiness to propose a lacuna. Nevertheless, it is conceivable that the procession is to be conducted only by women, of all ages; it is conceivable that the imperative is simply wrong by itself; and it is in fact likely that the name *Eumenides* as the title of the play was derived from what happens in the play, rather than from an explicit commemoration of it. With some ingenuity and an equal share of luck, an editor should be able to get by without additional lines.

In other cases, the stipulation of a lacuna seems unavoidable. At *Libation-Bearers* 243, there is no plausible link between Electra's assignment of a quadruple role to Orestes—he is to be father, mother, and sister as well as brother to her—and her invocation of Might and Right to assist Zeus in his support of the cause. The missing lines, one supposes, would have served to extend Electra's speech to a more respectable length. If so, they may have contained an appeal to Orestes to exert himself, a promise of help, and also perhaps an admission of her own weakness. If the hypothesis is acceptable, we should note the importance of this for our understanding of Electra's character and her role in the conspiracy. Few scholars, however, are likely to cast their vote for so massive a lacuna, unheralded by the usual telltale signs of faulty grammar or versification.

So much for possible losses. Related to this, but potentially more vicious in the hands of purposeful critics, is the judgment that the text is marred by dislocations. Initially such a view is by no means implausible. The scholia, and in some cases the texts themselves, give evidence that certain passages, mistakenly omitted by a copyist, were afterwards fetched up in the margin, with a reference to the place where they were to be inserted; and that subsequently, when a further copy was made, the marginal entry was reintroduced into the text, but in the wrong place. Where we have this information, as at *Seven* 517, which many manuscripts feature after 518 or 519, the restoration of the original order is relatively easy. Unfortunately, some readers are quick to propose transpositions where the textual history permits no such inference. Where the nineteenth century often fell back upon the hypothesis of a lacuna, the twentieth, less daring but more ingenious, prefers to appease its dissatisfactions by spotting cases of disarray. What renders this critical approach hazardous is our intuition that much of the power of a dramatic poem rests on the order in which the poet has seen fit to arrange his material.

Take *Eum.* 85–87, Orestes's address to Apollo:

> My Lord Apollo: justice is your craft.
> Do not, in justice, cut me off. The power
> To help stamps your authority.

Where this passage stands, it seems curiously late. It also appears to disrupt the continuity of Apollo's speech. Would it not be more convincing to have Orestes begin the conversation with his formal address before Apollo takes over? Apollo's strangely elliptic "I shall not betray" (64) might make better sense as a response to this address than as an opening of the scene. On several scores, then, a dislocation is indicated. But we cannot prove it; and in many ways the abruptness of Apollo's beginning, Orestes's slowness and ineffectuality, and Apollo's apparent disregard of the interruption have their own charm. Smooth logic, the standard tacitly invoked by most calls for transposition, need not be the leading characteristic of a divine epiphany.

Is *Libation-Bearers* 434–38, the stanza in which Orestes, singing, announces that his mother will have to die and that thereafter he will go off to his perdition, in its proper place? A number of scholars have argued that it must come later, nearer the end of the great musical exchange between Electra, Orestes, and the chorus, after 455. According to their argument, it is improbable that the chorus and Electra should continue with their admonitions, as they do in the received text, if Orestes has already decided on his action. In addition, metrical grounds are offered for the change; a transposition of the stanza would make for a greater degree of formal parallelism between the stanzas. Other critics have opposed the transposition on the proper grounds that it is required only by a modern feeling for terminal emphasis. The traditional sequence makes sense on the assumption that Orestes's decision is not climactic (note that it is sung rather than spoken);[20] that it is merely one of a series of such statements alternating with confessions of weakness and wonder; and on the further assumption that Electra and the chorus continue to work on Orestes so that he will not slip back. I am not happy with the psychological model implied in this further assumption. It presupposes that we are right in assuming, which we are probably not, that the words sung by Electra and the chorus are addressed to Orestes and not rather, over his head, to the audience as part of a massive tapestry of themes and memories invoking the precarious condition of the House of Atreus.

I have dwelt on the issue of transposition because we cannot hope to arrive at a satisfactory interpretation if we cannot be certain that the parts of a play succeed one another as the textual tradition says they do. If a critic can propose, as one has done, that the famous stanza dedicated to Zeus in the introductory ode of *Agamemnon* (lines 160 ff.) is not in its right place, then the task of the interpreter may well seem hopeless.[21] For my part, I firmly believe that the tradition is generally right, except for minutiae, and that modern attempts to transpose are often based on an inadequate understanding of what Aeschylus may have intended, or at least on an unwillingness to grant him the benefit of the doubt.

20. For evidence concerning speaking and singing, see below, chap. 2.
21. R. D. Dawe, "The Place of the Hymn to Zeus in Aeschylus' *Agamemnon*," *Eranos* 64 (1966): 1–21, gently rebutted by L. Bergson in *Eranos* 65 (1967): 12–24.

By comparison with the hypotheses of losses and dislocations, a third mode of challenging the received text is less weighty: the suggestion that the text contains more than Aeschylus originally wrote. We have already cited the theory of actors' interpolations and the case of the ending of *Seven*. Beyond this, it is thought that now and then we come upon what are called intrusive glosses—formulations and phrases which owe their origin to the attempt to explain something in the text and in the course of the transmission found their way from the margin into the body of the text. One modern scholar believes he has a more or less precise technique for the detection of such increments.[22] In the usual course of affairs, however, such intrusions are easier to spot than to explain, and everything about them must remain largely conjectural. A minor example would be *Agam.* 69–71, which translates literally as follows:

> Neither burning in the flame, nor pouring libations,
> Nor with the tears of a flameless sacrifice,
> Will [the sinner] soothe the savage wrath.

With these lines, the chorus caps its first hesitant words about Paris's foul deed and the punitive campaign of the sons of Atreus. It should be clear that there is something wrong with the middle line. Either the tears or the flameless sacrifice must go, a fact that is clearer in the Greek because they do not go together grammatically. It is probable that the set of actions with which the sinner might have hoped to assuage divine wrath consisted of three members: either burnt sacrifices, libations, and tears; or burnt sacrifices, libations, and sacrifices that are neither burnt nor poured. I rather suspect that "flameless sacrifice" is in origin a marginal comment on "libations" or perhaps even, extravagantly, on "tears"—an intrusive gloss that has squeezed out part of the original text. One may conjecture that the words that have dropped out spoke of the gods or Fate and their wrath. If this is accepted, a tentative reconstitution of the lines might be roughly:

> Neither burning in the flame, nor pouring libations,
> Nor with his tears will [the sinner] soothe
> The savage wrath of a stubborn Fate.

"Stubborn Fate" is *exempli causa*; it is less impressive than "flameless sacrifice" and may well be wrong. But the received reading cannot be right. To retain it is to pretend to a certainty that does not exist and to encourage enterprising critics to work from infirm premises.

Finally, a word or two about emendations. Emending, the fine art of

---

22. G. D. Thomson, "The Intrusive Gloss," *CQ* 17 (1967): 232–43, building upon the editorial theories of F. Heimsoeth and W. Headlam.

removing presumed corruptions and accretions by recovering a reading that has become obscured, does not these days enjoy the prestige it once held, except perhaps in Britain and Australia. The temperament of the emender emerges beautifully from this remark by one of Britain's most active practitioners: "The *Agamemnon* in its original form was decent Greek as well as good sense and elegant verse and fine poetry, and to such a condition I have endeavoured to restore it throughout."[23] One is inclined to envy the writer his serene confidence. When he gets through with *Agamemnon*, however, the play is not quite the same as before, as generations of perceptive and tactful critics have come to love and be awed by it.

Emendation carried out on a grand scale is bowdlerization. But the Aeschylean cause is not served any better by an undue respect for the received text where it is demonstrably perverse. It has taken a host of fine textual critics to bring order into a play such as *Suppliants*, which the transmission has left more damaged than others, and to give dimensions of meaning to its parts. Today it seems barely credible that, at line 1022, readers for centuries accepted M and had the daughters of Danaus sing: "Respond, friends, to our power [*menos*]," until Legrand in 1778 emended *menos* to *melos*: "Respond, friends, to our song." The work of emendation must continue. It is a measure of our need that so prominent a passage as Clytemnestra's beacon speech, *Agam.* 281−316, remains corrupt in a number of places. The same is true of the choral song separating the appearance of the Nurse from the entrance of Aegisthus at *Libation-Bearers* 783−837. The broad outlines of the thought are clear; but the fine texture of the language has, until now, defied recovery. There is much in *Suppliants*, especially in the second half, that still blocks our attempts to arrive at a convincing text.

The lover of ancient tragedy who has taken the trouble of comparing any two standard translations of, say, a choral passage in *Agamemnon* or *Persians* knows that two responsible translators may come up with widely differing results. In view of this, and of the textual issues noted above, the reader may be excused if he wonders whether there is any point in talking about Aeschylean tragedy as a valid object of critical inquiry. The answer I would give is a firm yes. The burden of this chapter has been to leave the reader under no illusions about the state of the text. But let me repeat that I do not wish to create an exaggerated impression of what is wrong with it. In subsequent chapters due notice will be given wherever the textual basis is insecure. In the absence of such signals, it may be assumed that the textual basis for the judgments advanced is adequate. In spite of certain healthy reservations,

---

23. A. Y. Campbell, ed., *The Agamemnon of Aeschylus* (Liverpool, 1936), p. xiii.

# _ 2 _

# Verse; Delivery; Evident Structure

In *As You Like It*, the princes tend to address each other in simple though playful prose, while Audrey and the Clown affect elegant verse. This appears to be Shakespeare's ironic comment on a courtly tradition which took it for granted that only noble minds should enjoy the privilege of verse. The tradition is at least in part indebted to a mistaken notion of what happened in classical tragedy and of the historical facts. In classical antiquity, lyric verse, i.e., poetry that was sung and accompanied and danced out, was understood to constitute a liberated popular response to the more controlled speaking voice of the reciter of aristocratic epic. In tragedy, also, the people's role, in the form of choral singing, was more "poetic" than the spoken iambs of the kings and queens who argued with the chorus or with each other. True, the ancient stage does not recognize prose, properly speaking. In fact, the first literary prose documents come from the time when Aeschylus was composing his plays. But prose literature was never, outside of the practical genres of rhetoric, history, philosophy, and related disciplines, fully accepted by the ancient critics, who went to the length of completely disregarding so popular an art form as the prose romances. Still, the range of versification on the Aeschylean stage is so great, and the iamb so natural a rhythm in spoken Greek, that by contrast with the choral hymns the dialogue may well be regarded as the dramatic equivalent of unmediated speech.

In what follows, we shall take up matters which some will regard as dry and mechanical. For those who have no interest in questions of meter, rhythm, and structure, the present chapter is eminently skippable. They should, however, be warned that the art of Aeschylus is in large measure a function of his skill in using sophisticated formal procedures which the audiences expected to see employed, though in some of them Aeschylus himself may have been the originator. In this, as in the next chapter, much will be said that would also apply, with minor modifications, to the other fifth-century tragedians. But Aeschylus stands at the beginning of the line, and he has his own unmistakable way of exploiting the formal requirements.[1]

1. There are many studies of the structural properties of Greek tragedy, and of Aeschylus in particular. Much useful information will be found in W. Jens, ed., *Die Bauformen der Tragödie* (Munich, 1971). The best study of the lyric meters is still that of A. M. Dale, *The*

The question what kinds of verse to employ in the theater, and how far to move from the cadences of natural speech to stylized rhetoric, has continued to interest dramatists. In Dryden's *Essay*, Crites argues that drama is better off without rhyme; Neander opposes him. The heroic couplets and the rhymed Alexandrines of neo-classical drama produce their own risks. When, in the last line of act 4, scene 3 of *Le Cid*, Don Rodriguez is reporting the battle against the Moors

> C'est de cette façon que, pour votre service . . .

Don Alonso enters on the run, with the first line of scene 4:

> Sire, Chimène vient vous demander justice!

The distribution of the couplet between two speakers, and its wrenching apart by means of a new action, is a poetic and dramatic gamble. The couplet may fall apart, and the house break down. It is to avoid such risks that more recent playwrights have usually abandoned verse altogether, or have, with Victor Hugo, called for a verse "that is free, frank, faithful, daring to say all without prudery, to express all without straining." [2] Others—Ibsen, Eliot, Auden, Maxwell Anderson—have experimented with verse types closely allied to the spoken cadences of living speech. [3]

Aeschylean drama is composed in a large variety of verse patterns. Some of them are easy to recognize; others, especially some of the choral rhythms, are among the most complex metrical creations known to man, and their adequate identification as verse is only about a century and a half old. Their recognition relies upon two principal assumptions. Ancient Greek verse operates not so much with stressed and unstressed units, as in English, but primarily with the succession of long and short syllables. With respect to the time taken to pronounce it, each syllable in Greek either has a predetermined vowel value or has its value determined by the consonants or consonant clusters that bound it. Someone who has learnt his Greek has relatively little difficulty in plotting the succession of shorts and longs. It is more difficult to determine, especially in the lyric passages of the chorus, where a poetic line ends and another begins. Without a recognition of these *termini*, no true assessment of the nature of the verse and of the relation of

*Lyric Metres of Greek Drama* [2] (Cambridge, 1968). M. Untersteiner, ed. and tr., *Eschilo: le tragedie* (Milan, 1947), vol. 3, "appendice metrica," diagrams all the choral passages of the plays.

2. *Théâtre complet*, ed. R. Purnal et al., vol. 1 (Paris, 1963), p. 441. When Hugo wrote the preface to *Cromwell* from which the quotation is taken he was twenty-five.

3. D. Donoghue, *The Third Voice: Modern British and American Verse Drama* (Princeton, N.J., 1959).

the lines to one another is possible. At this point we are aided by ancient writings on verse, both metrical scholia in our dramatic manuscripts and independent treatises on verse patterns, which explain how the scholars of the Alexandrian and the Roman periods understood the poetry.[4] With the help of these sources, and with due allowance for certain biases on their part, modern scholarship has arrived at a reasonably unanimous estimate of the raw data of metrical composition.

In the Greek plays, we distinguish between three kinds of verse: spoken verse, chanted verse, and sung verse. The distinction is probably too simple; it is quite likely that between the extremes of spoken and sung verse, there existed a sliding scale of intonations, ranging from almost speaking to almost singing. "Chanting," then, may cover various kinds of delivery. In a more technical sense, "chanting" is used of a delivery which is sufficiently musical to be accompanied by an instrument but not musical enough to be associated with dance, which is a virtually mandatory accompaniment of choral singing. The diverseness of the middle range is brought home to us particularly by the parodies of tragedy that we find in Aristophanes.[5] For our purposes, however, the present tripartite scheme should suffice.

The use of the iambic trimeter as the principal medium for speeches and dialogue is ultimately, it seems, indebted to the epic, in spite of the fact that the epic hexameter was not iambic but dactylic. We might compare the blank verse of *Gorboduc*, the first formal English tragedy (1562), which was associated with epic, especially Surrey's translation of Vergil, rather than with the native drama or even with the translations of Seneca then available. But the parallel does not take us very far. Whereas the authors of *Gorboduc* handled their blank verse in the primitive manner of metrical buccaneering, Aeschylus's iambs from the very first possess an authority and a range of usage which make it impossible for us to look on them as the first halting steps in a new medium. There is evidence that Aeschylus's habits in constructing his iambic lines changed over the years. In the matter of resolution, for instance—the use of two short syllables in the place of a long in certain designated places of the line—Aeschylus gradually became less permissive. *Persians* contains more than twice as many resolutions proportionately as *Eumenides*, with a fairly steady rate of diminution observable in the plays of the intervening fourteen years.[6] This means that he travelled a route

4. The chief document is Hephaestion's *Metrical Manual* of the second century A.D.

5. The Aristophanic scholia contain much useful information; see J. W. White, *The Verse of Greek Comedy* (London, 1912), pp. 396 ff. On the range of delivery, see principally A. Pickard-Cambridge, *The Dramatic Festivals of Athens*[2], ed. J. Gould and D. M. Lewis (Oxford, 1968), pp. 156 ff.

6. A. F. Garvie, *Aeschylus' Supplices* (Cambridge, 1969), pp. 32 ff., assembles the pertinent data and cites the authorities.

opposite to the one taken by Euripides, who with the years permitted himself more and more freedom in resolving his iambs. Precisely why Aeschylus became more severe in this respect we do not know. But it is proof of the care with which he attended to even the less obvious aspects of his art.

To describe the typical pace of an Aeschylean line of dialogue or rhetoric is difficult. Unlike the forensic transparency of Euripides's debates or the sinuous informality evident in Sophocles's later plays, Aeschylus's iambic speech always retains a formal, even lapidary character. It tends to be end-stopped, making of each line or couple of lines a weighty contribution to the massive build-up of the argument. Each of these building blocks needs to be appreciated in its own right. The usual rule of drama, according to which the line presses onward toward the completion or resolution of the larger structure, does not hold. This slowness, even obstructiveness of the verse is the rhythmic analogue to Aeschylus's universe, which is one of solid masses in loving or hating contention with one another. But within this scheme of metrical slow motion, Aeschylus is capable of lightning strokes that catch the listener off guard. The sudden refraction and colloquial ease of Cassandra's words to the chorus at *Agam.* 1239–41, coming close upon the heels of the slow march of her tangled visions of murder, are such a case. More will be said about this in chapter 4.

The large majority of spoken lines are iambic. But Aeschylus disposed of one other metrical unit for his dialogue, a trochaic line, longer than the standard trimeter but felt to be livelier and even closer to the rhythm of rapid colloquial speech.[7] Aeschylus uses it in only two of his extant plays: for a short section of dialogue at the end of *Agamemnon*, lines 1649–73, and for three longer sequences in *Persians*, lines 155–75, 215–48, 697–99, and 703–58, for exchanges between the Empress Mother and the chorus leader and between the Empress Mother and Darius. Other occurrences are found in the fragments of satyr plays. Silenus in *Champions at Isthmia*, for instance, uses trochees in the speech with which he calls on the satyrs to nail replicas of their masks against the house of Poseidon.[8] Exactly what the effect of substituting trochees for the expected iambs may be is beyond our understanding, though it is worth noting the incidence in the satyr plays and the comparative frequency of spoken trochees in Old Comedy. Nev-

7. T. Drew-Bear, "The Trochaic Tetrameter in Greek Tragedy," *AJP* 89 (1968): 385–405.

8. The text is given by H. Lloyd-Jones in H. W. Smyth, ed. and tr., *Aeschylus*[2], vol. 2 (Cambridge, Mass., 1957), p. 551; he ascribes the lines to the chorus. For the relation between iambs and trochees, see also A. N. Michelini's dissertation "Rhesis and Dialogue" (Harvard University, 1971), summarized in *Harvard Studies in Classical Philology* 76 (1972): 294–97.

ertheless, the power of a verse pattern that can be used to terminate the proceedings of a violent action, as in *Agamemnon* (the ending of *Oedipus Rex* is a parallel use), but which is also employed for the stately exchanges in *Persians* would be difficult to characterize with any degree of confidence.

So much for the spoken verse. Chanted verse is, for the most part, anapaestic.[9] It is distinguished from spoken verse by following a musical line that is not identical with the natural pitch of the language, which was, as we know, tonal. It is distinguished from sung verse by its greater rhythmic regularity and its more limited musical range. Its most common use is in the sequences which we may call "introductions"—that is, the lines with which the chorus makes its entrance into the theater, prior to singing and dancing the entrance ode; and in similar, though briefer, sequences with which the chorus heralds new turns in the play. The beginning of *Suppliants* may serve as an example of an anapaestic introduction. The chorus moves into the theater to the accompaniment of the double reed instrument (*aulos*) which supplied the musical line. The anapaests mark the regular pace which the chorus uses for the duration of thirty-nine short lines to arrange itself in position for the ode that is to follow. Such an introduction is designed to open proceedings on a note of calm. A fragment from *Edonians*, most probably from a choral entrance, employs anapaests to describe the tempestuous nature of Dionysiac music, with its castanets, drums, and other agents of ecstatic worship.[10] But the meter of the passage assures us that no such boisterous instruments accompanied the chanting. The lines constitute a detached report, not a mimesis of violent experience.

The other use of anapaests is essentially of the same kind, though we cannot be sure, or rather have reason to doubt, that the chorus changes its position. Relevant cases are *Agam.* 1331 ff., where the anapaests mark the moment in the play when Cassandra has made her exit and Agamemnon is about to be murdered; *Lib.* 719 ff., where the anapaests mark the beginning of the intrigue section of the play; and *Eum.* 307 ff., an introduction to the Furies' binding song, though this may equally well be explained as an example of the first kind, since the lines mark the entrance of the Furies after the scene is imagined to have changed from the temple at Delphi to the sanctuary of Athena.

Though the chorus is the main purveyor of chanted anapaests, some of them are assigned to individual characters. This happens especially in encounters between the chorus and a character. On such occasions, the chorus, singing and dancing, locks horns with a character whose verses show him to

9. W. Pötscher, "Die Funktion der Anapästpartien in den Tragödien des Aischylos," *Eranos* 57 (1959): 79–98.

10. Smyth, *Aeschylus*[2], vol. 2, p. 399.

be chanting (more about this below, chapter 7). Prometheus, in the play named after him, engages in a considerable amount of anapaestic chant, at the beginning, before the chorus enters (as well as in response to the choral singing), and at the end, where both he and Hermes and the chorus terminate the drama with an unparalleled sequence of fifty-three anapaestic lines between them. Ocean is also given anapaests, as is Io at the end of her scene.

The generous use of chanting in *Prometheus* is unique in the Aeschylean corpus. It is rash to speculate on the reasons why this play features so many chanted lines where, on the basis of what is found in the rest of the canon, one might have expected speech. But perhaps the playwright chose the anapaests because the action of *Prometheus* is, on the whole, rather more static than most. The slight increase in tonality, if not liveliness, that comes from the chanting may be felt to compensate. This would fit in with the fact that Io is Aeschylus's only character who has an aria, an ode structured along musical lines ordinarily reserved for the chorus alone. Such arias come to be more common later, especially in the plays of Euripides. In Aeschylus, characters normally adopt song only when they engage in an encounter with the chorus.

The third medium, in addition to speaking and chanting, is song. All three of the simple metrical patterns we have already discussed—iambs, trochees, and anapaests—are found also in song, though for that purpose their lines are less uniform and less evenly successive than in their proper medium. Especially a species of iambic called "dochmiac" (= "sprung rhythm"), a violently syncopated rhythm which in the end only distantly recalls the steady flow of iambs, comes to be a favorite pattern for the expression of horror and acute pain in song.[11] Dochmiac is singular in a number of respects. It is just about the only dramatic verse form of which we can predicate a distinct ethos—excitement, pain, revulsion; never joy, never elegiac grief, never sermonizing; it is unique to Attic tragedy, and may well be an innovation of Aeschylus's; and, because of resolutions, expansions, and refractions, it appears in so many shapes that some of them shade off easily into other kinds of meters: a great convenience when the playwright wants a rapid succession of emotions. Finally, unlike other meters, dochmiac encourages initial and terminal assonance and rhyme, which in serious Greek literature are on the whole considered plebeian, perhaps because of the ease with which the inflected language allows them. The following example, with initial assonance, shows the break in the middle of the line, stronger even than in an Alexandrine, that is typical of the meter (*Agam.* 1410):

11. N. C. Conomis, "The Dochmiacs of Greek Drama," *Hermes* 92 (1964): 23–50.

*apedikes apetames? apopolis d'esē*
cast off, cut off? they'll shut you out

Sung dochmiacs are, like spoken trochees, prominent in satyr plays: perhaps another indication of their fundamentally popular character.

Before we proceed to discuss the special features of dramatic song, a final word about the difference between singing and speaking. One of our greatest scholars has said that "the speeches of Cassandra add a strong element of causality to the visions and prophecies" of her singing.[12] To put the same thing in different words: song and speech often correspond to the opposing elements of passion and reason. At *Eum.* 143–234, the Furies start out on a note of violent wrath; hence perhaps their use of song, some of which is in dochmiac rhythm. The appearance of great passion is further driven home by the chorus dividing into groups singing and dancing in alternation. Choral division often suggests loss of control. At 179 Apollo, disdainful and calm, meets them with speech; and at 198 the Furies themselves, through their chorus leader, fall back on the spoken word to propose what turns out to be a pre-trial session. The anti-drama of the trial itself is speech from beginning to end. Only after the verdict is given do the Furies return to dance and song.

This equation of singing with emotion and speech with reason seems, at first blush, plausible enough. Io's aria is strong evidence in its favor. Unfortunately, the contrary evidence is at least as powerful. To be sure, Apollo and Athena never sing. They are gods, and thus removed from the mode of communication which is rooted in sacred hymns. Nor, understandably, does Pelasgus deviate from the controlled speech of political vigilance. But why should the Empress Mother, Clytemnestra, and Prometheus do little or no singing?[13] Some of the most passionate utterances in the repertory, such as Eteocles's exclamations upon finding out that it is Polynices who stands at the seventh gate (*Seven* 653 ff.), Orestes's vision of the Furies (*Lib.* 1048 ff.), and Cassandra's own vision of them (*Agam.* 1214 ff.) are put in the chaste garb of iambic speech. In the matter of choral pronouncements, it is somewhat easier to show under what circumstances they are sung and when the speaking voice supervenes (see chapter 8). But for the characters we can infer very little from the fact that one has a singing part and another does not. It may have something to do with the availability of good voices; we are prone to overlook the conditions of intimacy and trial and error in which Aeschylus prepared his works.

But if it is difficult to distinguish neatly between speech and song in terms of mental casts, it is even more difficult, not to say impossible, to say

12. E. Fraenkel, *Aeschylus: Agamemnon* (Oxford, 1950), vol. 3, p. 626.
13. P. Maas, *Greek Metre*, tr. H. Lloyd-Jones (Oxford, 1962), p. 53.

how one musical pattern, and that means one metrical genre, differs from another in mood and significance (for the dochmiac, which is an exception, see above). We must assume, I think, that the rhythmical and musical traditions upon which the dramatic singing was modelled created their special resonance in the perceptions of the audience. But if this was so, the links are lost to us. One variety of verse is called "Aeolic," after the patterns of the Aeolian poets Sappho and Alcaeus, whose rhythms the Aeschylean chorus takes up with some elaborations. It may, or may not, be significant that the choral sequence at *Agam.* 717–36 about the lion cub that grows up into a destructive beast has metrical affinities with Sappho's erotic verse. The implied reference to Helen might thus be underscored. But there are many Aeolic sequences which cannot by any stretch of the imagination be made to render up erotic overtones.

Now and then it is possible, by means of a careful analysis of metrical schemes, to set up a correlation between two passages within the tragic corpus. The lyric versification of the Furies' song of reconciliation at *Eum.* 916 ff. is anticipated, it would seem, at *Agam.* 160 ff., where the chorus cites the dispensation of Zeus, the power to learn through suffering, as a presumptive way out of the chain of punishments. In small details like this, it may be permissible to speculate about the implications of certain types of verse and music for identities of mood and theme. More ambitious efforts in this direction have proved abortive. For this reason I propose to dispense with a discussion of the types of musical verse used on the Aeschylean stage, a discussion whose technical demands would be out of proportion to the insight gained into Aeschylus's art, even if it could be conducted without constantly resorting to the Greek text. All that need be said is that the art consists of combining sequences of long and short syllables in what seem, at first glance, to be free associations but are, in fact, strictly governed and, as we shall see directly, repeated schemes, variations based on certain fixed traditions that go back to the art song and the communal hymns of an earlier period.

A Greek tragedy is composed of an alternation of choral odes and "episodes" (*epeisodia* = "intrusions"). The definition of an episode is simply this, that it includes everything that is not an ode.[14] To take the simplest example, *Persians* divides as follows: introduction and ode, 1–154; episode, 155–531; introduction and ode, 532–97; episode, 598–622; introduction and ode, 623–80; episode, 681–851; ode, 852–907; episode, 908–1077. It will be seen from this summary analysis that the chorus is active

14. Entrances at the beginning of plays and exit scenes at the end are not counted as parts of episodes. See also K. Aichele in Jens, *Bauformen,* pp. 47–68.

not only in the odes, of which there are four, but also in the form of spoken or sung exchanges with characters in some of the episodes. The speaking on behalf of the chorus is, if we can trust the ancient authorities, done by the chorus leader (*koryphaios*), a member of the chorus whose speaking voice is adequate for the purpose (see also chapter 8). We cannot tell whether this is always the same person throughout the play. In one instance, at least, Aeschylus writes for a number of speaking voices; in the scene of confusion after the murder of Agamemnon (*Agam.* 1348 ff.), each of the twelve members of the chorus has two lines in succession. But it is as certain as such things can be that choral speaking is never choral in the sense that several voices sound in unison. The ungainly practice of *Sprechchor* is a distinctively modern accomplishment. Only for the purpose of chanting, in introductory anapaests, and singing does the chorus function as a corporate body. And its most characteristic, and also its oldest, contribution is the ode.

The choral ode is defined by its structure.[15] The basic principle of this structure is "responsion," and the basic unit is the succession of two responding stanzas, which I shall call the *dyad*. That is to say, a stanza—i.e., a metrical and musical scheme of a certain, usually complex shape—is used twice, normally in direct sequence, to produce two different sets of words and phrases, which happen to be identical in their patterning of long and short syllables, and thus "respond." A new dyad, of a different metrical but equally duplicate patterning, is then introduced. In *Persians*, for instance, lines 548–57 and 558–67 form identical metrical schemes; so do lines 568–75 and 576–83, but their patterning is quite different from that of the earlier dyad. One may find parallels in the repetition of musical phrases, set to different words, in folk songs, carols, and hymns, except that the tragic stanzas come only in pairs and are often longer and more intricate metrically. In the later tragedians, the typical choral ode consists of two dyads, though the rule is by no means fixed. In Aeschylus a choral ode may have only one dyad, as in the case of *Prom.* 887 ff. and *Lib.* 466 ff., or as many as eight, for example, *Suppl.* 40–175. The number of dyads contained in a choral ode and the length of the stanza are a function of the role assigned to the chorus. In *Prometheus*, where the chorus has what might charitably be described as a subordinate dramatic part, its odes are appreciably shorter and more simply constructed than the odes in *Suppliants* and *Agamemnon*. Again, the predominantly contemplative character of the odes of *Agamemnon* and the slower pace of the action call for stanzas that are longer and more sustained than those in the odes of *Eumenides* and *Seven*.

In addition to its dyads, an ode may also contain stanzas whose verse pattern is not repeated. Such non-responding passages are not common, but

15. J. Rode in Jens, *Bauformen*, pp. 85–115, and the authorities cited there.

they are occasionally found at the beginning of an ode, or at the end, or between two dyads, or even—and this is a rare exception to the rule that the second stanza of a dyad must follow hard on the heels of the first—between the two twins of a dyad. But it is the dyads which form the heart and the substance of an ode, the guarantee of its musical and choreographic standing as a choral song. The replication is metrical and musical. In some cases, the twins are linked with each other or parallel each other in their structure of thought. This is especially likely to happen with dochmiac expressions of terror—for example, *Seven* 150–80. Mostly, however, the twins of a dyad, along with the non-responding "fillers," are merely consecutive units in the development of the larger structure, the ode, and avoid calling attention to their affinity except through their musical configuration.

An occasional doubt attaches to the question of the delivery of an ode or of a non-responding passage. The lines beginning at *Eum*. 254, a tracking song of the Furies, are non-responding but show certain similarities of thought and language with the dyad beginning at 143. The earlier passage is larded with addresses and exhibits a degree of disorientation that suggests, as I have already stated above, that it is meant to be sung by a succession of voices rather than by the full chorus as is usually the case with dyads. Because of this, it has been proposed that the later passage—less tightly organized as it is because of its lack of stanzaic responsion—was also sung by groups of three or four taking up each others' strains. Conversely, it could be argued that the thought of the second passage is rather more continuous than that of the first: the singers bear down on the ancient law of spilt blood and cite Hades as the supreme recorder. I happen to agree with those who prefer to regard these lines as sung by the full chorus. But it is clearly impossible to recapture the arrangements of the first performance, or to be certain of Aeschylus's preference in the matter.

The ode that begins at *Eum*. 143 also offers another problem that needs to be mentioned. Some of the lines that appear in its three sung dyads are iambic, and metrically identical with the iambic trimeters used in dialogue. Are we to imagine that some of the lines in choral odes were spoken rather than sung? The notion entails so many difficulties that the alternative appears unavoidable: some iambic lines, though externally indistinguishable from spoken verse, were designed for singing. Fortunately there is a body of evidence, even before the advent of drama, to confirm the conclusion. But once again a minor issue serves to alert us to the precariousness of many of our opinions concerning the delivery of tragic verse, and especially concerning the fixed relationship between verse form and mode of delivery.

Episodes—to return to this largely amorphous unit defined principally by what it is not—contain not only speeches and dialogue, but also what I have been calling "encounters," exchanges between a character (or, in the case of *Lib.* 306 ff., between two characters) and the chorus.[16] We distinguish between uneven encounters, in which one of the participants, usually the character, speaks or chants, while the other sings; and *even* encounters, in which both participants, i.e., both character and chorus, sing their lines. An example of the former is *Seven* 203–44, an exchange in which the chorus voices its fears through some violent dancing and singing while Eteocles, a law-and-order man, meets them with speech. Contrary to the rule of contiguity between the twins of a dyad which holds for an ode, in this kind of encounter the blocks of speech separate a stanza from its twin. Formally, the effect is one of rupture and dismemberment; the normal sequence of the dyad and the anticipated linking of a number of dyads are fractured by the interposition of the foreign element of speech. In another way, however, the dovetailing of speech and song makes for a dramatic fusion, a clashing and merging of energies which renders all expectations of a musical and choreographic continuum irrelevant. Aeschylus is the unrivalled master of this kind of encounter on the Attic stage. We shall have more to say about it in chapter 7.

An example of the even encounter that is, as it were, *durchkomponiert*, is *Pers.* 931–1001, the scene after Xerxes, in rags, has come on stage, in which he and the chorus engage in a joint lament over the fortunes of the Persian army. Both Xerxes and the chorus sing; to what extent the character as well as the chorus accompanied his singing with dance figures is not certain. Together, successively, they produce a stanza and then its twin, with further dyads following in the same fashion. As in the ode, therefore, the integrity of the continuous dyad is maintained, as is the sequence of dyads. It is only that each twin of a dyad is divided, with part of it sung by one participant and part by the other. I emphasize this pattern, for a modern reader might equally well have looked for one complete stanza to be sung by one partner, and its twin by the other. Greek tragedy does not favor the so-called amœbæan scheme (known, for example, from later European pastoral poetry) in which the second singer imitates the musical design of the first by fashioning a counter-stanza, or twin, to his stanza. Aeschylean drama, in spite of the supposedly agonal spirit embodied in its structure and in its conditions of performance, avoids such obvious formal competitiveness. Reciprocity and conflict are expressed in subtler ways than through the medium of symmetrical countersong.

The difference between an ode on the one hand and an encounter on the other is crucial for the articulation of the drama. An ode stands between two episodes, or what we might call scenes, and is usually relatively indepen-

16. H. Popp in Jens, *Bauformen*, pp. 221–49.

dent of them. An encounter, which may contain as much music and dancing as any ode and perhaps more (the great exchange at *Lib*. 306 ff.
contains as many as eleven dyads), is part of an episode, and therefore closely built
into the progression of the drama. It is of some interest to observe that
Racine understood the difference. Of the two religious plays in which he
uses a chorus, *Esther*, which is the more static, more like an oratorio, has its
choral sequences between the scenes, whereas *Athalie*, more gripping as an
action, exhibits its choral singing not only between the scenes but also
within the scope of the drama, in the form of choral encounters with Joad.
Some of the encounters in Aeschylus are among his most impressive creations technically and dramatically. In addition to the great exchange in
*Libation-Bearers* and the encounter between Xerxes and the chorus, we
might mention those between Eteocles and the chorus (*Seven* 686 ff.); between Cassandra and the chorus (*Agam.* 1072 ff.); between Clytemnestra
and the chorus (*Agam.* 1407 ff.); and, finally, between the Furies and
Athena (*Eum.* 778 ff.). Some are quite short, others extend through a major
portion of the play. The confrontation brought about in this manner, either
by means of speech or chant and song, or through the medium of insistent
song, gets us close to the very heart of Aeschylean drama.

That is what needs to be said about the modes of delivery and organization, with due apologies for the unavoidably taxing dryness of the exposition. A few words now about the larger structure. It has already been said
that each play consists of an alternation of odes and episodes, and that the
odes are of varying length. An episode, too, can be as brief as a speech
of twenty-five lines, as in Danaus's announcement of the favorable vote in
the Argive assembly (*Suppl.* 600 ff.), or as vast as the selection sequence
at *Seven* 369 ff., which consists of 351 lines, or the whole second half of
*Eumenides* (566 ff.), an episode consisting of 466 lines.[17] It may well be
thought that so protean a scheme leaves something to be desired as a standard of dramatic criticism. The fact remains that the articulation of the play
by the ode is fundamental: when the chorus takes over and all characters, or
rather those still on the stage, are sidelined, the drama gathers itself into a
quiescence from which the ensuing episode is a new beginning. Still, the
possibilities of variation for the episode are enormous, and in the light of
them it is doubtful whether it would be possible to construct a typical shape
for an Aeschylean play. In any case, as Charles Morgan has said: "In a play
form is not valuable *in itself*; only the suspense of form has value. . . ."[18]

17. But see O. Taplin, *The Stagecraft of Aeschylus* (Oxford, 1977), pp. 408–9, who
divides the latter half of *Eumenides* at 777 on internal, nonformal grounds.

18. C. Morgan, "The Nature of Dramatic Illusion," reprinted in S. K. Langer, ed.,
*Reflections on Art* (Baltimore, 1958), p. 97.

Each play has a configuration fitted to its particular needs, and this shape is not apparent until after the play has run its course—when, presumably, the dramatic experience is no longer at work. It may, however, be useful to say something about beginnings and endings.

Modern drama, from *Gorboduc* to Peter Shaffer, is likely to fashion its beginnings and ends along predictable lines. The beginning will be shaped so as to offer a modicum of information with a minimum of distraction; the end will be given over to the echoing of the crash, or triumph, or frustration which the play is intended to appraise or celebrate. There are exceptions. Some recent plays, Beckett's among them, refuse to impart information or to arrive at a terminus. They cannot really be said to begin or to end; they are truculently anti-Aristotelian in structure. But in the majority of plays that interest audiences, the conventional structure is maintained. For the beginning, conversation, often by secondaries, is a favorite device. Shakespeare's courtiers or plebeians quickly, though occasionally with a measure of randomness, establish the antecedents or the present conditions. At the least they set the mood. For the ending, once again, rather than a committed voice, Shakespeare is fond of introducing a character who, if not secondary, is relatively unaffected by the action to sound an echo, and often to affirm the survival of a larger world.

Similar arrangements are found on the ancient stage. Euripides's playbill prologues and *deus ex machina* epilogues are structurally related to Aeschylus's procedures, save that the Euripidean manner prescribes a virtual detachment of prologue and epilogue from the drama proper. More generally, an ancient tragedy may start in one of two ways, with a spoken prologue preceding the entry of the chorus, or immediately with the chorus. Contrary to what is sometimes said, this has nothing to do with the evolution of the drama as a literary genre. We know that some of Aeschylus's predecessors wrote prologues, and the role of the "answerer" or "interpreter" (*hypokritēs*) in Aristotle's reconstruction of the early history of the genre may have resembled what we find in some Euripidean prologues.[19] Two of Aeschylus's dramas, *Persians*, our earliest, and *Suppliants*, close in date to the *Oresteia*, lack prologues, or rather begin with the chorus which enters to the chant of anapaests and then proceeds to sing the entrance ode. The other extant plays have prologues, some of them spoken by one person, others featuring a succession of speeches or a dialogue. In *Seven*, the prologue, consisting of an address by Eteocles to a group of extras representing the people of Thebes, and a messenger's report about the enemy's preparations for battle, is followed by non-responding choral lyrics and then by an ode. This probably

19. Scholarship is still divided about the proper translation of *hypokritēs*, though the majority appears to favor the meaning "answerer" proposed by G. F. Else in *Wiener Studien* 72 (1959): 75–107. See also T. V. Buttrey in *GRBS* 18 (1977): 5–23.

means that the chorus of Theban women failed, in their entrance, to observe the choreographic decorum vouched for by introductory anapaests. In *Prometheus*, the prologue, for the most part a dialogue between two ministers of Zeus, is followed by solo anapaests—some of them, perhaps, sung rather than chanted—on the part of Prometheus, and then by an encounter, the chorus singing and Prometheus chanting. In *Agamemnon*, the prologue, spoken by a secondary who never reappears, is followed by extended systems of choral anapaests and then by a notoriously lengthy ode; in *Libation-Bearers*, the prologue, a speech by Orestes, is followed immediately by a choral ode; and in *Eumenides*, the prologue, a remarkably varied scene with four characters and a chorus, featuring both speeches and dialogue, is followed by a choral ode delivered with distributed parts. In this last play of the trilogy, the term "prologue" appears to be less than useful, for the segment of the drama that precedes the first ode is by itself a drama in miniature.[20]

It is a striking fact, therefore, that prologues can be different things, and that plays with prologues marshal the scene that follows in a variety of ways. It is especially surprising that the only prologue play which presents the regular anapaestic chanted entrance of the chorus is *Agamemnon*. In the other prologue plays, it must be assumed that the choristers enter silently while the prologue is being delivered, and place themselves in position to begin their singing; or, in the case of *Seven*, that they enter without the discipline expected of a chorus early in the proceedings, singing as they do so, with various members of the group spelling one another; or, in the case of *Eumenides*, that they are already in position when the action opens.

Notwithstanding the multiplicity of options, one or two intriguing similarities strike the eye. The closest parallel is that between *Seven* and *Eumenides*. They are similar in the length (though not in the dramatic nature) of the prologue, in the fragmented character of the singing, and in the structure of the ode, which in both cases consists of three dyads of cognate metrical composition. Next in degree of affinity are *Persians* and *Agamemnon*, except that the former has no prologue. The first ode of *Persians*, like that of *Agamemnon*, has in its center, separating one dyad from the next, a non-responding passage of considerable thematic importance: at *Pers.* 93–100, the chorus raises questions about the mysteriousness and potential fraudulence of the gods; at *Agam.* 140–59, a more extended interlude between dyads, the chorus completes its lyric report of the prophecy of Calchas, with hopeless appeals to Artemis and Apollo and reminders of the

---

20. For further details about initial scenes see H. W. Schmidt in Jens, *Bauformen*, pp. 1–27. Our knowledge of the beginnings of Aeschylean plays now lost to us is less firm than is suggested by U. von Wilamowitz-Moellendorff, *Aischylos-Interpretationen* (Berlin, 1914), pp. 56–59.

child-murdering tendencies of the House of Atreus. *Suppliants*, with a first ode of eight dyads and a large complement of non-responding units to relax the structure, stands by itself. *Prometheus* has no entrance ode.

What are we to make of this lack of conformity? Probably very little, except to say that it is not surprising to find structural similarities between the first utterances of the wise counsellors who form the choruses of *Persians* and *Agamemnon* and again of the distraught women who make up the choruses of *Seven* and *Eumenides*, though we may not be entirely prepared for the fact that the fearsome Furies should have much in common with the terrified women of Thebes.

Looking at the final scenes of the plays, the impression is once again one of variety rather than standard procedure.[21] In this instance, it will be useful to group the works according to their position, or presumed position, in their trilogies. Among first plays, *Suppliants* ends with a choral ode distributed between two half-choruses;[22] *Prometheus* ends with a long series of chanted anapaests distributed between the chorus and two characters; and *Agamemnon* ends with a brief series of spoken trochaic lines distributed between the chorus and two characters. Because of the briefness of this concluding passage (*Agam.* 1649–73), it is perhaps worth mentioning that it is preceded by an iambic dialogue between Aegisthus and the chorus-leader. The nearest singing and chanting are at a remove of about a hundred lines from the end. So much for first plays. It would be difficult to discover structural analogies in the examples given. For the second position, the middle play in a trilogy, we have only one certain candidate, *Libation-Bearers*. It ends with chanted anapaests, preceded by iambic dialogue. In third position, we have *Eumenides* and *Seven*. The former terminates with a brief choral ode in the simple ritual mode, preceded by a short iambic speech. *Seven*, on the other hand, concludes with a long lyric exchange between sub-groupings of the chorus (unless, that is, we regard lines 1005–78 as genuine, in which case the play ends with chanted anapaests). Finally, *Persians* stands by itself; it is now generally assumed that, though performed along with two or three other plays, it did not form part of a trilogy with a continuous subject.[23] For what it is worth, it, too, like *Seven*, ends with an extended lyric exchange, but this time between a character, Xerxes, and the chorus.

It should be apparent that in spite of the "rules" governing the architecture of a Greek tragedy, playwrights, and especially Aeschylus, permitted

21. G. Kremer in Jens, *Bauformen*, pp. 117–28.
22. M. McCall, "The Secondary Choruses in Aeschylus' *Supplices*," *California Studies in Classical Antiquity* 9 (1976): 117–31.
23. K. Deichgräber, *Die Persertetralogie des Aischylos* (*Akad. Wissensch. und Lit. Mainz, Abh. Geist. und Sozialw. Klasse*, 1974.4; Wiesbaden, 1974).

themselves considerable freedom in the shaping of the parts. One may note especially the structure, unique in the corpus of ancient playwriting, of the introduction of *Eumenides*, occasioned, I assume, by the initial step of giving the chorus a protagonist role, but also curiously at odds with it. The prologue is divided into three separate scenes: the initial speech spoken by the priestess, which is itself divided into two segments, separated by her vision of the Furies; the conversation between Orestes and Apollo; and Clytemnestra's ghost chiding the Furies, with the latter, out of the depths of their drugged sleep, responding with animal sounds. And when the chorus finally opens up, after a brief sequence of spoken iambs, it is not with the calm anapaests or the full-throated song known from other first scenes, but on a breathless, strident note, in the form of an excited, though metrically responding, interplay between several voices.

The burden of these remarks, which will have left the reader exhausted, has been to emphasize the plenitude of formal considerations guiding the Greek dramatist's hand, but also to signal the freedom with which a great playwright like Aeschylus was able to proceed. It was Aeschylus, we presume, who did more than any other writer to consolidate the forms which he applied with so much flexibility. Aristotle's testimony is fairly conclusive; modern scholarship is, if anything, inclined to assign to Aeschylus an even greater measure of responsibility than did Aristotle, whose preoccupation with the origins and the early development of tragedy may have blinded him to a full appreciation of Aeschylus's inventive genius.[24] Aeschylus's predecessors in the genre are little more than shadowy names. Only one of them, Phrynichus, "a student of Thespis" as the ancient commentators say, has left us a few fragments which, by their metrical variety, indicate that the genre was moving toward the fulfillment represented by Aeschylus. But the ancients also decided to relegate Phrynichus to oblivion, and to commemorate Aeschylus as the true founder of the tragic form.

24. G. F. Else, *Aristotle's Poetics: The Argument* (Cambridge, Mass., 1957), pp. 164 ff., esp. 179–80.

# 3

# Stage and Stage Action

Modern audiences deserve to see a play by Aeschylus in a modern production. To attempt a "classical" performance, complete with the trappings of a neo-classical revival, is to invite certain failure, and does not promote the cause of Aeschylus. The audience is not the same as the mixed assemblage of Athenians and foreigners, men and women, free men and slaves, rich and poor, intellectuals and illiterates, who gathered on a morning in late March or early April, hoping for blue skies so they would not be shivering in their improvised seats, and taking bets on the chances of victory on the part of the rival choruses whom they were getting ready to watch and judge. The modern audience is both more passive and more critical; it is also usually more familiar with a complex of dramatic traditions and types, each of which may have something to contribute to the effect that the director expects to achieve.

Imaginative directors and actors are drawn to the ancient repertory because a Greek play in its remoteness offers an unusual challenge of selection, combination, adaptation, and, in the end, recreation. To stage *Agamemnon* in the manner of Artaud, or by the rules of Stanislavsky, or in the form of a Handel oratorio, or as a Marxist passion play: some such choice is not only attractive but, to a degree, inevitable. But before a group decides what to do with *Eumenides*—an *auto sacramental?* a commedia dell'arte? both seem to me entirely legitimate—it is useful to find out, to the extent that this is possible, what the conditions of a performance in the Theater of Dionysus were, and how these conditions guided some of the writing that we have. A responsible director will wish to ascertain as much as he can about the ancient data before proceeding to his own version. A knowledge of Aeschylus's methods and of the material limitations that determined them is bound to enrich the modern director's understanding of his task.

The assumption here is that a play by Aeschylus is more than a piece of poetry. It was created in performance, not at a desk. What Gordon Craig said of *Hamlet*, that it was "complete when Shakespeare wrote the last word of his blank verse, and for us to add to it by gesture, scene, costume, or dance, is to hint that it is incomplete and needs these additions," though respectably Aristotelian, is odd enough as a statement about *Hamlet*, and even less acceptable applied to Aeschylus.[1] Aeschylus is, on all accounts, a

1. *On the Art of the Theatre* (London, 1911), p. 143.

remarkable poet. But his poetry cannot live without the stage action of which it is the verbal determinant. That it is often difficult for us to reconstruct the precise manner of the performance is another matter. There are, unfortunately, some popular misconceptions triggered by our knowledge that Greek tragedy was performed on the occasion of a religious festival, and that in its origins it may have been linked with the developing worship of Dionysus. This, it is felt, must mean that the Aeschylean stage offered grave motions, torpid speech, and music designed to stimulate a reverence for God.

Our information about the ancient stage derives, like some of the material discussed in the earlier chapters, from many different sources. Some of it goes back to ancient commentators, including Aristotle, Vitruvius, and others who were interested in the theater as an institution or as an architectural achievement. Even more important is the evidence of the anonymous writers of the scholia in the margins of our manuscripts. Much of this information is ambiguous; often the writers contradict one another; on other occasions the notices appear to be garbled or nonsensical. For example, the order of Might to Hephaestus to "step down, and collar his legs" at *Prom.* 74 has this note attached to it: "with his 'step down' he indicates the size of the god that is being enchained."[2] This scholar's view that Prometheus was a larger than life figure and that Hephaestus had to work on several levels to complete his pinioning and hammering has left its mark on a modern theory that Prometheus was represented by a huge wooden dummy, with the actor speaking his lines hidden behind it. There are other considerations that have contributed to this curious belief. But the "step down" has a much easier explanation: Prometheus stands on a wooden platform raised slightly above the level of the dancing floor, and if Hephaestus is going to work on his legs, he is well advised to step down from the podium to the lower level of the dancing floor instead of bending or crouching and thus endangering the audibility of his speech.

In spite of the occasional piece of wild speculation, there is a large body of impressive information to be gleaned from these writers, particularly when checked against the other two sources available to us: the archaeological evidence—both from excavations of ancient theaters and from ancient paintings representing dramatic performances or drawing on theatrical motifs or props—and the internal evidence from the plays themselves.[3] The

2. J. Herington, *The Older Scholia on the "Prometheus Bound"* (*Mnemosyne Suppl.* 20; Leiden, 1972), p. 82, line 74a.

3. Conditions of performance are discussed in many outstanding works. Among them are two volumes by A. Pickard-Cambridge: *The Dramatic Festivals of Athens*[2], ed. J. Gould and D. M. Lewis (Oxford, 1968), and *The Theatre of Dionysus in Athens* (Oxford, 1946). See also P. Arnott, *Greek Scenic Conventions in the Fifth Century* B.C. (Oxford, 1962). For Aeschy-

combined testimony of these sources is substantial; but each morsel of intelligence needs to be examined with caution. For the masks and the costumes and certain stage machines, for instance, we go to Pollux, a lexicographer of the second century A.D. who has assembled the pertinent data in a most orderly fashion.[4] There is just one difficulty; Pollux's date, six centuries after the time of the original performances, and probably at least four centuries after the Greek theater gave way to the Hellenistic and Roman theaters, with their raised stage, projecting wings, high buskins and elaborate headgear, and, most especially, the atrophy of the chorus. Though Pollux appears to have had access to early material, much of his discussion reflects the experience of the Greco-Roman world rather than of classical Greece.

Similar, though more subtle, doubts attach to the archaeological evidence. The southern Italian vases from which recent scholarship has tried to gather additional knowledge about masks and costumes are much closer in time to Aeschylus than Pollux's *Onomasticon*. But they, too, date from a period—that of Aristotle and after—which was more familiar with what we call "Middle Tragedy," a period which saw the building of the first stone auditorium and stage in the precinct of Dionysus and which prized certain conventions that had first been introduced by Euripides. Even the spade of the archaeologist, indispensable as the digging has been to a better understanding of the Aeschylean stage, cannot always furnish the kind of evidence that meets with unanimous approval. Not all experts, for instance, agree that Aeschylus's stage was equipped with the wooden platform mentioned above in connection with the task of Hephaestus. Was Aeschylus the first to use the shed at the back of the stage as an integral part of the dramatic setting? Once it *was* used for a scenic background, how many doors did it have? Did Aeschylus use the machine called a "crane" (*geranos*) or the *ekkyklēma*, a contraption to produce the corpses of persons killed off stage? These are some of the questions which have not yet been resolved to everybody's satisfaction.

For the purposes of this treatment, however, it would be unproductive to dwell on the uncertainties. Once again, I must ask the reader to believe that the area of agreement is large. With rare exceptions I shall proceed as if our information were fairly reliable—which it is, by and large. In matters where the authorities do not agree with each other, I shall adopt the proposal that seems to me the most likely or I shall cite the alternatives. Fortunately, many of the more controversial questions pertain to matters of

---

lus there is now O. Taplin, *The Stagecraft of Aeschylus* (Oxford, 1977). The archaeological evidence is most appealingly presented in A. D. Trendall and T. B. L. Webster, *Illustrations of Greek Drama* (London, 1971).

4. The standard edition of Pollux's *Onomasticon* is by E. Bethe (Leipzig, 1900–37).

secondary concern to the kind of understanding which this book is designed to supply.

We may begin with one of the more widely known facts: an Aeschylean play is, in keeping with official limitations, performed with a complement of three speakers or actors. It is true that three of the plays we have— *Persians*, *Seven*, *Suppliants*—can be performed with only two actors; and Aristotle suggests that when Aeschylus began producing his plays, only two actors per play were, as a rule, available to a producer. But, as *Suppliants* shows, the fact that a play could be performed with only two actors does not necessarily mean that no more than two were available. For we now know that the play was presented toward the end of the 460s, by which time, presumably, the city had made allowance for the addition of the third actor.[5] For all that, it seems that Aeschylus's earlier plays were written for a smaller set of characters, and avoided scenes featuring more than two speaking characters, with ample time allowed between appearances for the changes of costume which enabled an actor to play several parts. None of Aeschylus's extant plays offers the tightly joined scenes and the varied cast of *dramatis personae* of some of the later plays of Sophocles, which have challenged modern scholars to set up the most complicated schemes of changes of costume to abide by the three actors convention.

Aeschylus did not play hard and fast with the convention. It was well suited to his purposes, and often left him with personnel to spare. Even *Libation-Bearers*, with its cast of seven speaking characters and its accelerated intrigue plot, fits comfortably into the scheme. No more than three of the characters are ever on the stage together and there is ample time, usually in the form of an extended choral passage, between the exit of an actor and his reappearance in a different costume. Only once does there appear to be intolerable pressure on the convention: when Pylades, the constant companion of Orestes, pronounces his unique lines, *Lib.* 900–902, in the presence of Orestes and Clytemnestra and the attendant who has sounded the alarm. The solution of this problem seems to be that the part of Pylades was played by an extra, one of a group of subsidiary players who occupied the stage alongside the principal actors in the roles of servants, bodyguards, and citizens. This is not the only play in which a few walk-on lines must have been spoken by a supernumerary. But we find it in no other play of Aeschylus.

Of the size of the chorus, Pollux tells us that down to the time of Aeschylus's *Eumenides*, the tragic chorus consisted of fifty members, but that the fifty Furies on the stage proved so frightening and caused such a disturbance that afterwards the authorities limited the number of the choristers to fif-

5. For the evidence of the new date, see Appendix.

teen.[6] Some have accepted this charming tale.[7] Others have pointed to the structure of the choral sequence after the killing of Agamemnon (*Agam.* 1348–71) in defense of their belief that the chorus of the time consisted of twelve. All three figures—twelve, fifteen, and fifty—occur in the ancient evidence. The most likely solution is a fluctuating membership of roughly twelve to fifteen. The figure of fifty may have come in from the large choruses used in the dramatic performances called *dithyrambs* or from the legends from which many of the tragic plots were drawn, in which sets of daughters or sons—of Priam, of Danaus, of Aegyptus—typically numbered fifty. Since the training and the fitting out of the chorus was the financial responsibility of a benefactor chosen for the occasion, supporting a chorus of fifty, along with various other costs not required in a dithyramb, would have meant an enormous expenditure. As it is, the Aeschylean stage is peopled with secondary choruses—choral extras who add to the color and the movement but only rarely have their own words and music. When at *Libation-Bearers* 980 ff., Orestes shows the fatal cloak to the people, these are citizens who have filed in toward the end of the play and who will be used again in the latter half of *Eumenides*, *not* the chorus of servants who carry the choral action. Aegisthus, in *Agamemnon*, brings in his retainers, as Agamemnon had brought his own. The greatest splash of choral activity is found in *Suppliants*, where the main chorus of the daughters of Danaus is complemented by groups of Egyptians, Argive soldiers, and perhaps maid servants.

Many questions remain. In addition to the eleven judges who adjudicate the case of Orestes (*Eum.* 708 ff.), is there a chorus of Athenian citizens? Are the singing worshippers at the end of the play (1033 ff.) identical with the judges, or with the citizens, or are they yet another group of choristers? At *Lib.* 1048 ff., when Orestes has his first vision of the Furies, do they—i.e., extras in the costume later to be worn by the Furies of *Eumenides*—appear on the stage? One's first reaction is: probably not; Orestes hallucinates. But then one remembers the epic tradition whereby Athena appears to Achilles and to the listener, though seen by no other character.[8] Even more than the epic, drama favors the embodying of visions. Further, as we shall have occasion to note, the end of *Libation-Bearers* is already, in a sense, the beginning of *Eumenides*, precisely as the conclusion of *Agamemnon* is, in its way, the opening of *Libation-Bearers*.

These very summary remarks about the size and the number of Aeschylean choruses must suffice. About their dancing and singing, we are hope-

6. *Pollux* 4.110.

7. A. D. Fitton Brown, "The Size of the Greek Tragic Chorus," *Classical Review* 7 (1957): 1–4.

8. Homer *Iliad* 1.197 ff.

lessly uninformed, and what information we have is likely to be wrong.[9] The chief problem here is the lyric dyad, the very core of the musical action of the chorus. Because the twin stanzas are identical metrically, and that means, by and large, rhythmically, one would assume the dancing steps to be the same for each. On the other hand, many twins differ considerably from each other in content and mood. Does this mean that the dancing is not "mimetic," reflecting in its choreography the felt substance of what is being sung? On another point, some scholars assume that at the end of the dyad the choristers have returned to the position on the stage from which they set out at its start; are the movements performed to the singing of the answering twin counterclockwise, responding to movements in the opposite direction during the singing of the prior twin? These questions have something pedantic, even petty, about them. That they must be asked reveals the woeful state of our ignorance on the subject of the dramatic dance, but also our conviction that there were formal rules to guide the performance. It is entirely possible that dramatic dancing was not the sophisticated art which we indicate by the name of choreography, but consisted of simple progressions of steps that could almost be improvised by energetic chorus-leaders. The vase paintings, showing a large spectrum of bodily gestures, appear to argue for a more developed art of dancing. Conversely, at least one fragment from Aristophanes comments with surprise on the variety of dance movements in a play by Aeschylus, as if such virtuosity were unusual.[10]

The music is an equal mystery. We now have portions of some ancient scores for choral music.[11] But none of them have been read definitively, and in any case no trace of Aeschylean music has been preserved among them. It is assumed, though without very much evidence to back it up, that the singing was in unison, along with the double reed pipe and, for special effects, the great seven-stringed *kithara*. We also know that the musical line involved progressions that cannot be identified with the intervals on our half-tone scale and that particular tonic progressions went along with particular metrical schemes. But in the absence of adequate ancient records and

9. H. D. F. Kitto, "The Dance in Greek Tragedy," *JHS* 75 (1955): 36–41. A more confident view is expressed by J. W. Fitton, "Greek Dance," *CQ* 23 (1973): 254–74. See also Pickard-Cambridge, *Dramatic Festivals*, pp. 246 ff.

10. Aristophanes fr. 678, in J. M. Edmonds, ed. and tr., *The Fragments of Attic Comedy*, vol. 1 (Leiden, 1957). The reference is to the dance figures performed by the chorus that accompanied Priam to his ransoming session with Achilles in Aeschylus's *Phrygians*.

11. E. Pöhlmann, *Griechische Musikfragmente* (*Erlanger Beiträge* 8; Nuremberg, 1960). See the same author's "Die Notenschrift in der Überlieferung der griechischen Bühnenmusik," *Würzburger Jahrbücher* 2 (1976): 53–73. Our most tantalizing scrap of dramatic music comes from Euripides's *Orestes*; see D. D. Feaver, "The Musical Setting of Euripides' *Orestes*," *AJP* 81 (1960): 1–15.

persuasive modern interpretations of the scores, such abstract knowledge, derived from Greco-Roman handbooks of musical theory, does us little good. The music and the dance of ancient tragedy, the very elements which Nietzsche isolated as its essentials, are, alas, a closed book to us.

All actors, and all members of the choruses, were men or, in some cases, boys. Since Aeschylus presents choruses acting out the parts of women and girls in five out of his seven extant plays, and since some of the most memorable characters on the Attic stage are women, the limiting condition appears particularly striking. The staging of tragedies was an extension of the social and political life of the city. In fifth-century Athens, women were virtually without power. *Mulier tacet in ecclesia* is in its literal origins a comment on what was expected of a woman in the unlikely eventuality that she should stray into a public meeting (*ekklēsia*). Unlike a later age which associated the theater and acting with the demi-monde, and therefore willingly recognized the histrionic abilities of women, the Athenians of the classical age ranked acting on a par with pleading in court or delivering speeches at a senate session. A chorus granted by the public officials in charge of the festival was a group of men representing a borough of the city. It was expected to compete, in the fullest sense of the word, with other choruses representing other boroughs. It stood to reason that only men could be entrusted with so responsible a public role. It would have been unseemly for a woman to appear in a public gathering and address the crowd.

It would also have been unseemly for her to don rags, outlandish garb, or royal purple. Both actors and choristers wore elaborate costumes; further, they wore masks, made normally of stiffened linen. The original purpose of these seems to have been not so much histrionic as psychological; by putting on a mask, a man concealed the distinct features of his personality and identified himself with a larger group whose function required a limiting of his individuality. The roots of masking, it is assumed, are in religious ritual. Its use for embellishment and fun was prominent in ancient cults, especially in the cult of Dionysus, a god who required of his celebrants that they renounce their privileged standing and adopt the anonymity of members of the herd. This is of some significance for what happens in drama, especially as regards the role of the chorus. In addition, however, the painted features of the masks help the onlookers to identify the characters in the play and to follow them through the twists of their fortunes without having to rely solely on the subtler testimony of voice, gait, or physical shape, cues which in the vast hollow of the Greek theater could easily get lost. The masks also helped to maintain the dramatic effect which, if we can believe Ionesco, cannot work satisfactorily without the aid of the unnatural:

"If the actors embarrassed me by not seeming natural enough, perhaps it was because they also were, or tried to be, too natural; by trying not to be, perhaps they will still appear natural, but in a different way. They must not be afraid of not being natural." [12]

Two widespread misconceptions about Greek dramatic costuming should be cleared up before we proceed. The Aeschylean mask lay flat against the face, and contained no mechanism for projecting or enlarging the voice. And the buskin (*kothornos*) used by the Aeschylean actor was a travelling boot made out of soft leather, without elevator soles. Nor would there have been any point in an actor's footwear raising him above the level of the stage. The bulk of the audience looked down upon the stage from the hillside against which they were perched. The raised buskin came into its own only in the Hellenistic and Roman periods, when select audiences came to occupy the area once thronged by dancing choruses, and looked up at a stage raised high above their seats.

The costuming was lavish, outlandish, or derelict as the plot demanded. Euripides was not the first, notwithstanding the gibes of the comedians, to put beggars on the stage. When Xerxes arrives (*Pers*. 908) he is wearing the garments he has torn at Salamis at the sight of his troops suffering defeat (1030, cf. 468). The identity of character and costume outlasts the passing of clock-time—the all but interminable retreat that took Xerxes from the shore of central Greece through Thrace and Anatolia back to the royal court at Susa. In this case the costuming is uncontroversial. So it is, on the whole, for most of the characters on the Aeschylean stage, including the exotic Egyptians in *Suppliants* and Ocean on his hippogryph in *Prometheus*. That is to say, either the text provides us with some salient feature of the costume or we are at liberty to supply appropriate garb from vase paintings and other pictorial aids. But how are we to imagine Prometheus, spread-eagled against his rock? Does Hephaestus drive his wedge (*Prom*. 64) clean through a layer of clothing, or are we to think of him as stripped to the waist, i.e., dressed in tights like some of the more ribald characters on the comic stage? And how are we to picture the Furies in *Eumenides*, whose appearance is said to have made some women among the spectators faint and others miscarry? The great German scholar Gottfried Hermann pointed to the many pictorial representations of the Furies pursuing Orestes in which they are shown as stately, even attractive ladies rather than as fearsome or disgusting apparitions. [13] The conversion of the Furies at the end of the play, or rather the corroboration of the more positive aspect which has vied for recognition almost from the start, cannot be accompanied by a

12. *Notes and Counter Notes* (New York, 1964), p. 26.
13. *Aeschyli Tragoediae* rec., ed. M. Haupt, vol. 2 (Berlin, 1859), pp. 648–49.

visual change. Athena draws attention to the fact (*Eum.* 990) that their awesome aspect remains the same to the end. The only conclusion that seems possible is that the costuming and masking of the Furies struck a sober note, midway between fearsome and attractive, which could be useful and convincing in both parts of the play.

Here again the text is our best help. To start at the beginning: how do we discover that the creatures embodied in the chorus are the Furies? (For the sake of the argument I am assuming that the Furies have not appeared bodily to Orestes at the end of *Libation-Bearers*.) When the priestess first talks about them, she says that they are not women but Gorgons; then not really Gorgons either, but like Harpies: the comparison is implied by her reference to a painting she once saw of Phineus and his feast (*Eum.* 50–51). Apollo refers to them (68 ff.) as "loathed young women, wizened, ancient children" shunned by all, living in darkest Tartarus. Clytemnestra says (106 ff.) that she has sacrificed to them in nocturnal rites, and orders them to pursue Orestes with hot breath. Their own measure of themselves is that they are ancient divinities (150) whose task it is to pursue and punish killers, especially matricides (210). They describe their actions in terms appropriate to hunting dogs (246 ff.). All this is worked out in stronger and stronger language, but without a manifest or overt identification. At 312 they assert that their transactions are "fair and square" because they punish only the sinner and not the guiltless. Finally, in the first refrain of their "binding charm," the song designed to secure a magic noose around Orestes (331), they introduce themselves, though the wording of the line leaves a trace of uncertainty: "the song goes back to the Furies." It is as if Aeschylus were at pains not to single the Furies out specifically from among the various creatures and spirits associated with punishment and revenge. In any case the identification is short-lived; when Athena asks them who they are, they call themselves children of the night, and add that they are called Curses in the lower world (416–17). Athena answers: I know the family and the designations; as if to say: I appreciate your not stating outright who you are.

It is clear that the playwright wants their standing cloaked in some mystery. The mystery continues long after their general function has been established. With so much artful speech dedicated to creating a picture, or a non-picture, in the minds of the audience, we may, I think, conclude that specificity or even genre detail in the costuming and the masking would have run counter to the author's intention. The detail noted by the priestess (54) that the eyes of the creatures are dripping what the scholiast calls "a bloody flow" (the text itself is corrupt) is sufficient in the telling, and need not be duplicated on the mask.

Should it be at *Agam.* 1428? The chorus, by one of those anticipations whereby Clytemnestra, while still alive, is likened to the Furies, sings about her eyes: they have a dripping of blood upon them.[14] Are we to imagine that as Clytemnestra emerges from the murder, her mask is sprinkled with red dye? The answer must surely be no; the chorus, through its words, helps us to see her face as the mask never could. Such is the power of Aeschylean speech; through the grace of the song, we receive hints that take us beyond the rudimentary shapes on the stage, and enable us to create our own shapes in our minds' eyes. Athenian audiences were capable of imagining fire, darkness, and earthquakes. More commonly, they were invited to visualize the streaming hair and the torn cheeks dramatized in song by lamenting choruses. Racine's emphasis on tears, glances, eyes raised to the sky (critics have spoken of an eye-fetishism in Racine), a world of feeling established by means of facial expressions is missing from the Greek acting canon. But what the masks cannot provide is, in many instances, as in Racine, furnished by verbal cues; the imagination does the rest.

The stage on which the Aeschylean chorus and actors mingle is a hard-packed circular dancing floor (orchēstra) some eighty feet in diameter, and thus more than half the width of an American football field. The orchestra constitutes the space and the boundary of the dramatic action. In its origin, it probably goes back to the circular area cut into the hillside which even today, in countless Greek hamlets, serves as threshing floor and as a place to dry the grapes.[15] Unlike the modern proscenium stage with its simulation of bounded interior space, the orchestra breathes the freedom of the open air in which the Greeks exulted. The contrast especially with the drama that is currently popular is striking. Where the new wave emphasizes the closed room, the narrow courtyard, the tight ashcan, the Athenian theater shunned constraints. As in a painting by Giotto, rebelling against the Gothic enclosures, each character, including the members of the chorus, is enveloped in air and light, and contoured against the flat dancing floor. The configuration of the theater encouraged the feeling that all life, here sampled through dramatic action, is public life, untrammeled, open to the view of many, with a common sun shining down on all. Both the pressures of Racinian space—the chamber, the antechamber, the threatening feel of the sea beyond—and the limitless expanse of romantic space—of Faust, of Peer Gynt, of The Dynasts—are avoided in the clearly marked outlines of a dramatic space that combines freedom with definition.[16]

---

14. E. Fraenkel, Aeschylus: Agamemnon (Oxford, 1950) and D. Page, Aeschylus: Agamemnon (with J. D. Denniston, Oxford, 1957), among others, prefer to think that the line refers to Clytemnestra's (naturally) bloodshot eyes.

15. A. D. Ure, "Threshing-Floor or Vineyard," CQ 5 (1955): 225–30.

16. For Racinian space, see R. Barthes, Sur Racine (Paris, 1972), pp. 15 ff.

Five of our seven tragedies, all except *Agamemnon* and *Libation-Bearers*, require nothing further for their staging than this orchestra, with some limited use of a low wooden podium at the further edge of it, some fifty by nine feet in size, for those occasions when the loneliness of a character, or his dramatic importance, needed to be stressed by separating him from the chorus and isolating him in that location. As a rule, however, actors and chorus appeared on the same plane and within the same area, reinforcing the closeness of their dramatic relationship by a staging that emphasized their mutual dependency. Entrances and exits for both chorus and actors were at the two sides where the seating area of the auditorium sloped down to level ground. Materially speaking, they enter from nowhere and exit to nowhere; when they are not on stage, their location is of no immediate dramatic significance.

But in the first and second plays of the *Oresteia* this is no longer true.[17] What happens off stage—specifically, within the palace—is of great importance to the drama, and some of the movements on and off stage are plotted in relation to this palace. It is now assumed that what happened was this. When the great circular area had been cut into the southern slope of the Acropolis hill, some time early in the fifth century, the northern and eastern parts, before and to the left of the audience, were deeply gouged out of the living rock, while the portions to the west and south, to the right of the audience and at the furthest edge of the play area, had to be shored up with rubble and fill. The escarpment at the furthest edge was very steep; its height was sufficient to accommodate, below it and out of sight for most of the audience, a modest shed for storing properties, as well as for the few costume changes that Aeschylean drama required. To change his costume, an actor had to leave the orchestra via one of the side entrances and make his way down to the shed at the foot of it. This was sufficient for all practical purposes, especially in Aeschylean drama, which put no premium on light-ning-quick changes of costume.

At a certain point, however, it was decided to erect a further structure upon the roof of the old shed. This new structure, whose floor was roughly on the same level as the orchestra, or perhaps as the podium at the back of

17. For a thoughtful discussion of problems of staging, see O. Taplin, *Greek Tragedy in Action* (Berkeley and Los Angeles, 1978). In certain details, my conclusions differ from his, as also presented in his *The Stagecraft of Aeschylus* (Oxford, 1977). I hasten to add that my preference for a simple stage, without an elaborate stage building or *paraskēnia*, is not shared by all. For a contrary view, see S. Melchinger, *Das Theater der Tragödie* (Munich, 1974), and the important review by E. Simon in *arcadia* 11 (1976): 298–300. Ms. Simon is herself the author of a pertinent book: *Das antike Theater* (Heidelberg, 1972). All modern studies of the Theater of Dionysus in Athens go back to the decisive studies of W. Dinsmoor, especially his "The Athenian Theater of the Fifth Century," in *Studies Presented to D. M. Robinson*, vol. 1 (St. Louis, 1951), pp. 309–30.

the orchestra, could now be used to represent the palace—occasionally the cave—that so many of the later plays presuppose. What is more, actors could now enter and exit through the new structure, from which a ladder led into the shed below. Finally, the roof of the new structure could be used for appearances of divinities, though there is no place in the extant plays of Aeschylus where this is required. Only the watchman in the prologue of *Agamemnon* (3) announces the coming of day from a perch on the roof.

Once the structure is there, with its potential for a quickened and more complicated dramatic action, it is difficult to think away. As far as we know, it was permanent. Still, plays like *Eumenides* continued to be written which make no effective use of the new structure, and whose dramatic space is, in fact, the old undefined, flexible, open expanse of the orchestra. One might go so far as to say that the new scene building, or rather its front, which was the only part that really counted, remained, at least for Aeschylus and his immediate successors, a resource to be exploited or neglected as the occasion demanded and not a limiting condition of the art. There has been some discussion whether the front, or *scene* as I shall henceforth call it, had two doors, or only one. Because of the importance I assign to the sense of freedom, to the avoidance of anything that might suggest enclosure or confinement, I should be happy if it could be proved that there were two doors. Somewhat later, in Aristophanic comedy, two doors were probably the rule to designate the two houses of the antagonists. But for the Aeschylus of the *Oresteia* this needs to be qualified. In the second half of *Libation-Bearers*, the door of the palace, one door, has dramatic importance. Orestes knocks on it (653), it is an obstacle, a temptation; it can hide as well as release, and it is the boundary between conspiracy and achievement. Contrast the first half of the play, where space is not similarly subdivided between what is within and what is without. Electra moves freely between the palace and Agamemnon's grave with the same ease that characterizes movements in some of the earlier plays. Clytemnestra and Aegisthus, on the other hand, are killed within a space that Orestes has had to penetrate and conquer. And with the cries of death, Agamemnon's as well as Aegisthus's, the absorption of the further space into the acting area is fully documented.

It is, of course, unlikely that the arrangement of the doors could have been changed between the first and second half of *Libation-Bearers*. A modern director will have to make his own decisions without knowledge of how Aeschylus intended the movements. But the presence of the scene structure will have left some options to Aeschylus himself. When the slave reports the death of Aegisthus (875) and attempts to get the women's quarters opened to warn Clytemnestra, are we to imagine that he has emerged from one back door and is now hammering on the other? Or is he knocking on a central door, having, in the old manner, emerged via the long route from the side of the orchestra? Though it is my suspicion that *Eumenides* could have been enacted without the new scene, Aeschylus would, of course, have been tempted to use the new facilities. The hypothesis of two different doors remains attractive.

The issue of the doors pales in significance by comparison with what is now the most vigorously disputed problem in Aeschylean and fifth-century staging in general: the location of the structure which could variously serve as an altar or as a tomb or even merely as a lookout. Recent studies have taken cognizance of the rocky, unevenly graded area at the eastern intersection of orchestra and auditorium, to the extreme left of the audience, and have proposed that it served for a lookout, especially in the plays prior to the advent of the scene building, as in *Seven* 80 ff., and *Suppliants* 711 ff. where Danaus reports to his daughters the coming of the Egyptians.[18] But *Seven* 80 ff. is, in my interpretation, not a scene of reporting but one of imaginings, and hence does not require a lookout. Moreover, I cannot persuade myself that so important a stage action as Danaus's message to his daughters and their dances of fear could be tucked away on the extreme periphery of the orchestra against a wall of rock that would severely limit their freedom of action. I prefer to go along with those who place the structure in question on the central podium at the back of the orchestra. In *Suppliants*, the structure is called a rock (189) and a lookout (713); but the whole area of which it is a part is felt to be a holy grove, a place of worship (222 ff.) which the women are asked to enter (508). It is likely that as the women take refuge in the sacred area, they step upon the platform usually reserved to actors.[19] The same may be the case with the Theban women of *Seven*, whose temporary occupation of the platform would underscore their interference with the purposes and motions of the king. When the scene comes to be added to the stage, the closeness of the grave to the palace, evidenced in *Libation-Bearers*, descends in a direct line from the architectural arrangements at Mycenae and elsewhere.

This central structure, with its varied uses, is not to be confused with the small altar in the middle of the orchestra, which in Aeschylus's day had already become purely decorative, or perhaps served the exclusive purpose of marking the center of the area on which the chorus moved. We are told that dithyrambic choruses tended to move in a circular pattern, around the center of the stage, and similar patterns may have been followed by tragic

18. See, especially, N. G. L. Hammond, "The Conditions of Dramatic Production to the Death of Aeschylus," *GRBS* 13 (1972): 387–450.

19. For the movements of the chorus in *Suppliants*, I subscribe to the suggestions of Arnott, *Greek Scenic Conventions*, pp. 22 ff.

choruses. When the platform structure represented an altar, it could, as in
*Seven* and *Suppliants*, be embellished with the images of the divinities whom
the chorus addresses in its odes. Once again, however, it is conceivable that
the fullness with which the choristers list the divinities—at *Seven* 104 ff.
those named are Ares, Athena, Poseidon, Aphrodite, Apollo, Artemis, and
either Zeus or Hera—is the author's notice that we are to use our imagination rather than rely on visible stage presences. At *Suppl.* 354 f., Pelasgus
avers that he sees

> this host of umpire gods
> lowering their heads, darkened with fresh-cut branches.

It is difficult to decide between the assumption that the statues of the gods
flank the stage altar and the notion that the gods are present only in the
imagination. In the former case, their evident fixity would create its own
incongruity with what Pelasgus says of them.

Because of its interchangeability as an altar and a tomb—amusingly, at
*Lib.* 106 the chorus leader says that the chorus venerates the grave of
Agamemnon as if it were an altar—it may be assumed that no scenic
changes were necessary to convert the structure from one function to another. What is more, no fires were lit on the altar; there is little or no
sacrificing on the Aeschylean stage.[20] The choral references at the beginning
of *Agamemnon* to smoking altars are just what they seem to be: a conjuring
up of the vista of the precinct areas in the city beyond the stage, and not a
description of what is happening on the stage. In *Persians* (609 ff.), the
Empress Mother brings liquid gifts—milk, wine, honey—to feed her dead
husband in his tomb, who rises in response. The offerings to Agamemnon
at the beginning of *Libation-Bearers* fall under the same heading. But these
are not sacrifices to cult divinities. It appears that Aeschylus avoided a
mimesis of divine cult on stage. His dramaturgy retains no substantial link
with the sacred rites from which tragedy is said to have sprung. Even the
most fervently religious choral hymns are far removed in wording and content from what can be recovered of the ritual singing associated with the
cults of his time.

The scene, with its door or doors, was a boundary, not a purveyor of
illusion. There was, as far as we can tell, no scene painting in the fifth-
century theater. Agatharchus, who is sometimes named as the inventor of
scene painting, appears to have enlivened the view of the scene with simple
designs. But we are not to imagine caves, crags, and trees suggesting a
landscape, or an architectural ensemble. As far as the visible setting is
concerned, the scene building failed to modify the tabula rasa character of

20. But two fragments, frs. 26 and 208 Smyth, appear to call for sacrifices on stage.

the old acting space. The temple at Delphi and the palace of Agamemnon looked exactly alike; so did the cave of Philoctetes in Sophocles's play and the stable of the dung-beetle in Aristophanes's *Peace*. All interiors are, in any case, to be imagined; more commonly, are explicitly converted into exteriors and assimilated to the open space of the orchestra.

This can be compared with tendencies in the painting of the time. A vase by the so-called Codrus painter shows Aegeus, the father of Theseus, consulting the goddess Themis at Delphi.[21] We know that Delphic consultations took place inside the temple. On the painting Themis is located behind a column, while the consultant stands in front of it. The aim of the painter seems to have been to create a combination of interior and exterior space, to show more than the immediate, minuscule moment of consultation. On the orchestra stage, the playwright works not so much by combination as by assimilation or conversion. Especially in comedy, where we might often, especially in the scenes between husbands and wives, look for an interior, but also in tragedy, notably in intrigue scenes, all actions that might realistically be thought to take place within a house are moved into the open air of the public forum or of the promenade. The result is that we cease to distinguish between this or that setting; the scene of the drama is one, suitable for the presentation of all actions which in ordinary life demand their specific settings. I need not belabor the point that such visual universality can have a liberating effect. By forcing the audience to obtain its clues from the spoken word, rather than from scenic identifiers, the tragedy enhances its power.

This means that we cannot, properly speaking, talk of "shifts of scene." In *Eumenides*, the action supposedly moves from the Temple of Apollo at Delphi to the sanctuary of Athena in Athens, and from there perhaps to the Hill of Ares, the Areopagus. In another of Aeschylus's plays, *Women of Aetna*, we are told there were five changes of scene. Other playwrights furnish additional parallels.[22] In *Eumenides*, one might wish to contend that the action at Delphi is merely preliminary to the main action, which is in Athens. But this kind of argument assigns too great a significance to the topographical pointers. The final chorus of the play, with which the tamed Furies are conducted from the hill to their subterranean dwellings, offers no tangible information for anyone who wishes to trace their progress. In a larger sense, the Areopagus is merely a proto-Areopagus, spiritually part of Athena's domain, but beginning to claim its independence. And Delphi's difference from Athens is a vestige of the myth and, more important, the

---

21. Discussed by R. Hampe, *Die Gleichnisse Homers und die Bildkunst seiner Zeit* (*Die Gestalt* 22; Tübingen, 1952), p. 39.
22. Fr. 287 Lloyd-Jones.

minimal sketching of an Apollo on home base which the ideological dynamics of the play require. Dramatically speaking, Apollo and Athena
share the same ground, as indeed they do quite literally in the later part of
the play. Unlike Sophocles and Euripides, both of whom offer a more concrete sense of specific place and time, and who associate individual characters with habitats congenial to them, Aeschylus permits an ideal setting
which is the same, more or less, for all his characters. *Libation-Bearers* does
not present a succession of two scenes—one at the tomb of Agamemnon and
the second before the palace—but a comprehensive space that subsumes
both. (If the tomb is, in fact, immediately in front of the palace scene, with
two doors on either side of it, no shift need be imagined in the first place.) It
stands to reason that there are small variations from play to play; the setting
of *Prometheus*, with the protagonist standing up against the isolated rock,
calls for no identifying features whatever beyond the rich canvases of worlds
of travel out of reach, while the setting of *Eumenides*, with its trial procedure
familiar to the man in the street, is under some pressure, to which Aeschylus does not surrender, to forsake its ideality.[23] To the degree that the playwright elects to stress particulars, they are an attribute of the action, and in
the end of costuming, rather than of space.

   To revert to the mechanics of the staging: Aeschylus has two ghosts,
those of Darius and of Clytemnestra. There are no trapdoors; certain underground passages below the level of the orchestra date from a later period.
Ghosts rise from behind tombs. In *Persians* (681 ff.) Darius emerges on top
of the mound behind which he must have been crouching from the very
start of the play. After the conclusion of his exchange with the Empress and
the chorus, he withdraws to the same position. There really is no alternative, unless we accept a recent suggestion that at the end of his speech, after
842, Darius remained on stage for the rest of the play, as "a silent, brooding
presence."[24] In certain dramatic traditions, corpses get up and leave when
their presence is no longer required. The exit of a ghost imposes less of a
strain on our credulity; perhaps it is to be preferred to a prolonged stoop
behind the tomb. That we should have to ask these questions and ponder
the alternatives is a mark of our helplessness vis-à-vis a stage not equipped
for the enactment of *coups de théâtre*. The helplessness is complete in the face
of the ending of *Prometheus*; the language tells us that Prometheus and the
chorus are swallowed up in a cosmic cataclysm. Are we to imagine that they
fall down, and then rise and file out? Or do they, as has been suggested,
move toward the edge of the orchestra and jump the five or six feet to the
lower ground beyond?

   23. See U. von Wilamowitz-Moellendorff, *Aischylos-Interpretationen* (Berlin, 1914), pp.
181–82.
   24. M. Anderson, "The Imagery of the *Persians*," *Greece and Rome* 19 (1972): 174.

The scarlet fabrics upon which Agamemnon steps (*Agam.* 957) are evidence that drama is more than rhetoric and gesture. Aeschylus's use of stage properties is a far cry from what comes to clutter the actors' paths in nineteenth- and twentieth-century realistic drama. In *Agamemnon*, the chariot on which the king and Cassandra arrive—probably a modest transport vehicle rather than a triumphal carriage—and the scarlet material are the only major properties used prior to the revelation of the corpses when the fatal net, the "rank opulence of array" (1383), joins them as a third and last, unless we conclude from lines 1539–40 that the fatal bathtub is shown also in this demonstration of the tools of murder.

Elsewhere properties are equally sparse. The action of the trial in *Eumenides* demands voting urns and the pebbles brought to the judges for balloting. In *Persians*, besides the Empress Mother's vehicle, there are the vessels and baskets in which she, or rather her retainers, bring her gifts for Darius. No major props are needed in *Seven*, *Suppliants*, or *Libation-Bearers* save the branches and pitchers which, like the old men's staffs in *Agamemnon*, are part of the personal equipment identifying the agents. *Prometheus* is unique in this respect. The torture instruments with which Hephaestus fastens Prometheus against his rock, i.e., against the mound on the podium, include a hammer, a wedge, and chains; and Ocean's "swift-winged bird," the conveyance—a ship-cart?—carrying the chorus of Oceanids, and Io's hybrid accoutrements signify an interest in baroque adornment that sets the play apart from the others, though there appear to have been similar things in some of the lost tragedies. In *Libation-Bearers*, Aeschylus might well have anticipated Sophocles's treatment of the legend by having Orestes produce the urn with the ashes. Characteristically, Aeschylus mentions the urn without bringing it on stage; it is more effective in Phocia where he leaves it (686–87). Aeschylus knew how to use the stage for a spectacle. His mighty combinations of choruses with their ambitious dances, the lavish costumes often, as in *Suppliants* and *Persians*, highlighted by foreign and exotic touches, gave him a reputation as the most spectacular of dramatic poets. While an indiscriminate use of stage properties was not part of his manner, the few that he did use were endowed with a special power.

The most famous is, of course, the article which I have called the scarlet fabrics. Two prevalent misconceptions must be avoided. One is that the color was purple, a hue mixed of red and blue. The Greek words—*porphyrostrōtos*, 910; *porphyrās*, 957; *halourgesin*, 946—indicate the deep red dye obtained from the murex shell and widely felt to resemble the color of blood. For another, we must rid ourselves of the notion of a floor covering, natural enough in our society with its delight in wall-to-wall carpeting. If carpets were what is intended, Agamemnon's hesitation would not be intelligible. The word used by Clytemnestra (909) is *petasmasin*, "spreads," and the association is with fabrics consecrated to the worship of the gods. "Brocades and silks," though not the materials actually used, which were probably linen, create in our minds an analogous picture of precious inviolability. To think of their being crushed underfoot by the victorious general is to get some understanding of the coarseness and brutality which Aeschylus wants us to recognize in the act. No indoor theater can offer a staging device to duplicate the shocking force of Agamemnon's scarlet fabrics. The purely visual aspect must have been extraordinary. For an audience tiered up against the hillside and looking down upon the orchestra where Agamemnon's car had come to a stop, the mass of red engulfing him as he made his way from the vehicle to the scene door appeared to spell the death which it was known awaited him within.[25]

The subject of movements on the Aeschylean stage has its special charm, given the undifferentiated openness of that stage.[26] The movements of the gods were, one presumes, of great simplicity. In *Eumenides*, Athena, Apollo, and Hermes all entered and exited on foot; this, and not transportation via the machine called the "crane" which in later productions was used to swing divinities from behind the stage up to the roof of the scene building, is the force of 403–4:

> . . . I came, forcing my unwearied feet,
> wingless, the aegis swelling with a hiss. . . .

The simplicity of Athena's entrance and her unpretentious movement about the stage contrast with the violence of the dancing in the binding song of the Furies that precedes. In such contrasts, the extension of space becomes functional in its own right. The distance covered by Athena's calm and "unwearied" foot; Cassandra's exit into the doomed palace; the forward and backward surge of the daughters of Danaus in front of the altar; and, above all, Agamemnon's delayed descent from his vehicle: these and other stage events accord to space a dramatic role. Twice in the encounters between Clytemnestra and her victims on the chariot, the space between it and the door of the house becomes a felt substance. It turns into an obstacle, a tension that has to be broken down before the deadlock can be resolved. In the end, in *Agamemnon*, the resolution issues in error; the scarlet fabrics pervert the purity of the spatial barrier. Against this resistance, the principals move in isolation, without interruption, and without checking one another's progress. It is instructive to contrast this use of motion in space with what happens in neo-classical drama. In Racine, it frequently happens that the firmness of a character's purpose is broken by the entrance of an-

25. P. Friedländer, "Die griechische Tragödie und das Tragische," *Die Antike* 1 (1925): 18.

26. On this topic Taplin, *Greek Tragedy in Action*, is particularly instructive.

other; meetings brought about by chance turn into instruments of change. It is as if there was not enough room for the agents of the drama in which to move about. The likelihood of people's paths crossing even when they would rather be far away from each other is one of the great shapers of destiny. Historically speaking, this use of space derives from the practices of the Roman comic stage, and in particular from the plots of Plautus and Terence, in which comings and goings are similarly thronged, as if inscribed on the point of a pin. Euripides begins to move in this direction, but there is nothing of this in Aeschylus. His space is not constrained but resistant and vast. For meetings to be brought about, servants and messengers have to be dispatched, or the principals face each other across a gulf that makes of each act of communication a struggle against odds.

As the chorus tells us, Cassandra on her chariot has "the manner of a newly caught beast" (*Agam.* 1063); she is trembling. These are the words; but of course a tremble cannot be seen at a distance. To the eye, she stands still. Her stillness contrasts with the eagerness of Agamemnon, as her endurance contrasts with his easy surrender. In answer to Clytemnestra's Oriental salaams and prostrations (919–20), and only nominally in spite of them, Agamemnon steps down and marches across the "silks." He walks in silence, and the distance from the center of the orchestra to the door of the scene is such that the duration of his sacrilegious march seems interminable. Throughout this long interval, stretching between lines 974 and 975, Clytemnestra waits for him at her door. Slow progressions across the stage must have been frequent; in the case of Cassandra's walk, the movement is further slowed down by her repeated hesitation.[27] A modern audience, sophisticated and impatient, tends to be embarrassed by movement sufficient to itself extending some distance between two separate blocks of speech. An ancient audience would have seen the things differently, primarily as a result of the conditioning received from the Homeric epic. The epic procedure is to alternate speech and movement, and not to mix the two. Conversation is refashioned into substantial units of speech, each of them comprising within itself what in ordinary conversation would be split up into a series of small utterances, connected and underlined by action and movement. By the same token, action is freed of its speech components and exhibited pure. The organization of dialogue in Aeschylèan drama is, for the most part, indebted to the amalgamating technique of the epic. Hence speech and action were kept rather more distinct than is the fashion on the modern stage. This also permits the supposition that an actor temporarily disengaged—that is to say, sidelined by the singing of a choral ode or by an action being conducted between the other two principals—was not ex-

---

27. K. Reinhardt, *Aischylos als Regisseur und Theologe* (Bern, 1949), p. 104.

pected to register his presence through movements or gestures of his own. For the duration of his disengagement he became, as it were, a cypher, a part of the acting space, rather than a human sounding board to the action. To think of Pylades engaging in dumb show while he is being held in reserve for his single speech (*Lib.* 900–902) would be a mistake.

In chapter 1 we referred to the absence of stage directions in the ancient text. Internal references to the movements of actors and choruses which take the place of stage directions can be quite rare. In *Agamemnon*, entrances and exits are as a rule not noted. The only clear exception is the arrival of the herald, whose coming is formally advertised by the chorus. In *Suppliants*, likewise, there is no preparation for the coming of Pelasgus, no announcement of his arrival, no greeting on his part, only a perplexed comment, expressed in the third person, of what he regards as outlandish in the appearance of the women (234–35). In *Persians*, on the other hand, the Empress Mother prepares the audience extensively for her subsequent movements (521 ff.): she says that she will go off to pray to the gods, and then return to make her offerings to the earth and the dead. Later, with the same explicitness, she arranges what should be done for Xerxes after she leaves the stage a second time. What are we to make of the fact that some entrances and exits are fully prepared for and some introductions are made, while on other occasions characters enter and leave without a word being wasted on the event? The case of the Empress Mother is perhaps unusual; the circumstantial nature of her explanations is a mark of her concern for the welfare of her son. On other occasions it is tempting to conjecture that the absence of an introduction means that the character enters hurriedly or contrary to expectation, or that he is angry. But the cases of unannounced movement are too common to be satisfactorily accounted for by ad hoc explanations. We should remember that our text of a play is a descendant of the playwright's own master script, and that he was himself available, as director and actor, to arrange for the proper movements and entrances and exits. Since an Aeschylean tragedy was, as far as its author knew, destined for a single performance, no permanent indications were needed, unless the special features of a play or a character, as in *Persians*, called for them.

In the absence of instructions, it is intriguing to speculate on some of the possibilities. Gilbert Murray's "A Scenario of the *Agamemnon*" and accounts of the stage happenings by other scholars are justly famous, because they were willing to exercise their informed imagination in the service of a play's general conception as they understood it.[28] Some few demonstrable data are, of course, needed to begin with. Fortunately they exist. It is, for in-

28. G. Murray, *Aeschylus* (Oxford, 1940), appendix. Two other scholars who had a remarkable ability to visualize the dramatic needs of a play were Wilamowitz and Reinhardt.

stance, possible to start one's plotting of the action of a play by checking how often, and under what circumstances, the chorus is left alone on the stage. Surprisingly, *Libation-Bearers* wins the crown; the conspiratorial developments of the plot make it virtually certain that the chorus is left in control of the stage seven times: 22–83, 585–651, 719–29, 783–837, 855–74, 931–72, 1065–76. Most of these moments, each of them relatively brief, are found in the second half of the play, the intrigue portion, when the characters come and go at an alarming rate. The frequency with which the chorus occupies the stage alone sets *Libation-Bearers* apart from the other two plays of the trilogy, not to mention *Prometheus*, whose principal character is on stage throughout. In *Persians*, as in *Seven*, the chorus is left alone three times: *Persians* 1–154, 532–97, 852–907; *Seven* 287–368, 720–91, 822–1004; and in *Suppliants* twice, 524–99, 776–824. *Seven*, it might be noted, is ahead of these others in the length of the blocks of time during which the chorus is alone, with *Persians* running a close second. *Eumenides* contains only one brief moment during which there are no actors on stage, 140–77. This leaves *Agamemnon*, where the question is complicated by the prior question of Clytemnestra's movements. In anticipation of what I intend to say about them, I would conjecture that the chorus of *Agamemnon* is unattended four times, second only to *Libation-Bearers*. But the enormous length of these periods demonstrates how extraordinary the play is: 40–254, 355–502, 681–809, 1331–71, a total of 533 lines, to 269 in *Libation-Bearers*. Instead of the animation and swiftly changing pace of *Libation-Bearers*, *Agamemnon* offers a compact, not to say impenetrable, coherence.

But this is only the beginning, in response to the simplest questions. Once we turn to matters of detail, the answers are very much harder, and often mere guesswork. In spite of what I said earlier about our lack of information concerning the choreography, can we say something about the movements of the Danaids? At *Suppl.* 772 ff., Danaus tells his daughters to put their trust in the gods, which in this play, one assumes, means staying close to the podium and the altar. But in the ode that follows, the women seek salvation in escape and death. Does this mean they scatter all over the orchestra? At 850, however, someone (not only the text but also speaker assignments are disturbed throughout this section of the play) tells them to leave their seats; by this time, therefore, and probably by the start of the sung encounter which appears to begin at 836, they have recovered their sanctuary on or near the podium, cowering at the foot of the altar. More generally, the choral action of the play appears to have been one of see-saw movement, now gathering in a tightly huddled group near the altar, now streaming across the orchestra in a simulation of heedless flight. And what of the dancing of the Furies in the binding song (*Eum.* 307 ff.) with which the goddesses expect to paralyze Orestes and to bring him into their power? In the first stanza of the third dyad (368–71) and its non-responding supplement (372–76), the Furies describe themselves as both dancers and wrestlers, with the emphasis in both skills being on footwork. Is it legitimate to think of their movements at this point as being in imitation of the magic synthesis expressed in the words?

Later in *Eumenides*, what were the preparations for the trial scene, and did these preparations take place while the chorus was singing its preliminary ode (490 ff.) or rather after the termination of their song, along the Homeric lines indicated above? Because the play is one of the liveliest, and because we do not know to what extent choral dancing was formal and stylized and to what extent it was expressive of emotion or imitated the natural gestures of life, there is no limit to our uncertainties. What are the movements while the ballots are being gathered in and counted (711 ff.)? Orestes, Apollo, and the chorus are, we presume, worried about the outcome; is this worry exhibited in appropriate physical indications? After Athena has made her succinct announcement of the verdict and Orestes delivers his long speech of thanks (754 ff.), including at least one hint whose implication is less than complimentary to the Furies (761), are we to imagine that the chorus stands by impassively, like a sidelined actor? If not, what kinds of movements does the playwright allow his choruses during the intervals between singing? Does Apollo leave soon after the announcement of the verdict, at the start of Orestes's speech, or does he stay on until Orestes has done speaking, to leave with him? It is clear that, in the absence of reliable clues, the historical imagination is called upon to fill in much of the detail.

A like ignorance must be confessed concerning the finer points of acting. Do Orestes and Electra embrace when they recognize each other (*Lib.* 235) as they do in Euripides's version of the tale (*Electra* 576 ff.)? What are the gestures of greeting between men and women, and are they different from salutations of the gods? Does Eteocles, at the moment when he discovers that he is fated to fight Polynices (*Seven* 653) underscore the discovery and the horror with a violent motion of his body? Internal references to gestures and to what we understand by acting are almost entirely missing. And where they do exist, as in the speech of the watchman at the beginning of *Agamemnon* (3), their significance has lent itself to many different interpretations. The vase paintings give us the conceptions of the painters: translations into static shape of what the story, not the action, requires, rather than records of dramatic performances. It is best to leave all hope of assurance aside and to empower the modern director to determine the acting as his sense of style dictates it. Each interpreter will have his own preferences. I, for one, am doubtful about the proposal that in Sophocles's

*Antigone* (441–83) first Creon and then Antigone point at each other as they level their attacks.[29] The idea of two characters thrusting their outstretched arms at each other seems to me to be derived from the post-classical statuary of orators and emperors. My own inclination is to believe that acting on the fifth-century stage, and especially in Aeschylus, was less poised, and more tumultuous. At the same time we must be careful in our speculations to allow for a radical distinction between comic and tragic acting styles. Just as there were very few asides on the tragic stage, so certain movements and mannerisms would have been ruled out to keep the genres apart.

To conclude this chapter, I shall attempt a more detailed analysis of two issues whose difficulties are symptomatic of the problems we face when we try to reconstruct the Aeschylean stage action: the movements at the beginning of *Eumenides* and the entrances and exits of Clytemnestra in *Agamemnon*.

First, *Eumenides*. It will be remembered that the priestess delivers an initial speech designed to furnish information. Beginning with line 34, she reports her sight of Orestes and the Furies. We conclude that between lines 33 and 34 there is a pause, during which she has moved to a new position from which to give out her prophecies to the applicants before her, a position which enables her to see Orestes and the creatures. From this position she is now returning. In the end, she renounces her customary function and leaves it to Apollo to do his own prophesying. After she, and presumably the prophecy-seekers, have vacated the stage, Orestes and Apollo, the latter accompanied by an extra representing Hermes, are discovered in conversation. They, in turn, depart to make room for Clytemnestra's ghost and the Furies. Finally Clytemnestra's ghost exits, leaving the stage to the Furies, who are alone until Apollo returns to drive them out. Thereupon the stage is left bare between lines 234 and 235, a singular event in the extant corpus of Aeschylean drama, but paralleled in Sophocles and Euripides.

The oracular activity of the Delphic priestess took place, we are told, in the inner sanctum of the temple. Because of this, the great scholars of the past were convinced that the priestess's vision must have been obtained through one of the scene doors. Wilamowitz draws the logical conclusion from this and proposes that the subsequent developments, down to the

---

29. R. Williams, *Drama in Performance*[2] (Harmondsworth, 1972), pp. 20 ff. Note that F. L. Shisler, "The Use of Stage Business to Portray Emotion in Greek Tragedy," *AJP* 66 (1945): 377 ff., esp. p. 394, cites relatively little evidence from Aeschylus. For what might be gathered from the evidence of Greek art, see G. Neumann, *Gesten und Gebärden in der griechischen Kunst* (Berlin, 1965). I sympathize with Williams's view that in an ancient tragedy "the full detail of the performance is seen to be prescribed. . . . the dramatist is not only writing a literary work; he is also, by the use of exact conventions, *writing the performance*."

expulsion of the Furies from the temple, were enacted behind the scene wall, and must have been presented by means of a back door opening wide to reveal a sufficiently large glimpse of the interior.[30] But in spite of supposed parallels in later tragedy and Wilamowitz's belief that the imperfect visibility was useful in emphasizing the strangeness of the action, this solution must be considered a counsel of despair. We have no right to assume that Aeschylus disposed of a back door large enough to allow more than a faint and fleeting glimpse of what went on behind the scene wall. Further, I should argue that strangeness or mystery is the last thing the fairy-tale extravaganza of the first part of the play needs.

We have suggested that Aeschylean drama eschewed interiors. Scenes that in real life might be expected to take place within the four walls of a chamber or a courtyard are in tragedy drawn forth into the sunlight of the public arena. It is unnecessary, therefore, and indeed wrong, to locate certain scenes in conformity with their mundane locale. A disposition which, as Wilamowitz himself admits, would prevent the Furies from doing any dancing until the scene has "shifted" to Athens is condemned out of hand. Much better to imagine a series of actions all of which take place in front of the scene building, either in the orchestra or on the platform in the back of it. I have already indicated my belief that *Eumenides* could be produced on the old stage prior to the advent of the scene building. But since the other two plays of the *Oresteia* require the presence of such a building, its availability must be taken for granted in the final play also. The question before us is: where in the space at the playwright's disposal should the agents be placed, and which entrances and exits, including those in the scene wall, do they use?

We may start with the group that is hardest to accommodate, the Furies. The proper place for the chorus is in the orchestra, and it is difficult to conceive of any other place for them. This is one of the plays, of which there are a few in the combined repertory of fifth-century drama, in which the chorus has no entrance of its own, but is, at the beginning of the play, discovered in place. The choristers have entered before the play begins and, along with Orestes, have assumed their positions at the "navel" (40), the sacred center of the Delphic shrine; that means, here, around the vestigial

---

Performance, here, is a physical communication of a work that is, in its text, dramatically complete" (173–74). But quite apart from the question how exact the conventions were, and how little or how much was left to the director's ingenuity, Williams's position, if taken to its logical extreme, would take us to the conclusion of Charles Lamb that "the Lear of Shakespeare cannot be acted. . . . The greatness of Lear is not in corporal dimension, but in intellectual"; and that hence *Lear* must be read, not acted (*The Works of Charles Lamb*, ed. W. McDonald [London, 1914], vol. 3, p. 32).

30. Wilamowitz, *Aischylos-Interpretationen*, p. 178.

altar, the central marker of the orchestra. Orestes clings to it; the Furies are crouched on low stools around it (47). With this hypothesis accepted, the other movements can be traced accordingly. The entrance of the priestess is either through a door in the back or through a side access. Since she is accompanied by applicants, to whom she addresses her first speech, it is easier to assume that she comes in from the side and, narrowly skirting the further reaches of the orchestra, ascends to the platform, with the applicants positioning themselves at the edge of the podium, some distance away from the "sleeping" Furies at the center of the orchestra. This would, of course, mean that one set of agents does not immediately notice another set also present on the stage: a stage convention usually associated with comedy rather than with tragedy. *Eumenides*, of all Aeschylus's plays, is closest in diction, tone, and spirit to the comic model.

At 33, the priestess descends from the platform, which has served as tribune for her first speech, and walks toward the center of the orchestra. Stopped in her tracks by what she sees, she returns to the platform with agitated steps, and runs along its length, clutching its rim with her hands before finding the low steps giving her access to it. This may be the meaning of 36–37:

> My frame is bent, I cannot raise it high;
> My footing fails, my hands join in the running.

It is hard to credit the scholiast's view that the priestess returns from her vision of the Furies on all fours.[31] By line 39 she has regained the platform and recovered sufficient poise to present her account, at the end of which she exits through a back door. The applicants may have filed out earlier via the wings.

Enter Apollo and Hermes, also from the wings. They approach the center of the orchestra, where Apollo has his colloquy with Orestes, at the end of which all three of them leave, Hermes and Orestes through one side entrance, Apollo through the other. Next, the ghost of Clytemnestra rises from behind the mound on the platform representing her tomb. Her very first words are addressed to the sleeping Furies. Does she remain on the platform? If not, her progress toward the center of the orchestra is swift. A progress of this speed differs from the rather more stationary conduct we have predicated of that other Aeschylean ghost, Darius. Perhaps it is legitimate to make distinctions between ghosts as between other characters, and to plot the movements of a counselling ghost differently from those of a

---

31. Both "from the house of Apollo" (35) and "like a child" (38) put a strain on my interpretation. But the latter, rather than designating a crawl, may simply refer to the fumbling of a child that wants to draw itself up to a height; and I am prepared to believe that the central altar, the "navel," is for the present purposes made into a stand-in for a shrine.

bullying ghost. Still, a harangue from the podium seems equally plausible. When she has had her say, Clytemnestra disappears as she had come, crouching behind the mound, while the Furies bestir themselves to offer their first dance. The stools around the central altar remain, later to be used by the jurors. Finally, Apollo's reappearance might well be arranged through a back door, to give him the instantaneous dominating position on the platform which he must occupy in his contest with the Furies.

This scenario is one of several possible ones. An alternative sequence would start with the assumption that the Furies and Orestes are first discovered on the platform, with the mound serving as the navel of the shrine. On this assumption, the priestess would begin her performance in the orchestra, and move toward and up onto the platform. Her "running on hands" would then refer to a precipitate descent from the platform. The difficulties of this interpretation increase as one continues to plot the movements; a ghost that appears from the side entrance? An Apollo stationed in the orchestra as he scolds his opponents? What would be the chorus's cue for abandoning the platform for the orchestra? The debate concerning the proper staging of this series of scenes will continue unresolved; no additional evidence supplied by archaeology or philology will ever succeed in recapturing the playwright's own arrangements.

In this case, the general interpretation of the play is not greatly affected by what we decide about the disposition of actors annd chorus. In another case, however, the issue is graver. Our understanding of what Clytemnestra is to her companions, and thus to us, is closely tied up with the scenario that we create for her. Most critics believe that the Queen is on stage almost through the entire length of *Agamemnon*, and that with her powerful, brooding presence she dominates the play. Given the scarcity of incontestable proof, such a view must rest on what one might regard as the critical equivalent of *horror vacui*: the belief that if the presence of a character would, in the critic's view, enhance the meaning of a scene, that presence is to be assumed. The contrary position, corresponding to *horror pleni* or *amor vacui*, and analogous to narrow constructionism in law, would claim that if there is no demonstrable need for a character to be on stage, he must not be introduced or kept on. It would be foolish to presume that one position is intrinsically superior to the other. Once again, personal preference will tell.

Clytemnestra's first speech does not come until 264. But long before that there are lines 83–87, a formal address to "Queen Clytemnestra, daughter of Tyndareus," in which the chorus asks what news has prompted the Queen to initiate sacrifices. The sentence that follows describes the many sacrificial fires burning throughout the city. It is this address, a seemingly irrefutable stage direction, which has convinced most modern scholars that the Queen enters the stage along with the chorus, at 40 or soon thereafter, and that she is present, sacrificing, through all or most of the chorus's introduction and first ode.

Others, however, have doubted this. They see a close connection between the address to the Queen sacrificing, and the picture of ritual fires burning in the city, and conclude that the address is "in the abstract," directed to a Queen whom the chorus imagines to be taking charge of the ceremonies in a jubilant city. The evident impatience with which the chorus asks its questions may, in fact, be a formal index of their realization of the rhetorical nature of these questions. My own conviction that the Aeschylean stage does not favor the mimesis of burnt sacrifices to the gods points in the same direction. I go along with those, therefore, who suggest that Clytemnestra does not appear until after the first ode. She is not, as some translations have it, busy on stage, eerily silent, revealing her demonic personality by a slowness to speak that borders on aphasia. Nor is there the slightest evidence that she is present for part of the scene, coming and going in order to look after her religious duties. Clytemnestra is not a servant, a *servus currens*, bustling back and forth. The chorus exploits a number of opportunities to touch on its relations with the Queen. But the promise of her presence is not fulfilled until after line 258, when she enters from a back door. And this means that for the duration of more than two hundred lines of chanting and singing, our attention is riveted upon the chorus and what it has to tell us. Which is as it should be.

After Clytemnestra has entered, how long does she remain on stage? She leaves, I think, about line 354, just before the chorus intones its next ode. My reasons for saying so are as follows. First of all, the second ode, though not as long as the first, consists, with introduction and epilogue, of more than 120 lines, whose delivery may have taken, at a very rough guess, in the neighborhood of ten minutes. It is the kind of ode which, far from sustaining the action or giving the chorus an opportunity for voicing its role in the action, dwells on the moral and social implications of the legend and exemplifies the symbolic contribution of the chorus. Once again, at least by the standards of *amor vacui*, the choral achievement would gain from a stage entirely given over to the choral dancing. More important, when the herald arrives, advancing slowly across the stage to the accompaniment of fourteen long lines of speech by the chorus leader, he has a series of greetings, addressed to his native soil, Apollo, Hermes, and the royal palace. He does not address the Queen or the chorus. Only toward the end of his speech (582) does the herald deign to recognize the chorus's existence; he never explicitly acknowledges the presence of the Queen. It has been said that this lack of a specific greeting extended to the Queen is deliberate; the herald includes the Queen in the ill will he bears the royal house. But the absence of a greeting formula cannot be regarded as expressing the feelings of a newcomer toward the person or persons whom he appears to overlook. (See also below, chapter 7.) Others have cited the parallel of *Persians* 249 ff., where the messenger greets all except the Empress. But there is a difference. In *Persians*, the Empress Mother begins to speak at 290, after an exchange of about forty lines between chorus and messenger, and her first words call attention to the fact that she has been silent for some time, struck dumb at the news of the disaster. In *Agamemnon*, there are no grounds for silence. Clytemnestra has her first line only at 587, eighty-five lines after the entry of the herald, and after a great deal of information has been given out. In what she then says she pays little attention to what the messenger has reported. I suggest that she enters just before she begins to speak; the choral formula preceding her speech—Clytemnestra and the royal household must hear this message; I will earn a reward for letting them know—is intelligible only on the assumption that the Queen enters at the point when someone is sent out to fetch her.

A difficulty has been supposed in the circumstance that from the beginning of her speech Clytemnestra lets on that she knows the good news of Agamemnon's arrival. But there is no difficulty. What is happening here is once again based on good Homeric precedent, or rather on an understanding of the sharing of information that epic and drama have in common. A character, that is, may on occasion be expected to know as much as the audience knows, even if the dramatic version does not explicitly feature the imparting of the information. A good example in Homer is the scene in Nestor's tent (*Iliad* 11.661) where Nestor, in his conversation with Patroclus, is shown to know about events on the battlefield which he could not have witnessed in his capacity as a dramatic character, since he withdrew from the battle before they happened, but which he knows as a partner in the triangular process of story-telling which combines the bard, his characters, and the audience in a special network of communication. Achilles's refusal of Agamemnon's offer of reparations in book 9 receives its special poignancy from the same consideration: Achilles knows, because the audience knows, in what spirit Agamemnon has made his offer. Clytemnestra's awareness of Agamemnon's homecoming is a more straightforward specimen of the same stratagem; its plausibility is further strengthened by her readiness, after the flash of the beacon signal, for her husband's return.

A final obstacle: in our manuscripts, lines 489–500 are ascribed to Clytemnestra, 501–2 to the chorus. Almost all editors, however, have agreed with J. J. Scaliger that all the lines belong to the chorus, even though this may require a small emendation in one line.[32] The language and temper of the passage are choral, and the downgrading of the beacon-signal

---

32. For a recent attempt to retain all fourteen lines for Clytemnestra, see W. C. Scott, "Lines for Clytemnestra," *TAPA* 108 (1978): 259–69.

would be curious coming from Clytemnestra. Our conclusion is, therefore, that Clytemnestra is absent from the stage between lines 355 and 587.

It would take too long to analyze the rest of the Queen's entrances and exits at similar length. I propose the following: Clytemnestra leaves at the end of her speech, after 614; there is nothing to keep her on stage, and the remainder of the herald's scene is conducted entirely between him and the chorus leader. The Queen does not return until after the chorus has sung its next ode, 681–809. Is she present for Agamemnon's arrival? Once again, I venture to answer in the negative, though as before the case cannot be made to rely solely on the absence of greeting formulas. Agamemnon closes his speech with the announcement (851) that he will enter the palace to conduct a thank-offering to the gods. But before he can descend from his vehicle, Clytemnestra, addressing herself to the chorus, intervenes and introduces the action which in the end diverts Agamemnon's progress from the original pious objective. The intervention of Clytemnestra is dramatized as an interruption, a surprise; and it is the more effective if it is simultaneous with the Queen's entry. She has not met the King on his arrival; she will attempt to make up for the omission by extravagant compliments. Conclusion: the Queen enters at 855 and remains standing close to the door through which she came, working her will upon the King at a distance, until he leaves the car and, crushing the fabrics, makes his way to her. I have already suggested that, in spite of the intention expressed in line 957, he remains on the chariot while Clytemnestra has her speech about the riches of the sea. Only then does he begin to walk, in total silence. Both his perverted pilgrimage and their joint exit through the rear door take place between lines 974 and 975.

The rest presents no problems. The Queen enters at 1035 and exits after 1068; she enters at 1372, for what turns out to be her longest sojourn on the stage, and exits at 1577. She is not present for the appearance of Aegisthus; his remark at 1636,

> Yes, clearly, trickery was the woman's task,

could hardly be ventured with Clytemnestra on the stage. Also, dramatically speaking, the quarrel between Aegisthus and the chorus, rising as it does to the very pitch of murderous excitement, is more effective if Clytemnestra manages to choke it off only in the nick of time when she happens to enter at 1654, after which she remains to pronounce the final lines of the play.[33]

On this interpretation, Aeschylus's Clytemnestra is an active woman, a doer and a sayer, fully projecting her will in speech when she is on stage and

33. I am delighted to see that my scenario of Clytemnestra's movements, plotted some years ago, matches completely that of Taplin, *Greek Tragedy in Action*, pp. 280 ff.

kept off stage when her presence would constrict the action. The picture of Clytemnestra as a taciturn, omnipresent scourge haunting the stage with her formidable presence is a romantic fiction dreamed up by critics who share the modern lack of confidence in the validity of speech and accord to silence a dramatic power of its own. Aeschylus does know the value of silence; we know from Aristophanes and other witnesses that some of his most famous scenes struck dramatic capital from silence. As I shall try to argue later (see chapter 7), all Aeschylean speech is, as it were, carved out of silence in a way that is no longer true of his successors. But the silence of Niobe and the silence of the Empress Mother in *Persians* are the speechlessness of grief. The plotting of an intrigue, to judge from other plays that emphasize conspiracy, calls for lying speech rather than silence. That Clytemnestra is likened to a fury by Cassandra and, by implication, by the chorus, is not sufficient reason for the playwright-director to shape her function on the stage by analogy with the vision of the Fury crouched upon the gable of the house. Clytemnestra is an intriguer, a persuader, an active woman of speech. The frequency of her entrances and exits and the comparative briefness of her appearances on stage are suitable to her role in the play. It might be added that, with the romantic mask of the demon removed from her, she can be seen more easily to exist on the same human level as her husband Agamemnon, whom she defeats not as a goddess would overpower a mortal, but as a politician leads a rival astray. And that, I believe, is a gain for the appreciation of the play.

# The Poetry

# _ 4 _

## Style

Does Aeschylus have an "answerable style" adequate to the needs of his dramatic and poetic vision? It may seem like an impossible task to talk in English about the virtues and vices of Aeschylus's verse style. But the attempt has to be made. The Aristophanic parody of the grandiloquent old tragedian has distorted the picture to such an extent that most discussions, including some addressed to scholars of Greek, appear unable to free themselves of the catchwords of "weight," "bulk," and "bombast." In their view, Aeschylus is an early Greek Holofernes, who smothers his characters and his stage in a thick layer of verbiage. They forget that on occasion, and indeed on many occasions, Aeschylus can write with a simplicity and a grace that put Euripides's romantic plain talk and Sophocles's plastic springiness to shame. Even the small sample of Aeschylean drama that survives shows an enormous range of diction and syntax. Where *Agamemnon* offers the impacted cadences of metaphysical riddles, *Persians* shines with the brightness of epic word chains and *Eumenides* for long stretches appears to settle for the brusqueness of parliamentary contention. But the range is not a matter of artistic growth; the striking differences in speech between *Agamemnon* and *Eumenides* confound any attempt to explain stylistic variation in evolutionary terms. We must always remind ourselves that the plays we have come from the last decade and a half of Aeschylus's long life.

Aeschylean drama is a product of that crucial period in the intellectual development of Greece, and more particularly of Athens, which also witnessed the beginnings of a gathering of human knowledge in the form of disciplines such as medicine, natural science, and jurisprudence. It should not surprise us that the special terms and formulas hammered out by those responsible for the new disciplines should also crop up in that branch of artistic endeavor which more than any other in its time reflected the totality of contemporary strivings. Some portions of *Prometheus* and of *Eumenides* are palpably indebted to a medical vocabulary. The first choral reflections upon Zeus in *Agamemnon* (163–65) employ terms from geometry:

> I have computed all, but can find
> No approximation except Zeus . . .

though it is worth mentioning that the words that follow have nothing scientific about them:

If the mind has any hope at all
Of casting out the ballast of waste.

Much has been made of the presence of the technical vocabulary of law and jurisprudence in the *Oresteia*, and indeed in all of ancient tragedy. But perhaps it is equally important to show that, on the whole, Aeschylus has much less in the way of such privileged diction than might have been expected. It should not be lightly assumed that where a play turns on crimes adjudicated by a city-state and punished in a court of law, the language is necessarily that of a court procedure. In the *Oresteia*, the striking thing is how much of the talk of blood crimes does not fall back upon a technical vocabulary. The trial of Orestes is a special case, though once again we are impressed with the comparative simplicity of the speech. The repeated occurrence of a word such as *dikē* makes no specialized demands. Much that might be regarded as legal language is merely the unspecialized medium in which social and moral issues are naturally discussed, and had been discussed for centuries.[1] On balance it is fair to say that Aeschylus's use of "scientific" terms does not constitute a special challenge to critics of style. The terms are there, confirming that Aeschylus was not unaffected by the intellectual developments of his day. But on the whole they do not obtrude; they are sufficiently integrated into the larger sweep of the language not to push the speech into academicism or onesidedness. Only *Prometheus*, its diction guided by the central image of the engineer, is an exception.

Does Aeschylus use a vocabulary that stands apart from other kinds of poetic speech and that may be called specifically dramatic? The answer is no. Disregarding for the moment the stately and often daring compounds generated by the tradition of ritual choral song, what has always struck critics is the conventional quality of most of the tragic diction, its delight in the simple epic adjectives—good, bad, beautiful, ugly, just, unjust, and so forth—and in the compact nouns and verbs that reverberate with the social experience of the city-state. Translators have come up hard against this simplicity. Many have fallen victim to the temptation of substituting the more sophisticated, more tentative expressions favored today for the hard, squarely hitting terms of Aeschylus's Greek. The worst of them have replaced "bad" or "ugly" with the pejoratives of a Freudian scale of introspection. Some of this is probably unavoidable. A literal translation of the Greek would often result in the flat naivetés of a verbal poster art. It is important, however, that at every step of our exploration we remain aware of the concreteness of the vocabulary, of its closeness to the staples of a vigorous living tradition.

---

1. For a contrary view, see J. P. Vernant, in J. P. Vernant and P. Vidal-Naquet, *Mythe et tragédie en grèce ancienne* (Paris, 1972), p. 15.

If the contemporary sciences and other specialized concerns left only a light imprint on the tragic diction, are there other concerns which set it apart? In thinking about the neo-classical drama of France, one remembers the special sets of words—*amour, gloire, honneur, vengeance*—which Corneille and Racine manipulate in so tight a dialectical pattern that they may be said to lend a special color and impose a special limitation. *Gloire*, in *Le Cid*, or *amour*, in *Bérénice*, are magic words, foci for sensitive and impassioned energies through whose agency the verbal patterning takes on the semblance of a compact design. Does the speech of Aeschylean drama exhibit similar badges, resonant pointers in the verbal execution of its thematic conflicts? Once again, the answer is a cautious no. It would be extremely hard to find a Greek equivalent for the charged mass of connotations or the overtones of a national preoccupation with nobility that are contained in the word *gloire*. There are some rather more humble epic equivalents. But tragic speech does not stress them. It prefers a variety of words, each of them fitting in its context, but none calculated to set off the far-reaching vibrations that the French word carries with it. But that is not the same as saying that Aeschylus has no key words. In the entrance sequence of the chorus of *Persians*, for instance, *polychrysos*, "rich in gold," is used of the royal seat (3), the army (9), the city of Sardis (45), and Babylon (53); it occurs nowhere else in the extant corpus. Similarly the word *ochlos*, "[undisciplined] throng," occurs five times in *Persians*, and only three times elsewhere. The rare verb *timalphein*, "cheer with praise," occurs three times in *Eumenides* and only once elsewhere: it is part of the "gentle" speech used to overcome the "harsh" speech of the earlier plays of the trilogy. We read in a scholium that Aeschylus was made fun of for using the word. Thus each play and its complex of themes were likely to suggest a particular set of words, and Aeschylus was ready to venture out on a limb to secure the proper usage. We shall have more to say about this later. But such preferences do not constitute a special style.

It would be hazardous, then, to claim a decorum of dramatic speech for Aeschylus in the sense in which the term is applied to neo-classical tragedy and even to Elizabethan and Jacobean drama. There is, however, a rather more precise sense in which Aeschylean tragedy, in each of its sections, may be said to obey the rules of a decorum. Above all, the tradition requires that the spoken and the chanted portions of a play be in Attic, or, more exactly, in a dialect which expresses the essence of Athenian speech without some of its more colloquial forms; and that the portions that are sung and danced be in a form of Doric—that is to say, exhibiting, especially in its vowels, the patterns more at home in Sparta and Corinth and Thebes than in Athens or the neighboring islands. The tradition will appear surprising. Why should a type of communication which, more than any other in antiquity, is designed to appeal directly to a large and mostly unlettered audience make things difficult for itself by shifting back and forth between two forms of diction, neither of which corresponds neatly, but one radically less than the other, to the speech patterns heard in the polite society of Athens and imitated in the dialogue of comedy and of the Socratic writers?

Perhaps the formulation of the question suggests its own answer. Tragedy differs from comedy and from philosophical dialogue in requiring a psychic distance between what happens on the stage and what happens in the audience.[2] Too close an identity between the speech voiced in the orchestra and the speech habits of the listeners would lead to the kind of breakdown, to the banality, which modern opponents of psychic distance are often unable to ward off. The Greeks themselves, however, would have offered a simpler explanation. Choral utterance, they would have argued, was traditionally Doric; its greatest creators, from Stesichorus to Pindar, had been trained in a Dorian culture. Athenian audiences were used to the broad Doric $\bar{a}$ and Doric verb forms as the normal speech pattern that went with choral singing. An Attic vocalism in a choral ode would have rung a false note, just as modern aficionados of Italian opera feel that English translations of *Aida* and *Don Giovanni* are unbearable. The iambic "blank verse," however, though ultimately indebted to the recitations of the epic bards, is more immediately descended from the iambic poems of Solon and of the great Ionian authors: Archilochus, Semonides, and Anacreon. Their speech, though not Attic, came close enough to it to suggest, for the purposes of drama, a purified form of the native tongue.

Two dialects, then, and tempered dialects at that, out of the great number of idioms spoken in the classical Greek world, are employed, for specific functions, on the Athenian dramatic stage. But that is all in tragedy. In comedy much humor is struck from the imitation of the varied speech patterns of near and distant neighbors of Athens. Spartans, Boeotians, Corinthians, Megarians rub shoulders with Persians and nonsense Triballians; they exemplify the human capacity for misunderstanding and for condescension by means of a magnificent mélange of dialects ranging from the funny to the near-incomprehensible. This is especially true in Old Comedy, the fifth-century companion of tragedy. But the tradition persists in the New Comedy of the third century B.C. and after; Menander's recently discovered *Shield*, for instance, has a mock-physician who speaks Doric. Such realism is out of the question on the tragic stage. At *Lib.* 563–64, Orestes announces that he and Pylades will, to further the intrigue, express themselves like Phocians. But the promise is not fulfilled; there is nothing in the

---

2. The basic text is still E. Bullough, *"Psychical Distance* as a Factor in Art and an Aesthetic Principle," *British Journal of Psychology* 5 (1912): 87–118.

text that we have to suggest that their speech is anything other than standard dialogue Attic. It is of some interest that the promise is made in the first place; it is as close as Aeschylus comes anywhere in his extant works to the linguistic license of comedy. Here the venture is touched off by the beginning of the conspiracy. The "realism," though aborted, goes hand in hand with the affectionate vulgarities of the nurse. It should be contrasted with what Clytemnestra and the chorus say about the language of Cassandra (*Agam.* 1047 ff.): it is possible that she does not speak Greek, but even if she twitters like a bird—what is not Greek is not language—an understanding can be achieved through a communion of souls.

In the latter part of *Suppliants*, which, as we have said, has come to us in a rather unsatisfactory state of textual preservation, some scholars have proposed to recognize snatches of dialect, extravagant verbal forms that are supposed to characterize the Egyptian herald and his followers as barbarians. We cannot exclude the possibility completely. As *Eumenides* and parts of *Libation-Bearers* show, Aeschylus was more willing than Sophocles or even Euripides to adopt certain features of comic dramaturgy into his tragedies. But we must distinguish between comic speakers of dialect and the occasional use of a foreign word. *Suppliants* and *Persians* especially have been cited for their partiality to alien speech, and the suggestion is reasonable. The violent contrast between Greeks and Egyptians in *Suppliants* is characterized as a clash of cultures and ethical systems. In *Persians*, we never get a direct glimpse of the Greeks, but the clash is there, not so much between cultures as between human attitudes toward the gods. For dramatic reasons, therefore, the importance of barbarian words, and particularly of barbarian names, would be considerable. They introduce into the familiar flow of Greek speech an element of the unusual or exotic and an echo of the disorder or turbulence that in the Greek mind is associated with tales about a mysterious or shocking East. It turns out, however, that Aeschylus's use of barbarian words is surprisingly sparing: four or five in *Suppliants*, unless the largely corrupt section approximately between lines 825 and 900 hides more; and even fewer in *Persians*. If it was Aeschylus's intention to characterize the milieu of *Persians* or the roots of the refugees in *Suppliants* as foreign, his diction does not show him straining to do so. The distinction between tragedy and comedy appears to be preserved to a remarkable degree. But there are the names, the roll call of Persian nobles who lead Xerxes's troops into the field (*Pers.* 21 ff.) and, later in the play (956 ff.), the casualty lists of the choral lament. They succeed in establishing the foreignness of the locale and of the agents without interposing the obstacles of unintelligibility. The effect is considerable; the polysyllabism of the names goes hand in hand with the extravagance of Xerxes's grief when he is down and the outlandishness of his divine status while he was still triumphant.

One might compare the effect of biblical names in Racine's religious plays. Unlike the secular dramas requiring only a minimum of information for the audience to appreciate the dimensions of the conflict, the religious dramas are full of reminders of dynastic and theological contention. The rich tapestry of biblical names sets up a turbulence into which the characters themselves are drawn. Passion, violence, lack of decorum become the order of the day. Joad, the high priest in *Athalie*, embodies the fierceness of the biblical Elijah. Against this "barbarian" attack, the more secular Athalie, modeled on the familiar Greek and Roman heroines of the non-biblical plays, is in the end defenseless. In Aeschylus, Greek wins out over barbarian, though the Persian nomenclature articulates the crisis. But the economy in the use of non-Greek words confirms that in a deeper sense the struggle is between equals rather than between a familiar, moral West and an exotic, immoral East. The rarity of Persian or Egyptian or Thracian words on the Aeschylean stage confirms our contention that the Aeschylean language was shaped so as to touch the listeners directly, with the impact of an immediate appeal. Later in this chapter we will propose one or two qualifications of this general notion. But they will be no more than that.

As on the Shakespearean stage, the bareness of the setting ensures maximum impact for the spoken and the sung word. Without the distraction of fussy scenery, without the tangential mannerisms of virtuoso actors, the word may bloom as it cannot within the constrictions of the proscenium stage. Like the rhetoric of the public assembly and of the law court, but without the cluttering and the refracting that attend a political wrangle, dramatic speech is designed to influence souls. Renaissance critics talk of "instruction"; for them one of the principal objectives of drama, calling upon the spoken word to do its utmost, was "sententious excitation to virtue, and deflection from her contrary."[3] These critics, basing their claims on the importance of heroes and villains, of warning examples and paradigms to be emulated, had their ancient precursors, the first of whom, in his own impenetrable way, was Aristophanes, in *Frogs*. We cannot tell how Aeschylus thought of the matter, but I should think that if the issue had been presented to him as a choice between instruction and entertainment, he would have chosen the latter. Even so, the need for an appropriate rhetoric would have seemed obvious to him.

Serious modern dramatists, in the wake of Sterne and Joyce, prefer to have their characters move along the boundaries of meaningful speech rather than in the grooves prepared for it. In their hands, speech is a field of

---

3. George Chapman, in the dedication to *The Revenge of Bussy D'Ambois*, cited by M. E. Prior, *The Language of Tragedy* (New York, 1947), p. 23.

trial and error, a laboratory for demonstrating the precariousness of communication between man and man, and for showing up the chasm which lies between reality and illusion. In Bernard Shaw's best plays, speech is shaped in the manner of a game. It offers the staccato flashes of thrust and parry, the turns and counterturns of a set of articulate fencers. Without the players, the maneuvers would be as nothing. As it is, the sallies remain thin and transparent, and each of them dies before the introduction of the next. In Beckett's plays, speech undergoes a process of exhaustion. It is explored and tested and progressively discarded, until nothing is left but silence, barely reverberating with the possibility of speech. Since the days of Chekhov, this silence has affected all modern drama, however conventional. The characters use their language in such a way that we are led to believe that there is much that is not said but that is also dramatically important. The words of the text are merely an invitation to a more complete realization of the drama, one in which the spectator will have to cooperate. In drama the word is a seed, incomplete by itself; the worth of the play is a function of its ability to suggest a presence and stimulate an audience reaction which go beyond the verbal cues.

Contrast Shakespeare. His speech is athletics: the strenuous and joyful exercise of a rhetoric with no holds barred, sufficient unto itself, proud in the total efficacy of the medium. Aeschylus stands on the side of Shakespeare in this, as he does in so much else. What he lacks is Shakespeare's verbal acrobatics, the willingness to venture upon the high rope, to push against the barriers of meaningful speech and syntax. Aeschylus is not, as we shall see, averse to launching his own defiance of economy and easy intelligibility. But what in Shakespeare is more often than not a kind of verbal juggling, advertising itself as a joyous and energetic sleight of hand, in Aeschylus is likely to be a matter of brooding, of wrestling with a difficult or saddening thought. Typically, the Aeschylean passages that make linguistic demands on the listeners occur in choral songs rather than in dialogue or speeches.

But even in the most problematic sequences, where meaning emerges only with the greatest difficulty from strange and twisted speech, there is no question of concealment or imperfection. The characters—and that includes the chorus—always seem to be superbly certain of the adequacy of their utterance. The terrors and exasperations associated with the act of speech are due to understanding, not the lack of it. Where the moderns inquire into the nature and the validity of understanding itself, Aeschylus, and the ancients in general, display their skill by maximizing its shock. By understanding I do not mean learning. Aeschylus has no conversions, no *pater peccavi*'s. They were first broached by Euripides in a number of plays with which he laid the foundation for New Comedy. The only characters in the *Oresteia* of whom we might say that they learn a lesson are the Furies; and their conversion is not a consequence of the plot but part of the institutional arrangement which, in defiance of human resentments, terminates the proceedings of the trilogy. In any case, the conversion is not even that, for the Furies do not, at the end of the play, apprehend anything that they have not seen, or even stood for, before. By understanding I mean the enlargement of vision, the awareness of one's role in a more comprehensive scheme which sooner or later comes to all agents, and whose coming Aeschylus is able to formulate with all the fullness of his art, precisely because it is itself a consequence of the belief that speech is adequate to its purpose.

At the end of act 2, scene 4 in *Bérénice*, Titus's speech fails; he cannot avow to Bérénice that he must let her go for reasons of state. The emotion experienced is not unlike what we occasionally find on the Greek stage, where it would be characterized as *amēchania*, helplessness, or, more literally, the inability to find one's way out of an impasse. Characteristically, it is a feeling experienced by the chorus more often than by a character. In any case, such helplessness never announces itself as a failure of speech. In Aeschylean drama, speech is not controlled by the fluctuating fortunes or the wavering firmness of a character. There is no groping for words, no desperate surrender of verbal certainty, no forlorn suspension between alternative ways of saying things. By the same token, the character, if it is at all legitimate to divorce him from what he says, has, in any one scene, a decisiveness of conception that sets him apart from the irresolution of the modern hero initiated by Byron and Büchner. The linguistic assurance of the Aeschylean character, his unanalyzed conviction that speech is a tool, and not a proper object of dramatic analysis, carries the day.

Aeschylean rhetoric yields a full verbalization of what is thought, or felt, or pretended. There are delays, occasioned by the needs of a dramatic encounter or by the superior claims of a competing character. Cassandra remains silent so that Clytemnestra may be baffled, and her arrogance be given full scope. But Cassandra's silence is not designed to hint or to conceal; and when the silence is given up for speech, the speech tells all. Electra sees the lock which both she and the chorus immediately assume is Orestes's, and voices her feelings as follows (*Lib.* 183–84):

> My heart, like yours, was flooded with a storm
> Of bile; and pierced through as with an arrow.

The statement is in the aorist, a verb form which in classical Greek suggests both the suddenness of the experience and its present remoteness from the experiencer. Electra talks of her grief as if she were now capable of looking back on it. The remarks that follow, an elaborate two-line confection prosaically paraphrasable as "I am crying," are in the present tense which, under the circumstances, is as skewed as the aorist. The sufferer, it appears, can describe his sufferings to an audience as if they did not weaken his verbal skills—as if they were somehow outside him—but without surrendering his claim to their authenticity. Though there are anticipations of this in the lyric, it was drama, and specifically Aeschylean drama, which took this pioneering step in the history of the realization of the self. It is, once again, a testimony to the power and the unselfconsciousness of the word. In the end—though this might come better under the heading of "Character," in chapter 8—the distancing potential of speech fully and objectively embracing a feeling or a state of affairs moves counter to what we expect of a dramatic agent. An alarming example of this is found in Euripides's *Alcestis* (393–415) where, immediately after the death of Alcestis, one of her children sings a lament that does full justice to the grief in the house but is downright bizarre if taken as the response of a small child to the death of his mother.

As rhetoric, dramatic speech encounters two contradictory expectations. On the one hand, it is felt that it should be immediately intelligible. Because no doubt is felt concerning the complete expressibility of things, and because the dramatic artist is looked upon as a practitioner of persuasion, the audience demands not to have to puzzle things out but to have meaning and direction emerge unerringly from the guidance of the speech. The other expectation is similarly tied to the character of dramatic speech as persuasion, but the effect is the opposite. Experience in the public assembly and in the law courts lends color to the fear that persuaders may be deceivers. Listeners who have their own best interests at heart will look carefully behind and around the proffered rhetoric for telltale signs of prevarication and sham. But *pace* Plato's and the Platonists' message that drama, *qua* drama, is the deceiver, rhetoric as deception is to be associated with the purposes of particular characters in a drama, and not with the purposes of the dramatist himself, or of the play. Clytemnestra's flattery of Agamemnon, and Orestes's swindling of his mother, are savored as false because the playwright has furnished us with enough hints to prepare us for the truth. The idea that the playwright himself might, through delusive guidance and misleading pointers, get the audience off on the wrong track, only to put them right with a shocking twist, cannot be entertained for Aeschylus.[4]

In this respect, Aeschylus's compact with his audience is unique. With Sophocles, the mysteries and contingencies of private life, of unpredictable personal motivation, begin to soften the tough fabric of legend and plot.

---

4. This is not meant to deny the larger claim that all art is deception; see T. G. Rosenmeyer, "Gorgias, Aeschylus, and *Apatē*," *AJP* 76 (1955): 225–60. For a further development of the notion of persuasion as deception, see below, chap. 12.

Euripides goes even further; false signals and distortions of the traditional material succeed in keeping the audience off balance for much of the play. The Sophoclean introduction of the uncertainties of personal life is perhaps the more radical move. Certain things happen in the Oedipus plays because a sustained chain of perceptions on the part of a distinctively understood human life is in control. The mysterious progression of the aged Oedipus from beggar to saint in *Oedipus Coloneus* entails much that is only partially caught in what the audience is told. In Euripidean drama, the surprise inversions of *Alcestis* and *Hippolytus* and the shocking inexorabilities of *Bacchae* leave the audience in a fruitful state of perturbation. It is significant that in both Sophocles and Euripides the relevance of a particular choral ode is less immediately ascertainable. It is no longer, as it was in Aeschylus, an integral part of a consensus movement, but comes to be geared to more tenuous connections, with secret reverberations and rebellious second thoughts skewing the skein. The immediacy of Aeschylean speech is, therefore, a last vestige of public communication, of a rhetoric that stays, at every step, in tune with its listeners.

But is not a rhetoric that is equally explicit and open in all its parts a mirage, and would it not make for tedious drama? As we approach the Aeschylean text, we must ask ourselves whether all its details are equally powerful or deserving of the same degree of attention. The extended— some would say interminable—dirges at the conclusion of *Persians* and especially of *Seven* are composed for the singing voice, and in a manner that suggests that the singing (and dancing) was in this case the chief carrier of the dramatic meaning. The words, though obviously in tune with the larger issues of the plays, are shaped in response to the ceremonial traditions of the lament, and also in response to the need for a fully satisfying termination of the action, a need that has less to do with issues and themes than with a deeper rhythm below the threshold of verbalization.[5] To look at every word and phrase in a dirge, and to attempt to establish an intellectual pattern between them, and between them and earlier formulations, would be gratuitous. The musical urgency of the dirge works against the contextualist demand for poetic significance and integration.

But if this is true of laments, how can we be certain that we are not wrong in looking at other segments of the dramas with the magnifying glass of the modern literary critic? Is an analytic procedure that counts every word and measures every phrase against standards of unity and inclusiveness appropriate to what an Aeschylean drama hopes to achieve? For example, at *Lib.* 255 Orestes pleads his case with Zeus by claiming that his father was a

---

5. For the conventions of the dirge, see M. Alexiou, *The Ritual Lament in Greek Tradition* (Cambridge, 1974).

sacrificer; if Zeus is going to eradicate a race that has sent so many tendrils of fine sacrificial smoke up his way, where is he going to find similar satisfaction in the future? A close reading, fortified with a commitment to unity and its close auxiliary, irony, will pause delightedly over the gruesome implication of the son praising his father and expecting to be honored in turn for the one act of sacrifice with which Agamemnon is burdened in the trilogy, that of the sister of Orestes. An alternative reading, more plausible under the circumstances, neglects the immediate context in favor of larger affinities—in this case, the Homeric precedent. In the *Iliad* it is common for heroes who are hard pressed to call upon a god and cite either their own or their fathers' contributions to the gods' welfare. As we shall see in chapter 8, the character of Orestes is such that an epic reflex of this sort suits it well. The great formal encounter between Electra, Orestes, and the chorus that follows directly upon Orestes's prayer is complex enough, with its intricate network of professions and motivations. It would scarcely benefit from an irony casting doubt on the authority of a ruler whose ghost is the object of their addresses.

This example, and many others that might be cited, argue for a reading less meticulous, less probing than what our post-romantic timidities would demand. At the least, we must keep our critical responses flexible, and wade into the combat of close scrutiny only when we think the playwright sounds the call. This is a very subjective business, and no two critics will agree on what those moments are. Perhaps it is sufficient to have indicated that the nature of Aeschylean drama as public rhetoric, and the frequency within it of ceremonial occasions, should put us on our guard against overinterpretation. The compact between Aeschylus and his audience compels a ready assimilation and an immediate response. Under the conditions for which the performances were designed, subtleties and ironies that might reveal themselves to a protracted critical investigation are without objective standing. A legitimate distinction can be made between what the author may be thought to have intended and what the text can be made to deliver to modern sensitivities and techniques. But in the case of Aeschylus, the generic limitations of his art require unusual restraints.

The warning against reading too much into a line will appear quixotic when one comes face to face with one of the seemingly inscrutable passages with which *Agamemnon*, above all of Aeschylus's other plays, abounds. How is it possible for what we have called public rhetoric, assimilable without stratagems of translation, to contain such impenetrabilities? The end of the "speech of Calchas" (*Agam.* 140–55) is a case in point. We can translate it, but can we be sure what it means and how it contributes to the choral ode? The passage completes a statement in the preceding dyad concerning Artemis, the protector of defenseless beasts. Some of the words are rare, perhaps made up, though it is of course possible that Aeschylus's audience was more familiar with them than we are. My rendering is intended to be as literal as possible within the limits set by English syntax. Still, some of the details must remain mere guesswork. And for some of the extravagant words, whose meaning is explained by the scholiasts and lexicographers, only relatively tame English equivalents are available. I add parentheses to indicate what the more expressive Greek does not say but evidently implies.

> So gracious [she is], the fair,
> To the lumpish dewlets of fiery lions;
> To the suckling whelps of all wild beasts
> Of the open country a joy.
> Of this you are asked to generate tokens,
> Appearances propitious if also malign.
> On Healer Paean [Apollo] I call:
> Let her not block the Danaans with counter-blowing, lasting, ship-confining
>     calm, or urge
> Another sacrifice, lawless, not [designed for] eating,
> An inbred builder of quarrels, unheedful of men. There remains a fearsome,
>     risen-anew
> Householder of guile, remembering Wrath, child-avenger.

A prophet, Calchas is entitled to an element of mystification. Likewise the chorus, reporting his announcements, adopts the prophetic color the more enthusiastically because it conforms with its own natural talents (see below, chapter 6, for the "prophetic" function of the chorus). The difficulties of the language and the awkwardness of any attempt to connect the passage with its context are due in part to the dramatic purpose. Calchas's reading of the portent sent by Artemis is a conveyer of anxiety and a predictor of future doom. The last sentence is unusually pregnant: a dense series of nominatives, preceded by a simple verb; we are told what will be in store, lying in wait, after a feared sacrifice has been enacted. Resonant with terror, resurgence, the management of the house, trickery, implacability, child-avenging—*of* children or *on behalf* of children?—and divine anger, the nominatives close ranks like a swelling chord on the tonic. That these terms apply to Clytemnestra as well as to the Fury whom Iphigenia's killing will unleash is important. But what matters most of all is the nature of the aggregate music, the total mood of the sequence, with its violent juxtapositions of gentleness and viciousness, of grace and horror. This denseness, this obscurity, is functional where it stands. It is native to *Agamemnon*; in *Persians* or *Prometheus* it would have no place. With all its difficulties—of diction, of syntax, of reference—it is intelligible on its own terms. Characteristically, not even the most forbidding choral sequence of Aeschylus has been plagued with the kind of interpretive controversies that have left the

significance of certain Sophoclean odes in doubt. Our passage engulfs the
perceptions of the audience with its grand message, before a clearer, discursive understanding of the crime and its consequences is introduced. Aeschylus readies his audience slowly, with a musical conditioning rather than
with a forensic explication. He does not mislead, nor does he set up the
hurdles of queries or choices. The contractual rhetoric of the Aeschylean
theater keeps its promise of immediacy and dependability.

Because of this compact between playwright and audience, the speech
can on occasion get by with the merest scrap of a word. Danaus's "the ship"
(*Suppl.* 714) suffices to inform his daughters that the Egyptians have arrived. The anxious father follows this up in the next sentence with further
details to illustrate the hopelessness of the situation. But the simple "the
ship" was an ample dramatic cue. Thus the full formulation, the ringing
exploration of all the verbal components of what is to be communicated,
can alternate with the briefest pointers, mere ciphers of the verbal magic
which encompasses a thing. Both the exhaustive delineation and the dramatic shorthand are proof of the operation of the contract. It would be a
mistake to regard the brief pointers or some of the details in the fuller
phrasing as allusive. An allusion is a reference whose force emerges only
dimly, and which will not be fully appreciated until the progress of the
argument and the sleuthing work of the listener have brought together a
number of such references to throw light upon one another. This is not the
Aeschylean way. There is much that is cumulative, the fitting together of
verbal and intellectual stimuli reinforcing each other on an ascending scale.
But independent of the cumulation, each of the units has its own intelligible force.

Those who believe that Aeschylean writing can be allusive or even misleading point to such a passage as *Agam.* 1025−34, where the chorus darkly
hints at matters that are within its ken but which it will not disclose.

> And were it not that by divine decree
> One man's lot blocked another's
> From venturing far,
> My heart would rout my tongue
> And pour out its thoughts.
> But now it thunders in darkness,
> Its spirit pierced, and it cannot hope
> To unwind a sure thread
> From the fever flames of the mind.

As before, we must remember that the chorus has its own character, compounded of dignity, fear, and an aversion to all that is abnormal, monstrous,
or anarchical. The audience is familiar with this character. They know it not
only from the present play, in which Aeschylus has given the old men many

chances to confirm the impression, but from the whole tradition of tragic choruses. A tragic chorus tends to avert its eyes from unsavory or prodigious facts, or to talk about such facts with a mixture of half-recognition and blindness. Just as a modicum of lying is expected from an intriguer, so the choral mixture of insight and darkness is almost mandatory. There is nothing allusive about their song; it is the chorus behaving in its recognizable mode, brooding on hidden fears in a language whose tropes recall domestic concerns. (See also below, chapter 6.)

But does not the lyricism of ceremonial and reflection veil another dimension, the dimension of jealousy and plotting? Does not *Agamemnon* illustrate to the hilt the ability that public drama has of making the audience suspect private meanings and concealed purposes? And is this ability not a necessary corollary of the open form, the growing tension, the future-directedness that we associate with the tragic genre? The very first scene of the play, with the watchman crouched on the platform and hugging himself against the cold, would seem to confirm this. His avowal of silence sets the tone for the whole:

> Gods, I say you owe me a rest.
> The watch I keep is years of bedding down
> On Agamemnon's roof, hunched up dog-fashion,
> Eyes fixed on the nocturnal swarm of stars.
> I have seen them bringing winter and then summer,
> Bespeckled princes glowing in the sky;
> I know their settings, and have watched them rise.
> And now I watch for the password of the torch,
> The beam from Troy.

And, after he has greeted the beacon of light, and performed a little jig of joy:

> My hope is that I will get to press the hand
> Of my own Lord when he returns to his house.
> That is all I will say; my tongue grows huge and heavy.
> The house itself, if it could find a tongue,
> Would speak the truth. For me, my sense is clear
> To those who know, and dark for those who do not.

The distinction between those who know and those who do not appears to support those who see in the play a tension constructed from ill-understood or puzzling meanings. The fact of the matter is, however, that the watchman cannot possibly expect to find non-knowers in his audience. The disjunction is brought in to flatter listeners who would have had to be extraordinarily dense or recalcitrant not to know what the watchman feared to say. Their knowledge of the myth and their familiarity with the broad outlines of what Aeschylus was going to do in this play—a public announcement of Aeschylus's plans had taken place a short while earlier—left them under no illusions about the plot to murder Agamemnon. The pretended secretiveness is nothing more than a factitious mystery, a playful way of introducing a note of disorientation where certain knowledge is the key.

This is quite different from its modern analogue, *The Family Reunion*, which hides its truth under a veneer of quotidian prattle and nervous normalities. The watchman comes close to doing what Eliot's Downey does: "His Lordship is rather psychic, as they say" is the modern equivalent of the watchman's "My lady's masculine, confident heart wills it so." But in the *Oresteia* the lines that point to the "secret" are neither nervous nor pompous nor fuzzy but in their way as solid as what is pressing for recognition. And that recognition is not carved out against a resisting ignorance, but an actuality from the start, offering itself freely to the cooperating imagination, a fruit of the open disclosure policy of Aeschylean drama.

It stands to reason that we cannot, in this book, deal with the subject of the sound of Aeschylus's speech. This is fortunate on two accounts. First, it seems to me impossible today, even with the finely honed tools of scholarship, to recover the criteria on which Aeschylus relied to vary the auditory appeal of his language. There have been studies of Aeschylean euphony and frequency counts of assonance in spoken dialogue, particularly in epigrammatic sequences and in excited exchanges. But such studies can do little more than assemble the material. It is by no means clear what the evidence means and whether the phenomena observed, such as they are, reflect a conscious choice or, at least, non-random behavior.[6] And, second, I suspect that Aeschylus is indeed capable of choosing words for their sound and for the tonal stimulus they provide, but that other principles of selection have priority for him. In any case, a poetry that works with sound for intrinsic effect does not appear to have come into being until about a century and a half or two centuries after Aeschylus. As the playwright moves back and forth, now insensibly and now with a mighty leap, between the several styles available to him, variations in sound show no correlation.

To proceed from sound to a minimal unit of meaning, it is worth observing that Aeschylus uses few puns, and that their function is normally incidental rather than thematic. The éclat of the double entendre or of the

---

6. For a general study of the function of sound in Greek poetry, see B. A. van Groningen, *La poésie verbale grecque* (*Medel. Nederl. Akad. Wet., Afd. Letterk.*, n.s. 16.4; Amsterdam, 1953), and the critical review by H. Herter in *Gnomon* 27 (1955): 254–59; also W. B. Stanford, *The Sound of Greek* (Berkeley and Los Angeles, 1967). One of the best studies of the problem of alliteration in Greek known to me is I. Opelt, "Alliteration im Griechischen? Untersuchungen zur Dichtersprache des Nonnos," *Glotta* 37 (1958): 205–32.

etymological fusion is immediate; the ambivalence is not one that sets up a tension for the future, but one that confirms or merely adorns. The most famous word play in Aeschylus occurs in a choral description of Helen's voyage to Troy (*Agam.* 689–90): it is said of Helen that she is "truly ship-smashing, man-smashing, fortress-smashing," where the second element (in Greek, the first) in each of the compound designations is *hele-*, identical with the first two syllables of Helen's name. Again, take Cassandra's despairing play upon the name of Apollo (*Agam.* 1081, 1086), the sound of which she associates with that of a verb meaning "destroy." More often, however, the etymological games insist on the obvious and the routine, as when much is made of the traditional identification of *di-*, the first syllable in the Greek word for justice, and *di-*, the first syllable of the oblique cases of Zeus. Clearly, Aeschylus's inventiveness turns its back on puns and double meanings as a source for generating insight. They are relatively few in number, and they are retrospective; they confirm, briefly and in passing, what the audience already knows, or what the drift of a scene suggests. They do not jar the sensibilities; they seal.

Equally little need be said on the subject of riddles and of circumlocutions, two phenomena which in Aeschylus belong closely together and which, like puns and word games, tend to have strictly local standing. In the climactic exchange between Pelasgus, reluctant to admit the refugees, and the daughters of Danaus, they threaten to hang themselves (*Suppl.* 463):

> To robe the busts with novel signatures.

"A riddling word" is the king's response, and he asks for a simpler statement, which is immediately given. On another occasion the riddle promises to be more baffling, but its solution comes equally swiftly, though with a more explosive force. After the killing of Aegisthus in *Libation-Bearers*, the servant attempts to rouse the women; upon Clytemnestra's asking why he is disturbing the house with his shouting, he replies (886):

> My message is: the dead murder the living.

Clytemnestra immediately grasps the meaning:

> Alas, the word is riddling, but I read it.

The mystery is short-lived; it briefly marks a climax, but then recedes into the dead past of used material, without exercising the strenuous force that riddles are supposed to have, to detain, to worry, to enlarge the crisis.

Circumlocution is equally marginal, if by circumlocution we mean the circumstantial way of articulating a process or an event in the terms of a learned system, such as mythology or science. A typical example, very productive in the history of European literature, but quite absent from the

Aeschylean texts, is to refer to the setting or the rising of the sun by talking about the god Helios or Sol and his yoke of horses. It is not surprising that Aeschylus should shun the device, in spite of the ample precedent set by the Homeric epic. It is as if the decorum of the venture was recognized by him as operating counter to the immediacy of his intention. Even in the most Homeric of his plays, *Persians*, imbued as it is with the epic elements of a battle broached, sustained, lost, and lamented, the more mechanical ingredients of the epic style are avoided. Because the accent is either on simplicity or on originality, on eschewing the decorative conventions of the epic or the lyric, Aeschylus has some unusual kennings, i.e., circumlocutions that draw their substance from ordinary, non-learned experience, and that border upon the riddle. *Persians* has one (576–78): the drowned soldiers are said by the chorus to be mangled by "the voiceless children of the unpolluted." As a designation for fish, the phrase may seem remarkable, but the exotic force is blunted by a reference to the sea that occurs in the line just before this. Altogether, it appears that even with kennings, Aeschylus has no interest in keeping his audience guessing. Two conspicuous examples in *Agamemnon*, in defiance of the normal rules for the kenning, supply the designatum, hence unriddle the riddle from the start: "the cousin of mud, its thirsty yoke-fellow: dust" (495) and "shoes, the stepping minion of the foot" (945). With these kennings, even more than with the other figures we have discussed, one may well wonder what Aeschylus's purpose was. Their function seems to be unrelated to anything systematic; they do not create or deepen a mystery. At best, on the rare occasions when they make their weight felt, they can be said to invest humdrum things with substance, to personify and enliven them, and perhaps to spell out the connections which bind together some of the familiar parcels of our lives. But it is hard to avoid the feeling that these devices, rare as they are, have something excessive about them. The sense of an aggregate reality that they may be designed to inspire is undercut by their eccentricity. It is best, I think, to regard them as the odd excesses of a rhetoric not yet smoothed into predictable patterns.

It is now time to have done with the more general aspects of Aeschylus's speech, and with the exceptional features that might be found startling at first blush, and to turn to a consideration of what might be called the typical styles of the spoken, the chanted, and the sung portions of a play.[7] I start with a series of chanted anapaests. Anapaests are metrically the sim-

7. For some of the data relevant to an assessment of Aeschylus's styles, we are still indebted to three older books: W. Schmid, *Geschichte der griechischen Literatur*, vol. 1, pt. 2 (Munich, 1934), esp. pp. 290 ff.; W. B. Stanford, *Aeschylus in His Style* (Dublin, 1942); and F. R. Earp, *The Style of Aeschylus* (Cambridge, 1948).

plest system available to Aeschylus, less given to variation and resolutions even than spoken iambs, and the metrical simplicity is matched by the simplicity and the relative uniformity of the syntax and the diction. Here is a portion of what the daughters of Danaus chant soon after their entry on the stage (*Suppl.* 19 ff.):

> What country more gracious
> Than this could we reach
> With these suppliant branches
> In-our-hands, covered-in-ribbons?
> I greet the city, the land, the pure water,
> The high gods and those underground
> Who hold the seats of-heavy-punishment,
> And Zeus the Savior third, house-guardian
> Of honorable men. Welcome, I ask, the suppliant,
> The band born-of-woman, with a saving
> Breath of the land. But the arrogant swarm,
> Thronging-with-men, born-of-Egypt,
> Before they set foot on this land
> Of loam, chase them seaward in their hull
> Swiftly-oared. And there may they crash
> Running into a blast, a storm-wind-striking
> Thunder and lightning, and gusts, gloom-bearing,
> Of an angry sea. . . .

On the whole, one would agree, not a passage that presents great difficulties. The forward movement of the sentiment is easy to follow. The passages given over to chanting tend to be neither descriptive not reflective, but expressive in the sense that the chorus leader or the individual who does the chanting voices the feelings or the assumptions which are to serve as the basis for more developed structures. Consequently the syntax is usually one of straightforward statements or questions or exclamations, each of them brief and complete within itself. They have little of the bulk or the grandeur which is popularly associated with the Aeschylean style. The only elements that give an inkling of greater density are the items which in my rendering appear as hyphenated expressions. They are compounds, i.e., usually, adjectives, though occasionally nouns (very rarely verbs), put together out of two separate stems. Greek stands somewhere between English and German in the freedom with which new words may be formed in this fashion. That this freedom is not nearly as great in Greek as it is in German—not to mention in so combinatory a language as Sanskrit—is indicated by the humor Aristophanes strikes from such combinations. It is sometimes difficult to resist the thought that in Aeschylus, too, many of the more daring combinations hover precariously on the line dividing significance from farce, and that it is only the weight of the context, the dramatic excitement of which they are part, which prevents them from tumbling over that line, as they are made to do in Housman's famous parody of Greek tragedy. On other occasions the compound is introduced only in order to produce a word of sufficient length to complete a line of verse. Normally, however, the effect is one of packing into a relatively confined space the information, or the dramatic punch, that an extended phrase or clause would furnish more feebly. Even a random browsing in the text turns up such composites at every step. Attempts have been made, unsuccessfully, to determine whether Aeschylus's usage of compounds becomes more pronounced or less so in the course of his career, and whether there is a shift in the relative incidence as between dialogue, anapaests, and lyric.

One is tempted to associate the favoring of compounds with the notions of dramatic tension and dialectic opposition. If Aeschylus is, as can be plausibly argued, the master of dramatic confrontation, especially of a confrontation that works through the lyric as much as through forensic duelling (see below, chapter 7), the friction set up by the merging of disparate units into compound wholes might well be counted in support of that perspective. This is certainly true of much that is found in choral odes and encounters, and also in certain sections of dialogue. But in chanted anapaests, as instanced in our passage from *Suppliants*, the compound formations are more often than not devoid of internal friction. Though bulky and compact, and hence momentarily arresting the regular progress of the thought, the compounds are shorthand rather than oxymora. The units combined are complementary; the stems used usually represent suitable associations of noun and adjective or verb and noun. Externally, the compound adjectives go smoothly with the nouns with which they are linked. The total effect, therefore, is one of natural progression, with the compounds serving to supply energy and sometimes visual concreteness, but little more, to the easy rhythm of the anapaestic chant.

What we have said about the special quality of the compounds—their low level of dramatic tension and their relative semantic transparency—is true of anapaestic structures generally. There is emotional engagement, of course; nothing in Aeschylus has the dispassionate, even frigid, calm of a Euripidean prologue. But by comparison with what is found in choral singing or especially in spoken iambs, the chanted sequences constitute the troughs of the emotional curve. The diction and the syntax serve this purpose well; they conspire to create a sense of steadiness and homogeneity. The sentence structure is simple, with now and then an expansion via a brief relative clause modifying the steady march of main clauses. There are analogies with the parataxis of epic speech; and in fact the anapaestic introduction of *Persians* shows how well suited series of names and the type of adjective known as "ornamental" are to this kind of delivery.[8] The thought processes are leisurely, even slightly didactic, as if Aeschylus wanted to make sure that what his choristers chant at the beginning of a play or of a new section in a play would be fully understood by an untutored audience. In the present instance, the choristers introduce themselves as "factotums" of the departed Persians. The somewhat unusual term is immediately explained: they are caretakers, appointed by the absent Emperor. The thought of his absence at once introduces a touch of anxiety: they worry about the Emperor, for he has taken with him a huge force, and he is young. . . . Each thought creates its own successor in a smooth sequence, by means of elaboration, variation, or contrast. The grammatical means is, more often than not, the response of one word to another in the same case, or a development via relative pronoun or temporal particle. Syntactic violence is avoided; there are no gaps or breaks in the flow of anapaestic speech.

The word order, also, is one that corresponds to the patterns of mundane speech. This is an important point, for one of the most impressive and, to a textual critic struggling with a corrupt text, disconcerting features of choral odes is the frequency of *hyperbaton*, the separation and dislocation of units, usually nouns and adjectives, that in common speech would go together. The easy appositional chains of anapaests stand in strong contrast to such refraction, as does the clearly disposed articulation into smallish sense units, divided from one another by means of natural breathing spaces. The translator rarely has any difficulty in determining where to put his commas, his periods, and his question marks. All this goes hand in hand with the simple versification we have described above (chapter 2); the even pattern of longs and shorts and the regularity of line lengths conform to the steady progress of the thought. The short lines are filled with more or less complete thoughts, and bundles of three or four lines, corresponding roughly to stanzas in lyric song, are severely end-stopped, to maintain the clarity of the articulation. Only in *Agamemnon* are the chanted anapaests assimilated in diction and syntax to the choral complexities that follow. But that is only a matter of degree; even in that play, as unusual linguistically as in every other aspect, the stylistic distinction between chanting and singing is maintained.

From anapaests we now turn to choral singing, and especially the choral ode. Here the situation is less simple than in the case of the chanted utterance, for choral singing answers to a greater range of dramatic possibilities.

---

8. Aeschylus's debt to Homer has been studied by A. Sideras, *Aeschylus Homericus* (*Hypomnemata* 31; Göttingen, 1971). Cf. also A. F. Garvie, *Aeschylus' Supplices* (Cambridge, 1969), pp. 45 ff. Altogether Garvie's chapter 2, "Style," is a mine of information and considered judgment.

There are the laments and the prayers and the songs of triumph which communicate the fugitive motives of the group united in the singing. On the other hand, there are what we might call choral essays—sustained sequences of reflection in which the chorus voices tribal wisdom or issues of public debate. In spite of these variations, we approach an Aeschylean ode, or even a sung encounter, with certain expectations which differ from those brought to anapaests. These expectations are shaped by what the Aristophanic Euripides picks out for ridicule: the difficulty of the style seemingly verging on meaninglessness, the piling up of bulky adjectives, the clash of word upon word. Let us look at a sample passage (*Suppl.* 40 ff.):

Now calling upon
Zeus's calf, the avenger across-the-sea, the scion of the flower-cropping,
    ancestral cow out of the breath breathed
By Zeus; a touch, name-giving, was bestowed by destined Time,
A happy word: Epaphus he begot.

Him I ponder now,
Among the grass-cropping places of my ancient mother remembering the past
    labors. Now I will show
Firm proofs; improbable though they are they will stand out clear.
The fullness of my tale will prompt acceptance.

It is hard to imagine that to an Athenian listening to this ode for the first time—which, let us remember, was also thought to be the last—the details of the text were clearer than they are in translation. And yet we must assume that they were. The two stanzas are the opening salvo of an ode in which the chorus establishes its credentials: the women are descended from the Argive princess Io who, across the sea, in Egypt, in the shape of a cow, mated with Zeus, whose touch (*ephapsis*) and generative breath combined to produce a son named after the happy moment: Epaphus, himself bovine but also the grandfather of Danaus, the father of the women singing the ode. The listeners can be expected to have known enough of the ancient legend to assemble the appropriate recollections from the clues given. What is more taxing than the mythological conundrum is the language which makes up the lyric sequence. The translation simplifies and breaks up the structure; in the Greek, the whole dyad consists of one sentence, with three present participles—calling, pondering, remembering—as antecedents for the main verb, "I will show." Because the participial succession is interrupted by an independent, parenthetic clause concerning the touch of Zeus and its etymological consequence, the overall construction appears to be dissolved, with each unit pressing for recognition on its own, incomplete terms. The same pressure toward self-assertion and atomism is observed in the behavior of words. Often in an ode, it is difficult to establish the precise grammatical relation of a word to its context, and textual critics are hard put to it in deciding between two different cases handed down by the manuscript tradition. Thus, while in chanted anapaests the sentence is the principal building block, with sentences following one upon another in loose appositional sequence, in the lyric the sentence tends to lead a shadow existence, with words and phrases taking over as the chief conveyers of poetic and dramatic impulses. The extent to which this tendency is realized varies from ode to ode; an extreme case is represented in an ode which voices the confusion and disorientation of battle and its aftermath, *Seven* 345 ff.:

> Rumblings throughout the city, the turret-net
> Close, by man man is speared,
> Bloodied shrieks
> Newly-born
> Of [infants] at-the-breast howl.
> Snatchings, blood-brothers of random-running.
> Plunderer contracts with plunderer
> And calls [him] empty, [himself] empty,
> Wishing to have a partner. . . .

The impressionistic arrangement of wailing infants—not experienced as infants but as wailings, as units made up of blood and cries and fondling and death—of roaming plunderers and their frustrations, of leaning battlements and calculating eagerness, is untranslatable. It is a mosaic made up of words, of sense units violently removed from grammatical agreement— "newly born" is in the same case as "shrieks," and so is "bloodied"—as if to emphasize the abandonment of reason and order.[9] In this instance there are good poetic grounds for the violence. But it is merely the logical development of a bias native to all choral singing in Aeschylus. Instead of the breathing space between sense units favored in anapaests, the singing packs them close together, dovetails them, skews them, burdens them with a swarm of modifiers that get in one another's way, until it becomes a futile effort to look for the pauses subdividing a stanza or a dyad. The commas and periods employed in the translation above are at best approximate. A truer rendering would have to forego all punctuation marks save the stop at the end of the stanza. It is of course true that these features are more prominent in a hallucinatory sequence, such as the ode from *Seven* is; pure narrative or philosophical reflection tempers the lyric exaltation and smoothes the grammatical irregularities. The result can be a grand continuum of closely packed, inward-pressing descriptive detail, as in *Agam.* 437 ff.:

9. For a recent study of this type of grammatical disagreement, see V. Bers, *Enallage and Greek Style* (*Mnemosyne Suppl.* 29; Leiden, 1974).

The gold-changer, Ares, of bodies
And scale-balancer in war of spear
From the flame, from Troy
Sends home to the kin thick
Dust, burden-of-tears,
Of ashes, manpower-return,
An easy-fit in the casket.

There is nothing easy about the fit of the lines, of their magnificent, ponderous, unarticulated heaviness, to the slow syncopated iambs of the verse.
Once again, though the grammar may be construable, each word and word
combination counts for more than any sentence or clause. By the end of the
stanza, there is no sense of progress, as there is in the course of chanted
anapaests. The picture of Ares the banker of corpses endures and combines
with the other sense units to register an enduring impression of fullness and
compact materiality.

Perhaps the most important distinction between the diction of anapaests
and that of lyric song is to be found in the nature of the adjective compounds. We have already said that the compounds of chanted verse tend to
be traditional and transparent. Akin to the "ornamental epithet" of epic—
the conventional predication that does little more than affirm the essence of
the noun that it modifies, the anapaestic compound is designed to offer a
degree of stateliness but a minimum of resistance to the progress of the
sequence. Contrast the compounds of the lyric: "scale-balancer" as an epithet of Ares, "manpower-return" as an adjectival comment on ashes: these
are substantial and often ironic notes, elaborate commentary rather than
ornament. They slow down the argument and flood it with a spectrum of
illumination until the song swarms with a multiplicity of meanings and
sense impressions. The effect is furthered by the piling up of attributive
modifiers on which we have commented several times, and of which *Agam.*
150–55, quoted earlier in this chapter, is a striking example. There Artemis was visualized as

> urging
> Another sacrifice, law-less, not-designed-for-eating,
> An inbred builder of quarrels, unheedful-of-men.

Four complex phrases are accumulated to define the second sacrifice—i.e.,
that of Iphigenia—and the chain of hatred unleashed by it. As we move
away from the noun which serves as the pivot, the further predications
begin to take their cue not only from "sacrifice," but also from some of the
ideas expressed earlier in the ode. Each phrase, in turn, takes some of its fuel
from the phrase that comes before. The climactic term, "unheedful-of

men," which might also be translated "not-respecting-the-husband," connects not so much with "sacrifice" as with "builder of quarrels." The quarrels or animosities set off by the sacrifice will in the end lead to the murder of the husband, Agamemnon. The lyric, because it can say all this within its short compass, turns into an anticipatory mirror of the drama as a whole.

But this is only one side of the matter. After the lines about Ares cited above, the stanza continues (*Agam.* 445 ff.):

> Men groan, praising the man, [saying] that one [was] skilled in battle,
> that another fell gloriously in the fray, on account of another man's wife; thus a
> man growls to himself, and resentful grief creeps forth against the sons of
> Atreus, punitive-lords.

Suddenly the language turns simple, even plain, the syntax orderly, sharp. The gnarled compression of the grand lyric mode gives way to a brittleness—a nervous clarity that is of quite another world. Clauses are brief, even laconic, but grammatically complete; compound adjectives are infrequent and of the simplest formation. What distances this kind of lyric speech from the rolling cadences of chanted anapaests is the very nervousness of its internal directions. The mind turns this way or that; it moves quickly from description to inference; it imagines disparate groups speaking and complaining. In this way, in spite of the vast difference in style, the two lyric voices are one. Both the complex style and the brittle style are dedicated to the proposition that reality is made up of incompatibilities, of refractory data of experience, emotion, and speech. The ultimate distillation of such refractoriness is rendered in the form of *gnōmai*, of general truths and communal wisdom. It is surely not without significance that such wisdom sequences are an important element in the odes, and that it is the brittle style, rather than the complex mode, in which they are put (for more about *gnōmai*, see below, chapter 6).

Finally, a remark or two about Aeschylus's spoken verse. This is the most difficult topic to discuss. Unlike choral singing, whose verbal component is merely part of a larger communication consisting also of music and movement; and unlike chanted verse with its rather narrow range of dramatic function and linguistic effect, spoken verse comes closest to the natural means of human communication, and lends itself to the diverse purposes and moods for which that communication exists. Spoken iambic verse is also, metrically speaking, the most flexible of the patterns available to the dramatist. Traditionally, iambs had been used for scoffing as well as reflection, for political pronouncements as well as for essays on human behavior and diatribes. Still, prior to the advent of tragedy and of Aeschylus, the verse had been a limited and timid thing. In Aeschylus's hands, it blossoms into a versatile instrument, perfectly capable of catching the nuances and contrarieties of human intercourse. The central mechanism of the spoken line in Aeschylus is the sentence. In anapaests, sentences unfold by apposition, feeble structures that take their origin from the progressive stringing together of ideas; in the lyric, the sentence fights for survival, imperilled by the autonomy of the word or the phrase and the complexity of the vision; in the iambs, however, the sentence is an infinitely varied but always proudly sculptured organism, with its articulation and its confines openly laid out. Iambic speech—and that includes iambic exchanges—proceeds by sentences to build up to paragraphs; the spoken delivery checks itself against natural pauses and dividers that leave little doubt about the formal organization of the whole.

Iambic speech can be fulsome and laborious; it can also be mobile and dry. Clytemnestra's beacon speech (*Agam.* 281 ff.) dramatizes the orderly island-hopping of the fire signals into an excited, showy conquest of massive hurdles. The stages of the transit are clearly marked; though human effort is joined with physical momentum to produce an impression of vast distances strenuously spanned, the natural architecture of the verse prevents the energies from spilling over. The result is a rare balance of strong, though never extravagant, diction and transparent sentence structure. The solid, muscular words follow one another in a sequence that differs little from the arrangement of daily speech. I offer a small selection from the passage, 290 ff. What cannot be retained in translation is the liveliness of a language in which most of the subjects are masculine or feminine in gender, and thus seemingly participate in a personal struggle. What is more, the journey is one that many in the audience would have been familiar with, if not from their own travels, then from the accounts of others.

> Makistos did not hesitate; nor, overcome
> In thoughtless sleep, did it ignore the signal,
> But far away, to Euripus, goes the light,
> A beacon notice to Messapion's guards;
> Who, kindling their own blaze, relayed the message,
> And set the torch to a mass of last year's heather.
> The brightness waxes without languishing;
> Leaping across the valley of Asopus, like
> A moon in fullness, upon Kithairon's shelf
> It roused the next renewal of the tidings,
> Nor did the garrison shun the far-flung fire,
> But burnt another, large beyond their orders.
> High up, above Gorgopis lake, the signal
> Arched. . . .

This is from a descriptive section. The leisurely pace of the reporting encourages the mobilization at close quarters of nouns and verbs jostling one another for attention. The curve of the delivery stretches forward across many lines; the tensed arc of the recording gives the individual words room to ring out and hold their own. By way of contrast let us look at a piece of dialogue, *Eum.* 892 ff. The Furies have been won over by Athena; they now engage her in a spoken exchange concerning the privileges they may expect.

> *Cho.* Lady Athena, tell me about the place I'll own.
> *Ath.* A place that knows no suffering: yours to take.
> *Cho.* Assuming I take it: what will be my rights?
> *Ath.* No house will thrive unless you wish it so.
> *Cho.* You'll see to it that my power is so great?
> *Ath.* Yes, we will succor those who worship you.
> *Cho.* Will you endorse my power for all time?
> *Ath.* I would not promise what I cannot do.

If the translation appears unusually awkward, it is because the relaxed bartering, with its end-stopped lines, is difficult to accommodate in the shorter English units. But it must be added that the Greek dialogue, though fluent and idiomatic, has little in the way of poetic power. There is about it a conversational effortlessness that defies stylistic classification. The words are ordinary, the thoughts artless, the constructions unremarkable. This is the plain style, without frills, without dramatic tension or pretension.

Not all Aeschylus's dialogue is like this; in fact most of it is not. When the exchange is between opponents locked in a heated battle of wits or of fears, the increased tension is signalled by more forcible speech. The duel between Eteocles and the terrified women of Thebes illustrates this (*Seven* 245):

> *Cho.* But listen: I hear the neighing of the horses!
> *Ete.* Must you confess to hear more than you hear?
> *Cho.* We are encircled, and the city groans!
> *Ete.* It is my task to meditate on this!
> *Cho.* The hammering at the gates grows louder: Help us!
> *Ete.* Silence! Do not proclaim this from the housetops.
> *Cho.* O sacred gods, do not forsake our bastion.
> *Ete.* Damnation take you, if you can't keep quiet.
> *Cho.* Gods of the City, I beg you not to enslave me!

Unlike the sequence from *Eumenides*, with its easy, full-faced colloquy between two negotiators, the present passage features two partisans glancing away from each other, each to his own commitment. The language conforms. It is more angular in its constructions, more selective in its choice of words, more rapid in its changes from exclamation to question and from statement to command.

But, when all is said and done, and the three passages of spoken verse we

have cited are compared with each other, they can be shown to share a
common characteristic that sets them apart from both chanting and sung
verse. All three samples, it will have been noted, are singularly unam-
bitious in their use of adjectives, and the few adjectives that are present tend
not to be of the compound variety, either ornamental or contrived. It has
been said that spoken verse puts more emphasis on the verb. This is the
linguistic corollary to the obvious fact that the speaking voice is more
closely geared to the progress of the dramatic action than is the more ceremonial voice of the chorus. There is some truth to this. The great movers,
Clytemnestra, Eteocles, and Prometheus, have speeches that swarm with
action verbs in many different grammatical forms. Most choral utterances
do not call for the first and second persons of the verb as action speech does,
though choral encounters and those odes in which the chorus expresses its
anxieties or splits into two groups questioning or counseling each other do
not lack the appropriate verb forms. In any case, these differences are more a
matter of *what* is being said than of how it is said. The manipulation of
adjectives is more truly a function of the medium. In iambic speech they
come in as the semantic requisites of meaningful communication; they define or create the meaning for nouns that are neutral or uncommunicative in
themselves. They are not, as in chanting and singing, piled up in attributive or predicative chains in excess of the minimal needs of information.
Significantly, where the nouns are sufficiently informative on their own, the
use of adjectives may be reduced to the vanishing point, as in this segment
from Apollo's defense of Orestes (*Eum.* 660 ff.):

> The mounter creates the babe, the woman hosts it,
> The gods permitting, as if it were a guest.
> In proof of this I'll give you confirmation:
> A father can do his work without a mother.
> Here stands our witness, the daughter of mighty Zeus,
> Not hatched, like others, in the darkness of the womb.
> Not even a goddess could bear a child like this.

The precise, not to say perverse lines of the argument are adequately fed by
nouns and verbs; adjectives would only slow up the sophistry, and perhaps
expose its churlishness. The unadorned swiftness of the special pleading is a
far cry from the quasi-choral ponderousness, also in iambic speech, of Cassandra's prophecy (*Agam.* 1280–81):

> Soon there will come an avenger of our wrongs,
> A mother-murdering shoot, a father's lash.

But Cassandra is a special case; her speaking voice is a thinly disguised
singing voice; her prophetic fervor and inwardness, strongly expressed in
her many lines of lyric verse, break through also in her iambic passages.

In *The Common Reader*, Virginia Woolf enlarges on what happens to us "when we bruise our minds upon some tremendous metaphor in the *Agamemnon* instead of stripping the branch of its flowers instantly as we do in reading *Lear*," and concludes that Aeschylus "will give us, not the thing itself, but the reverberation and reflection which, taken into his mind, the thing has made; close enough to the original to illustrate it, remote enough to heighten, enlarge, and make splendid." [10] This stress on weight, bigness, distortion toward magnificence is repeated again and again in the responses of critics who love their Aeschylus but are also a little frightened by him. Aristophanes was the first. He recruited an Aeschylus so heavily armored, so swollen with "Scamanders, moated camps and griffin-eagles flashing" [11] that he could scarcely move, and would have been an easy prey for the comically agile Euripides if Aristophanes had not snatched him up unfairly and given him the victory in the contest. There is of course some truth in the picture of the muscle-bound giant of polysyllabic presence, as there is some truth in everything that Aristophanes tells us. But it is only one side of a more complicated situation. All one needs to do is leave *Agamemnon*, which has mostly served as evidence for the image, and turn to *Eumenides*, especially the second half of that play, to find that Aeschylus can vary his style to a degree not again found on the stage until we reach the linguistic self-consciousness of *Love's Labour's Lost*. Even disregarding the generic variations of delivery sketched above, Aeschylus is not a one-track stylist; nor is he, as Aristophanes humorously pretends, an original who does not really know what he is doing.

Aeschylus could indeed aim for loftiness "by stretching every phrase to the utmost, by sending them floating forth in metaphors, by bidding them rise up and stalk eyeless and majestic through the scene." [12] Longinus had this in mind when he spoke of Aeschylus's "conceits shaggy with ideas." [13] Aristotle introduced the term *onkos*, which literally means "bulky volume" and later came to designate the elevated pompadour on the Roman tragic mask. [14] Even a casual reading of the Aeschylean corpus furnishes some extraordinary examples of rhetorical bulk. Does Aeschylus really propose "eyes that wag their tails," as he appears to at *Agam.* 796–98, or should we suspect a corruption? The chances are that the phrase is sound, for there are some mild parallels. Eteocles's speeches at *Seven* 550 ff. and 597 ff. on behalf of the defenders of the fifth and sixth gates of Thebes contain similarly

10. *The Common Reader* (London, 1925), pp. 55, 49.
11. B. B. Rogers's rendering of *Frogs* 928–29.
12. Woolf, *Common Reader*, pp. 48–49.
13. Longinus *On the Sublime* 15.5.
14. Aristotle *Poetics* 1459b29. Note, however, that Aristotle associates the term with epic.

synthetic touches. In one case he says that a man's hand sees what is to be done; in the other he speaks of a "fleet-footed eye." It is as if Eteocles were attempting to oppose the vicious corporeality of the attackers by dissolving the bodily contours of the defenders who are, like Xenophanes's god, all ear, all eye, all hand—whereas even Parthenopaeus, physically the most disconcerting of the attackers, says that he prizes his eyes more than the gods. The attackers are bodies, and limited by the organic function of their bodies; the defenders are burning spirits, and Aeschylus falls back upon the resources of a radical lyricism to underscore the point.

Bulk can be created by a number of devices. It can be a matter of unusual expressions, such as the "tableting" of words, in the sense of inscribing them in one's mind (*Suppl.* 179); or of unusual compound formations, sometimes bordering upon the comic, such as "hollow-bellied" applied to a shield (*Seven* 496) and "nostril-ringing" said of the snorting of horses (*Seven* 464); or of unusual combinations of words, such as "voiceless messenger," a predicate of dust (*Suppl.* 180). We have already discussed circumlocution and kennings. Any of these would in the rhetorical handbooks of the ancients and their more recent successors come under the general heading of elevation. Elevation can be bombast, and Longinus felt that Boreas's big words in the lost play *Oreithyia* are pure rant:

> For let me see a single hearth-tenant,
> I'll corrugate a wreath of winter-storms
> And kindle and incinerate the roof.[15]

There are other things like this, reminding us of some of the funnier lines in Jonson's *Poetaster*. But after all, these are the words of the North Wind himself, who is known in Greek mythology for the violence of his aggression. Aeschylus's bulk is not a species of embellishment, accruing adventitiously to a text devised in the first place without its ornaments. While Aristotle regarded bulk and tropes as additions to an original stratum, earlier generations had understood that Aeschylus's language is creative communication, not refurbishment. But in their acceptance of his genius they tended to fall into the opposite trap of assuming that the playwright talked that way because of an innate fervor. The concept of Aeschylus as an original genius driven by spring-storms within him to utter oracular phrases over which he has only a minimum of control has been abandoned, along with the belief in an inspired Ossian or an automatically oral Homer.

Still, it is possible to be unhappy with this or that example of bulk. Evidently Aeschylus welcomed and delighted in opportunities for verbal extravagance. He lived at a time when the formulaic constraints of the epic

---

15. Longinus *On the Sublime* 3.1.

and its successor genres were being shattered by philosophers, Sophists, and others who had come to question the social values of the old traditions. The pressure for liberation, for democratic self-confidence, coincides with a greater emphasis on what the cult of Dionysus can furnish in the way of communicative enrichment. On the Elizabethan stage, the advent of religious ferment combined with a humanist pleasure in the resources of the language to produce a flowering of grandiloquence and of wit. Something very similar must be imagined for Aeschylus. An ounce of historical sympathy will permit us to accept even the more willful aspects of the bulk and to appreciate their larger function in the whole.

There is a sense in which the simpleminded identification of verbal extravagance with powerful emotion is true, except that the emotion is not that of the author, but of one of his characters. As Prometheus launches into his bravura description of the plight of Typhon buried for his rebelliousness in the roots of Mount Etna, his speech, ordinarily less flamboyant in this play than iambic speech elsewhere, takes on a splendor and a sweep which are the mark of Prometheus's anger and his sympathy with one who had fought Zeus and failed (*Prom.* 351 ff.). As the herald at *Agam.* 555 ff. recollects the sufferings of the ordinary soldiers at Troy, his passion generates a descriptive fullness which closely matches that of Clytemnestra's beacon speech. We have already cited the speeches of Boreas and of Cassandra. And let us remind ourselves that iambic speech gives only intermittent scope to bulk, which is more appropriate to the slower cadences of choral singing.

But in the light of a tradition that puts its emphasis on Aeschylean bulk, it is of the greatest importance that we also remind ourselves that Aeschylus can be startlingly simple and direct. His dramatic diction does not yet make a systematic distinction between tragic decorum and less stylized speech. When the Empress Mother tells the ghost of Darius (*Pers.* 714) that the Persian power has been "utterly-sacked," choosing a word normally associated with the conquest of cities and fortifying it with a prefix, she adds the qualifier "so to speak." The *maître de philosophie* who, as *Le Bourgeois Gentilhomme* teaches us, is responsible for the distinction between poetry and prose will throw up his hands in horror, as he will also when Darius says in language that can be found again in Aristotle, that "it is not the case that some [misfortunes] happen and others don't" (802). The tenuousness of the distinction between poetry and prose is instanced again and again, as in *Suppl.* 742, when the chorus leader terminates a remark addressed to Danaus with the deprecatory remark "but there is no need to tell *you*," or in *Lib.* 653 ff., where Orestes's language, as he knocks on the gate, is no different from what we might find in a Socratic dialogue or in comedy, which delights in offering the language of ordinary intercourse as if it just happened to fit into verse. The play in which this type of speech is most pronounced is *Eumenides*. Apollo, Orestes, Athena, and even the ghost of Clytemnestra (110–12) express themselves in cadences often indistinguishable from "prose" except that, as we have indicated earlier, the individual sentences are briefer and simpler than in, say, an early Platonic dialogue. Even the Furies, in their chanted anapaests, show no preference for bulk.

Simplicity, then, is as Aeschylean as its opposite. Even Aristophanes seems to have felt this, for one of the jibes which he has Euripides launch against his opponent is that Aeschylus has a habit of saying things twice over. In Euripides's view, this serves the Aeschylean grandiloquence, for the repetitions are variations, not duplications of the original statement. But the underlying idea is one that runs counter to Aeschylean concentration or complexity. "I have come and I have arrived in my own country" (*Lib.* 3) can at best be said to exhibit the kind of doubling which marks biblical verse. In addition to these doublings by variation, of which there are many, Aeschylean verse swarms with simple duplications and with words used twice or thrice over within a narrow compass. In the first stanza of the second choral ode of *Agamemnon* (355–66), the adjective "great" is used four times, with no apparent special effect intended. At *Pers.* 78 ff., within the space of ten lines, both captains and enclosures are said to be "secure"; at *Agam.* 1292, 1343, and 1372, Cassandra *hopes* that the blow which will kill her will be on target, Agamemnon *complains* that he has received a blow that is on target, and Clytemnestra *boasts* that during her earlier preparations she had said many words that were on target. On the whole, it is easy to distinguish such casual word repetition from cases of meaningful repetition—the recurrence of images and symbols that have a bearing on the developing drama, an outstanding example of which is the mention of garments dipped in dye (*baphas*) at *Agam.* 239 and 960; the latter instance cannot but direct the mind back to the circumstances of Iphigenia's murder. (More will be said about this below, in chapter 5.) Casual repetition, I would urge, should not be inspected too carefully. Whether we like it or not, we must accept the fact that Aeschylus, in spite of the richness of his vocabulary and the inventiveness of his grand style, eschews fine writing. The measured variation recommended in the nineteenth century, prior to the twentieth-century resurgence of oral publicity in the shape of radio advertising, is not Aeschylus's concern. One might wish to say that the repetitions serve some of the same purposes as formulaic repetition in the epic; that they help to underscore the constancy of the tragic rhythm and furnish an element of stasis in the violent motion of the drama. But as soon as the suggestion is made, its inadequacy, or rather its pretentiousness, is apparent. The repetition is just too irregular, too pervasive, to suggest any purposefulness at all. It is better to cite it as one more proof of the dramatist's willingness to emulate the unintentionalities of living speech. Many of Aeschylus's passages—both in iambic speech and, especially, in the choral odes and exchanges—exhibit the tightness and the bulk that later generations remembered as the special hallmarks of his style. But in the end we are forced to conclude that there is no one Aeschylean idiom. A lesser artist has his identifying mannerisms; he plays by rules. A great playwright like Aeschylus creates the rules. He fashions a verse that burgeons with a wealth of lexical and syntactic possibilities and that brims over with the directness of its attack. In the process he cannot always be held to the strictest requirements of literary polish. But his understanding with his audiences seems to have been such that he was accused neither of pretentiousness nor of slovenliness. More than his successors in the genre, he was the playwright of the people.

# _ 5 _

# Speech:
# The Larger Dimension

Before we turn to what, for want of a better term, is called "imagery," we must stop to consider one device which Aeschylus, along with many other writers, employs to order the reality circumscribed by the dramatic scene. This is the "catalogue" or, to give it a more general name that will be useful later, the "inventory," the relatively unadorned listing of names or things or properties. Such a listing has many uses and arouses a variety of responses. It may be severely didactic or informational, helping a character or the audience to learn the facts they need to know for passing judgment. Or the effect of the enumeration may be upon the imagination; the items of the inventory combine to compel the mind to change gears. Then again, an inventory may be so powerful, its diction and its vistas so splendid or frightful, that the listing is used as a weapon, to overcome a resistance or simply to terrify the listener into submission.[1]

The form is as old as the epic. The *Iliad* offers many lists, loving enumerations of objects appreciated for their beauty or their value. Usually the lists are in the dynamic mode; the objects are built into a system of action that is made to operate on or with them. Hephaestus *makes* arms; Agamemnon *will give* presents; a hero *dons* his battle dress. The static catalogue, a mere itemizing removed from the living context of action and interaction, is the invention of a later art. The so-called paratactic mode of the epic—its fashion of talking about the world and its events as if all consisted of an uninterrupted chain of data, each no more and no less significant than its predecessor or its successor and all held together by an energy whose loss is inconceivable—reappears, in miniature, in the inventory. Hephaestus's making of Achilles's armor is a workshop paradigm of how the epic bard fashions his poem. It exploits a sense of confidence, a familiarity with generic processes, that is ready for small variations in the scheme but not for large-scale deviation. The details of the ship-building process or the characteristic gestures and manipulations of a sacrifice or a meal are inventoried because within the rhythm of the epic world they are unchanging. Surprises and shocks are unique events that stand out in sharp relief against the faithful background of serial regularity. The inventory, in Homer's hand, is

1. There is need of a book on uses of the catalogue in ancient poetry. Some stimulating remarks will be found in M. L. West, ed. and comm., *Hesiod: Theogony* (Cambridge, 1966), pp. 356 ff.

an instrument of reassurance. It is the instrument whereby both the natural world and the civilized structure of the satisfaction of natural needs find expression and can be made to counterpoint the horrors of death. And even deaths on the battlefield can be savored as the stable links in a recurring cycle; hence the great casualty lists, with their suggestion of discipline, decorum, and beauty.

The lyric writers who succeeded to the epic legacy continued to employ inventories, but largely in a spirit foreign to the epic model, to lead up to, or offset, praise or condemnation:

> My hair is white, my beard is grey,
> My happy youth is gone;
> My teeth are old, my joys are small,
> So little time is left.
> Wherefor I sigh and think of Death
> And Hell's forbidding gloom.
> The trip is hard, but once you're down
> It's harder to return.
>
> Anacreon fr. 44 Diehl

The itemizing is placed at the service of an argument; it contends that the person at issue—in this case, the speaker—does not have certain qualities, or has them more singularly, or more fatefully than others. This introduces a forward momentum which strains against the internal democracy which is the epic birthright of the inventory. In Homer, the inventory encourages equilibrium, a fond preoccupation with each detail without prejudice to any other. In the comparisons and contrasts and appraisals for which the lyric uses the old technique, the terminal count is more important than anything that precedes it. The listener is forced to submit to a forward movement which deprives the terms of the inventory of their autonomy. Inventories of the epic type are not unknown in the lyric, especially in choral lyric. But the "epigrammatic" inventory, packing its explosive power into the final step, is the more common form.

As in so much else, the drama inherits stimuli from both the epic and the lyric. Aeschylus's art of the inventory is, if anything, more varied than what is found before him. Some of his lists are epic in every sense of the word. The description of the offerings that the Empress Mother is going to give to the ghost of her husband (*Pers.* 610–18) is of this kind. Registering in brief order, as it does, milk, honey, water, wine, olives, and flowers, the simple substances of a healthy and nourishing existence, the catalogue carves out a pastoral oasis to refresh us momentarily from the shock of the defeat. The simple costume she wears (608) underlines the intention: to wave the wand of humility and grace in the face of terror.

More typical perhaps, is another kind of inventory, of which I present the following example, once again a simple one, strategically placed at the beginning of a play, before tempers and identifications have had a chance to gather strength, and at a time when the didactic appeal is bound to succeed better than further along in the play. At *Eum.* 1–29 the priestess catalogues the gods that have had a share in the oracular activities at Delphi. She begins—and the double use of the word "first" (1–2) emphasizes the coincidence between serial listing and historical succession—with Gaia, the Earth herself, the founder of prophecy and the first (material) principle of it. The priestess then sketches the subsequent history, via Themis and Phoebe, to Apollo, whose advent is described at some length. Then, more summarily, she lists the other divinities that have a connection with the sanctuary: Pallas, the Corycian Nymphs, Dionysus, the river divinity Pleistos, Poseidon, and—to complete the list with the name of the great Completer—Zeus. Thus a list of ten divinities or groups of divinities located at a sacred site introduces a play which features, more concretely than any other ancient play we possess, gods in contention, and which at its conclusion memorializes the establishment of a group of divinities at a new site.

It is by no means a straightforward catalogue. For some of the listed tutelaries we have little more than the name; others are cited along with details from legend or sacred history. The mode is dynamic throughout, but the action component, and therefore the status of the divinity within the dynamic pattern, varies considerably. Sometimes it is the praise or veneration of the priestess that constitutes the action: she honors Gaia, Themis, Athena, and the Nymphs. Alternatively, it is the occupation of the seat by the divinity that furnishes the dynamism: Themis once more, Phoebe, Dionysus. The priestess herself at the end of the inventory sits down upon her chair as if in emulation of the powers who reside in the sanctuary. Thus her praise and her enthronement are the concrete gestures which determine the organization of the catalogue.

There is, of course, no question of her final gesture proving to be the moment to which the details of the inventory point. But the equilibrium is disturbed by another accent. The authority of Apollo, the principal divinity and the one whose power we shall see deployed directly, is removed from the shorthand staccato of the list and given a life of its own. In fact, the description of his journey from Delos to Parnassus, an important part of the official foundation legend of Delphi, is elaborated to form a secondary inventory. One of the elements emphasized in this auxiliary list is the escort given Apollo by the "pathbreaking children of Hephaestus," i.e., the Athenians, who guided him through a country that was uncultivated until they put the plough to it, "taming an untamed land" (13–14). Thus, at the very beginning of the play we find, not as a piece of dry information but built into the

concrete movement of an inventory, a notice that there was an ancient association between Apollo and Athens, and that Apollo and the Athenians
have something to do with the transformation of wild nature into a state of
cultivation.

The effect of the stratagem is twofold. On the one hand, the traditional
form, uncorrupted by lyric pressure toward a terminus, permits the full
savoring of every detail. The action verbs and the parallel implied between
the divine "occupations" and the enthronement of the priestess endow the
material with great liveliness. The special scope granted to the experiences
of Apollo and the special features of the tale of his accession rivet our attention precisely on those elements which will become most fruitful later in the
play. On the other hand, an inventory, even at its most leisurely, is something of a leveler; in focusing more broadly on one item than on the others,
it goes against its own egalitarian grain. The inherent rhythm prevents
Apollo, in spite of the prominence of his appearance, from engulfing all. By
being embedded in a historical process, Apollo's advent is, in a sense, cut
down to manageable size. Whatever may be claimed by the partisans of the
god, he is merely one of many; mythology joins history, in the shape of the
inventory that is native to both, in limiting Apollo's power vis-à-vis other
powers, real or possible.

That the priestess should be talking history at all is significant. Neither
*Agamemnon* nor *Libation-Bearers* offers a historical perspective. The events of
those two plays take up two or three generations. The agents are so closely
associated with one another that it is only by a wrench of the imagination
that they can be thought of as succeeding each other. Aegisthus does not
come after Thyestes, he repeats him; Agamemnon, the child-sacrificer,
merges with his father Atreus. We have Cassandra's assurance that Clytemnestra is a fury; we have the chorus's lyric vision that the eagles are
Agamemnon and Menelaus, and that the hare is Troy. Orestes, finally, conscious of his duty toward Agamemnon, becomes capable of action only
when the spirit of Agamemnon enters into him, just as Electra, in spite of
her loathing of her mother, seems a Clytemnestra *rediviva*.

Suddenly, at the beginning of the last play of the trilogy, by means of an
analytic catalogue, the liberating dimension of history enters and promises
to unclog the old inflamed congestions. The careful plotting of before and
after is a healing balm upon the gravid syntheses of the past. The informational inventory, with its emphasis on succession and newness and change,
initiates the resolution which the setting up of the instruments of justice
will continue.

More frequently, however, Aeschylus's inventories are not historical but
geographical. A small sample of this, as small indeed as the rules of the
inventory allow, occurs very soon after the priestess's introduction. It is

Apollo's announcement to Orestes (74 ff.) that he will go on a long journey, "along the land, beyond the sea, beyond the sea-washed cities . . . to the City of Pallas," where he will find satisfaction. One may well wonder why Orestes, to get from Delphi to Athens, has to turn into a globe-trotter. Like Aeneas, Orestes does not know what the name of his destination refers to. And like Aeneas, Orestes has some working out of his destiny to accomplish, a major mission which we cannot, in our minds, dissociate from moments of struggle, and lapses. Hence the wanderings, *errores*, tangible manifestations of what in another treatment might be analyzed as a process of inner growth. Aeschylus brings the wandering into connection with the need for purification (235–53). There is a suggestion that the purification, supposedly performed in the precinct of Apollo, will not be complete until Orestes has been received into many homes. Finally, the travels are a convenient way of pointing up the vigor of the pursuit conducted by the Furies. When they appear in the sanctuary of Athena, having tracked down Orestes, they can plead the exhaustion and the exasperation which come from following their victim over the length and breadth of the earth. His own effort is understood to be equally great; we are made to forget that Hermes guided him and stood at his side. In the end, the journey turns out to be a pleasant trick, a dramaturgical device. The brief inventory makes its appearance for the purpose of jolting us out of our satisfaction—just shored up by the priestess's historical catalogue—with settled civilization, and to expand the arena within which the conflict is thought to take place.

The geographical inventory can be a source of pleasure and entertainment. The Daughters of Ocean listening to Prometheus's tales of wandering find, in his accounts of strange lands and stranger customs, a welcome distraction from their preoccupation with their own limited anxieties. The pleasure taken in reports of exotic lands or distant times is the one means capable of making choruses forget, for a little while, their smallish fears.[2] Here again, the force of the inventory works toward expansion and liberation. The traveler, or the chronicler of other people's travels, opens up a world beyond the immediate setting and channels the currents of that larger world into the sterile desert of the here-and-now. The opening process can be painful as well as pleasurable; the faraway vistas hold their own terrors. Io's progress, as plotted by the Daughters of Danaus, is in fact an analogue to their own tortured journey (*Suppl.* 547 ff.). Though the final notice of Io's delivery of a blameless child (581) is a symbol of hope, their marital preferences are incongruously at odds with the choral praise.

For a look at the details of some crucial geographical inventories, let us

2. See B. Snell, *Aischylos und das Handeln im Drama* (*Philologus Suppl.* 20.1; Leipzig, 1928), pp. 49 f.

turn to *Persians* and *Agamemnon*. Though *Persians* is imbued with the spirit of travel—both the setting out of the troops and the retreat after failure are vast locomotions—there is, strictly speaking, only one travel catalogue in the play, the brief list of lands which the Persian army reaches in its flight after the battle of Salamis (482–97). The unhappy trek from Boeotia via Phocis, Doris, the Spercheios Valley, Achaea, Thessaly, Macedonia, and Thrace to the river Strymon is told with economy, with a few of the difficulties along the way picked out for emphasis. More important is a related kind of catalogue, the listing of the many contingents coming from all corners of the Eastern world to join in Xerxes's expedition (12 ff., 302 ff.). The force described by the chorus consists of units from Persia, Egypt, Lydia, Phrygia, Mysia, and Babylon, each contributing its special qualifications and resources. To the Greek audience listening to the rollcall of the masses beyond the Aegean and to the striking sounds signalling the names of their leaders, the inventory conveys a sense of mass and movement, but a movement choked by the magnitude of its components. Beginning with lines 73 ff., there is a portrait of Xerxes which portrays his progress as that of a royal monster, huge, demonlike, "of many hands and many sailors" (the Greek compounds blunt the rawness of the zeugma), moving his bulky mass forward against the Greeks. But even without this, the inventory of Persian might carries its own message: so varied a body of men, led by princes with exotic four-syllable names, cannot be expected to constitute a smoothly running war machine. The foreign names give the show away in this play as in *Suppliants* and *Seven*, for by way of contrast the Greeks emerge virtually anonymous. The heroic joy in names that is one of the glories of the epic is made suspect through an orientalizing refraction. Its indecency is aggravated by pitting it against the namelessness, and hence the presumptive unity, of democratic action. In fifth-century Athens, the great name had become a liability; ostracism was instituted to discourage those who invoked the old aristocratic principle of having the name ring out in public. So in *Persians*, the defense against the invader is credited to the gods and to the Greeks as a group, with no individual singled out by name. And in *Seven*, though both attackers and defenders have their names, it is the names of the attackers that are the famous ones transmitted by the legend, and their vain or brutal boasts are brought into close relation to those names. The names of the Theban champions, on the other hand, are relatively pale; they mean little, and as such are fitting labels for the dim personalities to which they are attached.

The resounding inventory of names, then, tends to emphasize the exotic, the un-Greek, and, where the issue is one of right and wrong, the less attractive cause. But the full tragic effect of *Persians* suggests that this is only part of the story. In a contest between presumption and modesty, ambitious names—of men and women or of cities and countries—are at a disadvantage. But tragedy transcends such melodramatic confrontations, and it cannot be denied that the Persian catalogues have a majesty of their own. One of the remarkable achievements of *Persians*, comparable to what Homer did with the Trojans, is the sense of loss that we are made to experience as Xerxes and his force go under. The catalogues inventory the loss, and compel us to face the substance and the beauty that, in spite of all thoughts to the contrary, earmarked the structure of the Persian Empire. There are analogous effects in Elizabethan and Jacobean drama. The ringing sequences of barbaric names in *Tamerlane* serve a similar cathartic purpose, except that the Christian tradition, with its message of humility and original sin, brings out even more forcibly the unattractiveness, or perhaps rather the dangerous attractiveness, of great personages and mysterious countries richly named.

At one point in *Persians*, we notice a curious countermovement. At 867–96 the chorus presents a catalogue of the Greek possessions of Darius. Here, of course, the names are by no means alien; the inventory has the quality of familiarity, even of indifference. Some of the listing is so bare that even the light sprinkling of epic epithets cannot save it from sounding jejune. Darius is said to have ruled—and, by implication, to have acquired—these possessions "without crossing the Halys, without rushing from the hearth." This contrasts him with Xerxes, who crossed a natural barrier of water and overextended himself to gain *his* Greek possessions. The centrifugality which the inventory has by its very nature is, in this instance, undercut not only by the bare-bones character of the list and the familiar look of the self-enclosed Greek world pictured in it, but also by its moral brief against political and military expansionism.

An undercutting of a different kind comes later in the play and helps to make it come to life in the end as a true tragedy. Beginning at 958, Aeschylus furnishes a series of inventories, shared between the chorus and Xerxes, of the names of the Persian and allied nobles destroyed in the war, all of them close companions of the Emperor. Xerxes longs for them and responds with desolation to the choral inquiries. Thus the circle is completed; the sense of loss of which I spoke above is concretely registered. In *Persians* the inventory starts out as an instrument of pride, even arrogance, a literary device seemingly brought in to eulogize the power and the wealth of the expeditionary force. Toward the end, the same technique is put in the service of a contrary purpose. By listing some of the same leaders, the last inventory ticks off the damages, the waste of valuable lives and of ethnic resources that Xerxes has on his conscience. In both cases, the chorus is the principal agent of inventory. Because a chorus is characteristically suspicious of any achievement that might exceed the bounds of decency and mortal limitation, the first inventory is pronounced with an undercurrent of fear. Acute ears—given the fresh memories of the war, the acuteness did not have to be excessive—could detect at the outset of the play intimations of mortality that stretched from the first encomium to the last casualty list. The text itself exhibits a radical metastasis, from the brutal confidence of the beginning to the elegiac awakening at the end. The catalogue of cities and of men, that old epic standby, now accommodates, and adjusts itself to, important internal developments in the drama.

So much for the earliest extant play. Probably the most remarkable geographical inventory in Aeschylus's work is Clytemnestra's beacon speech (*Agam.* 281 ff.), which we have discussed above.[3] The inventory of the stages of the journey traveled by the fire signal has a number of obvious functions. It broadens the horizon in canonical inventory fashion, and, as it were, anticipates Agamemnon's homeward journey, the details of which are not spelled out in its place. Because the rules of the play require that Agamemnon appear on stage soon after the announcement that Troy has fallen, the beacon journey comes in as a surrogate for the voyage that cannot be told, much less shown. The speech also highlights Clytemnestra's cunning and power. The details of the scheme prove that she has an organization stretching all the way across the islands to Asia Minor—one which the returning general cannot possibly match. Further, the catalogue introduces Clytemnestra as a speaking character. With its help she comes on with an authority unequalled on the Athenian stage. The "man-hearted" woman of the watchman's prologue demonstrates that she deserves the title. Beyond what the speech tells us about Clytemnestra, it introduces the language of light and shadow, of darkness and fire, which continues throughout the trilogy, and it does so with a virtuosity which only the form of the inventory makes possible. The light assumes phantastic shapes; it crashes against hard substances and is rekindled by them, as if they were crystals. We seem to be in a world of cosmonauts, of flaming meteorites racing through space. At the same time, because of the pressure of the tradition, the fire is made into a person, a runner in a torch race, triumphant at the goal. Through a succession of grammatical subjects, the initial hero, Hephaestus, remains the logical subject. The journey starts out summarily, an event to be grasped historically rather than pictorially. But soon the individual stops come to be given with more attention to detail. The result is not a slowing down but a growth of excitement and significance. There is nothing linear about the progress; the line zigzags both geographically and in the way the vignettes are developed. We are made to see not only the changing image of

3. The geographical realities and the text of this notorious passage are discussed by J. H. Quincey, "The Beacon-Sites in the *Agamemnon*," *JHS* 83 (1963): 118–32. See also E. T. Owen, *The Harmony of Aeschylus* (Toronto, 1952), pp. 70 ff.

light, which once or twice is on the point of flickering out, but also the islands and mountain ridges which strain to receive the message and invest it with their massive corporeal support. Also the crews, perched aloft, waiting, like the watchman of the prologue, and suddenly sprung into brief animation as the signal reaches them.

It is no exaggeration to say that the beacon speech serves as a paradigm for *Agamemnon*: note its motion virtually cancelling itself with its own angularities; its gloom of fitful brightness; its puppets dancing to the will of the Queen; its implication that time consumes itself rather than being fulfilled. The creative vigor of this remarkable inventory surpasses anything in Sophoclean or Euripidean bravura descriptions, such as Orestes's death told by the pedagogue or Ion's near-poisoning. In these examples, events are hastened to their inevitable conclusion. Obstacles are overcome, prophecies are fulfilled, and skewed lines are abandoned to focus freely on the final act, which consumes everything that comes before it. In the beacon speech of *Agamemnon*, there is no gravitation toward the end, only a feeling of progressively constrictive achievement. In this respect, the old epic color is maintained. We cherish the details of the journey; the arrival of the message in Argos is almost an afterthought, anticipated in the prior announcements of the watchman and Clytemnestra, and still not sufficiently climactic to be credited by the chorus.

Much more could be said about the Aeschylean use of inventory, both about its internal construction and about the differences between catalogues in dialogue and catalogues that are part of the choral song. It could be shown that spoken inventories are likely to constitute the principal if not the only burden of a given speech, while in the case of choral song the inventory is built into an ode in such a way that it is made to cooperate with other designs to produce the desired effect. As for structure, there have been attempts to show that all Aeschylean catalogues of any dimension are constructed according to the same fixed archaic scheme. Within the context of this essay, such speculations had better be left on one side. It is time, in any case, to turn to the subject to which a consideration of Aeschylus's style and structure is merely an introduction, and which has above all fascinated the readers of Aeschylean drama: imagery.

"Some sombre undertone sounds in the massed symbolisms of The Sea which None Can Drain, The Vine which Overshadows the House, and The Vintage of the Bitter Grapes."[4] The formulation, though happy, issues its warnings. Symbolisms, one would think, appeal to the active imagination; undertones register largely upon a passive or subconscious sensibility, if not

---

4. W. B. Stanford, *Greek Metaphor* (Oxford, 1936), p. 146.

purely sensorily. There is thus a question about the precise relation between the two, and how they work together. But this is one of the minor difficulties. Prior questions need to be asked. To begin with, it was the lyric writers Sappho, Ibycus, and Pindar who discovered the importance of the contribution of what we call tropes. The moon in Sappho's poem about a friend across the sea in Sardis develops from a simile into a trope whose presence colors and shapes the total poetic experience.[5] It may well be asked whether the density and the power of "imagery" in lyric poetry can also be realized in dramatic poetry. "Tragedies are so often based on violent and even brutal plots and are generally intended to endure the harsh test of performance before a miscellaneous audience."[6] Or, as it was put by Hebbel, who began his dramatic career with a liberal reliance upon tropes and images and gradually abandoned them in favor of the benefits of ordinary language: "The proper application of images is nowhere more difficult than in drama. If they are as easy to acquire as [an image used by a character in Grillparzer's *Ahnfrau*], the poet should reject them out of pride, for he will not want to pick up what all see around them."[7] If the appreciation of tropes requires an audience that listens critically or dispassionately, the conditions under which Aeschylean tragedy was performed would appear to make that difficult. But since tragedy, like the lyric, rejects the principle of complete verisimilitude, it needs tropes even more than the lyric, because the inducements to lapse into a trite realism are much greater.

I have avoided the term "symbolism"; nor am I entirely happy about its sibling, "imagery." The trouble is that no two critics seem to be able to agree on the precise meanings of these labels. One of our more influential commentators has said, "By 'symbol' I mean a particular thing, usually material, which may be taken to represent the idea," and proceeds to explore the symbolic function of the net in *Agamemnon*.[8] It has been urged, rightly I think, that "imagery" may "include anything from metaphor to a literal fact or scene poetically described," and that, as a result, symbolism and metaphor are often confused. "The literal fact or scene may have symbolic meanings, more or less evident, more or less private; but this is achieved by the connotation that words and even syntax may have acquired in any civilization or period, and not by means of the metaphoric relation of words to each other; the primary meaning of the symbolic word or sentence or poem is literal, indeed, the literal meaning is as much part of the effect

5. Sappho 6, in R. Lattimore, tr., *Greek Lyrics* (Chicago, 1955).

6. M. E. Prior, *The Language of Tragedy* (New York, 1947), p. 11.

7. W. von Scholz, ed., *Hebbels Dramaturgie* (Munich and Leipzig, 1907), p. 241.

8. R. Lattimore, in D. Grene and R. Lattimore, eds. (tr.), *Complete Greek Tragedies*, vol. 1 (Chicago, 1959), p. 15.

and intention."[9] "Imagery," it turns out, includes both "replacement-functions," i.e., metaphors, and "enlargement-functions," i.e., the symbolic use of words or word groups. That the two are closely interconnected is shown by the fact that similes and other devices of comparison may be said to fall under the heading of "enlargement" rather than "replacement"— though, psychologically speaking, metaphors and similes arise from the same synthetic potential of the language.

In spite of its shortcomings, the term "imagery" will continue to be useful, and I shall employ it in what follows. But another caveat is in order. "Images," both of replacement and of enlargement, were part of the tradition of the language which Aeschylus had available to him. The fact that compulsion and obsession could erupt in the form of net imagery says something about the thinking and talking of the generations that preceded Aeschylus; how much does it tell us about poetic design? The texture of life in fifth-century Athens had not yet removed the playwright from the energizing web of correspondences. Manual labor—agriculture; pottery; navigation, with its exposure to winds, cold, and heat—furnished a rich contextuality rooted in the life of the people. Furthermore, as Rhys Carpenter has shown for the visual arts, the Greeks tended to reshape inanimate structures as animate shapes:

> Greek art became symbolic, since its *representata* often stood for things other than themselves—as when a swan and nymph stand for a lake, a man-headed bull for a river, a marsh-bird for a marsh, or an object for its homonym (like Rhodes and the rose). But there was no mystic or mysterious intention and none of that deliberate obscurantism with which symbolism has so often allied itself. The symbolism of Greek coins was a kind of picture-writing; but it was not a hieratic script with an esoteric meaning for the initiate (as Christian iconography was at times).[10]

The *Oresteia* is a remarkable demonstration of the connectibility of the trope with the literal and of the apparent accessibility of the fusions. Still, we have to be very careful. The plotting of extended symbolic reference is a modern habit, derived from the Stoic insight into the pervasive cohesion of the cosmic body. Where it corresponds to a critical awareness of artistic objective and effect, classical perceptions may have been less ambitious, less given to kaleidoscopic reference.

It is, for instance, often stated that the Furies "represent" Orestes's conscience, and important conclusions are drawn from this, if not for the character of Orestes, then at least for the manner in which the audience is

9. C. Brooke-Rose, *A Grammar of Metaphor* (London, 1958), pp. 287–88. The best study of imagery in Aeschylus is A. Lebeck, *The Oresteia* (Cambridge, Mass., 1971).

10. R. Carpenter, *The Esthetic Basis of Greek Art* (Bloomington, Ind., 1959), p. 25.

expected to regard his standing in the moral universe. But we also know that the very concept of a "conscience" was slow to develop and did not, in fact, achieve some of the firm contours which it has today until long after Aeschylus. The Furies do not represent anything; they are a dramatic presence, a body of persons fighting for a certain right. We cannot deny that the palpable presence is, even for the Athenians of the fifth century, charged with "symbolic" enlargement. What matters is the degree of power, the decibels of the resonance, with which the enlargement is experienced. Because the Furies are conventional, a religious and mythological icon known to all, their appearance on the stage will have seemed entirely natural. This naturalness will have operated as a block on reading subtle psychological or philosophical meanings into their dramatic function.

The same warnings apply to Clytemnestra's statement (*Agam.* 866–68) that if Agamemnon had received as many wounds as rumor had it, he must have been more perforated than a net. Critics are tempted to see a connection between this extravagant comparison and the fatal net with which Clytemnestra later smothers Agamemnon before killing him. But Aristotle tells us that the Orphics compared the structure of an animate being to that of a net, and there are other passages to support the view that "tissue" and "structure" and "net" were closely allied concepts.[11] Once this is acknowledged, the net image seems much less startling, hence less in need of external buttressing from within the play.

The tale of the Amazons told by Athena at *Eum.* 685 is part of the charter story for the naming of the rock of Ares. Is it more than that? Are we to draw inferences from the virginity, or the battling spirit, or the anti-Athenian position of the Amazons? The pictorial use of Amazons, along with Giants and Centaurs, on friezes and pediments illustrating the struggle between barbarism and civilization certainly supports the case for symbolism. But once again I suspect that the personal standing of the Amazons in the cultural conditioning which the audience brought to the play was such that it would be unrealistic to speak of either enlargement or substitution. But this is a subject fraught with enormous difficulties, involving psychological issues that have not been successfully confronted. To what degree are we permitted to establish an enlargement function in the text even if we are relatively certain that the poet himself had no such design? This is, of course, the question Eliot attempted to answer for Virgil.[12] To what extent is it critically proper to assume that symbolic extensions within a text vary from generation to generation and from culture to culture? And,

11. Aristotle *Gen. Anim.* B 1.734a16.

12. With some modifications, the question looms large in the literary criticism indebted to the hermeneutic tradition of Heidegger and Gadamer. See, e.g., F. Kermode, *The Genesis of Secrecy* (Cambridge, Mass., 1979).

to come back to a question raised earlier, can we trace such extensions and links within a drama as we trace them within a poem? To give an example: at the end of the first ode of *Agamemnon* the recollection of Iphigenia's sacrifice is fresh and troubling. Very soon afterwards, Clytemnestra has her first words. We expect her utterance to be, to some degree, in response to that recollection and to the choral comments, no matter whether she has been on the stage to hear them or not. Images voiced affect behavior and action; this is one of the crucial ways in which drama differs from other genres. But it is also one extremely hard to trace and demonstrate.

Of the two staples of the traditional discussion of imagery, metaphor and simile, let us take up the latter first. Actually, it will soon be apparent that it is vain labor to distinguish between similes and metaphors on any but purely formal grounds. But on the surface, at least, similes are much rarer in Aeschylus than metaphors. It has been calculated that whereas there are four times as many similes as metaphors in the *Iliad*, and twice as many similes as metaphors in the *Odyssey*, the proportion in Aeschylean drama is the reverse. The count varies from three similes in *Persians* to twenty-seven in *Agamemnon*.[13] This is not a matter of artistic development. Clytemnestra's artful language of deception and the chorus's sage flounderings in the face of disaster lend themselves to the simile, while the disaster of *Persians* emerges more simply, without the ostensiveness of comparisons. When, at *Pers.* 424–26, we are told that the Greeks spear the Persians in the Bay of Salamis like tunny, the image is grotesque but it is also simple enough not to put an undue burden upon an imagination already weighted with geographical and cultural complications. The same extreme simplicity is found in the other two similes of *Persians*. In *Suppliants*, on the other hand, where the similes total ten or eleven, the defenselessness of the chorus produces a number of elaborate comparisons with timid animals from mythology (60 ff.) or from the world of stock farming (350 ff.). The most elaborate and most puzzling simile stands near the beginning of *Agamemnon* (49 ff.) and introduces the highly significant animal imagery which informs the whole trilogy.

The simple epic simile aims at surface clarity and neatness of logical relations (though the poetic effect can be far different). Almost without exception, therefore, the Homeric simile is in the form of an "as" clause followed by a "so" clause. Often a great deal of apparently tangential material is pressed into service between the two boundary clauses. But the boundaries mark the structure of the comparison, and the succession of "as . . . so" leaves the audience in no doubt about the terms of the maneuver. In

---

13. A. F. Garvie, *Aeschylus' Supplices* (Cambridge, 1969), p. 64.

drama there is greater formal variety, as there is less reliance on prefabricated patterns and transparency of relations. The series of compliments which Clytemnestra pays to Agamemnon (*Agam.* 966 ff.) may serve as an illustration of how the non-conjunctional or asyntactic simile works:

> The rootstock green, the foliage joins the house
> Spreading a shade against the Dog Star's burn;
> And as you come to join us at the hearth
> It means the coming of summer's warmth in winter;
> But when Zeus makes the wine from the unripe grape,
> Then coolness fans the torrid home. . . .

Simile turns into metaphor; as the return of the King is compared to a spreading foliage, to warmth in winter and coolness in summer, the epic articulation of "as" or "like" and "so" is dropped, though the "and" which introduces the comparandum (968) is a vestige of a more express coordination.[14] Since drama eschews the surface tangibles of epic and strives to convey an impression of the moral and aesthetic richness of the world of action, comparables enter into new relations that fuse them together more tightly. In the present case there is, toward the middle of the series, a linking word: A "means" B, which transforms the relation between "as" and "so," between comparatum and comparandum, into one between outer and inner, apparent and real, as if the summer's warmth were what mattered, and the King's homecoming merely a piece of preliminary evidence pointing in that direction. Thus the syntax appears to take the sequence out of the world of the simile; the grammar is sufficiently crabbed to stall any attempt to conduct an easy bipolar comparison. Still, the epic model of the simile is felt to operate behind the scene. Without the orientation that the model makes possible, the sequence would resist decoding. In this case, also, the underlying terms of the comparison conspire to kindle an extraordinary momentum. Critics have remarked on the vehemence with which Clytemnestra conducts her "Oriental" servilities. But even without this special effect, the "asyntactic" comparison, operating without explicit "as" and "so" connections, is a common feature of Aeschylean imagery, and indeed of all drama that cultivates an enriched speech.

The distinction between a comparison, in the narrower sense, and other types of trope is often difficult to establish, and Aeschylus's preference for non-epic structures often thwarts the critic's task of classification. The Empress Mother's dream at *Pers.* 181 ff. is a good instance of the difficulty. As the two women, said to stand for Greece and Persia, fight with one another,

---

14. For the convergence of simile and metaphor, see Aristotle *Rhet.* 3.11.1412b34. The most intensive investigation of the relation between tenor and vehicle in the simile is found in M. S. Silk, *Interaction in Poetic Imagery* (Cambridge, 1974).

Xerxes tries to restrain them, and yokes them to his chariot. That the two countries, or rather the two civilizations, can appear as two women has nothing of the simile about it. But the yoking of the women to a chariot implies the unspoken comparison: "as one would yoke two horses, so he yoked the two women." The rhetorical procedure is closer to the simile than it is to a substitution trope. But because of the suppression of the "as" statement, the image comes as a shock. The unexpectedness, the brutality of the conceit is a measure of the terror with which it forces itself upon the Empress Mother and the audience.

A more straightforward case of (at least partial) asyntaxis, without the suppression of anything but the conjunction, but with the major emphasis on the vehicle (the illustration) rather than on the tenor (the illustrandum), is the lion-cub sequence (*Agam.* 717 ff.):

> A lion cub, torn from its mother,
> Craving to nurse at the breast:
> Thus a man brought it up in his home;
> Sweet in the early flush of its life,
> Loved by the young, a joy to the old,
> Hugged it was, like a child in arms.
> And with its bright eye it fawned upon
> The hand that stilled the need of its belly.
>
> But in time it came to show the strain
> Of its race. To pay off its feeders
> It served a banquet of sheep-killing horror.
> The hall was stained in blood, a desperate grief
> For those who tended the house,
> Great carnage and much destruction.
> God willed that what grew in the house
> Became its minister and priest of Ruin.

Strictly speaking, the sequence is organized as a parable, not as a comparison. But the belated "Thus" (719) discloses the narrative, in the past tense, to be analogous to the preceding account of Paris's taking in of Helen and of the city's sufferings caused by the act. The parable, which is developed through a complete dyad, is remarkable for clarity of language, the simplicity of its narrative structure, and the symmetry of organization between stanza and responding stanza: the cub is the subject of the stanza, the grown lion of the answering stanza. It is probably the most discursive sequence in *Agamemnon*, as if told by a storyteller whose delight in straightforward narrative is enhanced by the moral direction of the tale. But the clarity is deceiving. There is, properly speaking, no obvious point of comparison. The lion cub is, by implication, comparable not just to Paris or to Helen but to the whole complex of factors—personal, environmental, divine—

which permit beauty and innocence to be metamorphosed into viciousness. The parable of the lion cub helps us to see that Helen is also a fury, and that Zeus, though *xenios*, a protector of the defenceless, is the prompter of disaster. The advantage of asyntaxis is precisely that it affords the analogical principle a wider scale of operation than the double tie of "as" and "thus" would tolerate.

In the end, tenor and vehicle are so combined that, as also in the extended Homeric simile, the result is not a clearer perception of the former but a new insight in which the original terms are subsumed, so that it is no longer possible or appropriate to decide which is the illustration and which the illustrandum. At *Agam.* 1001 ff., the thought may be paraphrased as follows: there is a point at which health, cultivated to excess, turns to ill health; and so with property, the man who has too much will come to grief. Excess of wealth is remediable, for the overloaded ship can be lightened by jettisoning part of the cargo; famine is remediable by Zeus's gift of an abundant harvest. We may regard this as a duplicate simile, comparing good health, i.e., a good diet, with affluence, with respect to two conditions: proneness to excess and capacity for recovering a balance. Now if it is asked which is the tenor and which the vehicle, no simple answer will do. The comparison is conducted not for the sake of illustrating one item by means of another, but to explore the workings of the "properties"—proneness to excess and resilience—in two related areas. Finally only the ability to recover remains as an issue with the assertion at the beginning of the next dyad that in a third area, that of bloodshed, no such recovery is possible. The text is difficult and some of it is corrupt, but there is little doubt about the thought pattern, which is paralleled elsewhere. The terms of the comparison, the members which in a syntactic simile would be related by means of "as" and "so," combine forces and lose their privileged status toward one another, and guide the eye of the imagination to the realization of a larger truth of which they are segmental manifestations.

This is a favorite Aeschylean procedure, employed especially in choral passages in which the chorus ventures to extend the perspective beyond the immediate transactions of the character and to locate them in a broader field of vision. The playwright restricts the autonomy of the terms of the comparison in order to reduce them to the status of mere phenomena signalling a larger truth. One mechanism, learned from lyric poets such as Sappho and Ibycus, is the introduction, into the vehicle, of language that is more appropriate to the tenor. This is well instanced, once again, in the lion-cub parable at *Agam.* 717 ff., especially 732: "the house was befouled with blood" is more easily associated with what happened in Troy or Argos as a result of Helen's coming into her own than with the lion grown unmanageable. The vista is that of a whole palace swimming with blood.

The procedure used here is akin to what is often found in the brief syntactic similes where an item from the vehicle comes to be transferred to the tenor. Sometimes this can become extraordinarily complex, not to say awkward, as in the double or triple comparison of *Agam.* 1178 ff. Once again, the translation must be approximate because of the condition of the text:

> And now my prophecy will no longer peer
> Like a newly married girl from behind veils.
> Bright it will shine, and with its blast will reach
> The rising sun, until, a mighty wave,
> It swells and brings to light our suffering.

As Cassandra turns from song to speech, the prophecy is the subject and the tenor. But the sentence is so constructed that the prophecy takes on successively the shyness of a young bride, the brightness and force of a westerly wind, and the massive propulsion of a great wave. The verbs grammatically associated with "prophecy"—"glance," "blow," and "swell"—are imported from the spheres of the vehicles. One could speak of metaphors; but with the tenor, "prophecy," clearly stated, the process is one of comparison and enlargement rather than substitution, and it seems more appropriate to appeal to the well-established tradition of the asyntactic simile. The extravagance of the cumulative broadening borders on rant; there is little to choose between a passage like this and similar things in Seneca or the European imitators of Seneca. What may save the maneuver is its very daring. Coming where it does, on the boundary between hallucination and explanation, the blending of disparate spheres seems intelligible and proper. And it is worth reminding ourselves that this kind of rhetoric is more prominent in *Agamemnon* than in the other plays. The brooding exploration of the workings of the ancestral curse attracts a flourish of amalgamation.

For a clincher, let us look at that extraordinary sequence early in *Agamemnon* in which the Atridae are compared to hawks. That is, of course, much too simple a way of putting it. Here is a detailed analysis of what happens, beginning with line 40. The Atridae moved out (40–47), shrieking (48) in the manner of hawks bemoaning the loss of their young (49–54); above, a god hears them and dispatches a Fury (55–59); thus Zeus Xenios launches the Atridae against Troy. Put as baldly as this there seems nothing complicated or alarming about this perfectly syntactic simile. The comparison of the Atridae with hawks bears on their motion, their voices, and their loss. The markers "in the manner of" and "thus" make the relations gratifyingly explicit. The mixture of tenses—the Atridae *moved* out; Zeus *sends* them— puts only a slight damper on the simplicity. But there is more. In line 58, Aeschylus uses a compound adjective, "punishing-at-a-later-time," which derives its force from the human tale rather than from the image of the hawks to which it belongs grammatically. And the whole idea of a god sending a Fury down to assist the hawks can be understood only in terms of what we said above about the shifting of attributes between proposition *A* and proposition *B*. Further, the motion of the Atridae, their dispatching of the expedition, stands in a curious relation to the high circling of the hawks. Does the latter, within the mechanics of the simile, have the effect of putting a crimp on the linearity and the promised success of the military undertaking? The god who is said to hear the plea of the birds is, we are told, either "an Apollo or a Pan or a Zeus." The vagueness, or exchangeability, of the divine succor (or strafing?) raises further questions. Apollo and Zeus are not likely to concern themselves with the fate of dumb creatures. Pan is more probably involved; he is a god of the countryside, and specializes in the excitement and the terror which wild nature suggests to civilized man. In this case, it seems, terms from *A* and terms from *B* are linked together in one subsidiary series to furnish additional cement for the comparison.

What is it precisely that connects the hawks with the Atridae? On the assumption that the equation tallies, who is it that corresponds to the lost fledglings on the human side? At a later point in the trilogy, Orestes appropriates the material of the comparison to establish his own and Electra's position: they are the starving young of an eagle, unable to fend for themselves and furnish their own food (*Lib.* 246 ff.). But at this early juncture of *Agamemnon*, the audience is more likely to undertand by the loss that of Helen: the Atridae move out crying their war cry *because* they have experienced a loss. Still, the listeners are not permitted for long to limit the reference so narrowly. Soon after the anapaests of the first simile, the same theme is taken up once more in the entrance ode (109 ff.). This time we learn that the expedition is sped by an omen which appeared to the Atridae at the palace. More important, the two birds of the omen are said to be royal, and their identification with the royal leaders is underscored by the emphasis on their number and their individuality:

> [. . . how the Atridae]
> Were launched, spear in warlike fist,
> To the land of Troy, by a fierce winged omen,
> The king of birds to the kings of the ships,
> One black, one white in the tail,
> Seen near the palace, on the spearhand side,
> Clear in their roost. . . .

Without the establishment of an explicit comparison, the audience is invited to draw the obvious parallels as the omen and its interpretation are developed. Initially the birds are seen as an omen, hence the singular "king of birds"; and the omen is understood to be the agent that starts the kings on their drive. But in the sequel the relation is converted to one of near-identity. Artemis is said to be angry at the eagles (= the Atridae) for feasting on (= destroying) the pregnant hare (= rich Troy) with its unborn offspring (= inhabitants). Our parentheses make the case more obvious than the poetry warrants. But there can be little doubt about the fact that the eagles—for that is what the birds appear to be in this context, rather than hawks—are an effective omen because their identity and their function converge upon those of the leaders. Even the distinction between the colorings of the two eagles was felt by the ancient commentators to have a bearing on the difference, in Homer, between choleric Agamemnon and the more genial Menelaus. Only in the last case, with the emphasis on pre-natality, is it difficult to be sure about an exact equivalent on the Trojan side of the ledger. The slight asymmetry is a help rather than a hindrance to our appreciation of the liveliness and the quality of the monstrous which inhere in the comparison.

From hawks that bemoan a loss, we have progressed to eagles that cause another's loss; from hawks that move in frustrated circles and obtain the response of some one god to eagles that attack and pounce and attract the punishment of a specific divinity. The application of this progression to the Atridae emerges so clearly throughout that no puzzling out is needed, in spite of the difficulty of the language and the horror of the imagined situation. In the end, as the ode continues, the sacrifice of Iphigenia binds the two comparisons further together and gives them a meaning of which the historical progression is only a mild foretaste. For it turns out that the loss of a dear one and the killing of the young are suffered and performed by one and the same agent, at one and the same time. Thus a syntactic simile (49 ff.) and an asyntactic simile (113 ff.) combine forces and find their ultimate validation in the description of an event. The orchestration of that event is fully prepared, from explicit parallel through implicit synthesis to a new and surprising totality. As the arc is completed, Helen is forgotten, and so is Troy, and Iphigenia takes their place as the most terrifying example of the truth that innocence and guilt, loss and crime, cannot be separated.

I have already suggested that some of the phenomena that we have discussed in our consideration of the Aeschylean simile—the transference of attributes from $A$ to $B$, the implicit identification of hawks and men—may fall under the rubric of metaphor. It is now time that we devote a section to this aspect of Aeschylus's imagery. It is generally acknowledged that Aeschylus has a more developed and a more daring art of metaphor than any other ancient Greek author, with the possible (and negligible) exception of the Hellenistic mannerists in whose hands metaphor declined into enigma.

The remarkable thing, once again, about Aeschylus's metaphors is that they need not be puzzled out. As is well known, when a poet uses a metaphor, *B*, the vehicle, can replace *A*, the tenor, altogether, leaving us to guess it; or *B* can be linked to *A* by an enormous variety of complex grammatical and syntactical devices. It would be too ambitious an undertaking to trace Aeschylus's procedures in all their astonishing variety. But it can safely be said that he prefers liaison, or at best partial replacement, to the total replacement of tenor by vehicle. He does not aim for the puzzle but for enrichment. Where total replacement is used, we can be tolerably certain that the metaphor is one sanctioned by tradition or by contemporary currency.

This is not to say that Aeschylean metaphor is simple. In fact, total replacement is, in spite of its proneness to privilege and secrecy, a far simpler procedure than the appositional techniques whereby Aeschylus brightens and occasionally encumbers his figurative speech. As with the simile, and roughly in the same ratio, the prominence and the daring of metaphor vary from play to play. In *Persians* and *Eumenides*, metaphor is much rarer and usually less complex than in *Agamemnon*, though it is also true that *Eumenides* repeats more images from *Agamemnon* than does *Libation-Bearers*. In *Suppliants*, again, metaphor plays a smaller role than in *Seven*. The difference between the plays is, of course, a function of their several objectives, and of the degree of lyric resonance Aeschylus locates in each of them. In spite of its highly developed art of choral song, *Suppliants* is primarily a problem play, the dramatization of a political issue rather than an evocation of primordial savagery, such as it might easily have been, being, like *Agamemnon*, the first play of its trilogy. Hence its language makes, on the whole, for clarity rather than reverberation.

Nevertheless, there is no play that does not exhibit at least a few, and normally a good number of, specimens of Aeschylus's inventiveness in the art of metaphor. On some occasions, the metaphoric force is blunted by an analytic addendum. At *Eum.* 196–97, Apollo calls on the Furies to

> Depart; un-goatherded disperse your flocks:
> No god takes pleasure in a herd like yours!

The second line clarifies the first, and makes the metaphoric reference explicit. The technique is one criticized by Aristophanes in *Frogs*, but interestingly it is Euripides rather than Aeschylus who has it cast in his teeth. And, in fact, Aeschylus is, by and large, averse to this kind of flattening. Nor does he need it, for his metaphors are built into the flux of the poetry with a minimum of resistance, so that their force registers on the imagination without trouble. This is true even where we might speak of mixed metaphor:

Channel the tale through your ears
With a calm stepping of the mind
*Lib.* 451–52

or

[The heart] growls, shrouded in darkness,
Its spirit in pain, never expecting,
Its attention feverish,
To find an easy opening for the thread.
*Agam.* 1030 ff.

The visions of tales marching through ears, but also piercing the eardrums like wire; or of the heart growling like a dog in the dark, but also (vainly) attempting to work the woof into the web: these are figurative ventures which in less favorable surroundings might bring a smile to wise men's lips. In the Aeschylean ambience, which presses for manifold combinations between the human and the animal spheres, between the natural and the professional, the effect is not similarly incongruous. The choral singing helps to blunt the edge of the extravagance. In both cases the key words, "tale" and "heart," are there, orienting the listener's attention to a relatively unambiguous reading of the passage.

Many attempts have been made to collect and classify the images which Aeschylus puts under contribution for his metaphors and figurative extensions.[15] Before we try to discover what can usefully be said about this, it is worth stressing that the image clusters and image relations in any one play derive from what Kenneth Burke has called the psychology of form, as against the psychology of information.[16] The image relations articulate for us not the characters in their thoughts and ambitions and actions, but the substance of the drama to which the characters are subservient, themselves often affected by the images that are called for by the "plot." At the same time, there are no absolute images and tropes; they do not appear in isolation. An image of a certain sort, developed at a certain length, is used in a particular context, at a measurable distance from other similar or dissimilar images. Much is gained from asking about the incidence and frequency of a specific image type or relation and from inquiring into the reasons why a context where we might, by analogy with other passages, expect to find

15. J. Dumortier, *Les images dans la poésie d'Éschyle* (Paris, 1935); O. Smith, "Some Observations on the Structure of Imagery in Aeschylus," *Classica et Mediaevalia* 26 (1965): 10–72; and many specialized studies such as D. Sansone, *Aeschylean Metaphors for Intellectual Activity (Hermes Einzelschr.* 35; Wiesbaden, 1975).

16. K. Burke, "Psychology and Form," in *Perspectives by Incongruity* (Bloomington, Ind., 1964), pp. 20–33.

a particular image, does not have it. But initially it is easier to ask what we find and how it can be classified.

One critic distinguishes between dominant images, stream images, and intermittent images.[17] The first signal the frame or theme for a play; the second, though less indigenous to the play, serve to communicate, through repetition, various forms of irony and ambiguity; and the third derive their validity from the immediate context. In *Persians*, the fight between the Greeks and the Persians is reflected, or perhaps fundamentally perceived, as a struggle between spears and arrows: 85–86, 147–49, et al. In *Seven*, the metaphor of the lot, the portion given to man, is clearly dominant, and developed with great virtuosity. In the *Oresteia*, the image of the banquet of children's flesh is part of the central core. Other images derived from this dominant figure help to give the trilogy its abundant texture. Images of devouring, biting, blood-sucking and the like prompt us to infer ironic relations between men and animals and between love and violence.

The tripartition is useful, though we might add that, beside the kinds of images that we may wish to identify with a particular play or scene, there are some images of which Aeschylus is inordinately fond, regardless of the context, and it is these that we are likely to find in the second and third categories mentioned above. What is more, the third type, the contextual image, is often linked to, if not virtually identical with, the stream image. Perhaps it is wiser to distinguish between only two categories: those images, in the first instance, which so dominate in a play that its very substance appears to be rooted in their prior existence; and, second, images which, though not unconnected with the first, draw their life from particular settings or structures, whether dramaturgic, ideological, or more strictly poetic.

Clytemnestra has had a dream about a serpent. When Orestes is about to kill her (*Lib.* 928), she recognizes that it is he who is that serpent. She does so just after she has compared him, in his insensibility to her entreaties, to a tomb (926). The comparison with the serpent is a metaphor; the comparison with the tomb is in the form of a simile. The two things which early in the play were said to have troubled her most—Agamemnon's tomb and the serpent in her dream—are now, in the last few seconds of her life, linked symbolically with Orestes. Somewhat earlier (794 ff.), the chorus had prayed to Zeus to assist Orestes in his chariot race:

> Know the orphan foal of the man who was yours,
> Yoked in his chariot of distress;
> Grant to him in his race
> The Proper Step; set up

17. T. R. Henn, *The Harvest of Tragedy* (London, 1956), pp. 135 ff.

A victory pattern, for us to see
Eager steps reaching the end of the course.

Orestes is the young charger racing with hooves lifted high, much as Paris
in a famous simile in the *Iliad* races through the grain field.[18] Is this what
gave Sophocles the idea of creating his bravura messenger sequence about
the race in which Orestes allegedly died?[19] In Aeschylus, Orestes's participation in a race is not the lying mechanism of an intrigue, it is real. The
Aeschylean Orestes attracts a manifold network of symbolisms, no doubt
because in his person, as a character, he is almost nothing (see below, chapter 8). All three images—the tomb, the serpent, and the race horse—are
common enough in the trilogy. But as one tries to decide how to classify one
against the other, one runs up against all sorts of difficulties. The tomb is
not only an image but a stage presence. The association between the Furies
and snakes is obvious. The notion of the racer is pervasive, from the torch
race of the beacon to the Furies attempting to catch up with their victim.
But can it be said that any one of the three images is more basic to the
conception of the trilogy than the others? Hardly. The more one studies
Aeschylean images and their interrelation, the harder it is to be certain that
some of them deserve special status as dominants.

The tomb is not only an image but also a stage presence. It is characteristic of Aeschylus's art that there is often little distinction made between the
figurative and the real. Greek mythological language encourages this habit
of ranging back and forth. Ares can be the god of war, or war itself. As war,
the name can stand for any destructive force, such as fire or drought. But
then, in addition, Ares can also be shorthand for one party in a war. Thus
the use of the word is varied, and might appear imprecise. What matters is
the emotional and semantic power associated with it. It is a frightening
word, and that is why it is used. Compare two occurrences, both from
*Libation-Bearers*:

Ares will meet with Ares, Right with Right
                        461

exclaimed by Orestes, and

There came to the house of Agamemnon
A twofold lion, a twofold Ares
                    937–38

sung by the chorus. In the first statement the burden of the name is difficult
to establish, but the doubling suggests an accumulation of hostility, sav-

18. *Iliad* 6.503 ff.
19. Sophocles *Electra* 681 ff.

agery, and perhaps also meanness, by way of contrast with the mustering of rights, of claims and counterclaims. My translation "meet with" is by no means certain; the Greek word, which means "come together," has a variety of shades, from violent hostility to coordination.[20] But where it stands, close to the end of the great exchange with which Orestes, Electra and the chorus ready themselves for the confrontation with Clytemnestra and Aegisthus, the line must be a vigorous assertion of the concerted use of fighting power, and the doubling of Ares serves the purpose, as does the doubling of Right—whose force is, if anything, even less narrowly defined. In the second passage, however, Ares is strictly a person: the two lions and the two Areses are Clytemnestra and Aegisthus. They are seen in tandem, as are other pairs in this trilogy (see below, chapter 8). But there is no doubt about their identity, in spite of the singulars.

The most famous use of Ares in Aeschylus's choruses occurs at *Agam.* 437 ff., cited above, chapter 4. The language of international banking exacerbates, by its impersonality, the nastiness and the waste of which Ares is the emblem. The sustained tenor of the comparison, the extended irony, permit the use of the term "allegory." But its Aeschylean quality sets it apart. The allegory is so pregnant, so full of internal strains, that the term sits awkwardly upon it. The exchange is of bullion—but also of bodies; the weighing is done on the battlefield; the commodity of exchange is ashes, transported like wine in well-wrought canisters. The talk of war as if it were a kind of business, a profitable activity that is to be conducted with a clear head, throws a merciless light on various aspects of the legend, including Agamemnon's sacrifice of Iphigenia. It is, apparently, a trope that Aeschylus favored. It is used again in *Seven* to highlight the mentality of the attackers, and especially of Parthenopaeus (545 ff.):

> He is not a man to haggle over the fight,
> Or to disgrace the journey's revenue.
> . . . An immigrant in Argos,
> He means to pay them back for his welcome there.

Parthenopaeus, "the girlish-faced," refuses to barter; Argos has made him a good offer, and he is going to give good service in return. The seeming irreproachability of the conduct, the good faith of the responsible businessman, drive home the absence of even the slightest spark of flexible humanity. This is, in fact, what Ares denotes: the unbending character of relationships and postures issuing in bloodshed, rather than the bloodshed itself.

One of the most prominent images in Aeschylus is the flashing light. In a lost play, *Bassarai*, which featured the tearing apart of Orpheus by Mae-

20. See also below, chap. 10.

nads, we read of the light of a torch filling the slope of a headland with sudden radiance.[21] It seems that the image of flickering flames in the dark, notoriously one of the effects that cannot be engineered on the Aeschylean stage, is one of Aeschylus's favorite touches. We have already talked about the beacon speech in *Agamemnon*: the beam greeted by the watchman (22–23) kindles the sacrificial fires lit by Clytemnestra throughout the city (91–96) and from that point on there is no stopping the parade of flames that punctuate the somber action of *Agamemnon*. By the time the herald enters, we understand that daylight has broken. But the flame imagery continues to rule in the speech of characters as well as chorus, as an advertisement that the light of day has not yet broken for the house of Atreus. But the symbolism is not allowed to stand unqualified. At the very end of the trilogy, when the Furies have reconstituted themselves as Eumenides, they are escorted out of the theater into their new dark abode to the accompaniment of the light, this time real and visible, of torches. The trilogy is thus framed by vistas of fire, while in the body of the trilogy that same fire is submerged into imagery, to operate symbolically rather than as a part of the setting.

Fire is not the only natural force to function as a trope. A recent study has stressed the importance of wind and storm imagery in the *Oresteia* and, indeed, in all of Aeschylus's plays.[22] Among the interesting findings, we learn that in *Agamemnon* and *Eumenides*, persons are said to "blow forth" their anger, though in *Libation-Bearers* this language is avoided, perhaps in deference to the more confined, domestic setting of that play. Each dramatic character of any importance is favored or disfavored, accompanied or opposed, by winds. The conciliatory characters are assisted by a kindly breath that furthers the resolution. Wind and breath, identified through vocabulary usage, help to advance the conviction that human action and cosmic action are locked into one. The winds at Aulis are transformed into a trope governing the power relations in the rest of the trilogy. Something very similar is found in *Suppliants*, where favoring and adverse winds form the matrix for the confrontation between the women and their pursuers and for the negotiations with Pelasgus; and in *Prometheus*, where the imagery of atmospheric pressure obtains its most powerful expression in the tale of Typhon (351 ff.).

An image can be so powerful that it supervenes upon the more palpable reality and reshapes it. The net image of *Agamemnon* appears to do this. It could be argued that it had its origin in the conception of Clytemnestra as a huntress, stalking her prey, just as later the Furies in *Eumenides* stalk theirs.

21. Fr. 12 Smyth.
22. W. C. Scott, "Wind Imagery in the *Oresteia*," *TAPA* 97 (1966):459–71.

The sources which Aeschylus used seem to have nothing about a net or a shroud.[23] The imagery, then, produced its own revision: Agamemnon had a net cast around him to hobble his movements. But once this happened, the question of the weapon with which he was killed took on a new complexion. In the majority of the ancient sources, and of the ancient pictorial representations, Agamemnon is killed with a sword. Others suggest that he was killed with an axe, or that one of the two murderers used the sword and the other the axe. Curiously, in that section of the play where we might expect to find a clear formulation of Aeschylus's version, the poet leaves the exact means of the murder undetermined.[24] The chorus (1492 ff. = 1516 ff.) pictures Agamemnon struck down after being enmeshed in a spider's web. The image is fully developed, only to be given up abruptly. This variant of the net imagery, with Clytemnestra as the spider and Agamemnon as the fly, is perhaps the most striking demonstration of what an image can do to the facts. Once the spell of the web or the net has induced the imagination of the author to relinquish men for beasts, it will be bad enough to continue to cite the murderous "hand" (1496) but the specification of the murder weapon will be entirely out of line. This may explain why Aeschylus never, throughout the trilogy, comes out unambiguously in favor of one version or the other.

The hunting net is spread over Troy as well as Agamemnon; hence again it would be awkward to isolate one instrument of execution. Add to this that Clytemnestra is not only a hunter or a spider, she is also the snake that strikes the eagle, only to be struck in turn by her snake offspring, as Troy is the hare killed by the eagle. And supporting these images of persecution and execution is a whole world of imagery that we may call cosmic: the sun, the moon, stars, interstellar spaces even; the sea and its treasure, both calm and in a fury; the snow of winter, with dead birds falling into it; but also ripened grain and fruits undoing the sterility of death. In a play like *Agamemnon* and in the further passages of the trilogy that are designed to recall it, the control of the imagery is such that it refashions the events of the drama. Or, better, the details of the plot are devised in conformity with what the poetic imagination is planning for the speech. Clytemnestra is, in some respects, what the imagery makes of her rather than the adulterous queen of the tradition. She is the snake and the spider as much as she is a royal intriguer with logistical support. The indeterminacy of the weaponry is part of the artistic scheme.

23. But note M. I. Davies, "Thoughts on the *Oresteia* Before Aischylos," *Bulletin de Correspondance Hellénique* 93 (1969): 214–60. He argues that the Boston Oresteia crater, which shows a net, antedates 458 B.C.

24. See E. Fraenkel, *Aeschylus: Agamemnon* (Oxford, 1950), vol. 3, appendix B: "On the Weapon with Which, according to the *Oresteia*, Agamemnon Was Murdered."

*Agamemnon* is admittedly extreme in this respect, as it is in so much else. The dominant image of doves pursued by hawks in *Suppliants*—note, however, the spider in the corrupt lines 885 ff.—is less inimical to the concrete mechanics of the action of the play because the two situations, the flight of the women and the flight of the birds, are easily identified, without remaining awkwardnesses. The image is developed most fully in the form of a simile, as the women take refuge near the altar (222 ff.):

> Here, at the joint and sacred altar-mound
> Pray to the gods, and huddle, like a throng
> Of doves, cowering in fear of like-winged hawks,
> Brutal polluters of a cousin clan.

The image is as old as Homer. But, once again, Aeschylus extends its power. In Homer, the stronger warrior's aggressiveness and the weaker warrior's fear are, as it were, liberated from their abstractness and set in motion: spiritual mobility is converted into the dynamics of locomotion; fear becomes fluttery flight; strength, fierce pursuit; and surrender, an alighting on the ground. Aeschylus adopts all of this. But he opens up the image to convey also notions of purity and impurity, constraint and victimization, vice and innocence, until in the end the perception of motion is left behind, and the impression of uncleanness and sin takes its place. There is no clash between this impression and the mechanics of the drama. On the contrary, the moral coloring adds a vital element to what we need to know about the plot, and what is difficult to dramatize if the play is not to degenerate into sheer melodrama.

One critic finds that the bird imagery is not as important to the meaning of *Suppliants* as another cluster of images closely associated with the legend of Io: the bull and the cow, male and female, gentle touch and violent seizure.[25] It is useful to be reminded of the importance of these images; it is also true that the use of the legend of Io, with its necessary components, points in a rather different direction, away from the core of the bird associations. Io and her story are important for the daughters of Danaus; the women orient their action, and in moments of distress recover their courage, by contemplating the successful career of their ancestress, Io, who went through many tribulations before she found her haven with Zeus. The tale of Io is a paradigm for internal consumption, analogous to one of the paradigms for action with which the old counsellors of the *Iliad*, the Nestors and the Phoenixes, rally their slackening comrades. But it is *not* part of the shaping texture of the play, not part of the imagery designed to help us find our bearings in a moral appreciation of the women's action. In allowing the imagery of the hawk and the dove to affect our feelings, we have a chance

---

25. R. D. Murray, *The Motif of Io in Aeschylus' Suppliants* (Princeton, N.J., 1958).

to understand why the women are escaping from Egypt, and why they must be received in Argos. The legal situation as such is unclear; in fact, Pelasgus suggests at one point that the sons of Egyptus have much justice on their side. The imagery effectively demolishes the claims of a purely legalistic response, and renders unto the Danaids what in the light of the larger drama is the justice of their position.

In *Suppliants*, as in *Persians* and *Seven*, the moral force of the central imagery is relatively uncomplicated. In *Agamemnon*, as expected, things are not so simple. The image of the pregnant hare (119) is a notorious crux. As we have already seen, the immediate reference is to the city of Troy teeming with men and treasure. But whereas the conquest of rich Troy, a military venture occasioned by justified complaints, is morally, if not admirable, at least defensible, the eating of the hare is monstrous. Whatever else may be involved, the chorus, and Calchas who is the reported speaker in their song, shape our judgment of the destruction of the city. But, as we have also seen, the imagery of violation and sacrilege signalled by the hare rebounds on Argos and the house of Atreus. The theme of viciousness, of the death-urge run rampant, engulfs the action until no one, neither aggressor nor victim, can squirm free. In *Persians* and in *Seven*, our feelings tell us, even if reason cannot, who is to be admired and who stands on the side of villainy. No such distinction is possible in *Agamemnon* or, for that matter, in the other two plays of the trilogy. In the *Oresteia*, the imagery does not clarify, it darkens. But the darkening is part of the understanding.

It is important, therefore, to distinguish between the kind of imagery without which our understanding of the moral meaning of a play would be greatly deficient and an imagery which is of a lesser kind, though often important and even essential for the sheer poetry of a work or for the internal direction of the characters and their ambitions. It is the former species which we should call dominant, no matter whether it occurs with some frequency or whether it comes in only once. It is Aeschylus's habit to make such imagery emphatic by repetition. By appealing to cognate images in the organization of discrete events, Aeschylus relates one act to another and gives meaning to the whole. The accent here is on "cognate"; we must speak, for each play, of a system of images, or of an image taking on a variety of forms. Images are not sprinkled through a drama like so many spices, but have a life of their own. A basic image is made to grow and develop until it becomes a commanding presence.

We have already mentioned the light imagery of the *Oresteia*. The torches which start out in the beacon speech as a poetic formulation of Clytemnestra's advancing victory end up in *Eumenides* as real torches in the hands of the escorts. This phenomenon, of the anticipation of stage realities on the level of trope, has been called *prolepsis*, which is merely the Greek for "anticipation."[26] The first uses of a dominant trope are, as it were, anticipatory in the sense that it is only through repetition and increase that the trope takes on its full significance. I would quarrel with the idea that at its first mention, the image is elliptical and enigmatic. No doubt the significance increases with each recurrence or variation. But the model of a puzzle which takes shape and approaches a solution only as more and more pieces fall into place seems to me mistaken. The understanding of the play made possible by the imagery seems to me to gain not in clarity but in power. The language of dyeing which is found in the earlier parts of *Agamemnon* (612, 959–60) finds its fullest completion in acts of dyeing or the display of dyes: Clytemnestra's person and weapon dyed by the blood of Agamemnon (1389–90) and the crimson fabrics (910 ff.) which transform the image of blood spilt into a material thing. The metamorphosis from trope to property is conducted with a rush of awareness that can be enlightening. At *Lib.* 997 ff., Orestes's disconsolate contemplation of the shroud forces the net imagery upon our consciousness more concretely than before. After wondering how it might be described, he concludes that it is the kind of thing a poacher or a footpad might use. The effect of this upon our retroactive understanding of Clytemnestra's deed is immediate. Though the net imagery had not held any mystery before, the meanness of it had not emerged quite so graphically. Now Clytemnestra has been branded a marauder, a sordid hunter of game not her own. Orestes's preoccupation with the shroud—he talks about it, addresses it, despises it—is the scenic equivalent of Clytemnestra's preoccupation with the red textiles. But the development is significant. Heroism, gigantic corruption, the endless flow of blood—in the house, in Aulis, in Troy—give way to palace cabal, lying tales, and stealthy action. With the demonstration of the pitiful shroud, the past takes on a new, vastly reduced meaning.

The lament of the Furies in *Eumenides* mourning the passing of justice and decency is anticipated in the "Fury's Dirge" sung by the chorus at *Agam.* 990 ff., which is itself anticipated by the dirge voiced by the hawks of the simile and heard "by some one god" (55 ff.). Like them, those other lost fledglings, Electra and Orestes (and the chorus) direct a song of mourning to Agamemnon and to Zeus to invoke help against the usurpers. Thus a network of laments, moving in and out, from the imagery to the action and back, articulates the movement of the trilogy. But the theme of the lament, the dirge shrilled by the desperate victim, is not restricted to this play or that, and thus is unlikely to constitute a dominant image. It is a feature of the genre as a whole. The cry of grief and terror touches on the heart of the tragic business—on the fear which informs so much of the choral action,

26. Lebeck, *The Oresteia*, pp. 1–2.

and which Aristotle had in mind when he spoke of pity and fear. Artaud's theater of cruelty distorts this dimension. "I propose a theater in which violent physical images crush and hypnotize the sensibility of the spectator seized by the theater as by a whirlwind of higher forces," he asserts.[27] There is much in Aeschylus that, in the violence and harshness of its imagery, would seem to come close to this demand:

> It is the rule that drops of blood
> Shed on the ground summon another
> Death. Murder invokes the Fury; she
> Brings from those who died before
> Blight to pile on blight.
>
> *Lib.* 400 ff.

Aeschylus works with subtler means than Artaud. Above all, his practice affirms the referential interconnection of systems of imagery, while Artaud makes no such provision. But the cruelty is there, and it is particularly prominent in a class of images on which we have had occasion to touch already, but which it may be worthwhile to take up as a special subject: images taken from the world of the beasts.

Aeschylus's imagery whereby men are turned into animals is an extension of the Homeric simile, but now for a larger purpose, not to hint at the raw but majestic forces operating in the world and through men, but rather to emphasize that the forces work only in animate beings, and that it is difficult from case to case to isolate the particular being invoked. When the general at the beginning of *Agamemnon* is compared to a bird, and also *is* a bird, the effect is both to join and also to separate the two orders. Generally speaking, the tragic world is not as easily construed as that of the epic. Often the tragic mode merges instead of separating; it views synthetically rather than articulately. That is why the satyr, who is both man and animal, is appropriate to it, bringing out into the open, at the end of the tetralogy, a way of seeing which in the tragedies is kept out of the plot and held within the poetry. Helen the lion-cub, Xerxes the serpent, and Clytemnestra the tracking-dog are merely a few of the syntheses that are realized, and pushed remarkably far, in the language designed to affect our feelings. But there is no question of hypnosis or of battering the sensibilities into acquiescence. Aeschylus's animal imagery, like that of Homer, is part of a syllogistic structure. It informs, enriches the understanding, and adds to our appreciation of the nature of an action or of the moral state of the world.

On the whole, the beast in Aeschylus has negative value. It affords to the context in which it is used a sensation of harshness, of lack of discipline, of

27. A. Artaud, *The Theater and its Double* (New York, 1958), pp. 82–83.

want of moral insight or commitment: of that neutral or repulsive world which exists prior to the advent of civilized man and his gentler accomplishments. The lion, the snake, the hawk, the horse stand for what man occasionally can be—when, that is, he renounces the advances of tolerance and cooperation.[28] On this score, the difference between Aeschylus and Sophocles is enormous. The Sophoclean hero—Antigone, Ajax, Oedipus, Philoctetes—is, much like the Homeric warrior, a rugged fighter for privilege. His singlemindedness, the sheer force of his striving, and his positive contempt for the gentler arts represented by civic institutions prompt an animal imagery that shares in the values which we associate with the hero. In Aeschylus, too, the beast can be noble, even heroic. More commonly, it is invested with a terror that undercuts any pretensions to dignity or grandeur. In the first ode of *Persians*, Xerxes relentlessly advancing on Greece (81 ff.) emerges from the alchemy of the poetry like a hellish monster from a Bosch painting:

> With the blue-black stare of a murderous serpent,
> A crowded corps of limbs, of sailors, he drives
> The Syrian chariot and advances
> Bow-taming War on spear-famed men.

Just before, and on other occasions also, Xerxes is, with some irony, said to be divine. He is, as it were, the archetypal beast, as well as the royal shepherd: a polymorph functioning with the assistance—or through the agency?—of fierce minions. With his "many hands," or arms, he is like one of the Hesiodic hundred-handers, monstrous beings who help Zeus to overcome his enemies. The picture is that of an *adventus dei*.

This is from a choral song. The singers are Persian elders—by no means, at least at this point, haters of Xerxes or of Persian military strength. The accents are what they are, however, because aggressive might invites this kind of treatment, no matter where the speakers' sympathies lie. Once the formulation is part of the record, of course, it can be developed further. This is the advantage of choral speech, which, because of its initial impersonality, tempers the natural human tendency to approve or condemn. When the speakers are inividuals, the moral direction is more obvious from the start, or at least should be. But in spite of Aeschylus's general association of the beast with the forces that hinder progress or endanger the city, there is a further difficulty, and that is the apparent exchangeability of animal identities. Cassandra has no cause to love Clytemnestra, and she talks about her and Aegisthus in most savage terms (1258 ff.): Clytem-

---

28. Kenneth Burke is particularly interested in this aspect of Aeschylus's imagery; see his *Language as Symbolic Action* (Berkeley and Los Angeles, 1966), p. 135.

nestra is a two-footed lioness (sleeping with a wolf); a witch preparing a witch's brew; a murderess sharpening her knife. There is mention of a chopping block; Cassandra will provide the ritual equivalent of an hors d'oeuvre. Aegisthus is a wolf. But this identification is made in the same sentence in which Apollo is given his divine name of "Lykeios," which in Aeschylus's time was certainly understood to mean "Wolf-God." One might argue that much of the speech is anti-Apollo. But it would be silly to think of Cassandra as regarding Aegisthus and Apollo in the same light. It is fair to conclude, from this and other examples, that some animal imagery, even in the speech of individuals, fails to convey a particular positive or negative ethos, and that it is only the context, such as the tone of voice, the gestures, and the other language associated with the image, which guides our responses. On the whole, however, Aeschylean beast terms are inescapably derogatory. Lions, wolves, snakes—the Homeric bestiary preying on the weak and the defenseless—are rarely appreciated for the majesty of their attack.

The horse occupies a special position. Three times (four, if a repetition is counted) in *Eumenides*, the Furies refer to what they feel the younger gods are doing to them and to the older order as the breaking of horses. Presumably the young gods (i.e., the divinities succeeding the Titanic order) would agree with this estimate; the new dispensation, replacing the law of the jungle with city ordinances, is a breaking of the old bestial spirit. One is reminded of Anacreon, whose slippery pride in his cleverness as a breaker of horses furnishes a rococo parallel to the thought of the Eumenides.[29] But then there is also the Xerxes of *Persians*, who in the Empress Mother's dream (181 ff.) attempts to yoke two horses, Greece and Persia, to his chariot, and fails in the effort of making them pull smoothly together. Like the unskillful charioteer of Plato's *Phaedrus*, he attempts to coordinate and tame what is too impetuous and self-willed to be so treated. The nobility of the untamed horse, like the nobility of the royal bird, the eagle, and even of the charging lion, can be appealed to by Aeschylus as a reminder that the old has a strength by comparison with which the present can look paltry. This is what creates the special poignancy of the Empress's vision (*Pers.* 205 ff.) of the hawk lacerating the eagle. The hawk is the newcomer—from the Persian point of view, the aggressive, undecorous Greek who deals unbecomingly with the royal bird, the representative of an ancient civilization.

For one interested in Aeschylus's beast imagery, *Persians* is a rewarding play because, unlike *Agamemnon*, it insists on spelling everything out with

29. Anacreon 84, in J. M. Edmonds, ed. and tr., *Lyra Graeca*, vol. 2[2] (Cambridge, Mass., 1931), pp. 180–81.

the utmost clarity. Images reinforce one another, events work in concert, and the design of the action is of great simplicity. In this respect, *Eumenides* is like *Persians*. The animal imagery of *Eumenides* is so unambiguously connected with the role of the Furies as hunting dogs or snakes from underground that there is rarely room for anything else. In *Libation-Bearers*, animal imagery is markedly absent from the texture of most of the play, or at least not dominant, until we come to the end and the reemergence of the snake. In *Eumenides*, the original Thyestian offense of cannibalism is repeated in a whole series of images of biting, blood-sucking, and disgorging. They stamp the Furies as a grotesque and brutal band from an earlier era that desecrates the purity of Apollo's shrine, and they seduce the audience into a false security regarding the moral standing of the divine orders battling each other. Clytemnestra, a well-wisher of the Furies, ascribes to them a dragonlike corporeality (137–39); she calls on them to

> Blow against him with bloody breath,
> Wither him with your vapor, the flame of your maw,
> Dry him up in fresh pursuit.

Later, in retrospect, with a knowledge of the benign issue of the play, the notion of Orestes as a deer to be hunted by the Furies is not devoid of humor. But in the world of blood-guilt, prior to the liberating invention of the city court, all behavior is animal. The Furies are asleep when Clytemnestra comes upon them; their drugged baying is a mark of their failure. Is the distance between this savage ineffectiveness and their later moral pathos too great?

Certainly Aeschylus's way of introducing the Furies is a daring experiment. It must be admitted that the playwright does little to ease the transition or to bring out its miraculous paradox. Once they have shown their other side, the side of the upholder of moral law and social stability against the rootless freethinking of Apollo's defense, animal imagery is given up except for occasional, fitful use. This happens as soon as they have sung their great ode about the "catastrophic" new order (490 ff.), which introduces, or anticipates, their conversion. Apollo continues to employ animal imagery for purposes of abuse (644, 729). He refers to the poison that they will be spitting out, and they themselves use the same image in their final exchange with Athena (782–812), though now it is a poison that comes from the heart and that blights nature and men: a great metaphor which helps them to recover their daemon status, the force of a Hecate rather than the more restricted beast role by which Apollo measures them. In actual fact, Apollo had put the Furies even beyond the pale of beasts when, at the beginning of the play (70), he said that not even animals would associate with the Furies. This, in a sense, begins their conversion.

To conclude this consideration of Aeschylus's imagery, it is worth restating what we have said before, that Aeschylean tragedy is human drama, unlike comedy and satyr play, which locate dramatic action in a no-man's-land between human civilization and the kingdom of animal instincts. The animal imagery, like all other imagery in this civilized drama, is subordinated to a purpose that is narrowly defined: the purpose of formulating, as sharply as possible, the limits and the implications of human conflict. It does not assert itself, as Tieck and the romantic dramatists or Ghelderode and the expressionists want it to assert itself, as a dramatic reality in its own right, competing with and in the end swamping the human—or, as Artaud would put it, the psychological—reality. The exception is Io in *Prometheus Bound*; Io's exemplification of the tension between man and beast is one of the many unusual features that set this play apart from the Aeschylean canon. In Io, Aeschylean beast imagery, normally contained as a trope and owing all of its power and subtlety to the magic of language, breaks out of that confinement and emulates the scenic realization of the other kinds of imagery which we discussed above. But nets and torches, when realized on the stage, are nothing more than props. And so Io's hooves and horns, the allegorical trappings of the pre-civilized existence for which the character stands, fail to compel with the force of the trope which generated them, and work as props only. The exception proves the correctness of Aeschylus's normal procedure, which left visible hooves and horns to the dehumanized riotousness of the satyr play.

# The Agents

# _ 6 _

# Chorus

*"Ben. Jonson* . . . had stumbl'd (I know not how) on a *Chorus*: which is not to be drawn through a Key-hole, to be lugg'd about, or juggl'd with an *hocus pocus* hither and thither; nor stow'd in a garret, nor put into quarters with the *Brentford* Army, so must of necessary keep the Poet to *unity of place*; And also to some Conscionable *time*, for the representation: Because the *Chorus* is not to be trusted out of sight, is not to eat or drink till they have given up their Verdict, and the *Plaudite* is over."[1] By adopting a chorus, Thomas Rymer suggests, Jonson forced himself into the unities, or a facsimile thereof. The chorus that Rymer has in mind and that Jonson used is not exactly what we find in Aeschylus. Even if we had more final plays of the corpus than we do, it is unlikely that we should find a comic "plaudite" expressed at the termination of any of them. And the insistence on the unities and on the role of the chorus in ensuring the unities points to Renaissance theory rather than fifth-century practice. Still, the steadying factor which looms so large in Rymer's drolleries is an important element in the Aeschylean use of the chorus. Since the chorus is, or at least used to be, one of the less immediately appealing among ancient dramatic practices, it merits special discussion.

Used to be, rather than is, because recent theorists and directors have once more come to acknowledge the usefulness in certain dramatic situations of a body of men or women, or both, setting off by their peripheral presence the doings of the main characters. In fact, some considerable ingenuity has been lavished on devising ways of making the chorus conduct itself as intriguingly as possible. In his preface to Barrault's edition of the *Oresteia*, Claudel insisted that throughout the performance the chorus be seated, with their scores on lecterns in front of them. Roland Barthes, who reports this, approves of the idea and wonders why it was not tried.[2] Others have proposed other stagings, not so much to get out of the awkwardness of following the traditional choric production, but rather because they have seen the value of deploying the chorus in a fashion that might underscore their specific conception of the play.

The usefulness of the chorus is, above all, psychological. The audience

1. C. A. Zimansky, ed., *The Critical Works of Thomas Rymer* (New Haven, Conn., 1956), pp. 171–72.
2. R. Barthes, *Essais critiques* (Paris, 1964), p. 76.

recognizes in the chorus an institutionalized part of itself, a delegate, within the body of the action, of the community, connecting the two worlds without removing the barrier necessary to maintain psychic distance. The choral function is that of a witness, with all the social and ritual implications of that term. When Cassandra cries out at *Agam.* 1315 ff., the purpose of the cry is, she says, to bind the chorus to her as a witness for the future when another woman and a man, Clytemnestra and Aegisthus, will die in turn. We are reminded of the old Germanic institution of the *Notruf*; the cry is needed to legitimize a subsequent complaint at law. The chorus of *Libation-Bearers* is not the same, dramatically speaking, as that of *Agamemnon*. But in an important sense it is, for it is acted by the same persons, and in any case there is a larger identity that binds all choruses together. More important, the audience, to whom the appeal is ultimately directed via or over the heads of the chorus, will add the echo of the cry to the moral perception in which they will view the death of the tyrants. Cassandra could not have addressed herself directly to the audience. That would be the manner of comedy, in which the playwright and his actors and characters play cat and mouse with the psychic barrier. The cry to the chorus takes the place of the cry to the audience; as an added advantage, it permits the address to be more narrowly focused. By remaining within the world of the play, the cry retains a clarity which it might otherwise lose.

But the chorus is more than just a built-in representative of the citizenry and a sounding board for characters. Two of Aeschylus's plays feature a chorus which, though not the protagonist of the action, certainly must be regarded as one of the principal agents of the plot. The Furies and the Daughters of Danaus are more characteristic of what Aeschylus does with his choruses than the nameless Athenian judges who also appear in *Eumenides*. The daughters of Danaus are vital personalities with a dramatic life of their own. The Furies act powerfully on their own behalf, besides constituting a significant symbolic force. With their defeat, or rather their transformation, something important happens to one branch of Attic drama, for Aeschylus's successors did not again try to put on the stage a chorus of quite the same autonomy and power. The choral use of supernatural forces remained an Aeschylean hallmark. The daughters of Ocean appear in *Prometheus*; the daughters of Nereus in the lost *Nereids* and perhaps also in one other play. Sophocles and Euripides employ only human choruses.

But these considerations pale before the most important contribution of the chorus, which is that of music. The chorus is the principal instrument guaranteeing the musical nature of Greek tragedy, if not its birth from the spirit of music. But this poses a grave problem. "When words enter into music they are no longer prose or poetry, they are elements of the music.

. . . Music swallows words." This is the view of one important critic.[3] On the other side, we have the suggestion that in drama, music is subordinated to words, gestures, and actions, and that it strengthens the poetry by contributing all the power of expression it can supply. In the history of musical drama, the two positions are exemplified by Gluck and Wagner, the former permitting words at best a role auxiliary to the power of the music, the latter attempting to weld the two into a combination which would preserve for the word its fullest auditory and semantic autonomy. Where in this controversy does Aeschylean drama take its place? Because only scraps of Greek dramatic music, mainly from Euripidean plays, have come down to us, there has been an understandable tendency to proceed as if the words were all that mattered. We have already noted (above, chapter 4) that some of the final choral odes and exchanges appear to use words routinely to fashion predictable laments. Yet it would be a counsel of despair to suppose that the words of the choral odes in our manuscripts do not have their own power as words. Aristophanes jests about the disproportion between words and meaning in Aeschylus, and other conservative critics of his time complain that the music in the latest dramatic presentations was obliterating the words. These are exaggerations. We have reason to believe that the average Athenian audience expected to understand the verbal components of choral singing. The conservative complaints would not make sense without this expectation.

We need no longer be apologetic about the chorus. The day when a play was supposed to be all action and interplay of characters is long past. The late romantic development of combinations of human and orchestral sound, from Mahler through Schönberg and Berg to Berio, has brought home to us some of the possibilities. How are we to imagine the effect of those massive blocks of choral singing, against which the spoken portions of the drama appear, at first glance, to have so little chance? A modern performance can hardly suggest the merits of this musical distribution. Since the art of dramatic singing in unison is lost, a modern director has to organize things differently. In the first choral ode of *Agamemnon*, for instance, one might suggest that where the singers call attention to their status as characters, viz., to their advanced age (104–7), a modern production might have them speak, or chant, with divided roles; but where the choral utterance is, as it were, disembodied from their role as old men, the lines might be sung by one amplified virtuoso voice, with the members of the chorus merely furnishing dance movements. But such a division of labor is artificial and precarious, and will immediately run up against a host of difficulties. Are lines 174–78, for instance, presenting one of the crucial "proverbial transi-

3. S. Langer, *Feeling and Form* (New York, 1953), p. 150.

tions" (for this, see below), to be regarded as in character or detached? The ancient practice of handling all choral stanzas in the same manner means, apparently, that convention lightened the director-author's load. But it also means that it is hard today to appreciate the wealth of musical nuances which choral singing commanded.

The music is lost. But by scanning the rhythms of what is sung and taking a cue from the verbal patterns we have, we can make some judgments about the variety of the choral singing. Equally important, we can make some guesses about where the music underscores and where it strains against the manifest burden of the plot. In the third choral ode of *Suppliants* (538 ff.), the accent is on compulsion. The compulsion is, this time, not of the kind which the rest of the play tells us the women are trying to avoid, the violence practiced by men claiming their rights. It is the compulsion of the (male) god who also stands for Right, for fruitfulness, and for the beneficent truths of legend. The singing creates a counterpoint to the dominant theme of the play, the women's aversion to marriage. Through their singing, the women offer a qualification of their stand which is nowhere explicitly argued. They are, it would appear from the ode, not opposed to sexual union. What they are trying to escape is the one union which society has prepared for them. Their attempt to escape it is, in the long run, fated to fail. The marriage was probably dramatized in the second play of the trilogy, *Egyptians*, which has not survived. The earnestness with which they sing about Zeus's union with Io introduces a note of compromise which may have come into its own in the final play of the trilogy.

Or take the choral action of *Seven*. The plot of the drama requires of Eteocles and his warriors an extreme simplicity of decor and stage action, to set off the barbarian exuberance of the reported enemy blazoning. The simplicity of the action is such that in itself it would scarcely create the momentum needed for dramatic effect. The chorus, with its musical and choreographic counterpoint to the dialogue, furnishes the missing turbulence. The music embodies the confusions and the despair of war, and this gives body to the more abstract reflections of Eteocles and his fellow-speaker.

The difference between what the chorus contributes and what the characters offer emerges unusually clearly at *Lib.* 246 ff. In a formal speech of complaint addressed to Zeus, Orestes compares Clytemnestra to a snake that has choked an eagle, whose young are now starving. He suggests that Zeus will have to go without a prior sacrifice unless he helps the young to grow up to be eagles in turn. The formal and pictorial reference is obvious; it is to the choral passages early in *Agamemnon*, which we have considered above. The similarity is striking, but so is the difference in tone. In the place of the complexities and the full intonation of the lyric, the speech of

Orestes puts everything out in the open. From a mystery linked with the central issues of organic growth and responsibility, we have arrived at a business proposition. The speech may make more transparent what had been partially hidden before. But the choral singing is what produces the overtones and tensions which help to determine our sense that we are dealing with a tragedy. In Sophocles, the choral utterance often follows, and quite directly, upon the spoken communication on which it enlarges. In Aeschylus, the choral statement usually precedes it, and often at a considerable distance. It is a preparer, a shaper of expectations, and a mood setter, permitting us to read the terms of the dialogue against a magnifying screen.

Somewhat analogously, a choral utterance may serve as a substitute for an action off stage. At *Lib.* 855 ff., the chorus recites the gist of the struggle between Orestes and Aegisthus before the death cries of the latter break in on us. Contrast what happens at 935 ff., while Clytemnestra is being killed. Here the chorus sings a more formally structured song, an ode to the house and its rescue by Right. It is a kind of psalm, hosannahs of joy hymning the destruction of the hellish beasts by the forces of light. The choral stand-ins for the two scenes of execution make possible a richer appreciation of what they mean and of how they differ than on-stage killings or even messenger speeches could have accomplished, because of the greater range of the chorus. Since the chorus can dispense with the restrictions of time and place in its meditations and paeans, its guidance of our sympathies and antipathies is more compelling. This is true even in so "unmusical" an action as the latter half of *Libation-Bearers*. Contrary to what readers of this intrigue play might initially gather, none of its spoken sections is as long as certain spoken sections of *Agamemnon* and *Eumenides*. The intrigue is saved from turning into closet drama; the musical enlargement mandated by the chorus transforms cabal into deliverance.

George Thomson has pointed out that in *Agamemnon* each song is shorter than the one before it.[4] The economy of the music makes for an increasing acceleration of pace until finally, between the exit of Cassandra and the murder of Agamemnon, no scope is left even for a vestigial ode, and a few chanted lines take its place: the denouement, so artfully postponed, cannot be delayed any further. In other plays, the economy of musical structuring is less tight; we have no other Aeschylean tragedy whose end-directed rhythm is as grandly conceived as that of *Agamemnon*. *Libation-Bearers*, as

4. For the structural properties and the distribution of Aeschylean choruses, see J. Rode, *Untersuchungen zur Form des aischyleischen Chorliedes* (Tübingen, 1966). The classic treatment remains W. Kranz, *Stasimon* (Berlin, 1933), in spite of certain untenable speculations about the origins of choral forms.

we have already seen, is really a diptych, with the Great Exchange stretching the first section to bursting point. *Prometheus* is singularly poor in choral
singing, a circumstance that has been cited in support of the view that the
version of the play we have is not by Aeschylus, but which has, one may
speculate, something to do with the concerns of the play. In *Persians*, *Seven*,
and *Suppliants* the choral scope declines, in some small measure, from the
initial ode to the subsequent odes, most of which retain a respectable
length.

The importance of the Aeschylean chorus is a critical commonplace.
Some modern scholars have attempted to show that choral singing in the
*Oresteia* advances the development not only of the dramatic themes, but of
the action, with an assurance not yet available to the earlier Aeschylus. But
nobody would deny that in all of the extant plays (with the exception of
*Prometheus*), the chorus is an authoritative part of the organic whole.
Aeschylus is our first and our last writer of unified choral plays—plays
which cannot be disassembled by taking them apart at the choral joints. To
be sure, Aristotle's reference to *embolima*, "inserted choruses," does not
seem to apply to the plays of Sophocles and Euripides that we have. But
their choral practice initiated the gradual severing of the chorus from the
dramatic action which was completed in Senecan drama and became the
rule in neo-classical tragedy. In Ben Jonson's *Catiline*, the chorus takes up
its functions at the ends of acts—i.e., between acts. Aeschylean tragedy has
no acts.

The organic linkage of the chorus with the play is mirrored in the internal structuring of the ode. Aeschylus's odes have a tendency to develop and
change direction to an extent unknown in the odes of his successors. The
internal progression either mirrors the progression of the play or furnishes
significant links between one episode and the next. In Euripides, the ode,
which usually consists of two dyads, generally organizes its thought patterns *by* these dyads—$a \rightarrow a'$ $//$ $b \rightarrow b'$—with the result that the two
dyads appear to be distinct and autonomous. In Aeschylus, as also in Sophoclean drama, there is a tendency toward breaking down the coincidence
between thought structure and stanza structure. It is common for the
thought of a dyad to spill over into the next stanza. As a consequence the
responding stanza is conceptually isolated from its peer: $a \rightarrow a' \rightarrow b$ $//$ $b'$.
The effect is one of greater fluidity. See, for example, the second ode of
*Agamemnon* (681 ff.), prompted by the mention of Menelaus. Here is a very
rough breakdown of the dyads, by the topics taken up:

$a$ :  Helen's ominous name; her exit from Sparta and arrival in Troy
$a^1$:  The doom she brought on Paris and her new in-laws
$b$ :  The lion cub

$b^1$:  The lion cub continued
$c$ :  Application of the parable to Helen

_____

$c^1$:  Old tradition about wealth, and criticism of it
$d$ :  Hybris and its economy
$d^1$:  Right distinguishes between the good and the evil house

It should be obvious that the main suture in the later part of the ode lies between stanza $c$ and the responding stanza. Stanza $c$ goes with the preceding dyad, while the responding stanza goes with what follows. But a warning is in order. This purely formal reading of the connections can be balanced by other ways of looking at the ode. There are striking analogies between the first stanza and responding stanza $d'$: Helen's arrival in Troy balances the departure of Right from the unclean house. The parallel in turn reinforces the vision of the Fury given in stanza $c$, and complements its application: not just to Troy, but also to Argos. Thus the ode turns out to have a larger unity, in spite of the seeming break between the leave-taking of the Queen and the allegory of the discriminating powers of Right. It is such a whole because dyads are not cut off from each other. And further, to illustrate the linking function of the ode, its preoccupation with departure and arrival, with Right and Ruin, and especially with the unanticipated growth of hubris, provides the link between the messenger's ruminations about Menelaus (620–80) and the entry of Agamemnon (782). The messenger, in a succession of speeches and responses, had started out with the fall of Troy and the imminence of Agamemnon's arrival, and then backtracked toward shipwreck, disaster, and the possible salvation of Menelaus. The chorus traverses a similar arc from good fortune to suffering—a movement which every single unit in the play, both episodes and odes, may be said to reflect—but with its terminal emphasis on hubris and *dikē* and its questioning of the moral standing of the house, it can also be said to have readied the scene for Agamemnon's reception.

The unifying virtue of the chorus is also in evidence *between* the odes of a play. This is especially true, to the verge of monotony, in *Suppliants* and *Agamemnon*, which, on this score at least, exhibit obvious parallels. In *Suppliants*, the opening anapaests (1 ff.) have for their central theme Epaphus, the son of Io and Zeus, ancestor of the Danaids; the opening and closing focus is on Zeus. Zeus also forms the central theme of the ode that follows (40 ff.), while Epaphus looms large in its opening and closing portions. In the following ode (524 ff.), the topic of the opening and closing lines is, once again, Zeus. Apart from the prevalence here of the scheme known as ring composition—the featuring of the same topic, and often of the same wording, at the beginning and at the end of a structure—the sequence of topics exhibits an almost stultifying degree of dovetailing. Compare *Agamemnon*: the central theme of the first ode (160 ff.) is Zeus; Zeus is also the theme of the opening and closing sections of the second ode (367 ff.). The central theme of the second ode is Helen; Helen is also the theme of the opening section of the third ode (681 ff.) and of the anapaestic passage which follows it (783 ff.). The facts as given cannot possibly be ascribed to chance. They signal a thematic inertia which only a playwright of Aeschylus's visual energy can afford to favor.

Throughout the history of Greek tragedy, one of the principal functions of the chorus, perhaps dating back to the old passion play, is the lament.

> Hurled from the house I come,
> To escort my offerings with sharp-cleaving beat.
> My cheek is brightly stained with a scratch of the nail, a fresh-cut furrow.
> The heart through life is nursed with shrieks;
> My clothing is linen-shred, rags torn with grief,
> Fine tailoring struck at the breast
> With cheerless affliction.
>
> *Lib.* 22–31

The conventional gestures of beating, tearing, and scratching are here, as elsewhere, reserved for the poetry sustaining the music of grief. In *Seven*, *Suppliants*, and *Libation-Bearers* a mourning or disconsolate chorus supports an action that climaxes in disaster or despair. In *Persians* and *Seven*, lamenting terminates the play. Such terminal grieving is, by tradition, of considerable length. It is hard to imagine an ancient critic raising as many questions about the expansiveness of the dirge in *Seven* as later critics did about the length of the music in the last chorus of Racine's *Esther*. The conventional nature of the grieving is especially marked in tragedy, where many forces are continually pulling the chorus away from a simple execution of communal grief. In the Great Exchange of *Libation-Bearers*, for instance, the chorus suddenly bethinks itself of its traditional role as mourner (423 ff.):

> I strike my breast like a Median
> Or a Cissian keener:
> Hammer beats and a rain of blows,
> The close-on-close outstretching of hands,
> Up and down, up and down: they strike and crash
> Upon my battered and luckless head.

The violence of the language, always close to generic parody, especially in translation, has in this instance an excessive air about it. It is as if the chorus were making a special effort to recollect a passive stance, a canonical, even contractual role, which its active interest in the conspiracy and its expectation of success set off somewhat awkwardly. Especially given the Aeschylean preference for strong, enterprising choruses, the lamenting function is harder to accommodate, and for that reason produces, if not frictions, at least rapid alternations of mood which have their own dramatic and psychological interest.

Closely related to lament is prayer. There are some who argue that all choral odes were, in origin, prayers addressed to gods, and that this root experience continues to affect the audience response even to those odes which have severed their connection with prayer. With the exception of *Prometheus*, all Aeschylean plays contain prayers or passages modeled on prayer.[5] Sometimes the model will inform a whole ode; sometimes, and apparently more so toward the end of his career, Aeschylus reserves the prayer elements for part of an ode. He has two choral imprecations for the purpose of raising the dead: the Great Exchange in *Libation-Bearers*, and the second ode of *Persians* (633 ff.). In essentials, these are little different from odes addressed to living gods, such as the first ode of *Suppliants* (524 ff.) and the entrance ode of *Seven* (109 ff.). All prayer in Aeschylus is more urgent, anguished, and fear-stricken than in the epic and the lyric models on which he draws for his language; prayer in drama is intimately linked to the choral impasse formula "What are we going to do?" In Aeschylus, this question guides the singing of the chorus, less so the debates or reflections of the individual characters. To the extent that wondering about the future and despair about the present play a significant role in Aeschylean drama, they crop up in the choral singing, and particularly in the choral prayers for help.

*Suppliants* 1–18 is an anapaestic opening:

> May Zeus of the Home-coming readily look
> Upon our band. We have come with ships
> From the fine-grained sands of the mouth
> Of Nile. We left the godly land, near Syria,
> And escaped into exile, convicted of no crime
> By a city's court for deeds of blood,
> But ourselves electing flight from men.
> Marriage with the sons of King Egyptus
> We spurn and loathe.
> Danaus, our father and first in counsel,
> Leads this band. He set up the pawns
> And moved the play of noblest grief,
> To flee with haste through the waves of the sea,

5. See esp. R. Hölzle, *Zum Aufbau der lyrischen Partien des Aischylos* (Marbach, 1934), pp. 105 ff.

> And to land on the Argive shore, from where
> Our race, the race of the fly-crazed cow,
> Boasting its birth from the touch and breath
> Of Zeus, has been defined.

Here the prayer, expressed as a wish rather than in the more urgent form of the imperative, is little more than a token. It claims the first line, after which the choral statement immediately glances off into descriptive and historical narrative, concluding the sequence with a further reference to the deity, but now as part of a solemnized historical past. But it is of some importance that the chorus needs even this vestige of a prayer to launch itself into the narrative, which at the beginning of the trilogy is the chief desideratum. What is more, both syntactically—the narrative is a continuation and elaboration of the prayer impulse—and scenically—the women are approaching the altar, suppliant branches in their hands (21–22), the whole section may still be called a prayer. And, as a prayer, it continues almost immediately when the women call on the city, the land, the pure water, the divinities represented at the altar (23 ff.), and finally on Zeus to receive their entreaties.

It is possible to argue that all subsequent choral utterances in the play, and much of what is said by the characters, are little more than an exploitation of the key terms of the initial prayer. The prayer thus functions as the nucleus, the generative force of the dramatic action. By means of prayer, the conditions and the boundaries of that action are first adumbrated. But though the initiating prayer is indeed common and important, choral prayer is found in all sections of an Aeschylean play. At *Lib.* 783 ff., after the nurse has been dispatched and before Aegisthus arrives, the chorus addresses a prayer to Zeus to protect Orestes; a prayer to Hermes to see to it that the house emerge unscathed; and a call to Orestes to disregard a mother's pleadings by clothing himself in the courage of Perseus. The coordination of addressees suggests that this kind of prayer, more closely geared to a particular juncture in the action, is less likely to furnish the key terms by which to gauge the drama. At the same time, it is, one imagines, closer to the kinds of prayers uttered on the spur of the moment by ordinary people on ordinary occasions. This gives it an authority which fully balances that of the initial prayer.

Prayers to the gods within the body of a play often precede or herald acts of violence. The chorus invokes a god or several gods to lend comfort and protection. The reaching out for help from above or below signals to the audience that a situation requiring such help is about to occur. The hazardous world of tragedy affords many occasions on which this form of prayer becomes operative. In Euripides, toward the end of the play, usually after all hope is lost, the call for help is often answered by this or that divinity coming bodily forward, or rather downward. In Aeschylus, at least in the plays we have, such epiphanies are reserved for the blessed dead answering summonses; the gods do not appear. The prayer is experienced as a psychological mechanism and as a supplier of thematic clues, not as one phase in an intercourse between mortals and gods.

Similar to prayer but, one assumes, quite different in effect are those passages, notably in the entrance ode of *Agamemnon* (160 ff.), in which the chorus does not address itself to a god, but discusses the nature of the god. In a prayer, no matter whether the god is addressed in the second person or in the third, the chorus assumes that the god's power is sufficient to overcome the difficulties which their fear has conjured up. But where the nature of the god is discussed, and particularly where the god is Zeus, the greatest but also the least easily defined divinity, the fear enters into the heart of the speculation. Such pondering of the nature of the divinity, though formally related to imprecations, with their voicing of divine attributes, is at the opposite end of the emotional spectrum. Instead of raising hopes, it serves to deepen despair; instead of introducing what is known and respected to shore up a fluid situation, it suggests that human instability is merely a part of an even more enormous obscurity. Such reflections are akin to what is found again later in certain odes of Sophocles and Euripides in which the inscrutability or hostility of the heroic world is memorialized. In Aeschylus, these reflections are rarer, but when they occur the impact is perhaps the more powerful. They clash with what is conceived to be the more confident outlook presented by Aeschylean characters.

Speculations about the nature of the gods can occur only when the chorus divests itself of its personal status and turns into a disengaged commentator on the action and its implications. Another type of song related to prayer requires that the chorus express itself with the full stake of a dramatic personality. I am thinking of songs of thanks, and their converse, songs of malediction. Contrast their modern analogues: in *A Midsummer-Night's Dream*, Titania's complaint (2.1.89–115) and Oberon's charm (5.1.396–415) produce a poetry of sterility and fertility which, because of the play's fairy-tale substance, impresses with the power of incantation, but fails to frighten or to sustain. Because of the suspense of disbelief prompted by the magic of the Night, we can savor the incantations as poetry, but we know that with the passing of the Night, their spell will have vanished.

In Aeschylus, such incantations are pronounced not by spirits of doubtful standing, but by deputies of the community, by bands of men and women whose own fate is substantially determined by the response to their evocations. In the second ode of *Suppliants* (630 ff.), when the daughters of Danaus give thanks to the Argives for receiving them into their land, the relief at the danger narrowly averted is profound. Their joy will turn out to have been premature; we gather that in the following play of the trilogy the protection offered by Argos proved inadequate. But for the time being the sense of joy communicated by the ode of thanks is substantial. The optatives and the imperatives of the grammar correspond to a series of corrective wishes, undoing the threats previously invoked, when the women had promised to hang themselves if their supplications were not heard.

In their ode of thanks, the chorus proposes to avert war, killing, sickness, and strife. The middle portion of the song invokes honors for old and young, and hopes for safe births; then back to one more threat which is to be averted: pestilence. Finally, assurances of fertility, at home and in the fields, and compliments, and a last warning to the city fathers to honor strangers, gods, and ancestors. The ode is a fairly routine example of its kind, by no means adventurous in wording or sentiment. One may even wish to speculate that its comparative simplicity is an index of its affinity to odes of thanks sung by satisfied worshippers. The shifting fortunes of Greek polis life and the uncertain relations with neighboring cities will have provided frequent occasions for such communal expressions of gratitude or concern. The listeners would, therefore, easily fall in with the formulas used near the termination of the trilogy (*Eum.* 916 ff.), the more so since the thanksgiving in this case is actually addressed to Athens herself.

The vote of thanks offered by the Furies is even more straightforward—though also poetically, it seems to me, more satisfying—than the song of the Danaids. After an introduction and encomium of Athens, success is sought for the city's trees, plants, fruits, sheep, and silver supply; the chorus asks the Fates, cousins to the singers, to protect the young men and marriageable women; and, most important, the singers express the wish to see the citizens living in unity, without suffering civil strife and murder. The wish will become true, the thought runs on, because Athena, Zeus's favorite, shelters the city. The last responding stanza of the encounter (1014 ff.) calls upon the citizens, and also the gods who run the city, to be happy. The exorbitance of the notion that the Furies can expect to influence the conduct and the success of the gods of the city is tempered by the clear understanding that such gods are merely a figurative way of talking about the city as a whole. The thought sums up the argument of the whole passage and nails down its comprehensive application. Athena's own anapaestic contributions—the encounter is between a singing chorus and a chanting character—do little more than underline the authority with which the blessings are pronounced and formalize the grateful acceptance of the gifts.

The function of prayer, of obsecration, of praises and curses in choral song is in large part to remind the audience that the human world is linked with a higher order, and that the workings of the gods among men are affected by, as they indeed affect in turn, the operations of the human intelligence. To what extent we are to accept the implications of this literally, and to what extent Aeschylus means these truths to register allegorically, is difficult to say. In some ways, as we have remarked before, Aeschylus is the least religious of the three tragedians. His heroes—Pelasgus, Eteocles, even Orestes—must make their decisions without the help of the gods, and often in opposition to, or under the constraints of obstacles linked with, the gods. In the chorus songs, we find both "realistic" religious coloring—the singers call on the gods or talk about the gods much as a Greek worshipper might think or talk about the gods outside the theater—and poetic formulations of what seem to be the same issues without recourse to the language of religion. What matters most is the enlargement. By introducing the gods, human actions and reflections are endowed with a sonority which enhances their standing (but see also below, chapter 9).

In that respect, the use of the gods is parallel to the use of legend—of the ancient past employed as a paradigm for the present. The paradigm from myth comes into full force for the first time in drama. Both the epic and the lyric know it, to be sure. Nestor reminds himself and his fellow Greeks of the ancient wars in which heroism stood out in purer form than it does in the degenerate modern world. Sappho attempts to gauge her suffering by contrasting it with notorious events in the legendary tradition. A past action or series of events, of clear outline, stable and measurable, radiating through the dark of the intervening ages, is held up against the fluid, uncertain reality of the present by way of contrast or affinity, warning or encouragement. The effect is to make the present appear even more poignantly deficient than before. But because of its isolated position within the text, its adventitiousness, the paradigm is experienced as a literary device. Because the voice that points to the paradigm—that of the epic hero or the lyric poet—is a single one, the comparison has the force merely of one of several such comparisons. Consequently the tie between present and past is arbitrary and loose; it is devoid of any stipulation that present and past are virtually one.

In tragedy and in the choral lyrics leading up to tragedy, the paradigm from myth comes to exercise much greater power. Since the voice making the comparison is a communal voice, the tie between present and past gains in authority. Moreover, because the "present" of the dramatic plot is itself a situation taken from legend or past history, the paradigm merely asserts a dimension which is already, by definition of its own share in the past, invested in the plot. To be sure, the main action of the epic is also taken from legend. But the epic offers us a past rather than a present; whatever one may wish to think about the ultimate temporal standing of the tale, the bard is at some pains to emphasize the temporal distance of his narrative from us. In the epic, the introduction of the paradigm from legend works as a piling of past upon past, as an extension of the past into an even more remote past: a mechanism which carries its own penalty in the rather limited force of the maneuver. In tragedy the paradigm has its full force; the past of the mythical example is experienced as different not in degree, but in kind from what the plot-present has to offer.

It is always difficult to draw persuasive conclusions about Aeschylean trilogies in general from the facts of the one trilogy that we have. But granted that the *Oresteia* is not untypical of the tradition, we may suggest that the paradigm is more prominent in the choral singing of the first play than in the second or third. The first play has the function, among others, of dwelling on the sicknesses and confusions of the characters' present, before the second and third plays introduce the consequences and, perhaps, the resolution. *Agamemnon* has choral singing with sustained sequences of mythical material. Its dramatization of the present is invigorated—both set off in relief and compounded in its terrors—by a repeated confrontation with the past. The same is true of *Suppliants*, where the story of Io and Epaphus shores up the position of the Danaids and provides a means of orientation. It has been observed that for the women to identify themselves with Io betrays a lack of insight; the daughters of Danaus do not seem to realize how different their fate is from that of Io. The identification therefore helps to define their character. The present tense which the women use in the first ode (540 ff.) to trace the wanderings of Io reveals too confident an assumption of identity.

The song is exceptionally simple, with an uninterrupted gliding motion from stanza to responding stanza and on to the next dyad. The women call on Zeus to help them; prayer often introduces an ode given over to a mythical paradigm. They remind him of Io; the god prayed to and the principal persona of the paradigm happen to be linked in the legend, which means that the women's claim on Zeus is twofold. Io started out from the country in which they now find themselves. The chorus describes her progress, her arrival on the banks of the Nile, the horror of the natives, then the resolution: how Zeus released Io from her labors, and she gave birth, and nature rejoiced. Finally, a revoicing of the prayer to Zeus, and the conclusion couched in theological terms: Zeus's counsels prevail.

This may well be the most singleminded choral use in tragedy of the paradigm from myth. But its very simplicity is dramatically intriguing. It involves an element of deception which will become only too apparent as the play continues. The earlier entrance ode, essentially the same in mythical content, is rather more complex, though its formal structure is just as simple. One may well wonder why Aeschylus should have chosen to have the two odes in this order. Here is a tentative breakdown, by dyads, of the thought sequence of the entrance ode (40–175):

1. We call on Epaphus, son of Io and Zeus, and propose to tell the story of Io.
2. Our lament may remind the residents of Metis and Tereus.
3. Our own misery is like theirs. We pray to our ancestor gods to protect us.
4. The obscurity of Zeus is great.
5. So is his power; may he recognize how unfairly our pursuers treat us.
6. We sing our lament; may the gods help us.
7. We call on Zeus and Athena to render our future as mild as our arrival has been.
8. If Zeus does not listen, we shall turn to the Zeus of the Underworld [i.e., Hades].

The formal simplicity is modified by the intercalation, after each of the last three dyads, of refrains; each of them is voiced twice, once after the stanza and once after the responding stanza.

Refr. 6. Further emphasis on the lament, and on its barbaric sounds (the women stress their Egyptian characteristics).
Refr. 7. We pray not to be forced in the bed of [the?] men.
Refr. 8. We recollect Io's sufferings at the hands of Hera.

Tabulations are a feeble makeshift resource. This rough breakdown of the thought pattern of the entrance ode of *Suppliants* fails to do justice to the artfulness, the willful obliquity of the thought sequence. It is composed of many different elements, of which the paradigm is only one. The reminders of Io and Epaphus crop up several times; the tale of Tereus and Metis and Aedone is brought in to point up the kind of grief of which the present song of lament is recognized to be a pale echo, but also to make an implied connection between lament and bestiality which ought to bolster their case with the Argive authorities. Unlike the easy identification of Io's fate with theirs which is the burden of the later ode, the introductory ode relates but does not equate. The suffering of Io—and that is the note on which the song ends—is held up as a turn of fate which the singers contemplate as a fearful possibility for themselves. As is characteristic of mythological exempla, one and the same legendary figure may furnish cause for fear and cause for satisfaction. It is the fear, the unresolved suffering, which is embodied, as one among various topics, in the earlier ode. In the later ode, more exclusively given over to the evocation of the paradigm, the fear is largely surrendered on behalf of the satisfaction derived from reflecting on Io's ultimate salvation. The progress is tantamount to what in Sophocles would be called irony, specifically the irony of false joy. For the sequel of the play will show that the thoughts of the entrance ode were more adequate to the intricacies and the dangers of the whole than the easy assumptions of its successor.

The combination of a paradigm from myth with other elements in the formation of an ode is the norm. But in the lyric utterance of the chorus, the paradigm can never be degraded to the polemical utility which is its standing in some passages of dialogue, such as the wrangling between Apollo and the Furies (*Eum.* 711 ff.). In choral song, the legend elevates the tone and lends respectability. This happens even in the low-keyed, almost decorative song that follows the excitement of the Great Exchange at *Lib.* 585 ff. The theme is evil women of the past, or female monsters, fired with a furious passion. Theoretically, the ode is about the passions of men as well as those of women, as the beginning of the first responding stanza (594–95) makes clear. But the examples cited are all women, and the narration concentrates on their "unsmiling exertions" (623).

Curiously, in *Libation-Bearers*, the character of Clytemnestra, world-weary and shrewd, is less easily associated with the great passion figures of the past than is Electra (or even the chorus itself). Still, the chorus has Aegisthus and Clytemnestra in mind. Their names are not mentioned; their crime is, if we can trust the text, couched in the vaguest terms; and the adjective "woman-hearted" (*gynaikoboulos*) at 626 would seem to contradict the attribute "man-hearted" (*androboulos*) that is attached to Clytemnestra at *Agam.* 11. But they are the logical contenders for filling the position of the one present-day monster countenanced in the song (623–30). The skewed character of the analogy is probably responsible for the poet's unusual step of placing a stanza about the unnamed Aegisthus and Clytemnestra within the sequence of mythical harridans, between the section about Scylla and the episode of the Lemnian Women, as if the present sinners could easily be ranked with the great paradigms. Logically, this should create havoc with the scheme, for the mythical exemplum should be effective only if the figures of the past and the figures of the present for whose sake the past is conjured up are kept distinct. Dramatically, the infraction of the rule works; as the Clytemnestra segment itself becomes one of the illustrations from the past and the precise nature of Clytemnestra's crime is left unclear, the confluence of past and present makes for an even greater horror. I have called the ode low-keyed. It is rather Sophoclean in structure and language, and philosophical in tone. Only the fourth dyad raises itself above the restrained level of the rest; it calls for the punishment of the transgressors by Right and the Fury. The vigor of this appeal is buttressed by the legendary parallels.

Perhaps the most famous use of the paradigm from the past in Aeschylus is the sacrifice of Iphigenia in the entrance ode of *Agamemnon* (205 ff.). Since the event is recent, and Iphigenia is closely related to the principals, "paradigm" is perhaps the wrong word. The technique is more like that of the parade of Darius's power in *Persians*—recent history, eyewitness information rather than remote parallels. If I cite it under the heading of "paradigm," I do so because it is worked into the ode very much in the way mythical exempla are worked in, and also because the effect of the choral recital is to nudge us into a better understanding of the dimensions of Agamemnon's burden and the limits of his responsibility. And it is, of course, true that the sacrifice of Iphigenia becomes in retrospect a paradigm for what Clytemnestra plans for Agamemnon, and Orestes for Clytemnestra.

The subject of the sacrifice is introduced discreetly, by way of a secondary clause, a narrative trick from the tradition of choral lyric. It announces, in the most general terms, that the priest-prophet, citing Artemis, proclaimed yet another mechanism for stopping the bitter weather (198–202). Only the reaction of the Atridae, and of Agamemnon in particular, solves the puzzle for us. The sacrifice is described fully, crowding the body of responding stanza 5 and stanza 6, the final section of the ode being reserved for a series of proverbial formulas designed to insulate the violence of the tale against the triumphant opening of the Queen's speech. In responding stanza 5 (228 ff.), we learn about the physical arrangements of the ritual. The movements are clumsy; the language and the syntax produce an impression of sullen violence and brutal containment, as the attendants bind and muzzle the girl and the father issues his commands. In the next stanza (238 ff.), we witness her glances, her wish to speak, and her recollection of previous ritual chants which, she feels, entitle her to have her say now: a subtle variation of the conventional: If ever in the past I have . . . , now grant me this wish. . . . Because the accent is on the violence done, not everything in the language is clear. But the power of the scene is undeniable; it casts its long shadow, paradigm-like, forward upon the scene of triumph and homecoming.

The paradigm, like the prayer, is a vivid instance of the resonance, as I have called it, that choral song may contribute to the dramatic action. But the Aeschylean chorus is not only a sounding board, an enlivener of more immediate concerns. It is not only an accompanist, responding to or chiming in with the transactions of the principal characters. An Aeschylean chorus does not stand outside the action, and it is certainly not an instrument for supplying entr'acte music. It is, on the contrary, a corporate character in its own right, essential for the purposes of the confrontation which, in most cases, forms the nucleus of Aeschylean drama. This confrontation, as we shall see later, is not primarily between characters, as it tends to be in Sophocles and Euripides and in the later European dramatic tradition, but between a character or characters and the chorus. This is true even in a play which is more or less pure intrigue—a genre which, one would suppose, lends itself least conveniently to the development of choral autonomy.

One way of organizing the rich material is to distinguish between narrative song and what we might call "personal" song, though it is difficult to make a radical distinction and isolate pure specimens of either. The narrative song is to be found, for instance, in the ode about Io's progress (*Suppl.* 538 ff.) which we have just discussed above. In that ode Io is not only an ancestor but also a paradigm: a forerunner in the art of overcoming obstacles and finding happiness. Hence it would be a mistake to regard the song as pure narrative; its paradigmatic function introduces into its understanding a biographical element which puts it somewhere between the two poles, but closer to the narrative end of the scale. In the ode about the monsters of the past (*Lib.* 585 ff.), the personal stake of the choristers emerges rather more forcibly through the intercalation of the surprising stanza concerning Clytemnestra and Aegisthus.

At, or near, the opposite end of the spectrum, we place the song in which the chorus, or rather the persons constituting the chorus, sing about their needs, their wishes, their present or past experiences—for example, the brief sequence at *Suppl.* 418 ff. in which the chorus calls on the King to terminate his reflections and to decide in their favor. The language of such "personal" song tends to be simpler, even more nearly colloquial—though we must stress again that true colloquialism is extremely rare in Greek drama—than the diction and the syntax of the narrative odes.

That is not to say that personal odes are more subdued in mood than others. One of the most common kinds of personal ode is the type we may label "asking the way," representing a vastly expanded form of the question: "Where are we to flee?" It is in the nature of the tragic business that the chorus must remain on the stage. There are several plays in the repertory in which the chorus temporarily vacates the stage, usually to indicate a change of setting; *Eumenides* is one of them. Nevertheless the tendency for the chorus to remain, and by its continuing presence to ensure a unity of action, if not of place and time, is evident. With this convention clearly understood, situations which cause the chorus to fear for its safety or for the safety of characters to whom it is loyal can be exploited to great advantage. The question "Shall we flee?" or "Where shall we flee?" is asked with greater poignancy precisely because the audience knows that it will not be answered, and that the desires of the chorus will die aborning. Such an ode— for example, *Suppl.* 776 ff.—shows a speech more adventurous, and a rhythm more excited, than a personal ode prompted by a lesser sense of urgency. One of the common features of "asking the way" odes is mythological and geographical amplitude. Monstrous prospects and faraway lands are rehearsed before the choral mind's eye to highlight the options available—or rather not available.

Agent choruses, the active participants in *Suppliants* and *Eumenides*, are not the only ones to invest their personal statements with the strong passions of love, hatred, or jealousy; or to furnish, with their successive choral utterances, an emotional curve simulating the ups and downs of a lived life. In *Libation-Bearers*, the chorus identifies itself so closely with the plans of the rebels, and has so much reason to hate the Queen, that some of its singing may be said to outdo in the vigor of its animosities what is found in *Eumenides*. The slave women give voice to a degree of ferocity which is barely equalled by Electra, not to speak of Orestes. Aeschylean choruses are full-fledged participants in the action, but as a body they are too unwieldy to permit themselves the rapid changes of mood and intent that individual characters can, if they so wish, assume. Or, to put it differently, the chorus has so many functions over and above its function as a dramatic participant that when it is made to express an emotion or a stand, the force of the expression cannot be kept moderate or subtle. It has to be projected with maximum liveliness.

This is especially true because one of the important functions of the chorus, and one that needs to be added as a third to the narrative and the personal, is the chorus's role as a voicer of tribal wisdom—of the adages and the distillations of experience which we group together under the heading of *gnōmai*, and about which more will be said below. Odes consisting of nothing but gnomic material are rare. More commonly, the wisdom language is used to balance other constituents, either narrative or personal. It is especially common in reflections about the nature of justice, of the city, or of the gods. Depending on their dramatic and musical integration with narrative or biography, such reflections furnish a varied texture of emotional engagement. Where the wisdom language is put in the mouths of old men, as it is in *Persians* and *Agamemnon*, the mood arches furthest from the passionate involvement signaling personal stakes. The lyric reflections of the aged counsellors of *Persians* and the unquiet ruminations of the elders of the city of Argos give evidence of their growing alarm, but even so they establish zones of calm which offset the passions of the engaged men and women whom they accompany or oppose.

Because of the compound function of the chorus—as narrator, as enunciator of wisdom, and as a potential agent—the playwright can leave the audience in suspense about what may be expected from it. In *Agamemnon*, the sympathy of the elders for their king, in spite of certain scruples about

the rightness of his cause, cannot be questioned. We might expect, therefore, that the death cries of the king from behind the scene wall (1343 ff.)
might move them, if not to action, at least to passionate remonstrance. Like
most characters on stage, the chorus cannot perform actions; it can only
speak or sing. Hence a realistic appraisal of the chances would result in the
admission that there is nothing they can do to help their king or to avenge
him. But what happens is surprising. The chorus splits into a group of
twelve individual speakers, a rare occurrence on the Greek stage. Instead of
a corporate lyric response to the act of murder, such as we know from other
plays, the frustration of human instincts imposed by the needs of the drama
is channeled into speech, and futile speech at that.

In *Libation-Bearers*, on the other hand, the chorus under parallel circumstances (869) declares that by refraining from action, it will avoid the
charge of complicity: a demonstration of cowardice surprising in a group of
women who earlier, in the Great Exchange with Orestes and Electra, clam-
ored passionately for doing away with Aegisthus and Clytemnestra. It is
this very chorus, however, which achieves something that the chorus of
*Agamemnon* fails to achieve: by speaking at the right moment, it succeeds in
changing the course of the action. The women's instructions to the Nurse
see to it that Aegisthus returns without his bodyguard. Thus the playwright can exploit the multiplicity of the chorus's functions to keep the
audience in a mild state of suspense about the effect the chorus may have on
the progress of the drama: a license that is of no small advantage in a genre
as predictable in its conventions as Greek tragedy.

We have talked about the structural properties of the chorus and its
unifying force within the play; about its contributions to the mood and the
thought of the drama, in the form of lament, prayer, and paradigm; and
about the scope of its role as a dramatic agent, stretching all the way from
detached narration and disinterested reporting to the impassioned pleas of
partisanship. In what remains of this chapter, I would like to enlarge further on this last topic by listening in to the choral voice and trying to
distinguish the various modulations of that voice (no matter, in this context, whether spoken or sung). Even if we accept Aristotle's dictum that the
chorus at its best is a character, integral to the clockwork mechanism of the
drama and helping or hindering the fortunes of the principals, the cadences
of the participant chorus are many. For the most part, however, in spite of
this variety, the choral voice is a product of its fundamental role, which is
that of commentator or responder, and not an initiator of action.

Its role as a commentator is, at its lowest level, one of furnishing information. In a larger sense, much that we associate with the chorus may be
grouped under the rubric of information: the narration of ancient legend,

the introduction of characters, and the warnings issued to principals who do not seem to be paying sufficient attention to the circumstances around them or down the road. A great deal of the information given out by the chorus is not so much for the benefit of the dramatic agents, but over their heads, aimed straight at the audience. Such direct communication between chorus and audience is extremely common, especially in the plays in which plot interest is reduced, i.e., *Persians* and *Prometheus*. Often the intelligence delivered is of a kind which the chorus, in its personal aspect, can be expected to possess, but which is awkwardly related to the contingencies of the action. Then again, the chorus may produce information or use expressions which are not especially appropriate to its dramatic function, but which happen to be dear to the audience. At *Pers.* 230 ff., the Empress Mother suddenly, without the kind of provocation upon which Sophocles might have insisted, asks where Athens is, and the chorus, through its leader, provides the answers. It could be argued that the question is psychologically defensible because the Empress has been pondering Xerxes's absence and the dream vision of the unruly women. But significantly the question is about Athens, not about Greece. It is being asked because the audience needs to learn more about the adversary, and Athens can be talked about more concretely than Greece. But it is difficult to suppress the suspicion that the question-and-answer session that follows was written to confirm the bond between playwright (and his chorus) and listeners. And yet the cause of internal economy cannot be dismissed altogether. The learning session, dispassionate, even pedantic, precedes the entry of the messenger of doom reporting the disaster which emerges as an Athenian victory.

I add further instances of information-giving, mostly from *Persians*, which comes down heavily on this aspect of the Aeschylean choral manner. In the introduction to the play, as the chorus describes the composition of the Persian forces, vaguely uncomplimentary touches creep in: the Lydian contingent is said to be from a people that is "soft-living" (41−42); the Babylonian advance is said to have been pell-mell, without discipline (53−54). This is, of course, the Athenian perspective; the chorus takes on the task of a commentator with an Athenian bias. Later (532 ff.), the chorus reproaches the absent king, mourns the dead, and pronounces the new freedom of the peoples of Asia now that the Persian power is broken: they will no longer have to pay tribute, they will no longer have to prostrate themselves, their tongues will be free to speak, their necks will be free of the yoke. Ostensibly, this tallying of the effects of the Persian defeat is an expression of fears. But the spirit of the passage argues against this. The little phrase "they are no longer under Persian rule" in which one compound word does duty for everything except "no longer" betrays the Athenian perspective as clearly as one might wish. Information-giving has been combined with the voicing of patriotic bias, and their integration in the larger dramatic purpose is a matter of some uncertainty. In fact, the information is as much the author's as it is the chorus's; and it is given out because the audience looks for it. The author is keenly aware of the expectations of his listeners and knows how to build them into the artifact. The action of the play rests upon the political and social experience of the listeners. In that limited sense, we may speak of audience control, of the poet taking into consideration the kinds of issues which the audience thinks important and returning them to the audience in the form of information. The separation of the two worlds, the world of the stage and the world of the auditorium, puts only a minor strain upon this process.

In the comedy of Aristophanes, where humor could be struck from the breaking down of that separation, audience control and author response gained recognition in a special mechanism called *parabasis*. At a certain point in the action, at a cue understood by all, the chorus would, as it were, divest itself of its dramatic role and become simply an instrument through which the poet might address the audience on topics of the day. The positions taken in *parabases* were always, as far as we can tell, those which the author could be certain would appeal to the majority of the audience. They would represent what the majority felt or was prepared to feel, though the comic playwrights were always at pains to make it appear that they were urging an unpopular view upon a slow-to-learn crowd of incompetents. Hence the notion, widely accepted, that the *parabasis* was didactic and improving, and that the comic playwright was a teacher of his people.

Tragedy knows no such convention as the comic *parabasis*, set off from the body of the play by its own metrical and histrionic characteristics. But the idea that the tragic poet should be addressing his audience in his own person is not unknown. The Romantics felt that the most useful activity a chorus could engage in was the voicing of the poet's personal philosophy. Recent critics of Greek drama have allowed for the possibility that some choral utterances may be giving us the playwright's own thoughts, though there is no formal pattern to indicate that they do. It is only natural that these critics look for such avowals in statements that appear unusually important or impressive and at the same time are tied only loosely to the action. One of our greatest scholars feels that Aeschylus uses the entrance ode of *Agamemnon* to let us know the religious and ethical principles which are to guide our appreciation of the drama.[6] According to this view, the chorus is, at this point, not merely one agent among others, whose notions about justice and injustice we are meant to regard with critical reserve.

6. U. von Wilamowitz-Moellendorff, *Aischylos-Interpretationen* (Berlin, 1914), p. 166. For a critique of the concept of a tragic parabasis, see D. Bain, "Audience Address in Greek Tragedy," *CQ* 25 (1975): 13–25.

Rather, the chorus's stance at this juncture is binding because it is the poet's, in his capacity as a moral thinker and as a formulator of the people's values. All this gets us very close to what was thought by A. W. Schlegel and the Romantic theorists who reflected on the function of the chorus in a revitalized drama along Greek lines.[7] 

There is much that is difficult about this. The common assumption that drama differs from the essay or the lyric precisely in that the poet does *not* speak directly or through the guise of a persona to the listener is difficult to dismiss. With a plurality of dramatic agents expressing conflicting views and ambitions, what gives us the right to assume that one of these characters speaks for the poet, more than his peers? The same skepticism should prevail in our interpretation of the views of the chorus. There is much about Aeschylean tragic choruses, notably fear, simplicity, even cowardice (characteristics to be discussed below), that would seem to disqualify the chorus as an appropriate mouthpiece for the poet's moral or philosophical ideas; nor does the chorus function as a credible representative of popular causes in these moods. But the issue is clouded. At *Eum.* 919 ff., the placated Furies, identifying themselves with the greatness of Athens, call the city "a citadel of the gods, the altar-protecting jewel of Greek divinities." It is difficult not to conclude that the words are as much to be identified with the poet, the audience, or the festive spirit authenticating the trilogy, as with the Furies who have earlier harbored little but resentment for the "jewel." But once we say this, what is to prevent us from regarding other pronouncements of the Furies in the same light? The great "change-over" ode (490 ff.), for instance, is addressed directly to the audience. Unlike the more fully orchestrated and more complex odes of *Agamemnon* and *Libation-Bearers*, this ode makes its appeal with the least deviation from a central message. Athena calls the Furies "more intelligent than I am" (849), and they prove it in this instance by stating what would appear to be some of Aeschylus's most positive political thoughts. As the trilogy nears its end, the poet's own standards—which is to say, the mature thinking of his time—emerge more clearly than before, and are put in the mouths of the characters whose imminent conversion makes them a more suitable body of informants than the Homeric divinities who oppose them. It is generally felt that by comparison with the other two plays of the trilogy, *Eumenides* is a drama diminished in pathos and suffering. This diminution in affective power makes it easier for the poet to come out into the open, not as poet, but as citizen, as political and ethical commemorator.

At one point in the "change-over" ode, which is largely trochaic and

---

7. See Victor Hugo, *Théâtre complet*, ed. R. Purnal et al., vol. 1 (Paris, 1963), p. 142: "What is the chorus, this bizarre body located between spectacle and spectator, if not the poet enacting his epic?"

iambic, a dactylic series, evocative of epic rhythms, raises the tone (528 ff., 540 ff.). The versification furnishes the advice at its center with added emphasis. The stress on the mean that is found here—the talk of health, of reverence, of piety, and of what is dear to the gods—is, of course, not unique to this ode; it is a common choral theme. But its occurrence here, in the mouths of the Furies, whose conversion is just beginning, lends it an unusual force. The golden mean is not a standard that one would readily associate with the world to which the Furies belong—at least as they appear to us in the early part of the play. The earnestness and the detachment with which moderation and piety are preached here point to an authority which lies somewhere beyond the traditional Furies' ken.

What happens here is that the Furies relinquish their partisan status—the special role they have under the dictates of the plot—in favor of a characteristically "neutral" choral stand. In spite of the differences between choruses—between the virgin truculence of the Danaids, the old men's wisdom and feebleness of the aged Argives of *Agamemnon*, and the single-minded vengefulness of Electra's companions in *Libation-Bearers*—there is an underlying choral psychology, if that is the term, which binds all tragic choruses together, and which emerges now and then in all the plays, even where the chorus is characterized in a way that would seem to take it some distance from this choral mentality. We should remember that the chorus is always, in spite of its momentary disguise, a deputy of the community. The playwright wishes to say something about issues touching his life and the life of his city.

Some of those issues will be discussed below in chapter 11. They are, above all, the great questions of freedom and slavery, of war and peace, of justice and injustice, and the like. The great dramatists have something to say about them, but differ in the means they choose. Some—Euripides, Brecht, Schiller—associate what they have to say closely with the speeches of the principals. In Aeschylean tragedy, it is more difficult to trace a direct connection between authorial position and the utterance of an agent. But given the root function of the chorus—which is that of witnesses, commentators, and representatives of the community—the author has a relatively free hand in coopting them for his purposes. They have both the virtues and the vices which the playwright sees all around him. They are the little people—with their decency, their capacity for some limited compassion, their unwillingness to get involved unless revenge gets in the way, their superstitions, their horror of extremes, their occasional moments of cruelty, their periodic hunger for compromise. It is by no means a simple picture, this choral mentality, life's wisdom poised against the extravagances of the major characters. Nor does it matter whether the specific role of the chorus is that of free men, women, or slaves. In whichever capacity, the chorus can either bear itself with dignity or display a servile or a childish demeanor. At *Agam*. 259–60, the chorus's deportment toward the Queen is proud and stiff; they are jealous of their masculine privileges and unwilling to play the courtier. At 586, on the other hand, when they say that they will be rich, they are referring to the time-honored servile notion that the messenger of good tidings gets a reward. The latter passage stands in a transitional position; it is obviously important to distinguish between what is expressed in the odes and in the great encounters, on the one hand, and what is said in passing. But it is not untypical, an indication of the many faces that the people's representatives may assume. And it is because of this variability, this openness, that the playwright is able to use the chorus for the dispensing of information and for the affirmation of values which may now and then plausibly be identified with his own desires. We cannot ever be entirely certain in answering the question where choral voice and authorial voice coincide. But that such moments exist, and that certain patriotic touches may empower us to recognize them, is more than likely.

Euripides and Sophocles are more radical than Aeschylus in constructing a choral personality at opposite poles from the heroism—or the abortive heroism—of the principals. But we cannot overlook the same emphasis on a "popular" psychology in Aeschylus. It emerges most clearly in the one play we have repeatedly recognized as standing apart from the rest: *Prometheus*. At *Prom*. 526 ff., the daughters of Ocean deliver themselves of what might be regarded as the popular sentiment par excellence; in effect they tell the hero: I do not want to have anything to do with principle; because you do, you have brought on your own troubles. This is the choral unwillingness to go along with the hero as he ventures upon his untrodden paths. (It is the side of the chorus which in T. S. Eliot's recreations of Greek drama becomes so pervasive that, in the wake of Euripides, it colors the pronouncements of some of the characters, such as Agatha and Mary in *The Family Reunion*; and which in his choruses is stressed to the point of parody.) Elsewhere, also, Aeschylus is capable of similar exaggeration. The timidity of the chorus in *Seven*, as castigated by Eteocles, is conceived as a counter-heroic extreme. For those who read the early choruses of the play in translation, the effect borders upon the ludicrous. The Englishing exposes and leaves raw whatever is incongruous and laughable in the expression of popular feelings. Our impatience with what we feel to be pedestrian prevents us from recognizing that the complete portrait is by no means laughable.

The Aeschylean chorus is a strong supporter of the weak versus the powerful, and tends to identify poverty with justice and wealth with injustice. The famous passage in *Agamemnon* (750 ff.) in which this identification is challenged is unique in our extant corpus. It occurs in the ode which

opens with the etymological exploration of the name of Helen and proceeds
to the simile of the lion's cub. After a stanza in which it transforms the
arrival of Helen in Troy into an ominous pattern of gestures, feelings, and
god-sent disaster, the chorus, picking up on a mention of wealth, starts in
afresh:

> An ancient saying, age-old report, persists
> Among men: if a person's wealth grows great and matures
> It breeds and bears before it dies:
> From a prosperous lot there grows
> A clan of unquenchable griefs.
> My own thought is one, distinct from others: what produces the brood
> Resembling itself
> Is an unclean act.
> Where the house is just
> It is blessed always with a handsome seed.

In the dyad that follows (763–81), the distinction between wealth that
begets crime or trouble and wealth that stays healthy in its offspring is
dropped. It is as if the choral tradition for which all wealth is suspect is
simply too strong to permit the lone voice crying in the wilderness to
endure. For the briefest moment, we hear a single voice, emphatically distinct from the corporate voice of the chorus, breaking in on the recitation of
tribal wisdom. If the voice is that of Aeschylus, it is the chorus that does the
singing. The view that Justice may respect wealth and help it to flourish is
part of the same choral utterance as the view that follows, and into which it
shades off without a noticeable break: that Justice shines in the smoke-
stained dwellings of the poor and honorable, but shies away from the gold-
plated establishments of the rich and corrupt. Reasonable men may argue
over whether the reference is to Troy, Argos, or both. But no one can mistake the reassertion of the old popular ethic—so different from the Pindaric
identification of wealth with the potential for justice—over what started
out as an unorthodox separation of ethics from economics. But we have seen
enough of the many faces of the chorus to conclude that this also, however
unusual, can become part of the choral amalgam.

The sense of justice and the support for the poor and downtrodden can
soften into something like pity or compassion. In epic, compassion is rare,
or at least little talked about.[8] Aeschylus is the first to introduce a number of
characteristic compassion terms into literature. But it is significant that,
prior to Sophocles, compassion for the sufferings of one's fellow men is not
expressed by the principals; it is reserved for the chorus. What the chorus of
*Agamemnon* feels for Cassandra, for instance, is complicated, but ultimately,

---

8. But see J. de Romilly, *La douceur dans la poésie grecque* (Paris, 1979), pp. 13–22.

in spite of momentary hesitations, reveals itself as pity (1069). The chorus of *Persians* has a greater sympathy for the lot of women than any one character or, for that matter, other male choruses. This has something to do with their "Homeric" role; they furnish the perspective of the Eastern kingdom defeated, with its Hecubas and Andromaches facing a dismal future. Aeschylean principals who might be expected to voice a similar compassion, like Pelasgus pondering the application of the fugitives, do not. Pelasgus's thinking is guided only by his interest in his community. He is not a free agent; indeed, nobody on the tragic stage is. Only the chorus can be said to have the latitude, unencumbered by role-playing or obligations toward family or city, that permits the full flowering of compassion. And it should not come as a surprise that the shedding of tears, also, is in Aeschylus a strictly choral business. A chorus will freely admit that it is weeping, or the choristers will encourage one another to weep. There are references to individual characters, usually absent, crying or having cried or about to cry. But no character refers to himself in the process of weeping. At the end of *Persians*, Xerxes asks the chorus to respond to his cries with cries of their own; he makes no mention of any tears on his part, but calls on the chorus to weep, and they comply.

The Aeschylean chorus hates war. Far from having a fixed opinion about the rights and wrongs of the Trojan War, it dwells on the viciousness of all war. In *Agamemnon*, this is clear from the start, with the image of the hawks devouring the pregnant hare, and the comments of the seer (126 ff.). In its ode (367 ff.), the chorus is equally critical of the conquered and the conqueror. Desire and temptation are said to be at the source of all these disturbances; for itself the chorus would wish nothing better than a peaceful life, one of retirement and calm. Throughout, the chorus succeeds in keeping the message of aggressiveness humbled so general as to make it applicable not only to Paris, but to all conquerors, all men and women in high places, all princes and oppressors. In the third dyad of the first ode of *Agamemnon*, the royal house of Argos replaces Paris as the object of anger; the argument, which had been moral, turns political. This is as far as choral restraint allows blame to go. The chorus backtracks at once and, characteristically, uses a pious generality (471 ff.) to temper the attack.

The hatred of injustice and of war is by no means militant. The canon of the golden mean is always ready to be cited to cushion the more impetuous instincts. Note the sentiments uttered just before Clytemnestra attempts to lure Cassandra into the house (1001 ff.). The chorus here tells us that man's strength presses for excesses and is therefore likely to come to grief even if its course is true. Caution, "jettisoning some of the cargo with a subtly balanced rope-tackle," may minimize the loss and save the house or ship. Zeus with his seasonal largess relieves our hunger, but no miracle worker can bring back blood that has been spilled. The moral is tame, not to say resigned. Destructive excess and saving husbandry are both available. Men must steer a middle course between heroism and despair, avoiding irremediables, of which the spilling of blood is one. The only fruit which the shedding of blood produces is vengeance and further violence.

The passage is full of the key words favored by the oppressed: *oknos*, "hesitation," *eumetros*, "measured," *agan*, "too much." To be sure, in histories of fifth-century Greek political and social thought, the terms signifying moderation, calm, avoidance of excess, and the like are usually associated with the views of the landed gentry and their partisans, who looked with disfavor upon the undisciplined energies of the democratic majority. And it is quite true that, if we look at the writings of Thucydides, Plato, and Aristophanes, the "people"—those who voted in the assembly to set up and maintain an island empire and who manned the ships to support this policy—are branded as hubristic precisely in the sense in which such behavior is abjured in the choral ode. But this is only part of the picture, and what I have called the choral mentality should serve as convincing evidence that the people who followed their leaders into brutal wars could, when they thronged the theater, applaud another kind of ethic. More recent history has shown abundantly that men and women who think of themselves as decent peace-loving citizens can, on a national scale, commit or allow great horrors without becoming fully conscious of the contradiction. The antithesis between the quiet virtues and heroism which comes to be sketched in Aeschylus and is fully worked out in Sophocles's heroic dramas is, among other things, a portrait of the ambivalence within the character of the Athenian populace—of a culture which for a while seemed to succeed in combining the building of an empire abroad with the practice of tolerance at home. The choral mentality reveals an important and often neglected aspect of the people's aspirations.

The "conservative" color should not cause surprise. Both tragedy and comedy suggest that, given half a chance, the commoners are happy to follow their more privileged leaders and to fall in with the cultural ideals championed by them. Loyalty counts for more than moral conviction. Once Agamemnon is dead, the chorus abandon their former skepticism toward the king's actions (799 ff.) and talk about him as a "beneficent guardian." Their integrity as citizens, their prejudices in support of the male role, (1453–54), and their natural circumspection pull them back to the side of the king. No psychologizing explanation is needed for this swing. The chorus members simply recover their native point of view, after an interim during which other sentiments, more ideologically structured, but equally conservative, have temporarily skewed their relation to their prince.

The vengefulness of the chorus of *Libation-Bearers* does not, in spite of appearances, tell a different story. Like the Furies of the first part of *Eumenides*, the companions of Electra take a stand against what they regard as a wrong, the disappearance of the mutual respect which makes for a humane life. The philosophy of the second dyad of their entrance ode (55 ff.) is clear and to the point: "Respect, once incontestable and unconquered, once distilled through ear and heart, now renounces its claim." It is because of this that they close ranks to oppose Clytemnestra and Aegisthus. That in the course of their opposition they allow themselves to be drawn into a spiritual intemperance of their own is, as it were, dramatically unavoidable. Like the Furies and like Cassandra, with whom they share much in language and thought, they are frenzied by the justice of their cause. They are older than Electra and Orestes; they are more keenly aware of the importance of the right moment for action. But the impulse from which their murderous counsel springs is roughly the same traditional mood which prompts the choral anxieties of *Agamemnon*.

The play which appears to depart furthest from this choral norm is *Suppliants*. If we expect the chorus to represent ordinary people (and, to repeat, it does not matter whether the people are free or bond; Greek literature, from the *Odyssey* to pastoral poetry, commonly minimizes the cultural and social difference between slaves and free men) thinking the thoughts of common men and women, the Danaids fail to satisfy our expectations. They are of a background which produces heroes and heroines. Far from constituting a nameless body of followers or, like the Furies, a body of women personifying an abstraction of popular thought, they are the children of a specific man at a specific time. They are capable of action as well as reaction; the flight which motivates the play proves this. The principal issue of the play discussed by them again and again, their refusal to marry, is rather more specific than the issues usually reserved for choral discussion. All this gives them an exceptional status among Aeschylean choruses. It also explains why a Danaus is needed. It is he who furnishes some of the contemplativeness—the voicing of the moderate values which elsewhere are supplied by the chorus and which are apparently so fixed a part of the tragic synthesis that the poet needed to supply their want in this manner. The advisory role of Danaus and the "protagonist" role of the chorus are not, as used to be thought, signs of immaturity or evidence of an earlier type of tragedy, but daring experiments.

But even in *Suppliants*, the choral norm manages to assert itself. Toward the end of the play, when the young women appear to be temporarily successful in their attempt to escape marriage with their cousins, our text shows (1034 ff.) that second thoughts creep in:

> But in our cheer let us not forget Aphrodite.
> With Hera she shares a power closest to Zeus. . . .

Whether the lines are sung by some members of the chorus, who thus take a stand in opposition to the rest, or whether the whole chorus, in anticipation of developments to follow, relaxes its former rigidity, what matters is that the lines give us the typical choral insistence on the wrongness of excess. In this case, the one-sidedness condemned is the flouting of Aphrodite's law. The warnings are similar to others pronounced by choruses, and by such "choral" characters as nurses and attendants, in many Greek plays, including above all Euripides's *Hippolytus*: that moderation and compromise are to be preferred to one-sided worship, or neglect, of specific divinities. The self-criticism of the women toward the end of *Suppliants* rights the balance and restores the choral norm, after the experimental use of the chorus in this unusual play had for a while effaced the distinction between chorus and principal.

Let us return once more to the "change-over" ode of *Eumenides* (490–565). It happens to be the last ode sung by the Furies, even though it starts before the play is even half done. They sing it at a time when Athena has gone off stage to pick the jury. It will be useful to tick off the sequence of thoughts, in order to indicate the distance the Furies have traveled from the "bestial" personality embodied by them earlier (and again later) in the play. The units are roughly those of the stanzas.

1. If the law upholds the matricide, that will pit man against man, and parents will no longer be able to defend themselves against their children.
2. We shall have to surrender our wrath and permit aimless killing.
3. If so, let no father or mother try to call on us.
4. There must be a place for fear and respect to remain intact. Acting rightly, on the part of a man or a city, is based on fear.
5. I speak for the middle road, halfway between anarchy and despotism.
6. Respect the altar of Justice; that way respect for parents and the survival of homes is assured.
7. In justice, a man will be, without compulsion, moderately well off, and certainly not miserable. The man who acts otherwise will be shipwrecked.
8. And the gods will rejoice in his destruction.

The ode is entirely without the venomous quality of the Furies' earlier singing, without the animal imagery that informs so much of it, and without their usual insistence on rights and privileges. In fact, they barely refer to themselves, and talk of the *daimon* rejoicing when the sinner fails (560). The ode is simply an encomium of the middle way, with plain justice and the principle of fear providing the guidance. The emphasis is on law and order, and on the dangers posed to them by permissive courts.

One might wish to say that this is where the conversion of the Furies from clan agent to political and institutional guardian begins. And, in fact, the speeches of Athena, Orestes, and Apollo that follow must be read against this new orientation. Yet we cannot properly speak of a conversion at this point, because almost immediately after the song, the Furies once more settle back into their old bugbear habits, to be definitively converted only very much later, after Apollo and Orestes have left the forum.

Where it comes, the song is as much of an anomaly as the second thoughts of the daughters of Danaus. It is a reassertion of the old choral stance. For a brief moment, the chorus sets aside its personal role and provides a battery of traditional, impersonal themes which will prove their worth toward the conclusion of the play, and of the trilogy. Dramatically, the interruption, if that is what it is, presents a difficulty. How can an audience be expected to see-saw back and forth between these transformations of choral identity? The answer is, probably, that the audience expects to find the traditional choral patterns asserted, even in contexts where the direction of the plot might seem to put them out of court. Perhaps endowing the chorus with a distinct personality creates a dislocation of a sort, so great that only a periodic or occasional reversion to the more impersonal norm can reconcile the audience to it. This kind of reasoning is, I think, to be preferred to the argument that the Furies can sing as they do in their ode because they are between two "acts," the departure of Athena and her reappearance with the jurors. To be sure, the depersonalization we have discussed is more easily accomplished at moments when the dramatic tension is relaxed. In its most extreme form, this is seen in the "terminal tag," the Euripidean manner of closing a play with a brief, mechanical choral statement which is nothing but a prefabricated compound of the choral mentality. Aeschylus's closest approximation to the Euripidean tag comes at *Lib.* 1065 ff., a superficial voicing of common choral fears, completely devoid of personal engagement, and designed to lead quietly into the last segment of the trilogy. But the timing of this phenomenon is, I think, less significant than the simple fact that the depersonalization can take effect at all.

The choral commonplace is not calculated to impress with its intellectual profundity, though the poetry can be very beautiful. It has been said that "in the choral odes the action is lifted out of time and place on to the plane of the universal."[9] Does this mean that the chorus embraces a greater truth or a greater insight into the meaning of the action? On the contrary, there are many occasions when the insight of the chorus is more limited, and certainly more comfortable, than that of the principals.

9. F. M. Cornford, *Thucydides Mythistoricus* (London, 1907), p. 144.

Sometimes, indeed, the choral thinking takes its cue from what is read into the thinking of the principals. We expect this to happen, of course, when the chorus consists of the retinue or the companions of a prince. Rosenkrantz's speech in *Hamlet* 3.3.11 ff. is a depressing caricature of the people's dependence on their leader. What befalls the prince affects the well-being of the subjects. The corporate significance of the king's role can shape the values of the subjects. In *Persians*, where some of the formulations suggest that the wise counsellors are little more than the beloved chattels of the royal household, the choristers introduce themselves in the neuter plural, the grammatical form which the Empress Mother (171) and Darius (681) use to address them. The Emperor is everything, and all other members of the household take on the guise of prized possessions. The case of *Persians* is extreme; the paternalism which stifles the self-confidence of the chorus is an exotic touch, designed to bring out the oppressive nature of non-Greek institutions. But the uncertainties and the indecision which flow from this are not restricted to *Persians*. In *Agamemnon*, the trepidations of the elders are motivated by their extreme old age. They emphasize their years from the start (72–82) to give a semblance of verisimilitude to their decent timidity. But this is just about the only thing we find out about the character of the chorus. It is no exaggeration to say that the chorus of *Agamemnon* are the least individually characterized in the Aeschylean corpus. The insistence on their decrepitude has an almost comic air about it. Their council session after hearing Agamemnon's death cries progresses like a parody of democratic procedural wrangling. There are similar things in Ionesco and in Beckett; various words are tried, until in the end silence is found more substantial. The near-comedy cannot gloss over the lack of substance.

Their response to Agamemnon's death follows a pattern that has been built up in earlier scenes. Their extended questioning has nothing dramatic about it; the metrical clues point to a stately delivery in the manner of a political discussion. The stage action complies; it would be a mistake to think of the old men rushing furiously about the orchestra. The length of the debate has the effect of underscoring the vanity of their scheme. It is the fullest dramatization of choral irresolution that has come down to us in the Greek repertory. To the question of whether the chorus has been unaware of the Queen's plotting, the obvious answer is that the death of Agamemnon does not come as a complete surprise to them. Earlier insinuations, especially 542–50, and the clear message imparted by Cassandra (1225–26, 1246) have given them all the information they need, though they refuse, or pretend to refuse, to profit from it: they assume the killer will be a man (1251). But is this the right way of looking at the difficulty? Perhaps, once again, the question should not be: "Has the chorus had an inkling of what is in store, prior to their council session?" but: "Is the session an adequate mechanism for further emphasizing one important element in the choral performance, the chorus's susceptibility to guidance by the principals, and its lack of resolution on most issues?" After initially criticizing Agamemnon's policy of war, the old men identify themselves with his purpose, and positively acclaim his generalship after his death. Similarly, in spite of certain reservations prompted by the masculine bias in which all male choruses share, they respect and honor the Queen. The chorus, in its role as a thinking and cooperating personality, may suspect and fear the worst; but the choral tradition requires that, far from fully voicing or acting on their suspicions, they should largely disregard them.

Irresolution, uncertainty, resignation: this is the other side of the coin to the positive virtues of the "people's" psychology. Songs of triumph are unsettled with reminders of the precariousness of life and of man's inability to escape death. The association of memento mori with the feeling of joy and pride is an old lyric heritage. In tragedy it comes to be vindicated as the people's voice. The most extreme and also the most effective dramatization of choral uncertainty is choral fear. Aeschylus is the great creator of the drama of fear, and the chorus is the carrier of it.[10] Aristotle's formulation of the function of drama as involving the provoking of pity and fear goes back, in major part, to the situations fashioned by Aeschylus, though the philosopher's quasi-intellectual *phobos* is not quite the same thing as the sheer terror produced on the Aeschylean stage. Even in Aeschylus, the fear may range from small trepidation to an obsession with danger, from a circumspect realism to the unleashing of demons on the stage. In *Libation-Bearers*, the chorus, in spite of its desire for vengeance, is keenly sensitive to the unfriendliness of the environment. At 264 ff., it warns the principals to lower their voices so as to avoid being heard and denounced. This kind of realism is abortive—no such overhearing takes place, or is expected to take place, in tragedy, except in so experimental a play as Sophocles's *Philoctetes*—but it is all the more striking for it. Aeschylus here wants to raise certain spectres, to bear down on the danger. Orestes, the divine agent, and Electra, with eyes only for her cause, are too committed to serve as appraisers of circumstance. The chorus, ordinary women who know what life holds in store, will do.

But usually the choral expression of fear is not so controlled. In Sophocles, choral timidity interferes with a full development of choral fear. In Aeschylus, where restraint and moderation are more often talked about than realized, fear is given free range. It has been said that choral fear is

---

10. B. Snell, *Aischylos und das Handeln im Drama* (*Philologus Suppl.* 20.1; Leipzig, 1928), pp. 45–51. Also J. de Romilly, *La crainte et l'angoisse dans le théâtre d'Éschyle* (Paris, 1958).

related to the very heart of the tragic experience, which finds expression in the cry: "What am I to do?" The difficulty with this is that choral fear is often most fully registered when no such question about action is at stake; and, as we shall see later, the question "What am I to do?" is relatively rare in Aeschylus in any case. Aeschylean tragedy furnishes rather few occasions for a choice of action or for contemplation of the future. Fear, especially choral fear, is incited by the contemplation of the present, of the inevitability of suffering and pain. What rings out from the great choral utterances of fear is not a only limited preoccupation with imminent ills but horror in the presence of inexplicable injustice. Unlike Sophocles, in whose plays fear can be plotted and explained in its relation to an orderly world, and Euripides, who turns fear into a matter for argument and pathos, Aeschylus enfranchises fear as an autonomous, primary fact of the tragic world.

A conventional representation of choral terror occurs in *Pers.* 215 ff. The chorus prays to the gods to avert trouble and to grant good. They also turn to Darius with the same request. Human weakness, the chorus implies, is such that we must put our trust in higher (and lower) powers. To gather from this that the chorus expects the gods to produce a changed outcome for it at some future time would, I think, be a mistaken interpretation. Rather, the prayer is founded on an insight into the incorruptibility of the evil that is already present. Prayer flows from fear not in the hope that its causes will be removed, but as a psychological correlate. As the deputy of common humanity, the chorus has the proper function of underlining and acting out fear as a common human condition. The Furies remind us (*Eum.* 517 ff., 696 ff.) that without fear men would scarcely submit themselves to the regulations of law; a just existence is possible only upon a foundation of fear.

The third choral ode of *Agamemnon* (975–1034), on which we have already touched above, is a song of fear. In spite of textual uncertainties, we can understand the sequence of the thoughts which anticipate the message of terror to be delivered by Cassandra. Here is a paraphrase: "My song is sad, my thoughts are fearful. I have seen the return of the troops. Still, the dirge of the Fury wells up in my heart. I have a clear notion of what the future will bring; would that it were otherwise! It is all a matter of fullness; in health, luck, wealth, only self-restraint can avert disaster. Blood spilled cannot be restored; Asclepius was punished for attempting to restore a life. My heart, which has knowledge of what is to come, cannot empower speech to be clear." The final insistence on the disproportion between vision and speech is important. Clytemnestra hides the truth because she is conducting an intrigue; the chorus cannot come out with the full truth because it is too frightening to admit even to oneself. The elders say that they know what they fear, but that their tongue cannot or must not express it. We have already seen that their avowal of knowledge is to be taken with a grain of skepticism—or, better, that it should be defined by the usual limitations of the choral ken. The theme of inexpressibility has a dramatic advantage. It helps to produce a modicum of suspense, which converts terror into anticipation and assuages its rawness.

A choral song that dwells concretely on the causes of fear can be as affecting as a song that embodies the fear itself. But the acting out of terror has a dramatic power all its own. As the Theban women of *Seven*, by way of a hallucinatory anticipation, contemplate the conquest of the city by its Argive opponents, the strains are more frantic and the communication of terror is more direct. To maximize the force of the terror, Aeschylus is capable of creating special situations. In *Suppliants*, Danaus leaves his daughters (775) at the very moment when the Egyptians are about to arrive. At the time when the play was written, Aeschylus had three actors available to him; the withdrawal of the actor who plays Danaus cannot answer a technical need. The absence of their father and protector will leave the women isolated, and this immediately augments the urgency of their terror. In a similar move, the chorus of *Libation-Bearers* makes much of the singleness of Orestes as he faces his several opponents in the second half of that play. At first glance, the chorus of *Libation-Bearers* is less subject to fear than some of the other choruses. Their identification with Electra's hopes and their confidence in Apollo's support of Orestes's plan should take the sting out of fear. But their choral function requires that they engage in it, and the thought of Orestes's exposure to peril provides the necessary motive. In actual fact, of course, Orestes has help to fall back on, whereas his opponents are dramatically isolated from each other. The audience will recognize the choral stratagem for what it is. But the credibility of the chorus is not thereby affected, since the choral avowal of fear has the sanction of the tradition.

At *Pers.* 115–25, the fears of the chorus are said to be caused by the failure of messengers to appear, and by the chorus's worry about the host venturing on the high seas. Both allegations are easily refuted. We are not told that it has been an unduly long time since messengers have made their reports; and, militarily speaking, there is no reason why a Persian emperor, with seasoned fleets available to him, should not be able to manage transport across the water. Once again, the choral reasoning is a special, even specious, contrivance to give a semblance of plausibility to what otherwise might strike the audience as unreasonable terror. The terror is primary, the reasons averred are subsidiary. The royal elders are to worry, and Aeschylus helps them along with the necessary fuel, which no audience will subject to an unseasonable scrutiny.

Choral fear is not without an occasional admixture of prudential wisdom. In Sophocles and Euripides, it comes to be quite common for fearful choruses to speculate on ways of saving themselves from disaster. There are similar touches in Aeschylus, though the tendency is not nearly so strong as in his successors. We have already referred to the type of song in which a chorus wonders where in the world to flee. Likewise, it is not unusual for a chorus to respond to an announcement of disaster by first thinking about its own status in the changed circumstance. At *Pers.* 262–65, the chorus answers the messenger with the cry: "That we have lived so long to see this!" Elsewhere, as in *Prometheus*, the chorus worries about what is going to happen to it, only, in the end, to overcome its self-centeredness and go under courageously in support of the hero. And this is, in fact, more typical of the Aeschylean resolution. Aeschylus's choruses are by and large able to avoid the extremes of a concern with their own safety that later authors wrote into the choral parts. His choruses are afraid, and even terrorized, but they do not buy their salvation at the cost of their deference to the principals or their attention to the issues.

Let this suffice about choral fear, uncertainty, blindness, decency, and compassion: all in varying degree manifestations of the central choral stance, which is the chorus's in its capacity as the voice of the people and asserts itself in the face of strong characterizations pulling the chorus in other directions. The poet uses the central core at crucial junctures in the play to cool or invigorate the action, to refresh the moral climate, to create a foil to the actions and thoughts of the principals. A band of Furies interrupts its harsh pursuit of the prey to sound the solemn strains of Justice and Injustice; a host of refugee women, their faces set against marriage, take thought of what in their conduct might offend an authoritative sector of Olympus; a group of elder statesmen voice their terror in the face of a reality only dimly perceived. These are moments in the choral music which break the dramatic momentum and exhilarate the audience with the recognition that the chorus of the moment is, in its essence, the same as all tragic choruses.

I have reserved to the last a discussion of the *gnōmē*, the aphoristic wise saying sanctioned by the communal experience. A heavy dependence on such saws often highlights the moments when the chorus reverts to its exemplary standing. But the subject cannot be discussed without some attention also to the way in which maxims, as we shall call them, structure the speeches of the principals, who will be the topic of a later chapter. The maxim has been of particular interest to the present generation of scholar-critics because of the widespread concern with formulas and other impersonal or suprapersonal devices which help to organize and shape poetic speech. The study of encomiastic poetry, for instance, and especially of

Pindar, has gone a long way toward explaining form and intention almost exclusively in terms of conventional formulas—not so much verbal as conceptual units which in varying linguistic guise are felt to account for the creative design.[11] It is tempting to recognize, in the manner in which Aeschylus deploys the central personality of the chorus, analogies to the conventions traced in Pindar and other choral lyric poets. This is most easily done within the realm of maxims—the pithily expressed, easily recognized adages with which Aeschylus, probably more emphatically than his successors, laces the more impersonal stretches of his choral poetry.

Just before Agamemnon's murder and just after Cassandra's departure from the stage (1331 ff.), the chorus has a series of anapaests that introduce the last movement of the play.

> No man ever says "enough!" to the joys
> Of Doing Well. No one says "no!"
> And bars its way into heralded halls
> With the words "Don't enter here!"

For the last time in this play, as often before, the chorus proposes that good fortune has a tendency to grow beyond the point of decent enjoyment. As an instance of this truth, they point to Agamemnon, whose lot is about to change. If so, they conclude, what man can say he is safe? The structure of the passage is typical of the way maxims are handled in tragic choruses, especially in Sophocles. First comes a maxim, often complete with personification, as in this case; then the application to an individual or a house; and finally a general conclusion, which can be implicit rather than explicit. In the present case, the progress of the thought has a special subtlety: the application in the middle step exploits more than is furnished in the maxim. Agamemnon, the chorus suggests, will pay the penalty not only for his having exceeded the bounds of moderate well-being, but also for the crimes of earlier generations of his house. The deviation from the pattern lessens the mechanical quality of the application and provides richer fuel for the conclusion that follows. There is a similarity here with the dynamism of some of the more complex Homeric similes, in which the points of contact are more manifold than is implied in the formal terms of the comparison.

The maxims contained in these anapaests can be paralleled elsewhere. More important, at this point, is the fact that the passage follows one in which Cassandra voices similar thoughts. It so happens that Cassandra's formulations are more vivid, with metaphors from painting or drawing (1327 ff.):

11. See esp. E. L. Bundy, *Studia Pindarica* I and II (Berkeley and Los Angeles, 1962).

Man's fate is pitiful. If he fares well,
A shading-in might turn it; and if ill,
A wetted sponge will wipe the picture clean.

The imagery reduces the simple power of the aphorism. But it is worth noting that these wisdom sequences, with their depressingly pessimistic message, come at the end of one scene or appearance and at the beginning of another. It is a common feature of maxims that they are used to work a transition from one theme or unit to the next. Sometimes the transitions are terse. But Cassandra's language shows that they can be elaborate or even awkward, as if Aeschylus tried to conceal the routine nature of the thought under a mantle of pomp. This is especially true of the prefatory remarks of messengers and the first responses of their listeners.

The transitional nature of the maxim, or rather of the chain of maxims—they rarely come singly—carries with it two implications. For one thing, a traditional maxim must be general enough to fit in, however loosely, both with the preceding and with the following context. And, two, it would be a mistake to look for the enunciation of important truths, keys to the understanding of the whole work or parts of the work, in these sliding remarks. It is instructive to compare similar techniques in the speeches of political orators reported in Thucydides. Maxims are adduced when relevant because they reverberate with the ring of the familiar and thereby ease the burden of the understanding. But their intellectual contribution is minor; they are the accompaniment, not the tune. The role of the maxim, especially of the brief, highly abstract maxim, might be compared with the role of the epic epithet, the attribute habitually used with a particular subject in clearly defined slots of Homeric verse. In the matter of thematic or conceptual contribution, there is little to choose between "fleet-footed" Achilles or Hera "of the white elbow" and Aeschylus's "things are as they are; they are being completed to the point of their destiny," introducing a series of maxims squeezed between a brief report on the causes of the Trojan War and the chorus's revoicing of their own left-behind status (*Agam.* 67–71).[12] Both the Homeric epithet and the Aeschylean maxim furnish a verification of the ethos of the text, but little more.

It is worth emphasizing this because there has been a tendency to assign too much dramatic significance to some of the dominant maxims of Aeschylean drama. This has been the case particularly with the notorious maxim "learning [comes] through experience," a thought which occurs several times in *Agamemnon.*[13] At its first occurrence, the thought (176–78) that

12. But cf. A. Lebeck, *The Oresteia* (Cambridge, Mass., 1971), pp. 70–73, on *telos*, completion.

13. For "learning through experience", see M. Gagarin, *Aeschylean Drama* (Berkeley and Los Angeles), appendix A: *Pathei Mathos*.

"he who laid down that learning comes through experience was correct" appears to mean little more than that having things done to you prepares you for the future. Since Zeus is identified as the one who laid down the truth, the assurance here has relief value. Along with five additional lines of maxims, it enables the chorus to proceed from the narration of the Hesiodic succession of gods to the description of Agamemnon's quandary at Aulis, with the comforting suggestion that all hardships have some profit built into them. But to ask how the notion of the maxim can be made to apply to Agamemnon and, more specifically, how Agamemnon might avail himself of the lesson for his own guidance in the horrible dilemma at hand: such an insistence on the helpfulness and truth content of a maxim would run afoul of the very idea of what a maxim does.

This is further borne out by the next occurrence of the maxim (250–51). Once again, it is the first in a chain of maxims which are, as often, strung up side by side without obvious links between them. The generic looseness of the liaison here degenerates into extreme choppiness:

> Justice weights the scales for some, so they
> learn from experience. The future:
> You hear it when it comes. For now, let it go.

In the presence of thoughts like these, one is reminded of what Northrop Frye has said about Milton's use of the chorus in *Samson Agonistes*: "For most modern readers, I should think, Milton's creative imagination is always right and his justifying apparatus always wrong: the imagination is that of a poet who is for all time; the apparatus comes from seventeenth-century anxieties which . . . were as dead as mutton even before *Samson Agonistes* was written."[14] The ideas expressed in Aeschylus's justifying apparatus were probably not dead in his time. But neither can they be said to startle us with their vivacity.

What ought to be avoided, especially in the case of choral maxims, but generally with the lyric utterances of the chorus, is an interpretation that exaggerates their psychological appropriateness. This, it seems to me, is as mistaken as the view that they always represent Aeschylus's personal ideology. I have in mind language such as this, about "learning from experience": it "is no final pronouncement of Aeschylus on the particular case of Agamemnon's quandary . . . it is . . . the chorus desperately trying to retrieve the situation their song has created, to find the saving word, to discover the purpose of heaven discernible in this dark story and turn their reading of it somehow to good omen."[15] The give-away here is the word "desperately." It works on the assumption that the choral contribution can

14. N. Frye, *Spiritus Mundi* (Bloomington, Ind., 1976), pp. 224–25.
15. E. T. Owen, *The Harmony of Aeschylus* (Toronto, 1952), p. 68.

be measured by the standard of a consistent and fragile personal interest. As a rule, and especially in the segments of *Agamemnon* where choral maxims run strong, the special character of the chorus is swallowed up by a larger-than-individual role, a tribal presence which leaves vulnerabilities far behind and counterpoints the ambitions and the weaknesses of the principals. The choral maxim confirms the continuing strength of the life of the group; it does not mark the fleeting stages of a mental struggle. Its intellectual content is often uninteresting, especially to our jaded taste. But without it the choral position, and the play, would lack an edge of toughness which the reminders of the communal experience contribute.

By the same token, it will not do to regard the network of maxims used in a play as structurally and semantically analogous to that of the imagery. In fact, there is no network of maxims, only a series of general reflections, some more immediately relevant than others, some more closely tied in with one another than others, but all of them arising directly out of a body of popular and prudential wisdom. The imagery of an Aeschylean play is creative; it answers to poetic demands that are more or less unique to the play. Choral maxims have a way of asserting themselves almost at random, certainly without the specific purposefulness and the calculated patterning that moderns expect in a poetic design. On that score, Aeschylean maxims are not too different in kind from the practice of Seneca, where whole sequences of dialogue are formed by concatenations of maxims and the speakers' dramatic profiles and the movement of the dramatic action are blocked out by the tattoo of chains of adages.[16] The difference is, of course, that in Seneca the maxims turn into attention-seeking casuistry; that they are in the mouths of the principals as much as, or perhaps even more than, a function of the chorus; and that their neutralization of dramatic tension is a major ingredient in Seneca's design. In Aeschylus, the confinement of larger chains of maxims to choral delivery leaves the action relatively untouched, though it is not always possible to distinguish between a choral utterance that stands aloof from the action and one that aids it.

After Aeschylus, especially in Euripides, who prepares the Senecan practice, general reflection begins to gravitate to dialogue and speech, away from the musical anchoring in which the older generation preferred to safeguard it. The usage of Renaissance English drama, deprived of the musical advantages of Greek tragedy, occasionally suggests that there is something embarrassing about maxims pronounced by the principals. In Webster's *The White Devil*, for instance, the villain Flamineo is at his most exasperating when he feigns madness and spouts maxim after maxim, as if sane men

---

16. B. Seidensticker, *Die Gesprächsverdichtung in den Tragödien Senecas* (*Bibliothek d. klass. Altertumsw.* 32; Heidelberg, 1970), pp. 180 ff.

could be expected to listen patiently to maxims only out of the mouths of fools. And indeed it is Shakespeare's fools—themselves, if not mad, at least ill-attuned to the appetites of princes and ordinary men—who continue the Aeschylean choral tradition. The conversation of the fool has an edge to it; it owes much to the riddling sharpness of British folk humor. But the difficulty that so many modern theatergoers have with the fool's language is as much a function of its intellectual and ethical flatness as it is of its verbal indirection. And that flatness is a relative, if not a successor, to the flatness of the Aeschylean choral commonplace. A fifth-century B.C. audience would not have attempted to ferret out points of contact between the fool's cautionary adages and Lear's passion. On the contrary, they would have relished the incongruity between the two, and the certainty that in the ultimate scheme of things the noble ambitions of the king would be shipwrecked and the painful wisdom of the fool proved true.

The fool's sayings have a barbed sharpness because they are playful modifications of larger insights, but even more because they are addressed to the principal. Aeschylus's choral maxims move only a short distance from the broadest formulation of what they are about; what is more, they are not addressed to anyone, but voiced, sung, turned in upon themselves without dramatic aggressive intent. The same lack of dramatic momentum can be observed in those maxims which Aeschylus puts in the mouths of speaking characters rather than the chorus. At first blush, it looks as if the plays of which only fragments have reached us contained more dialogue use of maxims than the ones we have. But that impression is deceptive. It so happens that the scholars and collectors of later antiquity who gathered together bits and pieces from Aeschylean drama were often especially interested in pithy statements that could be reused in other contexts—once again, note the separability of the maxim. John Stobaeus of the fifth century A.D., to whose collecting zeal we owe a great many of the fragments we have, supplies very little but one-line commonplaces. Many of them were presumably spoken by the chorus leader, but others must have been pronounced by characters, especially, once again, near the beginning or the end of a speech, or at the point in a speech or dialogue where the topic was changing direction. From the extant plays, we know that the characters who make these pronouncements are not necessarily nurses or watchmen or other representatives of the people. Here is Athena at *Eum.* 694–95: "If you mix clear water with mud, you will not get a good drink." In this instance, the formulation comes closer to the folk wit of the fool; the light touch is in tune with the special quality of the play. As in the case of choral maxims, we should note the "provisionality," the low semantic force of the speaker's commonplace. At the end of the remarks with which he displays to the citizens of Argos the two corpses of his enemies and the net with which Clytemnestra had immobilized Agamemnon, Orestes adds (*Lib*. 1005 – 6): "I hope I'll never have such a partner in my home; I'd rather die first, childless, undone by the gods." These lines have worried some critics greatly, and they have proposed to eliminate them on the grounds that they do not match Orestes's character. About that character we shall have more to say in a later chapter. Here it should suffice to say that the lines are not designed as a summation or conclusion of the speech or as a quintessential statement permitting an insight into the speaker's motivation. They are useful precisely because they veer away from the ethos of the speech and move us, by way of a transitional mechanism, back to the fund of popular wisdom where everything is anchored. The sliding maxim is serviceable because it is a disengaged utterance.

I would not want to leave the impression that maxims cannot be used differently. As the Empress Mother (*Pers*. 598 – 602) returns from her prayers with gifts for the nether gods, she begins her speech with a general comment on the psychological effects of adversity and good fortune. This is by way of introducing a speech about her fears. No such preface had preceded her earlier communication of her fears (161 ff.). There are two good reasons for the use of the preamble here. For one, the present announcement of fears is to have greater weight than the earlier one; the maxims serve to supply that weight. And second, now that the worst is known, there is more need for the comfort that "choral" wisdom can bring. The ancient tragedian is particularly given to marking these initial emphases. Because there is no pressure to assimilate the curve of the action to the time units of quotidian experience, more attention can be given to setting off the major blocks of development and analysis. As characters attempt to pacify the gods or avert the evil eye from what they are about to say; as they ready themselves to persuade their opponents or, indirectly, to swing the audience behind them, and perhaps heighten the suspense, initial underscoring becomes attractive, and the most obvious marking device is the sounding of a more or less relevant maxim, a move which also enables the playwright for a brief moment to touch base at the store whence the energies of the public performance flow. Relying on a maxim is refuelling at the source. It is the chorus which most persuasively conveys the values and the power of that source, of the near-anonymous life-preserving spirit which sustains civic life while heroes come and go. And it is Aeschylus who, more beautifully than any playwright since, knew how to give to that spirit a poetry and a drama of its own.

Mme de Staël once complained about the chorus in Schiller's *Die Braut von Messina*: "The chorus of that play is, unfortunately, only a chorus of chamberlains. A true chorus consists of all the people; they alone can be impartial spectators. The chorus must represent posterity. If it is animated by personal affections, it becomes ridiculous; for it is hard to conceive how several persons can, at one and the same time, say the same thing, unless their voices are understood to communicate eternal verities."[17] There is much in this statement with which we may want to quarrel: the criteria from ordinary experience, the appeal to posterity, and the echoing of Schlegel's ideal spectator. But she understands the truth that Greek tragic poetry, and that is especially true of Aeschylus's tragedy, is public in the broadest sense of the term, and that the chorus must be the authenticating agent of this openness. As Georg Lukács said, in reaction to Strindberg's preface to *Miss Julie* and its call for an intimate theater: "A theater cannot strive for victory over the perceptions of the primitive mass without destroying itself."[18] Unlike what the modern term "lyric" suggests, the lyric contribution of the Aeschylean chorus is to remind us of those "mass perceptions." Its reflections on common truths are not private, or "overheard," but declaratory pronouncements solemnized via song. That this need not be undramatic but can, on the contrary, help to create the drama should be clear from the choral passage which is as good as any with which to terminate this chapter. It is a passage which we have cited before, the picture of war and the fallen city at *Seven* 345–68. The mode of the dyad is descriptive, not ruminative or expressive of popular truths. The accent is on vivid visual and auditory perceptions, on the active, though near-mechanical, cruelty of man to man, and the special suffering of the women. What matters is the absence of names and of particularizing data. The mechanization of human conduct reduces it to a level where motivation and circumstance turn irrelevant, and only what is always unchangingly true is retained. In this case, the theme of the desolation of the city and the terror communicated by the chorus are directly relevant to the topic of the play and help to shape the narrower dramatic frame within which Eteocles, the hero, moves. In that respect, they cannot be compared to the enunciation of prudential wisdom, of which there is, in any case, rather little in *Seven Against Thebes*. But like the maxims and series of maxims which are so prominent in some of the plays and occur in all of them, the vision of the conquest of the city recalls to our minds the predictable patterns of life to which all men are exposed, whose inevitability heroes like Eteocles are prone to forget. The music may mute the terror or sweeten the message. But without the chorus, the principals would be paper dolls, flexing their muscles and testing their strengths in a world without substance.

17. *D'Allemagne* (1813), vol. 1 (Paris, 1968), p. 311.
18. G. Lukács, *Schriften zur Literatursoziologie*[2], ed. P. Ludz (Neuwied, 1961), p. 274, apropos of Strindberg's intimate theater.

# — 7 —

# Communication

Homer is our first conversationalist. The epic has as one of its glories the mutual testing and probing between opponents on the battlefield prior to armed engagement or after its conclusion. It also has the more intimate exchanges, less firmly shaped by the conventions of the genre, in which heroes and heroines voice their fears or comment on one another's accomplishments or weaknesses. In book 6 of the *Iliad*, Hector and Paris have two conversations (325 ff. and 517 ff.) which quickly establish for us the very special feelings by which the brothers are linked: impatience and affection on the side of Hector, respectfulness and gaiety on the side of Paris. Epic conversations are organized as successive speeches rather than interlocking speech. But in spite of this formal quality, epic communication forges a close bond between the speakers. In the face of the heroic conventions and the artificialities of the paratactic mode of composition, the men and women of the *Iliad* and the *Odyssey* are conceived as complex fictional characters. The length of the poems permits a full exploration of what they have to offer. Because the listener comes to live with the desires and fears of Achilles and Agamemnon and Odysseus and Nausicaa, the exchanges between them build upon one another toward a cumulative comprehension of their weaknesses and their strengths. We learn to appreciate a battle of wits, a scene of seduction, or an exchange between comrades in arms. The epic medium, formulas and all, is sufficiently flexible to secure from us a sense of complicity. We share in the expectations of the characters as they move toward and away from each other, and predict how they will respond.

The drama, especially Aeschylean drama, will not do this for us. Its compass is too brief to develop a familiarity or a sharing of feelings. Stage presentation, with its masks and its other obstacles to the audience identification achieved in narrative fiction, imposes a heavy burden. The kind of communication between characters that drama offers is more appropriately anticipated in the lyric, and especially in the choral lyric fashioned by Alcman and brought to perfection in the choruses of Pindar and Bacchylides. Alcman's *Maiden Songs* were written for two half-choruses answering one another in responding stanzas and pitting two rival leaders against each other in playful combat. The singing projects the intimate relationships between young women who have grown up together. But they, and the rival leaders of the choruses, are not only, like the heroes of epic, personal friends and enemies; they are also mimetic performers. They sing and they dance; communication between them is couched in the severe restraint of stanzaic responsion. The scope of personal feelings is broadened and reshaped by the choral voice. Tribal wisdom and civic experience blunt the particularity of the discourse. The voices of the leaders—women acted by women in the *Maiden Songs*—merge with the voices of the choruses. Intimacy, humor, and aggressive banter come through as they do in the epic, but they are carved from a medium that is much more resistant to them, and which continually presses for a greater generality and a muting of the personal engagement. The choruses of the *Maiden Song* transform conversation into contest and communication into formal exchange.

Something very much like this must be looked for in the dramatic performances that preceded the coming of Thespis, according to Aristotle's reconstruction of the early history of drama, before the first and second "actors" came to be separated from the choral ensemble. But the analogy can be extended further. Aeschylus's characters do not engage in conversation. Scribe and Shaw, with their imitation of the inflections of distinct personalities and everyday speech, are at the furthest remove from the uninflected, echoless exchanges of Aeschylean drama. One might say that the speakers of *Agamemnon* or *Persians* do not listen to one another, but wait patiently until it is their turn to speak; and when they speak their speech continues, or varies, or interprets what has been said by others, but a listener would look in vain for any signs of true responsiveness. Aeschylean speech is self-absorbed, isolated, marked off from what precedes and what follows by a gulf of silence. Interruptions, continuations, the meshings of natural conversation are the discoveries of a later drama. Each Aeschylean speech act is, as it were, enveloped in silence; the speaker is alone with his impulse toward communication. Communication is expression contained within the limits of its own self-sufficiency.[1]

*Agamemnon* is our best evidence for the constant weight of potential silence upon the junctures of tragic speech. In that play, the norm of isolation is experienced as a special horror. The soldier is a hawk; man is enveloped in blasts of wind; the Iphigenia of the choral song cannot speak out; the prophet speaks to all, and to no one; Cassandra converses only with gods. Agamemnon himself is a has-been; he has left his soul in Troy, and his speech in Argos is painfully turned in upon itself. Clytemnestra is the only one whose speech scores points off the wills of her fellow *personae*. But she, too, and perhaps even more than the others, listens only to herself; her

---

1. The best book on communication in ancient tragedy is still W. Schadewaldt's *Monolog und Selbstgespräch* (Berlin, 1926).

several victories are won without the attunement to sharing that conversation calls for. Like her person, her speech is larger than life-size; at its boundaries, it emerges from, and lapses back into, silence.

The vast space surrounding Prometheus cushions him in silence. He refuses to Ocean and to Hermes the rights and privileges of natural communication. His own speech is produced almost in defiance of his knowledge that it will come to naught and dissipate itself in callous space. Xerxes hurls his complaints to an answering but unresponsive chorus; Eteocles speaks, but there is no meeting of minds, and when we would expect to witness a drawing together of the purposes of Eteocles and the chorus, Eteocles falls silent, as if to ward off the debilitation that would accrue from the process of two parties bridging the gulf between them. It is remarkable to watch how the most magnificent language, the most absorbing phrases, are uttered in the spirit of an understanding that words are regressive, insular manifestations of intelligences that rarely reach or influence each other. Aeschylus's language is rightly admired. But the effect of the language is upon the listeners; the continuities between the consecutive speech acts are definable rhetorically. With respect to the linking of the *dramatis personae* in the bonds of a shared experience, continuity is the exception. Each speech act, whether it be a sustained oration or a line of rapid-fire exchange, is bounded by withdrawal.

Silence, sometimes, is better than speech. Aeschylus says this in a Prometheus play of which we have fragments:

> For many people silence is a boon.[2]

This may at first surprise in an art which prizes the grand articulation, the full-throated song. A distinction needs to be made between the silence we have been discussing, the silence that fills the interstices of speech, and a silence that replaces speech and appeals to the audience with the dramatic power of speechlessness. A chorus cannot be silent; in spite of an occasional admission of helplessness or awe it is the function of the chorus to communicate with the audience via speech and song. A cancellation of this function would bring the play to a stop. But a character can be made to withhold an expected contribution and thereby give added meaning to the drama. The famous silent figures in Aeschylus are Niobe and Achilles in two lost tragedies; Prometheus as he is being hammered to the rock; the Empress Mother during the exchange between chorus and messenger; and Cassandra as Clytemnestra tries to draw her out. There are, of course, many other speakers who remain silent for a while, and supernumeraries who have only

2. Fr. 103 Smyth.

two or three lines, if any. But here I am referring to those few characters who are silent at a point where they might, or in fact should, give voice.[3] It is up to the playwright to make certain that the audience understands this. Usually the other characters comment on the silence. This is the reason why Clytemnestra cannot be included among the ranks of the silent. Though there are certain points in *Agamemnon* where a modern, and perhaps an ancient, audience might have expected her to speak, nobody in the play voices this expectation or a regret at her failure to speak. It will be remembered that my conception of her stage movements (see above, chapter 3) is such that her seeming reticence turns out to be explained by her absence from the stage. The muteness of the Empress Mother while the messenger and the chorus have their exhaustive encounter, on the other hand, might be explained as a case of archaic concentration: the audience must not be distracted from attending to one polarity at a time. But it can also be understood as a deliberate exercise in reticence. The Empress herself explains her lack of speech (290–92):

> I have long been silent: suffering, and crushed
> By a misfortune so excessive that
> It clips the wings of questions and of speech.

This is a particularly instructive example. The Empress Mother never sings; she leaves the stage before the arrival of Xerxes, so she will not be a participant in the final lyric exchange. Aeschylus has designed her to play the part of a high-minded, self-controlled lady; participation in a dirge might have the effect of thwarting that impression. Her failure to be involved in the earlier exchange between messenger and chorus should pass unnoticed. Nevertheless, Aeschylus inserts his motivation for what is thereby tagged a deliberate silence.

The Empress's silence is one of grief, hence secondary, not essentially determined by character. Elsewhere also, as in the silences of Niobe and Cassandra, grief may be said to play a role. But now the silence is primary, it speaks to the conception of the figure. As Cassandra refuses to respond to the appeals made to her by a person she loathes, silence comes into its own as a heroic gesture, as the most graphic symbol of the isolation which is her lot. And as such it is merely a concentrated exhibition of the silence and the isolation which attend the speech of every Aeschylean character. Another dramatist whose speakers stand in splendid isolation and whose speech disregards the familiar cadences of human communication is Seneca. The Senecan *tirade* marks a degree of self-absorption which is natural in the Stoic

3. O. Taplin, "Aeschylean Silences and Silences in Aeschylus," *Harvard Studies in Classical Philology* 76 (1972): 57–97.

villain-saint jealously aloof in a frightening universe. Aeschylean insularity has very little in common with Senecan narcissism. When the Senecan Atreus or Hercules wraps himself in the protective shroud of his rhetoric, the aim is defensive, and the effect is pathos. Curiously, notwithstanding the self-conscious contrivance of the rhetoric, what emerges is an impression of vulnerability, of unsatisfied hunger and the weaknesses of the flesh. Aeschylean rhetoric carries no trace of such debility. Its strength derives from its lack of philosophy. Human want or cosmic precariousness are far from its concerns. The solitude of the Aeschylean speaker is, on the contrary, a token of his power. As a lyric voice, proclaiming, confessing, or merely informing, he is sufficient unto himself. The appeal is universal rather than clinical.

Silence, both at the confines of speech and as a substitute for speech, is a very Aeschylean thing. Aristophanes was so greatly impressed with Aeschylus's silences that he had his Euripides mock them as one of the old playwright's more bizarre features. On the modern stage, beginning with Chekhov and finding its extreme realization in the plays of Beckett, silence has once again turned into an instrument of great dramatic power. Chekhov's silences start out as self-absorption, as pregnant moments of lyric solitude; in this respect they have something in common with their Aeschylean analogue. But in Chekhov and his imitators, they move toward cross-talk, and end up as positive testimony to men's inability to commune with one another or even with themselves, a point which in Beckett and Handke and others is exploited with a fierceness that leaves drama as spoken discourse in the limbo of exhausted genres. Aeschylean drama is, indeed, nothing if not spoken discourse. Silence is not an existential obsession, but a tool, used rarely, and at a climactic juncture, to underscore the isolation of a hero. For the rest it is the ever-present but scarcely impinging matrix from which each speech act detaches itself as if it were a monologue but consented to play its part in the necessary interaction of the dramatis personae. In this latter capacity, silence is a potential, an amplifier, not a human condition or a penance.

Aeschylus has few monologues proper: the address of Prometheus to the gods and elements (*Prom.* 88 ff.); the watchman's speech (*Agam.* 1 ff.); Cassandra's vision (*Agam.* 1214 ff.); and two or three others. These monologues may be uttered on an empty stage—Prometheus, the watchman— or in the presence of the chorus or even of other characters. What they have in common is their total disengagement, their express advertisement that the speech has no addressee within the setting of the dramatic stage. It is a communication for which addressees or witnesses have to be created in the very act of speaking. For, in spite of the disengagement, the feeling of loneliness on the part of the speaker, a statement that is not formally directed at a recipient is unthinkable. The alternative is no speech at all, which is at that point considered unendurable or ill-advised. The manufactured addressee is either a god or, what amounts to the same thing, a relevant segment of the larger world—Night, or the Sun, or one of the social forces—Strife or Persuasion or Delusion—whom Hesiod bequeathed to literature. Critics have spoken of vertical relationships, and have said that Aeschylean characters often prefer them to horizontal links—that their nexus is with deities rather than with other men.[4] As long as this is recognized to be a statement about the directedness of speech, it is acceptable, but it would be hazardous to claim that the major Aeschylean characters engage themselves in any meaningful commitment to the gods.

In spite of its formal directedness, invented or given by the setting, most Aeschylean speech is like monologue. It is pronounced in the absence of, and often without an express interest in, the certainty that it will find a firm recipient. It is not that speeches are aimed so as to miss the mark. Rather, speech is rhetoric, and rhetoric, in spite of what Aristotle says about the various possible addressees, is essentially thoughts formulated with maximum attention to the aptness of the vocalizing. The Aeschylean theater, with its roots in choral lyric and ritual utterance, favors this dimension. It throws the weight of the utterance back upon the speaker and isolates him from the range of potential addressees. The insistence upon the addressee in the formal monologue is, in fact, proof of our contention that formal directedness and pronounced isolation can go hand in hand. Many other speeches begin with an isolating proem, an exclamation (*Seven* 597 ff.), or an adage (*Agam.* 636 ff.), which veers the utterance away from the nearest possible addressee. This does not necessarily mean, and usually does not mean, that we obtain greater insight into the soul of the speaker. Isolation and self-absorption is not the same thing as self-revelation or self-analysis. Monologue is not soliloquy.

It is remarkable how often characters enter and begin to speak without overtly addressing anyone on the stage. The practice varies from play to play. *Agamemnon* is more extreme in this regard, as it is in so many others. But by comparison with the social niceties of the entrance speeches in Sophocles and Euripides, Aeschylus's are generally less recognitional, if I may use this term to refer to utterances that indicate an awareness of an addressee. Because of this, it is more difficult for Aeschylus, if he has any such ambition, to characterize certain speeches as more outwardly directed than others. A proper study of this subject requires the raising of many questions. We need to distinguish between speech and lyrics, between brief and

4. Schadewaldt, *Monolog und Selbstgespräch*, pp. 53, 62–64.

long utterances, between messenger reports and reportings that are less radically set off from the context, between statements and complaints, between two-sided and three-sided dialogue. Most important, perhaps: how often within one scene (i.e., a sequence in which the same characters are on stage) do we expect specific addresses to be renewed? But even with all the answers to these questions in, it is not easy to appreciate the special quality of Aeschylean practice.

One straw in the wind is Aeschylus's penchant for "generic" forms of address, abstract or impersonal formulas which blunt the sharpness of a direct communication. "Blood," "seed," "race," "head," "eye," "force," "protection," "benefit," and others are Aeschylean locutions for the purpose of salutation.[5] Each of these is usually coupled with an adjective or a genitive to make the specific reference fully apparent. "But you, fraternal blood of a common father" (*Eum.* 89) and "O dearest vigilance of our father's house" (*Lib.* 235) have about them something of the kenning or riddle, though the reference is in each case unmistakable. They show a minor disinclination to focus speech on a recipient. This same disinclination emerges most strikingly in the comparative statistics concerning the presence or absence of any form of address. In the *Iliad*, 4.5 percent of all verses are expressly addressed to a particular person or persons; for the *Odyssey* the figure is 5 percent, for Sophocles 6.1 percent, for Euripides 6 percent, for Aristophanes also 6 percent, and for Aeschylus 2.25 percent. Such figures can be misleading, but the radical difference of the figure for Aeschylus requires an explanation. In the other playwrights, and to a certain extent also in the epic, the personal address is a matter of routine courtesy, a necessary artistic consequence of the understanding that speech is a social tool, a means of realizing a nexus with a worthy (or occasionally, especially in the *Odyssey*, an unworthy) partner. In Aeschylus, addresses are subject to a nicer discrimination. They come into use only when there is to be an emphasis on the closeness or the exceptional nature of the relationship. Add to this that both in addresses giving the name of the person and in addresses using generic periphrases, Aeschylus often extends the allocution until it stretches over two, three, or even four lines, a bulk far in excess of what is found in the earlier poets or the later dramatists. It is as if Aeschylus wanted to compensate for the comparative rarity of his addresses by enhancing the weight and the ceremoniousness of the ones he has. By the same token, as the address increases in bulk, the sharpness of its focus is diminished.

It has often struck readers that the messenger who brings the news of the defeat at *Pers.* 249 ff. greets the citadel, the land, and the Persian people but

5. T. Wendel, *Die Gesprächsanrede im griechischen Epos und Drama der Blütezeit* (Stuttgart, 1929). For relevant remarks about Aeschylean addresses, see also D. Bain, *Actors and Audience* (Oxford, 1977).

*not* the Empress Mother to whom his report will be delivered. Likewise in *Agamemnon*, the herald who confirms the capture of Troy does not greet Clytemnestra (which may, of course, be explained by the supposition that the Queen is not yet on the stage) or the chorus, but salutes the earth, the house, and the gods. This is sometimes excused on the grounds of tactfulness: the messenger, full of the horror, or the significance, of what he is about to say, avoids a direct appeal to the persons who will be most immediately affected by the news. Instead he establishes or reestablishes contact with the forces that had of old conditioned his life in the city. I have no quarrel with this. But quite apart from any personal motive or scruple on the part of the messenger, the lack of precise focus once more exemplifies a more general tendency on the part of Aeschylean speech.

We shall return to messenger speeches in a moment. Before we leave the subject of addresses, a few words about Clytemnestra. I am particularly concerned with the great speech that begins at 855, and which is initially addressed to the chorus,

> Reverence of Argos, honored citizens!

The speech dwells on her sufferings, and on her virtuousness during the long absence of Agamemnon. The exaggerations of the apologia continue the hyperboles launched earlier at 606 ff., but now in the presence of her husband. The address to the chorus and the references to Agamemnon in the third person—"this man" (867)—are in their own way appropriate. They avoid an immediate confrontation and stipulate a dependence on the chorus as a fellow complainant. But this must not be stressed. In the absence of a routine art of allocution, deviations are hard to pin down. By 878, however, Clytemnestra has apparently turned to face her husband, for now, in reporting on the absence of Orestes and on her grief, she uses the second person singular pronoun. Some fifteen lines later, as she plunges into her "low-crooked curt'sies and base spaniel-fawning" designed to undo Agamemnon's discipline, she is once more addressing the chorus, as is apparent from the fact that her references to Agamemnon are in the third person. Only at the end, with her invitation to step off the vehicle (905), does Clytemnestra again turn directly to the king, saluting him with the untranslatable phrase *philon kara*, one of Aeschylus's innovations and a typically impersonal expression, literally: "Our own head," but without the headman or headship connotation of that word. Freely translated, the phrase means something like "Member of the family" or even "Now that you have returned." She also calls him "Lord," a term that is ordinarily used only by the chorus, but not by social equals.

The specific addresses, then, are to the chorus at the beginning of the speech, and to Agamemnon at the end before Clytemnestra turns to the maids to bid them hurry up with their preparations. The first is a deflecting maneuver; the second is harnessed to deception. In the course of the speech, we can follow the restless inflexions of Clytemnestra's scheming mind. The overriding impression that remains is that, though speaking now in this direction and now in that, Clytemnestra refuses to rest her attention fully on anyone. This remains true even after she has committed the murder. Standing over Agamemnon's body and telling all (1372 ff.), she employs no addressing formula whatsoever, though the clear implication is that she is speaking to the chorus, and through them, or over their heads, to the audience. My point in all this is not so much that Clytemnestra's speech habits are remarkable, but, on the contrary, that they are merely an unusually impressive illustration of Aeschylus's normal practice. Speech is a voicing rather than a sharing, an act of indulgence rather than an attempt to reach another being. And allocutions are for the purpose of dramatic articulation. Far from registering a genuine desire for communication, they are, as it were, a reluctant acknowledgment of the need for speech to come to rest somewhere after completing its trajectory through the vast space separating speaker from speaker.

If there is communication, as we have said before, it is often with the audience, to furnish needed information. In that case, of course, it is as much the playwright, in his capacity as a shaper of the plot, as it is the character or the chorus that does the communicating. In the first scene of Racine's *Andromaque*, Oreste favors Pylade with a long exposition of antecedents. The list of particulars, and its matter-of-fact production, are perhaps less barefaced than a Euripidean prologue or its Shakespearean descendant, the introductory conversation. But the audience accepts all of them in the same spirit of accommodation, without boggling at the thin veneer of dramatic manipulation pasted upon the Racinian speech. Aeschylus has nothing quite so breathless and conventional as these initial crammings, principally because less knowledge of particulars is needed to understand what an Aeschylean play is about. The spoken prologues found in five of the seven plays (all but *Persians* and *Suppliants*) are, on the whole, minimally informative, with the exception of *Eumenides*, which assembles a string of details concerning divine establishments. The prologue of *Eumenides* is spoken by a priestess, who instructs an audience of Greeks gathered for a festival—and that means an audience identifiably like the one watching the play. This brings us very close to the special perspective of comedy. The recipient for which the historical information is designed is for once almost explicitly acknowledged.

It may come as a surprise that the baldest delivery of information should be found in the anapaestic and lyric entrances of the chorus in *Persians* and *Suppliants*. On second thought, it makes some sense that the formal entry of the chorus lends itself more easily to the unadorned or unweighted recital of antecedents than the entrance speeches of characters who are going to be involved in the action of the play. It has been said that "Aeschylus, unlike Euripides, seems to have tried in various ways to integrate his prologues"— and this includes the choral entrances—"in the dramatic structure of his plays."[6] This is claiming too much, though *Seven* and *Prometheus*, with their introductory dialogue, go rather further in this respect than the other plays. The Euripidean method of information-giving, at any rate, is not entirely eschewed by Aeschylus. It is common enough for an Aeschylean character—whether in the prologue or not, and, in fact, more prominently in the course of the play—to give information about himself as he enters, and before he turns to face another character. In *Eumenides*, Athena enters (397) eleven lines before she addresses the Furies. In the meantime, she discourses on the reasons for her coming, her port of embarkation, and her mode of transport, all of which conspire to identify her for us and to document her qualifications for the issue at hand. The postponement of the point at which she acknowledges the presence of others is more emphatic than elsewhere, but not uncharacteristic. The autonomy of speech and the need for information take precedence over the social amenities.

Where the information concerns events that happened in the (near or distant) past, and in a locale not included in the play area, we have the messenger speech. The messenger is, as far as his message is concerned, omniscient. He is the equivalent of the epic bard who narrates the past with only ceremonial admissions of ignorance. When the drama is a rehearsal of imperfect knowledge or of blindness, the messenger introduces the knowledge that liberates or kills, because it concerns events too violent to be comprehended within the visible scheme. Only once in the extant corpus does Aeschylus give us a report of events happening off stage but simultaneous with the action on stage. This is Danaus's account, from his perch at the altar on the platform, of the approach of the Egyptian ships (*Suppl.* 711 ff.), a parallel of the speech of the housekeeper who at the end of *Rosmersholm* reports, from her place at the window, the double suicide of Rosmer and Rebekka as it is happening. Ibsen's version is the more dramatic, with the housekeeper beginning unsuspectingly and giving way to growing horror as the meaning of what she sees dawns upon her. Danaus's report shows no such approximation to the feelings of an informant who imparts his information as he receives it and responds to it as the addressee might. He proceeds as if he has absorbed his data at one fell swoop, warning the women not to be frightened by what he has to tell them. His message is, therefore, structured much like a report of events that have taken place in

---

6. A. F. Garvie, *Aeschylus' Supplices* (Cambridge, 1969), p. 123.

the past and are accessible to hindsight as a unit, but which need to be strung out once again in order to produce the horror they would have awakened in an onlooker.

All three tragedians follow a set procedure in their presentation of messenger speeches.[7] The messenger arrives, usually introduced by the chorus. There is a preliminary exchange, with the recipient of the message asking "why" and "how" and "what" and inquiring about the source of the intelligence. This both prepares and delays the full announcement, rendering it climactic when it comes, and increasing the thrill of the comprehension. New information is always received reluctantly, the presumption being that it will not be good news. Sophocles, especially, structures his messenger scenes with consummate attention to the delaying tactics. Aeschylus uses the basic scheme, with some variations. Danaus, if we can call him a messenger, requires no introduction, and his exchange with the chorus is preceded rather than followed by the body of the message. The same variation is found in *Seven* (792 ff.) and *Agamemnon* (503 ff.), though in the latter case there is an introduction, and the part of the message that precedes the exchange is a grand elaboration of the greeting rather than the message proper, which follows after the exchange. In *Persians* (249 ff.) the canonical scheme is used. The lying speech of Orestes in the intrigue of *Libation-Bearers* (674 ff.) is not conceived as a messenger report; it lacks the narrative scope and the descriptive detail which define the typical messenger's performance.

Since *Persians* gives us the messenger speech in its purest and at the same time its most ambitious form, let us look at some of its features. The chorus leader makes the announcement. We learn that the new arrival is a Persian—it is his gait (or is it his means of transport?) that identifies him—and that he is bringing clear intelligence, either good or bad. The assurance that what he has to say will be clear is part of the convention; a messenger must not speak in riddles. (Cassandra is not a messenger but a visionary.) As for the disjunctive "either good or bad," it has a naive air about it, but its force is considerable. It shows the recipient prepared for the worst, but hoping against hope; it also shows him confident that the message will be heavily weighted in one direction, and not a delicate mixture of the good with the bad. The suspense is kept up some distance, until the messenger completes his report. The availability of the trilogic pattern, with its terminal compromise and its glimpse of potential triumph, reserves the option of introducing a happy outcome. But the series performed in 472 B.C., in which *Persians* stood as the middle play, was apparently not conceived as a continuous cycle of plays in the manner of the *Oresteia*. *Persians* is an independent

7. L. di Gregorio, *Le scene d'annunzio nella tragedia greca* (Milan, 1967).

play, unsupported by the prospect of ultimate relief. And the knowledge of recent history which the audience brought with them into the theater guaranteed the impossibility of the news being anything but disastrous.

After the messenger has had his summary announcement,

> How with one blow the flourishing multitude
> Was crushed, and the cream of Persia swallowed up,

and engaged the chorus in a first lament, the Empress Mother, apologizing for her silence during this preliminary phase, formally sets the stage for the full report by asking who has not died and who has. In this case the disjunction, and the order in which the questions are raised, are of personal as well as formal interest. The messenger understands, and prefaces his report with the news that Xerxes is alive. After this the floodgates are opened, and the messenger presents the first expansive installment of his four-part reportage. This first part furnishes the casualty list. Its progression of names reminds us of similar things in the epic, except that the names here are Oriental rather than Greek.

The summary announcement at the beginning provides the initial charge. The rest of the report is a slow disclosure of contents already delivered to the recipient. By announcing complete disaster, the messenger provokes a dirge, which takes its place before the listing of the losses. The quadruple division of the report proper is itself important. Aeschylus avoids the lengthy bravura pieces favored by Euripides and, to a lesser extent, also by Sophocles. Aeschylus is impatient with an exhaustive, consecutive detailing of events. He seems to have felt that an audience should not be exposed to an uninterrupted chain of facts without the occasional summary or moral and an ordering of the events into their proper categories. So, in *Persians*, the battle of Salamis is not reported in one block. It is broken up into a number of segments, of which the central panel, the account of the battle itself, is the longest. The segments are separated from one another by remarks of the Empress, or by exchanges between Empress and messenger. First comes the casualty list (302–30). Its roll call of the sonorous names of the leaders who have fallen casts a mournful shadow over what follows. After an appropriate question from the Empress, the messenger cites the numbers of the forces engaged, whose disproportion causes him to recognize in the defeat the hand of the gods. Once again the Empress raises questions, which prompt the major segment, the description of the battle. It is itself, though continuous, clearly articulated as a sequence of four parts: the trick of Themistocles (353–85); the advance (386–407); the battle proper (408–21); and the desperate stand and the suffering of the Persians (422–32). The preparations for the battle, the deception of Xerxes, and the unexpectedly joyous embarkation and advance of the Greeks take up much more space than the fighting itself. The context, the mood, and the sounds and the sights which make up the conditions under which the battle was fought count for more than the movements of the fighting units. In the place of tactics and procedures as a staff officer might describe them, the dramatist through his messenger of grief offers us a vista of oars striking the waves, of voices raised in triumph and in polyglot perplexity, of hulls crushed and corpses choking the sea. The central panel comes to an end with a picture of what happened to the fleeing Persian sailors. The Athenians (424 ff.)

> struck them and broke their backs, much like
> A school of tunny fish, their oars smashed
> And vessels gashed and wrecked.

The tale of woe would seem to be complete. But after a brief exchange between messenger and Empress there follows an account of the battle of Psyttaleia, which closes the series with the recording of a personal triumph, that of the—unnamed—Aristides, as it had opened with the report of a personal achievement. And in a further epilogue, introduced by an outburst on the part of the Empress, we learn of the fate of the survivors, including the disaster on the Strymon river.

By breaking the messenger speech up as he does, Aeschylus makes room for the raising of questions and immediacy of response. Facts are refashioned into visions and memories and into foci for grief, and that grief is articulated responsively as the narration progresses. As in the choral analysis of battle in *Seven* (345 ff.) discussed earlier, speech interprets and interiorizes as it reports. But the interiorizing stays aloof from any suggestion that grief might be sharable. It is the special virtue of the Aeschylean messenger speech that, in spite of its abandonment of pure factuality in favor of analysis and lyrical elaboration, it insulates both the events reported and the grief communicated by the very mechanism of its delivery. The Empress may interrupt and engage the messenger in question and answer. She may even, as before the final panel, have a speech of her own in which she inveighs against the deity responsible for her son's defeat. The clarity of the disposition of the messenger's contribution and its tidy setting off from the rest of the drama—the messenger enters, he delivers his tale, and he leaves—encapsulate the pain and arm the sensibilities of both dramatis personae and audience against it. Pity and fear are maintained at their proper level of moderation and do not degenerate into an excess of empathy, which Aeschylean tragedy shuns.

The closest that dramatic speech can come to taking account of the human relations which it is thought to reflect is in the exchanges to which we shall now turn. As we have seen, neither the epic nor the classical drama knows the flexible, seemingly random conversation which is the pride of the realistic novel and of some experiments in naturalistic drama. In the epic, set speeches, each complete within itself, and only minimally characterized as being addressed *to* another person, are the rule. The same tradition is available to drama, in varying degrees, depending on the conception of the play. The stiff, self-centered orations of *Suppliants* and *Agamemnon* have little in common with the more fluid structures of some of Sophocles's later plays. They do, however, share a dependence on formally organized speech which is at a far remove from the trial and error and necessary trivialities of everyday communication.

In its place, however, classical tragedy exhibits two innovations which leave the set pieces of epic rhetoric far behind them, and which may well be termed Aeschylus's most important contributions to the formal history of the genre. I am referring to the shorter, condensed scheme known technically by the name of *stichomythia*, which we shall call "shuttle speech"; and the larger, more elaborate exchange between a character and the chorus or the leader of the chorus, which we have termed "encounter." It will be recalled that in chapter 2 we distinguished between two varieties of encounter: the even kind, in which both parties sing, and the uneven kind, in which only one of them does. In this discussion, little distinction will be made between the two subspecies.

Shuttle speech and encounter are Aeschylus's way of producing an engagement or a confrontation between the functionaries of the drama. Through these schemes, he modifies their virtual isolation and brings them into closer formal relation to one another. At least that is the first impression. But upon further experience it transpires that the formal contact engineered by the two schemes often has a distinctly negative effect. Instead of meshing the purposes of the contending wills, the stylized symmetry of the schemes helps to underscore their separateness. Initially, the impulse appears to be one of mutual cognizance and potential cooperation; the mood is social, communal, communicative. But as the conflicting positions are taken with the severity of a perfect, unresolved equilibrium, the opportunities for a reconciliation dwindle. By the time the shuttle speech or the encounter has been run through, the distance between the participants may have become, if anything, even larger because of the exactions of equal time and tight equivalence. Screened and armored within the unremitting structures of reciprocity, the participants are left with none of its promise, but only with the same division with which they started out.

It is no exaggeration to say that the encounter is Aeschylus's special way of dramatizing conflict and isolation, and that it is thus at the very heart of Aeschylean tragedy. But when we say "conflict" we must be careful not to understand by this some of the elements which Hegelian thinking has introduced into the discussion of drama. Aeschylean exchanges, though clearly availing themselves of opportunities offered by human contention, rarely carry us beyond them to the larger issues—to the collision of philosophies or of values, much less to a sense that a world out of joint is being championed by heroes fighting to the death for what they believe, or in their persons symbolizing the cosmic engagement. Neither shuttle speech nor encounter is exclusively or even primarily given over to the function of dramatizing a collision. But even where what is at issue *is* a conflict, it rarely touches upon the larger questions raised by the play. More often, it involves the competition of men and women jealous of their privileges or uncertain of their stance in relation to others. Hegel emphasizes the collision more than the suffering. The collision is between two goods, whose goodness is confirmed in the very clash of the champions. Aeschylus cannot afford this solace. The players in his drama are human beings; the tension is not between what they are and what they stand for, but between what they aspire to and what they achieve.

Many later dramatists availed themselves of the benefits of shuttle speech. It is found in Shakespeare. The conversation between Gaunt and Bolingbroke in *Richard II* (1.3.528 ff.) demonstrates the line-by-line versification, the verbal self-consciousness, and the tendency toward aphorism that the structure favors. The same is true of the set-to between Le Comte and Don Diègue in *Le Cid* (1.3.215 ff.), where the dialogue prepares the explosion of the slap, and of the final conversation between Egmont and Orange in Goethe's *Egmont* (2.2), just before Orange makes his farewell speech. Each of these examples has its own special quality, tailored to the needs of the drama it serves. In Greek drama, too, shuttle speech accommodates a variety of purposes. This variety is more easily studied in Sophocles and Euripides than in Aeschylus, the reason being that Aeschylus's shuttle speech is usually shorter and less artfully developed than that of his successors. But even in Aeschylus there are some interesting and surprising variations.[8]

First some figures which, crude as they are, have something to tell us. From the available evidence, it appears that Aeschylus became more interested in the dramatic possibilities of the form in his later plays. *Persians* and *Seven* have only three occurrences each; *Suppliants* has five, as does *Eumenides*; *Agamemnon*, *Libation-Bearers*, and *Prometheus* have eight each. The figure for *Agamemnon* is, at first sight, surprising. One might have thought that there was little scope in this slow-moving play for the kind of quickening to

8. B. Seidensticker, "Die Stichomythie," in W, Jens, ed., *Die Bauformen der griechischen Tragödie* (Munich, 1971), pp. 183 ff. See also S. Ireland, "Stichomythia in Aeschylus," *Hermes* 102 (1974): 509–24.

which much shuttle speech is hospitable. But quite apart from the greater length of *Agamemnon*, facing-off or quarreling is only one of the situations for which the scheme is used. Equally often, in fact, shuttle speech is in the main informational. Information can shade off into instruction or persuasion; and there are cases, such as *Seven* 245 ff. and 712 ff., where a character attempts to persuade or guide another without much information being given out. Often a piece of shuttle speech starts out as information-gathering, and ends up somewhere else. One of the longest sequences of this kind is found at *Suppl*. 293–347. Strictly speaking, it is two sequences, joined by a brief unit (323–34) in which the rigid regularity of line-by-line alternation is relaxed in favor of a looser structure. In this transitional passage, Pelasgus and the chorus shift from a contemplation of origins and nationality to a scrutiny of legal and moral claims. Dramatically, the whole sequence is of one piece. Shuttle speech commonly indulges in this license of moderating its severity somewhere around the middle of its progress with a short-lived relaxation of the pace. In the present instance, as we have seen, our text does not permit us to decide definitively who does the asking and who the answering. But there can be no doubt that the inquiry furnishes the audience, like the King, with important information, and that by line 325 Pelasgus is satisfied that the women indeed have an ancient connection with the land of Argos. Up to this point the sequence is entirely in the narrative mold; the inquiry has for its purpose the establishment of facts. There is nothing about the calm progress of the shuttle speech that would suggest that Pelasgus is moving toward a decision of any sort. But, beginning with line 332, the mood changes. The pre-trial inquest turns into judicial proceedings; from dispassionate data processing, we advance to contest and polemic. Answers are formulated as questions, the question-and-answer linearity yields to statement abutting on statement, tempers flare, and in short order the battle lines are drawn.

Some shuttle speech signals a fugitive cooperation. The shared experience of worship finds its expression in shuttle speech at *Suppl*. 204 ff. and *Lib*. 479 ff. At *Lib*. 212 ff., the recognition of brother and sister naturally elects that structure. Likewise, joint deliberation is most easily dramatized by recourse to the shuttle structure, though it is questionable whether *Agam*. 1347 ff., the responses of the members of the chorus to the death cries of Agamemnon, can properly be put under this heading. Formally, with its unchanging sequence of couplets and its pondering of the news, it is. We have assumed, however, that all twelve members of the chorus participate in this mockery of a deliberation scene, and that should disqualify the passage from consideration. But its hesitations prompt another question. One may inquire whether the effect of shuttle speech is to retard or to further the action. No simple answer can be given. For the most part,

Aeschylean shuttle speech appears to grow naturally out of the preceding transaction, and to lead up naturally to what follows, without a radical shift in speed or mood. Our example from *Suppliants*, the scene between Pelasgus and the chorus, is in that respect unusual. In any case, the stiffness of the scheme lends itself to retardation, where retardation is desired.

It can be climactic, in the sense that the two speakers engaging in it turn to it at a point when tempers have waxed hot or the need for intelligence has turned pressing. Under the stimulus of a felt common emergency, the speakers take, as it were, unwilling cognizance of each other. The strain that this momentary surrender provokes is evident. Recalcitrance, defensiveness, and skepticism make for a formal austerity which sustains the sense of isolation. For example, *Seven* 712 ff. where the speakers are the chorus leader and Eteocles:

> Ch. Against your wish, take the advice of women.
> Et. Tell me what might be done; avoid long speech.
> Ch. Do not, we urge you, visit the seventh gate.
> Et. Your words will fail to blunt my whetted purpose.
> Ch. God loves a victory, however undeserved.
> Et. An armed soldier cannot support that notion.
> Ch. Are you then willing to reap fraternal blood?
> Et. When the gods command, one cannot escape disaster.

The appeal of the chorus comes to nothing, as does the brief willingness of the King to listen to the women. The mechanics of the shuttle speech virtually assure the outcome. Instead of drawing together, the speakers end up facing away from each other. The sequence is a pendant to an earlier shuttle speech (*Seven* 245–63) in which Eteocles attempts to persuade the chorus to give up its frenetic ways of worshipping. The balanced structure documents a skirmish between contestants who are evenly matched. In such a contest victories are unlikely, and at most short-lived.

On rare occasions, however, an agonal shuttle sequence terminates in the discomfiture of one of the speakers. The most memorable competitive shuttle speech in Aeschylus is the dialogue with Clytemnestra whereby Agamemnon is persuaded to step on the scarlet materials (*Agam.* 931–44). Unlike the wrangling between chorus leader and Aegisthus, which generates two shuttle passages toward the end of the play, the series between Clytemnestra and Agamemnon is charged with a weight and a significance which advertise themselves in every word used. Clytemnestra wins out, and Agamemnon gives way; we feel that maximum profit has been struck from a capital which is usually invested more conservatively in Aeschylus. For once, the deceitful rhetoric of the great temptress gives to the conventional form a power that thrusts it beyond the customary equilibrium. The magic of the great scene dissolves the balance and Agamemnon falls.

Aeschylus's measured virtuosity in the matter of shuttle speech can also be gauged by comparing two passages in *Libation-Bearers*, at 108 ff. and 908 ff. The latter, the disastrous exchange between Clytemnestra and Orestes, is competitive, climactic, and stiff. The former, the initial dialogue between Electra and the chorus leader, is exploratory, cooperative, and remarkably flexible. Indeed, it has several of the features which mark the greater fluidity and lifelikeness of some of Sophocles's shuttle sequences: repetitions, clarifications, and interpositions such as would naturally crop up in a conversation in which advice is requested; and, on the formal level, incomplete grammatical structures taken up and mediated by the questioner, in this case Electra (117 ff.):

> Ch. Remember those responsible for the bloodbath and . . .
> El. Say what? Dispel my ignorance? I should say . . .
> Ch. That some divinity or a mortal visit them . . .
> El. To judge, you think, or to impose a punishment?
> Ch. A simple answer : to kill in turn for killing.

In passages like this the speakers come as close as anywhere to collapsing their purposes into one. Punctuation at the ends of the lines would do an injustice to the near-surrender of separateness that this rare species of shuttle speech suggests.

The other example, the final conversation between Orestes and Clytemnestra, is full of the sharp weapons of a duel. Each speaker, in a desire to gain the advantage over the other, turns into a challenger. Each line is emphatically end-stopped; each statement is complete within itself. Thesis and antithesis, attack and counterattack follow each other in unrelenting sequence, until the last brittle (and untranslatable) shout by Orestes (930). I translate literally, without attempting to fashion a pentameter:

> You have killed whom you should not; now suffer what ought not [to be]!

Aeschylus's shuttle speech never approaches the nervousness or the forensic obsessiveness of the Senecan variety, where language and thought are repeatedly tested on the anvil of a recessive logic of greed and exhaustion. Unlike Seneca, Aeschylus rarely relies on key words moved forward and backward and juggled into bizarre perspectives. Aeschylus's dialogue is carried by solid feelings and steadfast loyalties and, in the case of the informational exchanges which form the basic stock of the pattern, by the sheer momentum of the narrative. Nevertheless, the range of rhetorical development is remarkable, as is its exploitation for the sake of the drama.

Shuttle speech is the *stretta* of ancient drama, the pared-down version of the meeting of two temperaments, or simply two intelligences vying for recognition. Similar in structure, and perhaps even more typically Aeschylean, is the larger kind of confrontation that we have called "encounter," to which we now turn.[9] It will be remembered that at *Pers.* 256 ff., the entrance of the messenger, who is given a few summary lines to speak, is immediately followed by an encounter between the chorus, singing, and the messenger, speaking; and that at *Seven* 203 ff., a similar encounter between the chorus and Eteocles is used to lead up to a stretch of shuttle speech, to modulate what might without it have come through as a piece of raw wrangling analogous to the acrimonious debate between Apollo and the Furies at *Eum.* 711 ff. In that scene, which takes place while the voting is going on, the specious arguments of Apollo prevent us from distinguishing between reason and unreason. Generally shuttle speech spikes the guns of those who want to isolate hero from villain or judge opposed temperaments. For that, the encounter is the suitable form, especially the uneven encounter. In such a confrontation, the speaking character often stands for the commands of reason or of reasonableness, while the singing character or characters—often the chorus—stand for the imperatives of unreason and occasionally of irresponsibility. (But see above, chapter 2, p. 35.)

The encounter between the Danaids and Pelasgus at *Suppl.* 348 ff. is typical of many such exchanges between women and a man, or between ecstatic worshippers and a secular head, or between grieving old men and a self-assured messenger. The lyric measures that define the sung portions of uneven encounters are frequently of the more extravagant kind, including dochmiacs, contrasting markedly with the cool iambs of the speech. The separation of stanza from responding stanza by means of speech produces an air of nervousness and irresolution. But while it accentuates opposition and struggle, it also holds out the promise of an ultimate understanding. Some scholars believe that the uneven encounter—i.e., usually, the scheme of a single speaking character contending with the singing and dancing chorus—is a vestige of the very origins of drama. There is, however, no evidence for this. It is, in fact, more likely that the encounter, in both its manifestations, is Aeschylus's special contribution to the young tradition of play-acting. Its function in Aeschylean tragedy is roughly the equivalent of what Euripides attempts to achieve by means of the diptych of aria and speech—the successive delivery, on the part of one and the same character, of a lyric statement that is sung and a forensic statement that is spoken, both going over more or less the same material. The Euripidean scheme charts a comprehensive understanding of how a person comes to grips with

9. Cf. H. Popp in Jens, *Bauformen*, pp. 221–49.

an issue. The aria formulates the response of what Plato would call the passions; the speech represents the stand of the reasoning faculty. The temporal succession of the two responses, which is always in this order, is by the nature of things unavoidable. But the listener is conditioned to convert the sequence into a simultaneity in his imagination, two powerful structures of consciousness being explored together and complementing one another. In Aeschylus, the dialectic that matters is not between the two dimensions of a single person but between contrasting human types. The encounter between the Danaids and Pelasgus; that between the women of Thebes and Eteocles (*Seven* 203 ff.); and that between the daughters of Ocean and Prometheus (*Prom.* 128 ff.), where the character chants rather than speaks, are typical instances of individuals and choruses in a state of confrontation.

The most remarkable, and least orthodox, example of the scheme is the Great Exchange in *Libation-Bearers* (164–465).[10] Its length is extreme; even with proper allowance made for the lines dropped out in the prologue, the encounter stretches through almost a third of the play; with its conclusion (466–584), consisting of a brief choral passage and a spoken coda, it covers almost two-fifths. The choral contribution is in part sung and in part chanted; the chorus is joined by not one but two characters, both of whom sing throughout. In spite of the regularly spaced incidence of choral chanting, this encounter must be regarded as closer to the kind that is *durchkomponiert* and not to the uneven species. Most important, there is no confrontation. All partners in the effort are working for the same aim; their faces are turned toward the tomb of Agamemnon more than to one another. Still, it is appropriate to suggest that the two confrontations in *Agamemnon*, between Cassandra and the chorus (1072–1330) and between Clytemnestra and the chorus (1372–1447), and the trial and resolution in *Eumenides* (566–1031) exhibit instructive formal analogies to the first half of *Libation-Bearers*. In each case an iambic sequence gives way to an encounter which in turn once again yields to iambic speech. It is the total system, with iambic introduction and iambic conclusion, which constitutes the complete confrontation. The concluding speech usually registers quite clearly the advance that has been gained by the encounter.

In the first lyric exchange between Cassandra and the chorus, for instance, the chorus acknowledges Cassandra's visions—the feast of Thyestes, Clytemnestra's preparations, the murder, the sufferings of Troy—by moving from skepticism to a bewildered empathy (*Agam.* 1072–1177). As a consequence, Cassandra turns to speech, and announces that henceforth she will express herself openly. That the pledge is imperfectly kept is another matter. What counts is the new tone, the feeling that a temporary

10. The Great Exchange will be discussed more fully in chap. 8.

agreement has been reached. Again, throughout the uneven encounter between Clytemnestra and the chorus (*Agam.* 1407 ff.), the two opponents gradually move closer to the middle, centering their sights on the avenging demon of the house and on Justice. It is only the appearance of Aegisthus which prevents the restoration of a dismal sort of harmony; nothing more than the question of who is to bury the king was keeping them apart. The development moves from heated accusations and charges of madness toward a resigned partial agreement. That is one way in which a confrontation can go.

The same movement is most clearly demonstrated in the reconciliation between Athena and the Furies in *Eumenides*. But here the approaching agreement does not begin to be felt in the lyrical segments of the confrontation. For once, Aeschylus has the Furies sing not dyads but repeats; *Eum.* 808–22 is an exact repeat, word for word, of 778–92, as 870–80 is of 837–46:

> Is this what I must suffer?
> Never!
> Me, my ancient wisdom, to be housed underground,
> Detested and spurned?
> Never!
> My strength, my anger live.
> Oh, oh, the twisted pain deep in my ribs!
> Hear my cry, Night Mother!
> A cunning I cannot match rakes me to ruin
> From the lasting demesne of the gods.

The effect of the repeats is one of deadlock rather than adjustment. Or are we to imagine that the rigidity and the atavistic bleakness of the confrontational anger hints at a resistance already broken? In any case, whether the freezing of the lyrical voice has psychological significance or not, once the singing is over and Athena initiates the shuttle speech which concludes the sequence (890 ff.), the Furies are ready to accept the compromise. The encounter that follows, with Athena chanting and the chorus singing, is no longer part of the confrontation proper, but a cooperative encounter of joy in celebration of the compact achieved.

The general scheme—speech, encounter, speech—is also found in *Suppliants* 176–417 and *Persians* 155–531. In the case of the encounter in *Persians*, we can hardly speak of confrontation; the exchange is between messenger and chorus, featuring an extreme version of the choral reaction to bad news. The messenger's speeches anticipate and enhance the weight of the concluding or, in this case, principal iambic passage. But fundamentally this is the Aeschylean tripartite scheme of speech followed by lyric exchange followed by speech, a scheme around which Aeschylus appears to have been eager to do his structuring. Only in *Prometheus* does the author proceed more in the manner of Euripides and Sophocles, with iambic passages, choral songs, anapaestic-lyric exchanges, arias, and non-responsive lyrics succeeding one another in a more fluid manner instead of conforming to the circular tripartite scheme.

Athena's struggle with the Furies has much in common with the way Pelasgus responds to the Danaids, but in *Suppliants* the encounter builds up to the conflict, which is then further exposed via speech, ode, and shuttle speech before it is precipitously resolved. In *Eumenides*, the politician, Athena, wins out. In *Suppliants*, it is the chorus that defeats the politician, at least temporarily. The victory of the chorus is recorded in a brief ode (418–37) attached as a supplement to the encounter. This is not the only unusual structural feature marking the encounters in *Suppliants*. In the encounter between Danaus and his daughters (734 ff.) which is prompted by Danaus's report of the approach of the Egyptians, Danaus's speech, designed to set the women's fears at rest, is answered by them in a sequence that combines speech with song. By this formal means, they convey a mixture of reactions, with some partial convergence upon the calming mood of their father and, for the rest, a continuing surrender to the fear of capture.

The Aeschylean encounter is a mighty thing. The large, and often complicated, but tightly closed structures which serve as the vehicle of confrontation are, to a degree, counter-dramatic. Their circular form resists dramatic development or psychological adjustment. No progressive recording of smallish changes prepares the ground for the new positions adopted at the end. The Great Exchange of *Libation-Bearers*, with its formal complexity and its low level of confrontational energy, is characteristic of Aeschylus's art even where he dramatizes competing passions. Aeschylus shows little interest in the organic mutations registered by characters moving closer to an understanding or to a final separation. Unlike similar sparring sessions in the later dramatists, confrontation in Aeschylus dismisses the flux of time. It is less a portrait of minds jockeying for position than a record of their systematic relations. Hence the pedimental form. The energies dramatized can best be exhibited in a scheme of weight and counterweight. When the resolution comes, it usually takes the shape of an abatement. The energies which had emerged from the current of iambic speech subside back into it again, but now with a new distribution of forces in control.

The public nature of Aeschylean speech attains its most balanced consolidation in the climactic encounters found in every play. It is not profitable to tag them as "rituals," as if the confrontations were in any important sense similar to the forms of worship from which drama is said to have sprung. The Aeschylean encounter is a mechanism for the tracing of thesis and antithesis on the part of representative human energies. In its carved symmetry, it borders on allegory, and more specifically on psychomachy, the battling of souls writ large. It is saved from such etiolation by the immediacy of the language, and above all by the simulation of human tempers. The basic moods are fear and confidence; the basic metaphor is that of the trial or the pursuit. It is Aeschylus's achievement that the trial or pursuit is felt to be real, the experience of individuals caught in a specific action, and not a mere paradigm. Through the elaborate structures which Aeschylus invented or perfected to dramatize communication, the voice of the playwright endows the speakers and the singers with believable voices of their own.

# _ 8 _

# Characters

Aristotle says that tragedy imitates action. That is to say, it is what people do and how they fare, rather than what they are or what is decreed for them, that is the concern of tragedy. We cannot be sure that this point of view was widely accepted in Greece. Theophrastus, Aristotle's right-hand man, is reported to have defined tragedy as the turn-around (*metastasis*) of a heroic fate. The formulations are worlds apart, but neither of them includes a reference to characters. In fact, Aristotle's *Poetics* does not have a word for our "characters."[1] When he speaks of the agents of the drama, they are cited simply as those who act, or who have certain moral features or conduct themselves in a certain way. The word "character" was invented for narrative fiction, where from the start it enjoyed an unsettling companionship with exaggeration and parody. But if by "character" we understand the simulation on the dramatic stage of a plausible human life (and the crudity of this and of many other similar formulations is a necessary initial gambit), we can then ask whether it is possible to determine if Aeschylean drama is a party to such simulation.

   Some fifty years ago, H. W. Smyth, who wrote the last major introduction to Aeschylus in English, could devote many pages to delineating the contours of the Aeschylean dramatis personae and their lives as they might be reconstructed from their utterances.[2] More or less in the manner of Bradley on *Hamlet*, he used the texts as a basis for larger questions about the characters, as if he were trying to make sense of the disturbing behavior patterns of a patient or a customer. He did not, it seems, approve of Tycho von Wilamowitz's attack on the very notion of a constant dramatic personality existing independently of the sequence of scenes in which the playwright develops the action.[3] He appears to have taken it for granted that a dramatic character approaches perfection as its outlines coincide with those of specific men and women whom we might encounter in the street. He did so in spite of his express recognition that the Greek dramatic conventions—

1. For Aristotle and character, see T. G. Rosenmeyer, "Aristotelian Ethos and Character in Modern Drama," *Proc. IXth Congr. Intern. Comp. Liter. Assoc.*, vol. 1 (Innsbruck, 1981), pp. 119–25. Also Charles Chamberlain, "The meaning of the Word *Ethos* in Aristotle's *Poetics*" (diss., University of California, Berkeley, 1980).

2. H. W. Smyth, *Aeschylean Tragedy* (Berkeley and Los Angeles, 1924).

3. T. von Wilamowitz-Moellendorff, *Die dramatische Technik des Sophokles* (*Philolog. Untersuchungen* 22; Berlin, 1917).

the masks, the verse, the music, male actors playing female roles—must necessarily subvert any attempt at psychological verisimilitude.

Critics have become more careful since those palmy days—or at least they have become less certain of themselves.[4] Obviously it is impossible to do away completely with the notion of character, even though stage drama imposes limitations and furnishes opportunities that are quite different from those associated with narrative fiction. Unless the speakers and singers in a tragedy bear some resemblance in their way of talking, reacting, and planning to what listeners have experienced in themselves and in their associates, dramatic *mimēsis* would be inaccessible or empty. It is important that we avoid importing into our understanding of "dramatic character" peculiarities which an ancient audience would have found either unduly idiosyncratic or altogether foreign to their expectations. On the one hand, it is wrong to look for arresting character studies, so unusual in their singularities that they exceed the demands of the action. On the other hand, the terms widely favored in discussing the heroes of Renaissance and post-Renaissance drama—weakness, presumption, passion, majesty, good manners, grace—may be derived from a model which is not that of Aeschylus. Neither Freud nor St. Paul nor, for that matter, Theophrastus or La Bruyère, furnish us with the proper guidelines.

We can start with the plain observation that Aeschylus's characters are limited and hence, by definition, artificial. Diderot, the theoretician of dramatic realism, deplores the unreality of theatrical characters in the tradition he is trying to demolish, and blames their acceptance on a convention going back to Aeschylus.[5] The limitations are obvious: Aeschylean characters do not faint, or cry, or laugh; they do not go to sleep—though the Furies are *discovered* sleeping—nor do they eat or drink on the stage. Though the dramatic action often hinges on the infraction of a rule, or on the threat of an infraction, the Aeschylean stage does not recognize the most pervasive social response to such an infraction: embarrassment. Aeschylus eschews any possible diminution of the full waking vigor of a person's vitality. Biological needs, gradations of consciousness or attention, and shades of perception are decidedly not part of the Aeschylean scheme of conduct. The maximization of vitality even has as one of its consequences that old men, though common among choruses, are rare among the princi-

4. Among recent contributions to the subject, one might mention J. Gould, "Dramatic Character and 'Human Intelligibility' in Greek Tragedy," *Proc. Cambr. Philol. Soc.* 204 (1978): 43–67; P. E. Easterling, "Presentation of Character in Aeschylus," *Greece and Rome* 29 (1973): 3–19; M. Nussbaum, "Consequences and Character in Sophocles' *Philoctetes*," *Philosophy and Literature* 1 (1976): 25–53. More generally, see "Changing Views of Character," *New Literary History* 5, pt. 2 (1974).

5. D. Diderot, *Paradoxe sur le comédien*, in F. C. Green, ed., *Diderot's Writings on the Theatre* (Cambridge, 1936), p. 261.

pals. The norm calls for persons that are wide-awake, serious, direct; they live, if that is the term, at a pitch of intensity which puts the audience on edge and obviates a facile fellow-feeling.

"There is, therefore, an absolute distinction between a dramatic character and a person in real life. . . . We can only understand [the playwright's] characters so long as we agree that we cannot know all about them and are not supposed to know all about them."[6] The words are those of L. C. Knights; he adds that, whatever its limitations, the dramatic character, to be effective with the audience, needs to be felt as if it were complete. That is to say, the dramatic character differs from an individual not in that it is more universal—"universal human nature is not a very human thing"[7]—but in that, though it is incomplete if measured by the standards of empirical reality, it registers upon the sensibilities of the audience "as if" it were a complete moral and behavioral organism. The lack of what Yeats calls the "minute particulars" from the selective aggregate on stage does not, it is claimed, prevent the audience from investing it with an identity which makes possible something very much like human interaction. Our question is: does our experience of Aeschylean drama indicate that this is how Aeschylus's characters are to be perceived?

The obverse of completeness is specificity. To seem complete, a character has to be distinguishable from other characters. To put it differently, maximal characterization would require that any one random statement made by a character could be identified as belonging to that character and no other. Now it is, of course, agreed that no known play satisfies this requirement. But of Aeschylus it must be asked whether the utterance of a character forces the imagination, as it does in Ibsen or Hauptmann, in the direction of one organically perceived life or not. The answer must be no, and not only because Aeschylean speech is formal and public and therefore blocks, on the level of utterance, the development of psychological specificity. Dramatic speech on the Aeschylean stage is often conducted by disembodied voices, borrowing temporary mouths through which to speak. One feature that helps to drive home this aspect of Aeschylean speech is the naturalness of self-praise. In *The White Devil* (5.1.100 f.), Francisco says: "I did never wash my mouth with mine own praise for fear of getting a stinking breath." In Aeschylus no such Christian humility prevents people from talking about themselves as if they were talking about somebody else. Speech in an Aeschylean tragedy originates from a source which lies beyond the center of gravity of an individual soul. It is not the segmental creation of a character, and thus needs no censoring by the character's sense of what is fitting.

6. L. C. Knights, quoted in N. Rabkin, *Approaches to Shakespeare* (New York, 1964), p. 55.

7. E. Goffman, *Interaction Ritual* (Garden City, N.Y., 1967), p. 45.

Over and above the pressure of public speech, however, the characters are incomplete, and do not seek completion in an audience response, because they are unfixed, and they are unfixed because, like the characters of Brecht, but in a more narrowly aesthetic sense, and therefore more profoundly, they are the function of a larger whole. They are the temporary means, both fragmentary and fluid, which the drama discovers for itself to enunciate certain truths demanded by the action. In Brecht's case, characters change as social circumstances demand it of them; capitalism forces the human amoeba into wayward shapes, and the drama traces the process with mirrorlike clarity. Aeschylus uses no mirror, nor does he think of people as oppressed by tyrannical social forces. The larger unity which dictates the conduct of his characters is precisely that dramatic action which Aristotle takes to be the primary datum of poetic organization. That we feel some of the characters to be detachable and identifiable on their own in spite of this enhances our respect for the playwright.

The colossal discovery of Aeschylus and his immediate predecessors was dramatic speech, the combining of sentences into a semblance of experienced life. Homer had made a beginning; but the formulaic nature of his speech and the requirements of heroic decorum kept the utterances of epic warriors and princes geared to a level of expressiveness which suggested the life of the moment rather than the life of a sequence. Aeschylean speech is the first we have that gives us the intensity, the surprises, and the connectedness that we ask of an extended curve. But precisely because it seems to get us away from the conventionalities of battle scenes, feasts, and other subjects that fix the mind's eye on the moment, and replaces them with the less familiar way stations of a developing movement, it is important that we keep certain distinctions in mind. In drama the pull is toward ideas, definitions, and contrastings—the monumentalities of a highly abstract art. What there is in the way of psychological continuities is once again reduced to the experience of brief moments, smallish enclaves, suitable foci for exaggerations or triteness. But for the principal agents of the drama, as we shall see, the matter is more complicated.

Let us begin with the simplest detachable unit: the chorus leader.[8] He is, of course, properly speaking no dramatic character at all. As the agent of the chorus, its spokesman more than its leader, coming into view only when the chorus ceases to sing or chant and subsides into spoken lines, he is in large measure a construction of modern editors. For it is by no means completely certain whether the spoken utterances of the chorus are to be assigned to one

8. M. Kaimio, *The Chorus of Greek Drama Within the Light of the Person and Number Used* (*Soc. Scient. Fennica: Comment. Human. Litter.* 46; Helsinki, 1970), pp. 157–59.

person only, or whether the members of the chorus took turns in assuming the role of leader. Ancient evidence on this head is wanting. It so happens that these segments of speech are rarely extensive enough to endow the speaker with an identity in excess of what is given for the chorus as a whole. For our purposes, then, it does not matter whether there is one chorus leader or several in succession. The anonymity is virtually complete; the speaker furnishes information, reacts to a piece of news, or responds to a position taken.

The longest spoken sequence occurs in *Agamemnon* (489 ff.). For the most part, the passage serves as an announcement of the coming of the herald. The speaker also expresses his satisfaction at the thought that it will now be possible to verify or refute the message of the beacon. The next longest sequences occur at *Pers.* 215–25 and *Eum.* 244–53. Seven other passages, varying from eight to five lines in length, complete the roster of extended choral statements (as against choral participation in alternating dialogue). Slightly more than half of these passages are similar in substance to the passage from *Agamemnon*: they are introductory, or explanatory, but do not take us far toward an appreciation of the speaker's motives or intent. Of the ones that seem to promise more—*Pers.* 215 ff., *Seven* 677 ff., *Suppl.* 328 ff., *Agam.* 1612 ff. and 1643 ff., *Eum.* 244 ff. and 652 ff.—the passage in *Seven*, consisting of six iambic lines, is perhaps the most interesting. Eteocles has clutched the Curse to his heart and broken out in maledictions against his brother; the chorus leader, abandoning the terror and the excitement that had characterized the chorus earlier, now warns Eteocles to go slow and not fall victim to an anger which he himself associates with the enemy. This is an abrupt change in the choral stance, and it is continued in the sung contributions that follow. The leader does little more than set the stage or strike the initial chord for a choral argument that will be developed by the chorus as a whole. He is an instrument of the developing action, not a shaper or bearer of it.

Having said this about the chorus leader, it is, on one view, hard to say more about the majority of the principals. As a recent critic has said, "the rare and remarkable action, the dramatically significant action, entails the actor who (almost literally) measures up to it."[9] A similar claim has been made for Racine.[10] This is, once again, the Aristotelian view, or at least a plausible interpretation of that view. The characters of the *Oresteia* are created so as to be adequate to the action asked of them. Now this way of putting things lends itself to terminological confusion. It might be argued, and indeed has been, that the adequacy position cannot be right, because in

9. J. Jones, *On Aristotle and Greek Tragedy* (Oxford, 1962), p. 114.
10. R. Barthes, *Sur Racine* (Paris, 1972), pp. 24–25.

Sophocles's *Philoctetes* Odysseus tries to measure up to the situation and fails.[11] The answer to that objection is of course that the action to which Odysseus is adequate requires that he fail. But is this not little more than a tautology, a proposition that is as true of any other conceivable play as it is of Aeschylean drama?

What makes the adequacy position intriguing is its emphasis on the control exercised by the traditional tale and by the formal structure of the play over the dynamism of personal life, and on the virtual exclusion by this control of the possibility of an autonomous character absorbing the audience's interest in and for itself. But, as Richmond Lattimore asks in an interesting discussion of this issue,

> Is that all? Is there to be no personality, no character, for its own sake? . . . The modern actor, playing Hamlet, will not be content with a character-in-action who is just sufficient to play his necessary part in the revenge drama. He feels he must *be* Hamlet. This is a man, and the play itself has interest chiefly as it concerns him. . . . Those characters are most like independent persons, to be so studied and played, who show some touch of the irrational, some privacies of personality, that escape the logic of the plot . . . who chop and change their choices, or threaten to: Medea inciting herself, Philoctetes and Neoptolemus, Ismene trying to reverse herself. Antigone. . . .[12]

It will not have escaped the reader's notice that there is not an Aeschylean character among them. And the chances are that what is true of Sophocles and Euripides is less true of Aeschylus. Conversely, as we shall see in our chapter on the plot, it is often harder in Aeschylus to determine the nature of the action, and the control it is supposed to exercise (see below, chapter 11). Nevertheless it is commonly perceived that the major Aeschylean characters fit less easily into the pattern sketched by Lattimore of those who "chop and change their choices" and attract our interest for their specificity or their quirkiness. That is not the same as saying that the major Aeschylean personages have a stereotypical quality that stands in their way of functioning as individuals, a position that is often argued by those who look at Aeschylus's dramatic action as the simulacrum of a sacrificial rite.

As a matter of fact, there is room for quirkiness in Aeschylus's scheme. We find it in the portraits of some secondary figures, of the auxiliaries who satisfy a passing dramatic need and are less closely dovetailed with the larger movement of the play. Here is the watchman at the beginning of *Agamemnon*, calling upon the gods—the first word of the trilogy—to grant him a respite:

11. Nussbaum, "Consequences and Character."
12. R. Lattimore, *Story Patterns in Greek Tragedy* (Ann Arbor, Mich., 1964), pp. 62–63.

Gods, I say you owe me a rest.
The watch I keep is years of bedding down
On Agamemnon's roof, hunched-up dog-fashion,
Eyes fixed on the nocturnal swarm of stars.
I have seen them bringing winter and then summer,
Bespeckled princes glowing in the sky;
I know their settings and have watched them rise.

Are these lines the dragging complaints of an exhausted menial, barely able to keep his eyes open, repeating himself and, with his head swimming, grinding to an inconsequential halt? Perhaps; and he has thirty-nine lines—enough to establish a minor identity for himself. He is afraid, he sings or whistles to avoid falling asleep, he compares both his night's work and his masters' lot to a game successfully played, and he gets ready to do a dance of thanksgiving. There is enough here, it seems, to pinpoint an air of slyness and relief, of bravado and lower-class directness; to catch our interest, and to throw into relief the unrelievedly solemn strains of the chorus about to follow. But there is a great deal else that is difficult to square with the Brueghelesque portrait of an anxious clown happy to be able to leave his post and report the news. There is the golden rhetoric about the stars and constellations as keepers of the season, about the dusky flame with its good message of the "cry of capture," and about the orders issuing from the hopeful heart of the man-willed lady. The verse is alternately taut and prolix; the language stiff and colloquial by turns. Is this mixture intended to have us laugh? I rather doubt it; laughter destroys mystery, and we are left with a minor feeling of mystification at the conspiratorial ring of the lines about what the house could say, were it to find a tongue to speak.

The watchman is a gargoyle, a smallish, overdrawn figure pretending to a semblance of vital familiarity, with a touch or two of grossness or of down-to-earth self-importance. The author is prepared to start a play with such a gargoyle because it radiates life without committing him to naturalistic standards for the whole. The watchman's quick changes of mood and pace, the juggling of the public and the private, are both disconcerting and exhilarating. The disrespect he shows the Queen in absentia—he imagines himself calling on her to get out of bed, to rise (like the stars of summer and winter?) and arrange for the celebration, with himself as the principal dancer—are welcome condiments to add to the sequence of suspense and relief. In all this he resembles the Nurse of *Libation-Bearers*. She, too, has her share of comedy, though she is not as such a comic person. Like the watchman, she is oppressed by the weight of the immediate, and fails to recognize larger issues. Personal loyalty, nostalgia, and even sentimentality control her thoughts. Her speech, too, alternates between a special desultory style in imitation of old people gossiping (743 ff.) and more solemn cadences. Through her appearance, the nurse acknowledges the hatred of the commoners for Clytemnestra and their love of Orestes. She rounds out the legitimacy of Orestes by dwelling on his privileged position as a baby. And she helps to immunize us against Clytemnestra's terror: Orestes is a child, he cannot help himself. His wetting of his clothes is a signal of his weakness: he is defenseless, and he has to kill.

It will have been noticed that in discussing the "character" of the nurse we have glanced off to look at her function in the play. In the end, she becomes an agent of the intrigue. But long before that, in a less dramatic but equally effective way, she performs a function vis-à-vis Clytemnestra and Orestes which helps to explain why Aeschylus introduced her. The same is true of the watchman. His main purpose is to prepare for the appearance of the beacon and to create a modicum of suspense in the waiting for it. His own waiting, uncomfortably, under duress, brings home to us the constraints that becloud the house and its members. As he tries to whistle his fear away, it comes out as a lament for the family. His special brand of black comedy gives us not only a gargoyle that is not quite a character—there is no time for that—but a situation. It introduces us to the theme of the sufferings of the house and conditions us to understand better the subsequent developments.

Aegisthus, in *Libation-Bearers* as well as *Agamemnon*, can be looked at in the same fashion. In *Libation-Bearers*, his appearance is even briefer than that of the nurse or the watchman. He speaks only fourteen lines; one may calculate that he is on stage fewer than two minutes. He has the bearing of a tired, small-minded administrator. He claims to be grief-stricken, but his skepticism concerning the news shows that he wants it to be firm. Curiously, his skepticism takes the same form as that of the chorus in *Agamemnon*: women are likely to be credulous, which obliges men to practice a healthy disbelief. Once again, however, these few touches are not sufficient to create more than the sketch of a man. What there is is grayer, more uniform, than the refreshing capers of the watchman and the nurse. Still, in his modest way, the Aegisthus of *Libation-Bearers* qualifies for gargoyle status.

In *Agamemnon* (1617 ff.), the same end is achieved by different means. Aegisthus's blustering answer to the complaints of the chorus and the clear evidence of his cowardice, advertised earlier by Cassandra (1223 ff.) and now verified by the chorus (1625 ff.), make for a divertingly scurrilous clown. Unlike the watchman and the nurse, Aegisthus plays his role in the trilogy because the tradition called for his presence. But because of the enormous emphasis placed on Clytemnestra, Aeschylus chose to reserve for

Aegisthus the inglorious part of a gigolo. First a young gigolo, and then a middle-aged one. His is a character by subtraction. It has its importance within the scheme of things. But its opportunities for deployment are too limited to assist us in our analysis of Aeschylus's art of fashioning human conduct on the stage.

The scurrilous and the ugly are not uncommon in Aeschylean dramaturgy. We know of one play, the *Cabiri*, which appears to have featured a group of drunks. Athenaeus, who tells us about it, calls the play a tragedy.[13] It is conceivable, though not likely, that it was really a satyr drama. But we can compare the viciousness of the Egyptian herald in *Suppliants* and the brutality of some of the things said by the Furies in *Eumenides*. Tragedy need not be noble. Xerxes enters the stage with his robes torn, and the impression created by his dirge and his self-abasement runs counter to the demand for decorum. Euripides, who is often credited with having introduced this sort of ugliness into European drama, was not the first. And Aristotle's proscription of what he calls *to miaron* (the ugly) came in the face of much evidence that it had its legitimate uses.

Ugliness is merely an extreme form of registering the animal energy and the "minute particulars" which, when held within enclave limits, enliven the experience of the classical play. The minute particulars can become too prominent, and even oppressive, as they usurp a leading function. There is a question whether *Eumenides* does not accord too much scope to this kind of gargoyle realism. It could be argued that the figure of Athena is harmed by Aeschylus's desire to bear down on the particulars. The homeliness of her initial speech (397 ff.) is a consequence of the poet's intention to avoid, at all costs, any suggestion of majesty or power that might stand in the way of a life-saving familiarity. Athena plays to the hilt her part of the tough, conciliatory, practical democratic committee woman. There are moments when she comes through as almost prudish (413–14); on other occasions she exhibits a fine streak of irresolution: the Furies cannot stay but we cannot send them away either (480–81). It is not just that Athena in her capacity as the woman in the middle, mediating between men and women, old and new, war and peace, becomes an instrument of compromise. The particular forms of her conduct are more sharply contoured and get us closer to the line where caricature begins than we should expect of a major character in a serious drama. For once, what Aeschylus usually reserves for his minor figures has spilled over into a larger design. This is quite different from what happens in the case of Danaus, the Polonius of *Suppliants*, whose cautionary sermonizing and protective fussiness are projections of the cho-

---

13. *Deipnosophistae* 10.33.482F.

ral personality, here transferred from chorus to character because of the special role of this particular chorus. Danaus is not an individual so much as a pooling of tribal experience. Athena is much more sharply drawn.

Normally, however, this gargoyle art comes into its own only in the case of minor characters, or minor developments affecting major characters. When the Empress Mother remarks that of everything she has heard what grieves her most is the news that Xerxes is not decently dressed (*Pers.* 832–34, 845–51); or when she finds a motive for his incursion into Greece in the shyness of a young man (753–58), these are sudden flashes of a subtle perception of life that electrify the stage action without necessarily enriching our understanding of the character of the speaker. The particularism involved is akin to the sharpness with which the herald of *Agamemnon* details camp life in the Troad. Where else in Greek literature, prior to the advent of Plato and the Alexandrians, do we find a similarly keen observation of the desiccating force of the summer heat (555–66)? Again, the herald's insistence (503 ff.) that the returning king be given a worthy reception has about it a curious element of deprecation—as if he expected, and perhaps desired, the opposite to happen. Such refining or psychologizing is what Aeschylus allows in his secondary figures or secondary scenes. But even here a doubt enters. Could it be that the herald's warning is a convention used with heroes come home? Is there not a danger that we may mistake what the Athenians might have regarded as a bit of traditional color for the unique utterance of an exclusive self?

The role of convention in the fashioning of dramatis personae and dramatic events is unmistakable. Aeschylus has the Military Man: Agamemnon, Eteocles; the Queen: Clytemnestra; the Divine Judge: Athena; the Dowager Queen; and many others, not excluding some of the minor figures whom we have already discussed. One of the conventions with which Aeschylus works is the opposition between princes and commoners, a contrast first exploited in the *Odyssey* when Odysseus acts in concert with his slaves and retainers. Unlike Odysseus, Agamemnon in the tradition is impatient with his inferiors. Agamemnon's speech of homecoming (810 ff.) is one we would expect from a high-riding prince: unprofound, even unattractive, with the chance of anger on the edge of what he says and what he does not say. He is the man of action left callous by his obligations and his experiences. His speech consists of four parts: he proudly announces and confirms the fall of Troy; he agrees with the chorus that people cannot be trusted to be free of the envy of success; he calls for a public meeting to decide on policies for the city; and he proposes to go to the palace and give a thank-offering to the gods. The mixture of pride and suspiciousness and the proclamation of a new broom reveal the tyrannical mentality which Greek literature, and especially Greek drama, uses again and again. Public dispositions take the place of the admission of private scruples; the possibility of error or of failure is discountenanced. Sophocles added a further dimension to the portrait of the public man, with Oedipus and Creon unlocking a rich reservoir of weakness and honesty, albeit after their fall. Agamemnon is given no such chance; he is made to go to his destruction with his arrogance intact. The only major character who is a king and who allows us a glimpse of his weakness is Xerxes. But it is significant that we do not get to see him directly before he is undone. In effect, Xerxes presents himself after he has ceased to be a king and after he has reverted to the status of a child mothered by the Empress.

Only in one play is the change of a king into something more than a king carried out, and that is in *Seven.* Under the impact of the curse on the house, Eteocles is shipwrecked as a king, and allies himself with the Fury. But we can hardly instance that case as a development or a lasting change. The bulk of Eteocles's performance is in the typical mold, as general and leader of the citizens. After the Curse catches up with him and he turns into a furious privateer bent on self-destruction, he has some twenty lines of speech and a brief exchange with the chorus before he goes off to his death. One might even say that the radical conversion on stage *is* his death, analogous to the conversion of Pentheus in Euripides's *Bacchae* from king to Peeping Tom. The enormity of the change and the brief duration of the new estate reinforce the validity of the type. The general cannot change except to die.

Agamemnon's collapse before Clytemnestra's temptation (930 ff.) is so swift, and Clytemnestra's arguments seemingly so inadequate, that it has been common to apply a psychological yardstick: "The truth is that he needed no more than this easy allaying of his religious and social scruples: there is no conceivable reason why he should now suddenly change his mind—unless he secretly wishes to do so."[14] This is getting hold of the wrong end of the stick, for it assumes that the real Agamemnon is the one whom we see making his way across the materials, and that his earlier proud demeanor was the result of dissimulation. Dissimulation is not unknown in Aeschylus; Clytemnestra, it turns out near the end of the play, has been practicing a particularly clever specimen of it. To that we shall return directly. In the case of Agamemnon, however, there is not enough of a personal core to hang dissimulation on. He is a victorious general, the embodiment of a literary type, but he has no dramatic life of his own. His only function in the play, other than his initial speech of homecoming, is to be tempted to step on the materials, and thereby to fall. Whatever else is said or sung about him in the play concerns the Agamemnon of tradition, and

14. Page in J. D. Denniston and D. L. Page, eds. and comms., *Aeschylus: Agamemnon* (Oxford, 1956), p. 151.

perhaps the Agamemnon whose underworld existence will be of some importance in the rest of the trilogy; with the dramatic character of Agamemnon it has nothing to do. That character has a total of eighty-two lines, almost half of which are given over to his temptation. There is a churlishness about some of his earlier utterances which conforms to the type—though it should also be said that it adds fuel to the flames of Clytemnestra's justification, if such is needed: his "Your speech was like my absence: long drawn out" and "Leda's scion, guardian of my house" (914 ff.) are evident sneers calculated to lose him some of the sympathy of the audience.[15] But they are merely the slight exaggerations or willful uses of a recognizable pattern.

Clytemnestra's "arguments," her sly appeals to Agamemnon's preoccupation with prestige and position, are totally effective. Agamemnon falls because the temptations offered are meaningful in terms of the type he is, no matter whether such arguments might have sufficed for a more complex flesh-and-blood personality. The discussion between them is a contest of pleas, as if from the handbooks of rhetoric which were just then coming on the market, with little to indicate a process of floundering and chaos and resolution. The suddenness of the collapse is like that of Hector in the face of Achilles (*Iliad* 22.136 ff.), itself an anticipation, on the psychological level, of his impending death. But, unlike Hector's crash, which is modulated with a maximum of pathos and inwardness, Agamemnon's yielding generates nothing that brings home to us either the pity or the justness of it. It is a mere datum: the King will be dead.

This explains also how Aeschylus can shift Agamemnon's standing in the trilogy without observing the rules of psychological or social plausibility. When Agamemnon goes to his death, his arrogance, his obsession with place, and his grim selfishness loom large. The evaluation initiated by the herald's narrative of the sufferings of the common soldiers and the desecration of the temples is fully borne out by the man himself. But as soon as he is dead, the support given him by the chorus appears to vindicate him, and this is corroborated in the subsequent plays of the trilogy, until Apollo, at *Eum.* 631 ff., can refer to Agamemnon as a successful, worthy, admirable leader. The resolving function of that last play requires that *de mortuis nihil nisi bene.* Does it also require that the sacker of Troy, the sacrificer of his daughter, the desecrator of precious materials be expressly and completely whitewashed? Whatever the intention of that development, it is effective only because the figure of Agamemnon fails to provide the personal authenticity that would stand in the way. It is not that Agamemnon is a flat

15. But A. N. Michelini emphasizes the conventional aspects of the phrase in "MAKRAN GAR EXETEINAS," *Hermes* 102 (1974): 524–39.

character; if he were, the problem would still exist, for a flat villain resists beatification as much as a complex one. It is that he is merely a type, an almost impersonal entity, inspired by the legend and its elaboration in various epics, furbished anew for the scenes in which he is needed and capable of adaptation as the circumstances require. The Homeric Agamemnon can show himself magnificent and lamentable by turns, a great king but also a sorry bundle of jealousies and resentments. As the *Iliad* develops, the narrative fiction, with its scope and its opportunities for "telling," permits the construction of a legitimate character. The Aeschylean Agamemnon has little but the label of "general of the armies" to sustain a dramatic identity.

Agamemnon is the most striking instance of Aeschylus's reliance on the type-character or, what is saying the same thing, the non-character for achieving important dramatic effects. Other principals, such as the royal ghost, Darius; the protector of the land, Pelasgus; and the distraught maiden, Io, owe much of their dramatic strength to their generic limitation. Even Cassandra, the misunderstood prophet, moves us with a power that is inspired by a recognizable typology, by the calling up of a literary tradition, or perhaps even of a folk memory, which Aeschylus knew how to animate without investing it with the perilous traits of a "personal" life. The one supposedly biographical touch, the love of Apollo for this woman, and his curse, is not a matter of biography or social intersecting, but a mythological reformulation of the type she is. The great creative act of the playwright is to bring the visions upon the stage. The scene has dramatic power by virtue of the horror that is communicated. But the instrument chosen for that communication is convincing precisely because it has no share in human complexity. We are not invited to consider why Cassandra acts and talks and sings the way she does. The curse is not an explanation; if it were, it would raise more questions, especially about Apollo's intentions, than it is supposed to answer. Cassandra's complaints are, in essence, a reflection of our own willing horror at seeing a semblance of human life sacrificed without cause.

Cassandra is not dead. Modern playwrights, in an attempt to get beyond the "psychological" concerns which Artaud castigated, have rediscovered the value of the impersonal. The blind Pozzo in act 2 of *Waiting for Godot* shows some of the same impatience, inwardness, and horror of life stamped upon a vacant die. The voice is that of a protester who protests not against a specific crime, but against all life to the degree that it is constraint. The comprehensiveness of the protest puts the protester beyond the pale of a particular human station. His voice is disembodied; as a character, he affects us because he lacks the specific life, the character, to back up, and diminish, the fullness of that voice.

If, in the remainder of this chapter, I have, once again, more to say about the *Oresteia* than about the other plays, it is because the trilogy offers us a more ample opportunity for studying the question of character, and also because it is generally admitted that the trilogy gives us Aeschylus at the height of his dramatic achievement. In the eyes of many readers—I wish I could say for many spectators—the *Oresteia* is identical with Aeschylus. My own interest in all of the extant plays should be evident. Even so, it is often the case that this or that feature prominent in one of the other plays is found again in the *Oresteia*, more powerful or more interesting and sometimes more artfully integrated in the dramatic sequence. Finally, many critics have felt that if Aeschylus can be said to move close to the creation of autonomous and flesh-and-blood characters, he does so in the mature work staged two years before his death.

Agamemnon's decision to sacrifice Iphigenia is often considered a keystone in the edifice of character-shaping which these critics regard as the most important discovery of Aeschylean tragedy. Because, it is argued, we are made to watch Agamemnon as he slides from irresolution and agony into vicious choice, Agamemnon's claim to the status of an idiosyncratic character is incontestable. But it will be remembered that the sacrifice, and the decision to perform it, are at several removes from dramatic immediacy. We must distinguish among what is enacted on the stage, what a character reports about himself as having been enacted (or being on the point of enactment), what is reported by a messenger, what is reported by the chorus, and what is referred to by the chorus or others incidentally, outside of a context devoted to reporting. One may quarrel about the precise details of this scheme of vanishing immediacy. But by every conceivable account, the manner in which Agamemnon's decision is introduced is certain to refract the immediacy of the experience. The little phrase "not finding fault with any seer" (186) is interesting. Is the chorus criticizing Agamemnon for giving in to the prophet too quickly? If so, the phrase might help us to sort out our feelings about Agamemnon's deed. It is more likely, however, that the chorus, at this point at least, takes no position whatever. The phrase chimes in with the detached air of their recital. The impersonal narrative emphasizes Agamemnon's near-automatic compliance with what the playwright calls the "blasts of fortune" (187).

The legend demands that Agamemnon, through membership in the house of Atreus, inherit his father's grim child-eating legacy. It is true that Aeschylus lays far greater stress on what the King has done himself than on the crime committed by his father. But the monstrosity of the action appears to arise out of a matrix of history and circumstance that dwarfs the King's initiative and provides the chorus with its cushioning language. The *Oresteia* illustrates the Aeschylean tragic fashion of putting the causative factors in front of the drama. Nothing that happens on stage can truly be said to produce effects, or to be caused primarily by something else that happens on stage. The events that make up the action are motivated by causes that antedate the play. Both in *Agamemnon* and in *Libation-Bearers*, after the bloody deed is done, the doer's awareness is deepened. He becomes conscious of demons and other forces beyond him as the ultimate causes or as the possible avengers. The repeated pattern suggests a significant mode of looking at human action. Aeschylus is not telling us that demons rather than men are at fault; the speakers are principals and choruses who have their own axes to grind. But the prominence of the scheme helps to blunt our sense of human freedom. It has been said that tragedy rests on a double reading of Heraclitus's *ēthos anthrōpōi daimōn*: a man's self is his presiding deity; or, conversely, a man's presiding deity is his self.[16] The demonic and the psychological coalesce.

The scene that is particularly instructive in this regard is the last scene of *Libation-Bearers*. Does Orestes turn mad, and if so, how are we to interpret his madness? As a psychological, i.e., clinical, development? Or as a realization of what he states to be the case, i.e., of being hunted and driven by forces beyond him? By the same token, can we say that in this scene Orestes is shown experiencing the pangs of conscience? Or is it the case that the real powers, the demons and Apollo, come to be ranged in the foreground, displacing, as it were, the precarious autonomy of Orestes as an agent, and prompting a dramatic dissolution of his sanity? Such questions must be answered before we can talk further about the nature of human action and of character-drawing in Aeschylus.[17]

Early in *Libation-Bearers* the chorus refers to Clytemnestra as an "ungodly woman." The main thrust of the adjective is clearly accusatory: Clytemnestra is impious, hated by the gods, a blot upon the purity of a god-fearing society. But other incidences of the word, as at *Suppl.* 422, indicate that it can also carry the sense of "ill-starred." The habit of seeing a person against a background of divine will is crucial; it is more than the use of a pale formula. It suggests that the dramatic agents can be *both* analogous to persons *and* foci for the understanding of larger currents. Only the gargoyles and features modeled on gargoyles escape this duality, but they are, relatively speaking, marginal to the tragic pattern. The larger currents can be variously felt and traced: as the play of demons, as the constellation of fate, as the working out of a curse or an oracle. They in turn represent the pull of legendary tales, or the vectors of verifiable history. Drama possesses an additional means of absorbing the incipient autonomy of characters, and

16. R. P. Winnington-Ingram, "Tragedy and Greek Archaic Thought," in *Classical Drama and Its Influence: Essays Presented to H. D. F. Kitto* (London, 1965), pp. 31–50.

17. For further remarks on this head, see below, chaps. 9 and 10.

that is the lyric mode, the human capacity for experiencing the world primarily not as a concatenation of causes and effects or purposes and results, but as a tapestry of sense impressions and arcs of energy operating directly upon the imagination. The force of the lyric perception in drama, nowhere more compelling than in *Agamemnon*, is to cancel the concreteness and the separateness of the understanding self vis-à-vis the understood object, and to force the two into a new identity. As the audience of the drama surrenders itself to the power of the choral song, it surrenders also its privilege of judging and objectifying human actions distinct from the experiential stream of which they are a part.[18]

The lyric mode is more compelling in some plays than in others. But as a generic expectation, it is pervasive, and counters an excessive preoccupation with character in isolation. It is as if we were looking at a crowded map, on which events, deeds, and actions are no more prominent than feelings, general truths, and fears. There is here none of the simple dialectic between the will of the universe and the individual will that Thomas Hardy presents in his theory of tragedy in *The Dynasts*, and which manifests itself in his novels as a deadlock of wills, paralyzing heroism and enervating the springs of action. On the contrary, despite the lyric mold and other factors limiting the exposition of human action in Aeschylus, the role of the heroic agent is by no means erased. His art has nothing in common with the modern stage, where pathos rather than praxis has become the norm, and where human initiative has been displaced by static condition and by a "decoratively anemic" reality.[19] Aeschylean tragedy celebrates man as agent, and focuses on action and achievement. But the matrix guarantees against the error of assuming that convincing action and convincing character-drawing presuppose one another. The words written about *King Lear* some fifty years ago by J. Copeau point in the same direction:

> Here nothing is cut to shape. Nothing leaves life behind. Life is superior to the beings who do not know her and do not know themselves. The external action exercises its immense power. The reflex, the response prompted in the living matter unravels all its consequences. It is pitiless. And the agent clings to the compulsion which his first movement triggers. . . . The enormity of events and of natural catastrophes goes together with the ferocity of characters and works with it to produce these vast combinations of things.[20]

18. See the difficult formulations of P. Szondi, *Theorie des modernen Dramas* (Frankfurt, 1956), p. 68. Note also the remarks on irony in F. M. Cornford, *Thucydides Mythistoricus* (London, 1907), pp. 148–49.

19. The words are those of D. Donoghue, *The Third Voice* (Princeton, N.J., 1959), p. 255.

20. J. Copeau, *Critiques d'un autre temps* (Paris, 1923), p. 164, apropos of *King Lear*.

To understand the power of the lyric mode, one more glance at the Cassandra scene may be permitted. Superficially it might be said that Cassandra is a messenger not of the past, but of the future or the present, an announcer of death-in-the-happening. But the fact of death is already more or less established. Cassandra does not talk about the deed of the killing—the human effort and the human consequences—but about its anchoring in the house, in the past, in the curse. The deed counts for less than the ambience: that is the lyric response. And Cassandra gives us the lyric mode at its most extravagant, severed from the choral conventions which ordinarily muffle it and concentrated in the sensory and moral energy of a single, outrageously isolated individual. When the chorus conveys the mode, there is less concentration and the dispersion of unity is more thorough. We have already discussed the process whereby the Furies oscillate between their role as hellish forces (*Eum.* 321 ff.) and their function as moral guarantors of justice (490 ff.). When, at 415–35, the Furies pay their respects to Athena and engage her in an exchange that is courteous, intelligent, and mature, it is difficult to recognize in them the same persons whose bloodthirstiness we witness at the beginning of the play. The fluidity is a function of the context. This is true of the individual scene; it is even truer of the larger unit, the play, in which action and character obey larger rhythms.

All this means that such character terms as "vacillation," "hesitation," "adaptation," and "change" may not be relevant. An Apollo who, after *Eum.* 748 ff., is no longer an interested party but an embodiment of the spirit of fairness cannot be said to have experienced a conversion, but is responding to new stimuli which have to do with the changed dramatic situation. When Eteocles, after the announcement of his brother's presence at the seventh gate, changes from controlling statesman to obsessed duelist, the change is not one of character, much less the realization of his "real" character, but the superimposition of an awareness of the curse upon the earlier conception in which the curse was only a minor motif. When Pelasgus changes from the imperious potentate, the leader of his country, which he is in the first scenes, to a mere functionary of the people, unwilling to risk their fury, the change is not to be measured in terms of verisimilitude. It answers to a set of changed circumstances, each of which has brought out one aspect of a complex aggregate, whose complexity is itself a function of the complexity of the situation in which the character is placed.

Aeschylus is not writing "heroic" tragedy in the spirit of Sophocles. An Antigone, an Oedipus, an Ajax are primary characters; the interest of the plays is largely in the way the characters are made to clash with sets of circumstances that prove too great for them. The Sophoclean hero comes to grief because he attempts to maintain a personal identity and a consistency of conduct which the social nexus will not allow. Prometheus is the only hero in the Aeschylean canon who maintains a similar stance, and of whom it could be said that the play is written around a character of stable dimensions, designed to battle circumstance. In the rest of Aeschylean drama character (and human action) and circumstance cannot be similarly separated or made to clash. A modern critic writes that "tragedy is a cadential form . . . [that] reflects the basic structure of personal life, and therewith of feeling when life is viewed as a whole."[21] The model is not that of Aeschylus. The life that controls Aeschylus's vision is not that of an individual, a personal life, but a life that extends forward and backward, horizontally and vertically, and embraces much else beyond the single curve of a heroic career.

Once this is understood, we may have less difficulty with a curious phenomenon which is especially prominent in that most lyrical play, *Agamemnon*: the coalescing of two persons into a new unit. In the entrance ode of *Agamemnon*, the king is referred to as the "senior leader" (184, 205). It is as if a special effort were needed to separate Agamemnon from the larger and, in terms of the house, more significant unit: the Atreidae. The house of Atreus is a more meaningful entity at this stage of the dramatic proceedings than any one individual. The brothers, Agamemnon and Menelaus, in their combination as a brace of generals, serve as shorthand for the house. The mention of one invariably turns our thoughts to the other. After the homecoming of Agamemnon by himself has become an issue in speeches by the herald and Clytemnestra, the chorus (617) asks the messenger about Menelaus; in its thinking the brothers belong together. The coalescence of the figures of Agamemnon and Menelaus is matched by the imagery of the birds who are their analogue (113, 122 ff.). Critics differ about the degree to which Aeschylus is attempting to distinguish the birds in temperament. Some identify one bird as aggressive and the other as soft, and proceed to distinguish the temperaments of Agamemnon and Menelaus. As far as we can tell, there is nothing in the complete tetralogy which requires Menelaus to be a coward. Hence the distinction would seem to be redundant. The language bears down on the doubleness rather than on the difference. Throughout the trilogy, the brothers are twins in action and in the burden of the house; it would be inappropriate for this glancing passage to suggest otherwise. The brothers work in tandem, and it takes a special act of discrimination on the part of the chorus to single out one of them, usually Agamemnon, for separate attention.

21. S. Langer, *Feeling and Form* (New York, 1953), p. 351.

Clytemnestra and Helen, the renegade daughters of Zeus and Leda, are treated similarly. At the very moment when the chorus complains about the Queen they also once again touch on Helen's guilt (1455 ff.): Agamemnon's murder is only the latest of the many losses Helen's departure has caused. Clytemnestra protests: do not blame Helen; include me in your criticism. This is in tune with the chorus's perspective. In the sequel, the concrescent vision is maintained, with Agamemnon and Menelaus (1469) and the two sisters (1470) combined into pairs. The linkage is an essential part of the house, that powerful shaper of many choral utterances, and also of the laments of Cassandra. The watchman contemplates the notion of the house itself taking on speech (37). The tandem formulation gets us a little closer to that awful contingency. And with the house finding its voice, the contribution of the individual is once again put in jeopardy.

There is much, therefore, to support the view that "there is something wrong in our critical isolation of the protagonist, and something wrong with our sealing-off of the principal figures . . . from the atmosphere of lyric commentary they live in." [22] At the same time, it cannot be denied that the concept of the "hero" is thought to be one of the most powerful legacies of Greek tragic drama, and that the persistence of the hero on the modern stage is felt to be one of the factors in the continuing relevance of ancient tragedy. Murray Krieger, writing on the tragic vision, sketches the difference between a reconciliation via universals—Aristotle, Hegel—and the fragmentation of the modern vision, whose particularity derives from Kierkegaard.[23] What remains untouched, in spite of the stress on difference, is the tacit belief that a tragedy has a hero.

It will be better not to employ the term "hero," with its Renaissance connotations and its suggestions of centrality. But as we train our sights on the principal agents in an Aeschylean drama, we realize that their integration in the lyric scheme, their absorption by the action, their corporate standing in a network of social and political filiation, does not after all diminish the force of their singularity. The Aeschylean tragic character shares with his modern counterpart an intrinsic social isolation. The matrix of which he is a part differs sharply from the neo-classical universe of overpowering attractions and revulsions. The Greek character is heroic to the degree that he is not fitted into a nexus of give-and-take; the Sophoclean protagonist is the clearest evidence of that. Aeschylus's principal also speaks by and to himself; the nexus which holds him firm is not one of human relations, but of the creative ensembles of legend and politics. He is not

22. Jones, *Aristotle and Greek Tragedy*, p. 82.
23. *The Tragic Vision* (New York, 1960).

uprooted, because there is no society to uproot him from. There is no estrangement, no fragmentation, because there is no accepted model of an integrated social experience to alert us to more harmonious possibilities.

But this also means that it is difficult for Aeschylus to create the impression of loneliness. If Aeschylus wishes to characterize Prometheus or Electra as suffering because of their isolation, drastic means have to be taken. The invocation of the elements and of the gods is Prometheus's way. His special standing, or rather, non-standing, within the human community is marked not only by the contempt he shows for men in general and in particular, but also by the truculence with which he sets up an abortive community of interest with larger than human forces. Electra's loneliness manifests itself in fantasy and the violent distortion of familial bonds. As she defines Orestes to herself as her father, her mother, and her sister as well as her brother, the piling up of kinship terms is a measure of the special nature of her isolation. In the absence of natural ties of human affinity, artificial bonds have to be created to argue, by exaggeration, the precarious position of Clytemnestra's daughter.

These are extreme cases; the feeling of loneliness, endemic on the Sophoclean stage, is relatively rare in Aeschylean drama. But isolation is the common birthright of the Aeschylean character. Conceptually, in the way we would define his being, he is part of a larger setting, or of several larger schemes working together. Dramatically, however, and in his relation to other characters, he is separate and insular. Agamemnon, after rendering his account of triumph, remarks on the envy of his companions (832 ff.) and their lack of cooperation, Odysseus excepted. Xerxes has reason to complain about his isolation; Eteocles has given up on his fellow citizens and resolves to take the whole weight of the required action upon himself. The Furies revel in their separation from the rest of the gods, in spite of the fact that they have their office *from* the gods (364 ff., 391 ff.). It could be argued that this thematic carving-out of aloofness from a potential sociability can register its effect only if sociability is accepted as the norm. But the intimation that social solidarity is possible is a delusion. Aeschylean tragedy repels the human bonds without which ordinary life would be unbearable. The singularity of the tragic voice is primary. Orestes is on his own; the fleeting assistance of Pylades, a small voice in the moral wilderness sounding just at the right moment, serves only to confirm the canon of isolation. The ebb-and-flow movements of Orestes and Electra toward each other, their need for cooperation in the interest of the intrigue, are shadowed by their own hopelessness; they are brought into play only in order to be proven delusory. There is no union of souls, only the formal steps toward a union which in the nature of things cannot come about.

Aeschylus's characters stand outside human relationships because they are seemingly invulnerable. Agamemnon is open to temptation, and Orestes's sanity crumbles within sight of the Furies. But none of them experiences the inner struggles, the pangs of conscience, the second thoughts that Euripides was the first to put on the stage. Sensitivity, openness, the labile construct of the ego: these are the fruits of a new vision which became possible after Aeschylus, and which was ultimately to lead from tragedy to New Comedy and the bourgeois *drame*. Euripides's plays are full of young and gracious persons who voluntarily elect death because of the delicacy with which they perceive the needs of their friends and foes. The bruising of beauty and of moral sensibility in a meaningless universe is a constant Euripidean theme. Aeschylus has none of this. He avoids the self-dramatizing which self-sacrifice calls for. The lust for life among his characters is too strong to permit voluntary resignation. In Aeschylus, life is both worse—it kills indiscriminately—and better—the city flourishes—than in Euripides, but it is whole, and the character identifies himself with it unreservedly. Suffering is not a matter of nakedness, of protective layers stripped off and nerves exposed, but of rights or claims injured and defended.

The softer human virtues, those that in civilized life bring men and women together into unions of feeling, are notable by their absence, save in choral comments which are, as it were, deflected from reaching the ears of the characters. Except perhaps for *Prometheus*, there is no Aeschylean play in which a person comes on stage and says: sorry, it is not *my* wish, but I have to do such and such. That is Euripidean philanthropy. In *Prometheus*, both Hephaestus and Ocean experience the pangs of bad conscience, and attempt to lend a helping hand. They are rebuffed by the hero, in whose eyes such assistance is demeaning; assistance would break in upon an isolation which is a necessary condition of being a principal. Even the daughters of Danaus do not ask for help; they insist on their rights. The only bond in which men may find themselves gathered together is the bond of a common crime or, to put it in the terms of the legend which sponsors it, the bond of a curse. But such a bond does not appease the sense of isolation.

How is it possible to speak of isolation, if the character resists our attempts to read into it the common need for drawing together with others in compacts of love or hatred? The answer to this is that weight, sheer mass—or rather the simulation of mass by means of solid speech—takes the place of the human identity. It is an ancient commonplace that the higher the tower, the more likely it is to attract the lightning of Zeus. Sophoclean drama utilizes the old Homeric image of the headland struck by the howling wind and raging waves to commemorate the hero's exposed stance. Each of Aeschylus's major characters is invested with the same promise of truculence, invulnerable to the inroads of the environment, in defiance of death and madness and the possibility of compromise freely chosen. What defines the Sophoclean hero is not his awareness of his singularity, his purity, or the strength of his action, but the tangible quality of his presence. In addition, the Sophoclean hero goes through a characteristic career, including a momentary weakening—which defines him as a social being and as a mortal—and a final hardening. The Aeschylean character has the presence without the career, the massiveness without the tempering through fleeting intimations of mortality. Even a Xerxes and an Aegisthus are vivid presences, massed bundles of speech and purpose refusing to be wedged into an awareness of fallibility or wrong. Indeed, their sense of importance, undiminished by any feeling of guilt or shared loss, is so great that it reminds us of the children studied by modern psychology who forget, or fail to perceive in the first place, their contribution to a chain of events, and hence blame others for what befalls them.[24]

The Aeschylean character does not need the advice directed by the chorus at Orestes (*Lib.* 832 ff.):

> Place the heart of Perseus
> In your mind. . . .

Orestes has the heart of Perseus naturally within him; he glances away from his fellows as he insists upon his rights. Euripidean heroes and heroines sacrifice themselves so that others may flourish. The Aeschylean hero is a mechanism for the conservation and expansion of energy, not for its snuffing out. Oaths are sworn and threats are issued to affirm the vitality of the character rather than to delineate future action. In French Renaissance drama, the fixity is one of values and of conventions. Rodrigue gives up Chimène in order to preserve their love. This radical juxtaposition of persons and values is possible on a stage committed to the appraisal of a moral and social code, and especially of Christian standards. In Greece, perhaps the epic, and perhaps the new humanism of Euripides provide parallels. In Aeschylus, a person does not choose between ideas or values, but seeks to advance his personal stakes within the specific conditions created by the poet to make the character loom as large as possible. The Cornelian hero may fail in his attempt to match the measurable, fixed good which exists outside him or to embody within himself, or within himself and his beloved, the norms against which he gauges himself. In Aeschylus, no such fixed terms are given; no anguish can accrue from the clash of two conflicting norms. Conflict exists only between persons, and the roots of these

24. See, e.g., F. Redl and D. Wineman, *Children Who Hate* (Glencoe, Ill., 1951), pp. 108 ff.

conflicts are not to be sought in anything so abstract as moral positions. It is simply a case of towering presences going to their doom for want of a world that is large enough to allow room to all. This helps to explain why it is difficult to determine why the Danaids act as they do or why Xerxes fails. External factors count for less than the impact of mass upon mass; reasons given for the clash tend to be felt as rationalizations. It may also help to explain why Aeschylus can, in the case of the Danaids and the Furies, use a multiple protagonist. Unlike Sophocles and Euripides, who lodge heroic suffering within the contours of a single career, Aeschylus can realize his conception of dramatic collision by means of group action as well as individuals. Where a meaningful commitment to courage or duty or virtue is secondary, the dimensions of the tragic personality need not be confined narrowly. On the contrary, the power and the fury of the impact of a human presence invites the configuration of a group. In this kind of tragic art, where weight counts for more than psychological finesse or biographical pathos, the choral protagonist has some decided advantages. The sidelining of the chorus after Aeschylus constitutes a flight from the full utilization of what the genre has to offer.

Because the tragic engagement in Aeschylus is dramatized without a significant reference to issues—here *Prometheus* is an exception—the scope of the impact appears to be the greater for it. Twice the playwright uses the expression "testing the demon," which reformulates the action as a combat with the unknown, commencing with a reconnaissance. Once (*Agam.* 1663) the phrase is used by Aegisthus to characterize the foolhardiness of the elders. In *Libation-Bearers* (513), it is the chorus leader who in the ensuing intrigue thus expresses his expectations of Orestes. A similar usage is found at *Seven* 230 ff.: it is the business of the men, not of the women, to do homage to the gods when enemies are probing (or when they, the men, probe the enemy). These are merely straws in the wind, but they suggest strongly that conflict is visualized by analogy with the simple business of measuring one's strength, preferably in a climactic situation where the rival is conceived to be of towering strength: a daemon. To be sure, Electra and the chorus at the beginning of *Libation-Bearers* cautiously feel their way and sound out potential opposition before proceeding to more overt action; they shrink from the forthrightness of an Antigone or an Oedipus. But this greater carefulness has nothing to do with a reflecting upon causes or a weakening in the face of controversial and debated values. Rather it gives us the more cumbersome preparations of a human force entering upon the plain. Because the causes of the conflict are not clearly felt or enunciated in intellectual terms, the aggression need not emerge with lightning swiftness. (See also the section on shuttle speech, above, chapter 7.)

The characters who waver or respond readily to the provocation of an issue clearly drawn tend not to be the leading characters. Pelasgus and Ocean are secondary in the sense that their irresoluteness—one is tempted to say: their humanness in the face of a troubling dilemma—throws the inflexibility of the principal or principals into greater relief. As we shall see, neither Orestes nor the Furies can be said to waver, although it is evident that in *Eumenides*, for reasons that will become clearer later, the contest of massed energies is not given the lasting scope it has in the other plays. This can be measured by entries. We expect that the forcefulness of a character's engagement be balanced by the steadiness of his stage presence. Where there is a great deal of coming and going, the impression of massiveness that we have been discussing is, of course, diminished. In *Agamemnon*, where we have found that Clytemnestra exits and returns on several occasions, the effect is due to the intrigue, dissembled though it is. In *Eumenides*, the frequency of personnel changes, especially early in the play, has to do with the ethos of the play, which is counter-heroic. For the resolution offered by this last play of the trilogy, it is important that the uncompromising intransigence of character be diluted. Everybody in the play is a newcomer; the Acropolis is used as a kind of assizes, in which nobody is quite at home—a neutral arena for consultation and appeals, but not for heroic stubbornness. There are moments when it is questionable whether a particular character needs to be on stage or not. At the point when Athena has closed the debate, Apollo, the attorney for Orestes, could decide to leave to go on to his next trial. His observation that he will remain to see how things will come out (677) is amusing because a little later (713 ff.) he surrenders his bystander's role and gets himself drawn into a wrangle with the Furies.[25]

But *Eumenides* is the exception. Elsewhere Aeschylus's principals are securely lodged within an action and bulk large where they stand. And their bulk is in large part supported by Aeschylus's refusal to diffuse the massiveness and refine their conduct along the lines of what Aristotle called the probable or the plausible. No wonder that neo-classical emulators of the ancient drama preferred Euripides or Sophocles. It is a fact that most dramatic criticism prior to the turn of the century remained hostile to Aeschylus. For the Renaissance, a comment by La Harpe is representative of many: The character of Clytemnestra is of a revolting atrocity; she is neither amorous nor jealous nor ambitious; all she wants to do is kill her husband, and that she does. "Voilà la pièce."[26]

25. For the distribution of lines 676–79 I follow Winnington-Ingram in the apparatus of D. Page, ed., *Aeschyli Tragoediae* (Oxford, 1972), p. 272.

26. J. F. de La Harpe, *Cours de littérature* (Paris, 1825), vol. 1, p. 84, cited by W. H. Matheson, *Claudel and Aeschylus* (Ann Arbor, Mich., 1965), pp. 5 ff.

In what he says, La Harpe is undoubtedly right. Nevertheless his remark gives me a chance to reconsider what we have been saying, and to make an important qualification and in the process to show that Aeschylus, like any other writer of genius, is not easily caught in the trap of a general definition. Without wishing to go back on my skepticism concerning the operation of "character" in Aeschylus, I hasten to confess that Clytemnestra seems to me to constitute an important exception to the standard for which we have been arguing. The Queen is too prominent a personage to be included among the gargoyle figures of the second rank. On the other hand, she is too interesting a personality to be explained largely in terms of a prefabricated type, or as a paradigm of unselfconscious isolation, or as merely adequate to the requirements of a plot. The intrigue which she conducts is of a very special sort, ill-calculated to explain the secret of her power or her lurid charm. To see how the engineers of a proper intrigue deport themselves, we need only glance at the role of Orestes in *Libation-Bearers*, not to mention the more fully developed intriguers in Sophocles and Euripides. It has been said that there is no intrigue in *Agamemnon*. As Reinhardt puts it: instead of concealment and warnings, the dominant signals of an intrigue in progress, *Agamemnon* has divine signs and voices of doom, sometimes pronounced by the very men and women who should be in the position of receiving the warnings.[27] Disaster spreads everywhere, gathering strength toward its fulfillment. There is no dividing line, properly speaking, between those who do the plotting and those who are being plotted against. *Agamemnon* is the story of a wrath; Clytemnestra, like Pinter's Goldberg, is embodied Wrath. It is difficult to tell who or what she is, but we can speculate, not always accurately, on where she is going (153–55):

> There remains a fearsome, risen-anew
> Householder of guile, remembering Wrath, child-avenger.

From the beginning, information about Clytemnestra comes in in bushels. She is a woman with the mind of a man (11). Her authority and her initiative are acknowledged in scene after scene. She is the doer, the preparer; the emphasis is on her power, her independence of action. The chorus attempts, in vain, to assert against her the traditional prerogatives of the male sex. When they voice their reluctance to accept Clytemnestra's interpretation of the fire signal, she comes close to regarding their disbelief as a pointed insult. Given the conventional nature of such question-and-answer sequences, Clytemnestra's resentment is revealing: we learn that the Queen has an ego, a measure of self in excess of her public role, subject to discomfi-

---

27. K. Reinhardt, *Aischylos als Regisseur und Theologe* (Bern, 1949), pp. 82 ff.

ture as well as satisfaction. Hers is the will, the design, against which everything in the play comes to be measured. The chorus's "You could be a man" (351) in answer to Clytemnestra's "I am a woman" (348) is a feeble acknowledgment of the singularity of her person.

The feminine charm must not be forgotten. Clytemnestra is, after all, the sister of Helen. The charm becomes a weapon as she persuades Agamemnon to step upon the crimson stuffs. It is a charm that kills, a fatal handmaiden of corrupted Eros. Refinement and violence, cultivation and cruelty, come together in a compelling mixture. The lines in which the chorus elaborates the meaning of Helen's name (687 ff.) may, *pari passu*, do duty also for Clytemnestra. They dwell on the collocation of the soft with the harsh, merging luxuriousness with wrath:

> Her name is right; she spells Hell
> For the ships, the men, the city;
> Brocaded canopies opened up as she sailed
> With the breeze of the giant wester;
> The pack of the hunt, shield upon shield,
> Through trackless tracing of oars
> Unloaded her at arboreal shores
> In the East;
> And Strife, blood-soiled, saw it done.
> Wrath helped; sights trained on the end,
> She gave her to Troy, an ominous trust,
> Preparing to crush. . . .

The virulence of the lines, progressing from delicate and civilized pursuits to the abyss of Strife and Aggression, applies equally to Clytemnestra in her Argos. It is a cruelty which, when resisted, degenerates into vulgarity. Clytemnestra's address to Cassandra (1035 ff.), holds the menace, the delight in having victims squirm, which intellectual brilliance tinged with evil commands: "You there, I mean you, Cassandra. You will be one of many household slaves. The same happened to Heracles. Be glad that your masters are not *nouveaux riches*; they would throw the book at you." For contrast, to see how a humane mistress may receive a slave consort of her husband's, Deianira's kindness toward Iole, in Sophocles's *Trachinians*, is instructive.

Clytemnestra's act, the murder of her husband, has little to do with any passion for Aegisthus or any profound anger over the affair of the sacrifice of Iphigenia. Nothing in the play suggests that Clytemnestra is intended to appeal to us in her function as mother, or as a disappointed or cheated wife. Her references to Iphigenia are not to be taken as the pleading of extenuating circumstances for the crime undertaken, but as an almost impersonal recording of the past sins of the clan and their most recent outcropping. As for Cassandra, the Queen's belated reminder that she was Agamemnon's concubine (1440 ff.) is not a mark of jealousy but of Clytemnestra's contempt for the world of Agamemnon and everything contained therein. Domesticity, the family, are too narrow to contain her greatness. Clytemnestra is rather more like one of the remarkable woman culprits in Elizabethan and Jacobean revenge tragedy, except that Aeschylus does not play with the disharmony between domestic filiation and demonic revenge which equips many of the Renaissance heroines with their perverse seductiveness. Like Iago, she combines pure vice, radical and gratuitous, with parochial motivations and social ties.[28] But the domestic aspect emerges only as part of the deception, through the flattering speech with which she succeeds in laying Agamemnon's scruples to rest, and whose dissimulations are meant to be perceived.

There can, I think, be little doubt that the element of deception is carried openly into court. It is mistaken, in fact, to speak of dissembling. Nothing is dissembled or hidden; the contempt implied in the flattery is so palpable that it is no longer a truth obscured by a veil of pretending but an outright weapon leveled against Agamemnon. Agamemnon is unnerved because the contempt is out in the open. The kowtowing and bowing and scraping sit ludicrously upon the lady whose man-like heart was brought to our attention earlier. Agamemnon is not tempted by cajolery; he is unmanned by open defiance clothing itself, transparently enough, in servility. There is no point in comparing this kind of psychological warfare with the simulations of Sophocles's Ajax and Deianira or with the even more creative trickery of Orestes at *Lib.* 674 ff. They are meant to deceive; Clytemnestra's orations are designed to irritate.

As Reinhardt saw, it is difficult to speak of intrigue. Clytemnestra is a conspirator whose plans we must guess. She has no fellow conspirators; Aegisthus's share in the murder, and in the preparations for it, is, as we learn later, too slight to warrant much attention, and the shape of the drama forbids any early concern with him. Hence, Clytemnestra's traffic with her husband proceeds from silence, from a lack of material clues, to outright attack. There is no middle ground, no halfway stage at which both her desires and recollections of an irrecoverable past are bound together in a mixture of hesitation or regret. Ambivalences there are, but they are minor. Her speech employs none of the smallish, clever stratagems of deception that go with the dramatic realization of a plot. The weight of Clytemnestra's aggression rules out the playfulness of allusion. It has been suggested that with her remarks to the chorus (345−47),

28. Cf. B. Spivack, "Shakespeare and the Allegory of Evil," cited by N. Rabkin, *Shakespeare and the Common Understanding* (New York, 1967), p. 78, n. 33.

Even if the men return unfaulted by
The gods, the suffering of the dead would stir
And rise. . . .

Clytemnestra is alluding to Iphigenia, but that the chorus understands her to mean the dead at Troy. I prefer to think that Clytemnestra's words refer generally to those who have died in the war. But the threatening implication is obvious.

Clytemnestra does not prevaricate; she is a mighty liar. Her lies can be monumental in their simplicity. She responds to the arrival of the herald (600 ff.) by comtemplating the joy a husband come home will give her. She launches herself on a career of conventional greeting formulas whose spuriousness is apparent to both audience and chorus. Her statement that she has had no more to do with another man than with the tempering of bronze (611–12) is curious, both for its needless apologetics—is this how one meets a returning spouse?—and for the terms of its comparison: what is the aptness, under the circumstances, of "I know nothing of the smith's art"? It will not do to look for subtle echoes and reverberations—to speculate, for instance, that the tempering of bronze harks back to the murder of Iphigenia or forward to the murder of Agamemnon. The thought stands on its own, set apart by its extravagance, as does the excessiveness of the lyric "beloved" (605). The audience's knowledge of mythology and the disquiet of the chorus are assaulted head-on. Clytemnestra is a liar who wishes her lies to be recognized as such. The more widely the recognition is accepted, the greater the affront to Agamemnon. Her sleepless nights, the mosquitoes that keep her awake, and the dreams that perturb her (887 ff.) form a tissue of creative invention that would put Odysseus to shame. But their purpose is aggression, not caution.

In the face of this cruel joy in inventing a world whose falseness is designed to hurt, the critic must dispense with his custom of tracing the long-distance connections so dear to him. At 868 Clytemnestra says, apparently jokingly, that if all the reports she had heard about Agamemnon's difficulties had been true, the King would have been a tissue full of meshes, so lacerated would his body have been. The reference to the net has proved irresistible; it has been claimed that the Grand Guignol picture of a sieve-like Agamemnon reveals Clytemnestra's secret hopes, and that these hopes center on an image which is an anticipation of the very tool she will employ later to immobilize Agamemnon for the kill.[29] That there is something grotesque about her imaginings is undeniable. In the sequel, Agamemnon turns into a three-headed monster, with a threefold covering of earth. But there is nothing secret about the wishful imagination at work. The raw

29. See also the discussion above, chap. 5, p. 120.

visions, so lacking in the decorum that might be expected of the usual queen, are an advertisement of Clytemnestra's belligerence. They are fabricated for the moment; to affiliate their imagery with earlier or later elements or endow the Queen with hopes or sensibilities that function independently of the rhetoric of the moment is to glance away from that moment and blunt its force. As Clytemnestra's speech dwells on the imagined scenes of Agamemnon's death, the crushing demoralization communicated to chorus and audience is immediate.

Cassandra's portrayal of Clytemnestra (and Aegisthus) at 1223 ff. is the first explicit account by another of Clytemnestra's real being. But, coming as it does after the brutal spectacle of the Queen's assault, its shock value is minimal, especially so since Cassandra's revelations are not exactly sharp of focus and require the filling in of details, either from Cassandra's earlier lyrics (1100 ff.) or from the action yet to come. The audience is not in a position to advance far beyond its earlier understanding that Clytemnestra is aggressive, hostile, possibly destructive; more precise confirmation is still to come. It does not come until Agamemnon's death cries are heard, or rather until the death cries are put in perspective by Clytemnestra's speech of admission (1372 ff.).

It is a remarkable speech, for a number of reasons. Agamemnon is not named; the name is held in abeyance until the end, when it is produced like the solution to a taxing puzzle (1404 ff.). The weight of the statement is on the deed, not on the victim of the deed or on the justice of the case. The deed is described in vivid presents, as if Clytemnestra were now, for the first time, capable of experiencing the action with the detachment of a connoisseur. It is also described defensively, as the final phase in a preventive war (1374 ff.). The earlier exuberance, the nervous joy of the attack, is forgotten, to be replaced by apologia. The quarrel and the planning for the deed are now alleged to have been long in the making. The killing, we learn, was the final explosion of a slowly maturing enmity. This is an entirely new perspective; nothing in the earlier part of the play has prepared us for it. The effect of the argument is to approximate Clytemnestra's campaign retrospectively to the rhythm of the intrigue that we are about to witness in *Libation-Bearers*. Dramatically, that is a falsification; psychologically, it comes close to saying that the action has broken Clytemnestra just as it has undone Agamemnon. The man-hearted woman, the vital artificer of aggressive fiction, is transformed into a weary plotter, drained of heart and grandeur. The process is completed in the exchange with the chorus. The emphasis on the concreteness of the blood starts out as joy in the tangible evidence of a manful deed heroically accomplished. It shades off into preoccupation with blood-guilt, which increasingly moves Clytemnestra into the position of distinguishing between herself as an instrument and "the ancient, acrid avenger" (1501) as the real agent. This is her way of renouncing complete identification with the deed. The chorus understands her; it counters (1507) that the daemon may have helped, but that the true originator of the calamity must be sought elsewhere.

Clytemnestra, then, turns into a woman, and a complaining one at that. If one looks for something like psychological realism in Aeschylus, it will be found in these scenes, after the killing of Agamemnon, when Clytemnestra is beginning to turn into the figure whom we will meet again in *Libation-Bearers*. Unlike Lady Macbeth, she feels no remorse; she does not go through the agony of a Christian soul damned. But neither does she turn relaxed or contented. There is a new watchfulness, a hope that things will quiet down now that her duty, if such it was, has been done. Because the time for lying, for playing with the truth, is gone, she reveals herself openly as an emancipated woman who realizes that her emancipation has cost her dearly.

Clytemnestra's remarks on Agamemnon's burial, 1551 ff., convey the bitterness of her disillusion. She no longer sides with the Fury; she admits her sole responsibility; but the spirit is one of resignation. Toward the end, she puts on the hair shirt of the proto-Cynic: If only I could put a stop to the murderous madness of the house, I'd be satisfied with a pauper's portion (1567 ff.). The language, of property and of diet, helps to establish the new Clytemnestra. She wavers back and forth between her concern for the chorus and her contempt for them. The woman who had killed to free herself from the ties of one union now finds another, lesser union too much for her. Her complicity with Aegisthus forbids reconciliation with the chorus. The man-woman, now depressingly all woman, contemplates peace, but sees her new role *within* the social structure, with Aegisthus as the new king, thrust peace out of her reach.

Clytemnestra's new desire to compromise, her new incapacity for action, prepares her role in *Libation-Bearers*. In that second play, her reception of the fictitious news of the death of Orestes is characteristic (691 ff.). She blames the curse, says she will communicate with her associates, arranges to have the messengers lodged: everything with a calm considerateness that is now the substitute for an emotion that has been burnt out of her. Perhaps the moderation of the response, in spoken iambs, not, as usual in such a situation, followed by lyrics, is deceiving. We note also the fantasizing about Orestes's flight, that he had "wisely snatched his foot from the muck and left," as if Orestes had been, at the time of the death of Agamemnon, in any position, or of an age, to flee by himself. But a certain amount of pious fabrication, designed to relieve the pressure of the guilt, is not unexpected. Its defensiveness goes on all fours with the managerial circumspection in evidence at the end of *Agamemnon*. Now it is Orestes, in the report of his "death," who is the brutal one; Clytemnestra is merely pitiful. This points ahead to the issues of *Eumenides*—but that is another matter. In the exchange after the intervention of Pylades (908), Clytemnestra's reasoning sounds plausible enough. She does not cite Iphigenia; she offers another argument used earlier, the argument from the loneliness of the woman whose husband is off to the wars. But the argument is now querulous, without the malevolent verve of the earlier version.

What do we make of all this? Do we say that in enacting the collapse of the original Clytemnestra, Aeschylus traces one woman's career from plotting and triumph to disenchantment? It is more appropriate, I think, to regard the great aggressor of the first part as quite distinct from what happens later. The earlier segment is made up of echoes and dreams of another order, a world of visions and nightmarish shapes. Down to the death of *Agamemnon*, Clytemnestra is off by herself, not responded to by others, unresponsive to them, designed for the express purpose of leveling her assault upon the King. Her rhetoric takes its cue from that purpose; it functions *as* rhetoric, as speech in support of a crusade, without attuning us to the human potential whose engagement might produce such words. Nevertheless, precisely because she is isolated; because she hides the truth, if not from the audience, at least from her fellow principals; because her real purpose has to be tracked down and reconstructed by the fascinated spectator, she comes through as something vastly richer than just an aggressive queen. Reading between her lines, and digesting the enormities of what she says, we perceive that we are in the presence of a being certainly more powerful, and probably more complex, than the princely figures upon whom Aeschylus usually hangs his tales.

The point is, however, that this extraordinary being appears to have no organic connection with the circumspect, self-revealing lady who has to deal with Aegisthus and with Orestes. It is the Clytemnestra of the middle portion of the trilogy who furnishes us with the data of mundane experience that we associate with the concept of character. "Character" comes into being only after Agamemnon's death, and that means, for practical purposes, with the beginning of *Libation-Bearers*, which may be located somewhere near the entry of Aegisthus in *Agamemnon*.

Unlike *Agamemnon*, *Libation-Bearers* shows human beings interacting in precisely calculated ways. The recognition scene between Electra and Orestes at the start of the second play shows us what may be expected. In the place of the hieratic, unyielding stiffness of the meetings and reunions of the first play, *Libation-Bearers* presents familiar relations, including the careful adjustment of a person's expectations to the arrival of another. The process whereby Electra identifies first the lock and then the footprints as those of Orestes has been criticized not only by some modern scholars but also by Euripides, who has *his* Electra say (*Electra* 283): "I would not recognize Orestes if I saw him." In actual fact, as Reinhardt has shown beautifully, the version of Euripides, the conventional recognition by means of a scar, is less interesting and makes smaller use of the possibilities of the dramatic stage than Aeschylus's drama of a desperate woman whose hopes are centered on the return of her brother; who is willing to jump to some very large conclusions, expressed in some very rash language, to satisfy those hopes; and who proceeds to shrink back from her own conclusions when confronted with the object of her desire.[30] Here convention bolsters psychology: new information is always resisted, so as to enhance the power of its impact and to allow it to be absorbed slowly. We do not need to fall back on the extreme speculations of one scholar, who believed that the house of Tantalus was endowed with specific Lydian features which would make it easy for Electra to recognize the presence of a blood relative; or those of another, who thought that sister and brother shared between them the peculiar condition of one foot being shaped differently from the other.[31] The "measuring" of line 209 is little more than a token of Electra's feeling that her desperate gamble, and her joyous hunch, can be translated into empirical proof. The order of Orestes's lines (226 ff.) also seems to me psychologically effective and grammatically possible, though most scholars, beginning with the judicious Robortello, have proposed to scramble them:

> And when you saw this twist of mourner's hair
> You were amazed, and thought you were seeing me
> (and measuring footprints, also, in my tracks).
> Here is your brother's, commensurate to your head,
> The lock! Come match it to the cut of my hair.

Line 3 is a kind of footnote, added after the mention of the first reaction. The tracing of the tracks is never more than an addendum; it is the business of the lock that matters. And indeed the fourth line follows as if the lock were still the subject of discussion. First, a reference to Electra's earlier joy: the lock matches her hair, and then, in line 5, a demonstration that it actually comes from the head of Orestes.

The circumstantial, looking-glass quality of this is quite different from the stark silhouette art of *Agamemnon*. From the start, we are taken into the confidence of Electra's secret thoughts. The chorus, reminding Electra of Orestes's existence, prompts her to admit to herself and to them that she is

---

30. Reinhardt, *Aischylos*, p. 111. On this topic, see also F. Solmsen, *Electra and Orestes* (*Med. Nederl. Akad. Wetensch., Afd. Letterk.*, n.s. 30.2; Amsterdam, 1967), pp. 7–8.
31. The critics in question are A. W. Verrall and H. J. Rose.

always thinking of her brother. When she finds the lock she treats it as if it were human, i.e., Orestes himself: she wants it to have a voice so she can either reject it or sorrow with it. By the time Orestes himself appears, the completeness of trust with which she has given herself over to the identification of the lock (and the tracks) forces her to shrink from the further recognition. Orestes's tactfulness, his refusal to burst out with the truth or even to address her as "sister," rounds out an exercise in delicacy. It is in the same spirit of refinement that Aeschylus, the recognition barely completed, chooses not to burden Electra with further indulgence in grief or joy, and has her ponder the role Orestes is to play in saving and repossessing the house. At this stage, as at her entry, she continues to think of herself as a woman in need of protection. And the impersonal, almost coy use of the passive voice at 241—"she is most justly hated"—suggests that her feelings toward her mother are still not fully crystallized into the need to act.

The recognition scene is pivotal. It is a fully developed reaching out of two human beings toward each other, a slow tracing of the irrational dovetailing of recoil and embrace which ties two beings together, in their thoughts as well as their addresses. The scene that follows, the Great Exchange, could not be more different. But before we turn to it, it is proper to ask a few more questions about Electra and Orestes. Electra is, if we can trust the manuscripts, completely dropped during the intrigue that occupies the second half of *Libation-Bearers*. Her last words (508–9) are among those that terminate the exchange. It appears that, for the purposes of the conspiracy, Electra is a negligible character, especially by contrast with Sophocles's and Euripides's versions of the legend. Aeschylus's principal concern is with the house, hence with the heir who must set it right. To employ Electra in the intrigue might have complicated matters beyond the simple objective of restoring the house and removing the cancer. It might also have put Electra in a compromising situation, too close for comfort to what is associated with Clytemnestra. The fact that we can recognize the risk means that we look for a pattern of consistency and an economical use of characters.

What is it that motivates Electra in this play? She is not expected to protect the house or carry out the vengeance. She is there, one presumes, partly because without her Orestes would lack the social involvement demanded by the scheme of progressive socialization which the trilogy dramatizes. The recognition scene is a harbinger of the gifts of gentleness and togetherness which in *Agamemnon* had been out of reach. But once Electra is on the stage, what attitude is she to take toward the task ahead? Aeschylus starts her out on a note of uncertainty. With her first words she wonders how to approach the gods (84 ff.) and how to do the sacrificing Clytemnestra has asked her to undertake. She even wonders whether it is right to ask the gods to punish the villains (122). Altogether there is something peculiar about Electra's approaches to the divinities. She asks Hermes to help her by getting the nether gods and Earth herself to listen to her; and she calls on her father, and all the dead, to pity her and Orestes. In the end, the father becomes the chief addressee. Why the introductory series of addressees? Safety in numbers? Uncertainty to whom to appeal and how to secure their attention? Further, unlike Orestes (18–19) and the chorus (117–23), she is slow to cite the theme of revenge, and needs instruction in the matter. Nor does she, when finally adjusted to the thought of the death of the killers, give any indication of realizing that her wish for moderation and purity (140–41) might be difficult to reconcile with her hope for an avenger. She seems, at first, to assume that the revenge will not involve her, and indeed this turns out to be correct. Yet before Electra disappears from sight, her growing sense of kinship with her brother has made her more resolute in calling for punishment. The Great Exchange consolidates her new attitude, for it compels her to remember her past sufferings. Under the impact of the memories, she turns into a promoter of vengeance. Finally her new confidence (487) occasions thoughts of marriage: a far cry from the hesitations and humilities of the initial scene.

But the development is not rapid; especially her new firmness toward her mother takes time to mature. The dramatic focus on the house as the major entity always cramps the opportunity for private relationships between individuals, and serves as a buffer on the growth of Electra's hatred. Even toward the conclusion of the exchange (429 ff.), Electra denounces her absent mother for having buried her husband—not Electra's father—without honors, as if the breach of decorum counted for more than the murder or Electra's deprivations. At the same time (418 ff., 444 ff.), she frets over the indignities heaped upon her, and makes much of them to bring Orestes round. Her major role in the exchange, like that of the chorus, appears to be to overcome Orestes's seeming reluctance to face up to the full implications of his duties. She is a living reminder of what the cruelties of Clytemnestra and Aegisthus have produced. But, in that capacity, she is a reference rather than a person, an incentive rather than an individual. Her development is not primarily a maturing, or the portrait of an exhausted young woman collecting herself. It is a construction put together for furthering an action that in the end can do without her.

Does Orestes succeed in satisfying our expectations of a living character, with a plausible set of motives and an organic curve of conduct? More particularly, does Aeschylus give us an Orestes capable of doubt and moral scruple, of suffering by virtue of a conflict experienced deeply within? After the recognition scene, Orestes makes a reference to Clytemnestra (249) which is more emphatically hostile than anything Electra or the chorus have yet produced. Calling upon Zeus, he asks him to look upon

> the orphan brood of eagle father,
> Dead in the coils and winding spirals of
> The gruesome serpent.

A little later, he falls back on the threats and commands of Apollo to furnish a motive, but adds that he has his own reasons and desires. Here the tone is one of patient explanation, even of defensiveness. Once we are launched into the exchange, resolve has to be built up anew, as if Orestes had not already made up his mind to do what needs to be done. Only by 434 ff. do we find him once again firmly committed to the thought of revenging his father, but now with an added note of desperation—"Thereafter, let me die." It seems that Orestes moves through a succession of feelings which, in their very inconstancy, hold out promise. Curiously, Electra and the chorus continue to pressure him *after* he is already committed to the deed.

Orestes is confident that Apollo will not forsake him (269). In this trilogy, the god's command and protection are of even greater thematic importance than the family curse. By comparison with a play such as *Seven Against Thebes*, it is remarkable how little use Aeschylus makes in the *Oresteia* of the old tradition of the curse upon the House of Atreus. Only Clytemnestra, and the chorus and Cassandra in talking about Clytemnestra, remind us of the old crimes and of the demon triggered by them. In *Libation-Bearers* and *Eumenides*, the curse is virtually dropped in favor of another perspective that stresses the culpability of Clytemnestra and Aegisthus. One presumes that the altered perspective was needed to permit a satisfactory resolution. In any case, by throwing the weight of explanation behind the will of a god— or the gods, for Apollo, we learn to our mild surprise, is simply an agent of Zeus—Aeschylus simplifies and rationalizes the scheme of crime and punishment, and extracts Orestes from what might have been an impossibly opaque situation. Eteocles must die; the curse demands it, for a curse cannot stop but must have its victim. Orestes can live, because the curse has been stopped in its tracks by the arbitrary action of the god.

But once the god has been introduced, new problems present themselves. A character identifying his lot with the demands of a curse can impress us with the authenticity of his action, and with a flourish of freedom. The Homeric hero fated to die as he pursues his combat and the Sartrian hero carving a precarious freedom from all-embracing constraint are our evidence. But a man who takes orders, and quite specific orders at that, from a divine controller? Orestes ponders the threats at considerable length; their effect seems to be to relieve him of the need for taking a personal position in the matter. It comes as a surprise, therefore, that he adds, by way of a codicil, that there are also personal reasons guiding him. The reasons he gives are remarkable, in spite of the briefness of the passage. First, in addition to the god's commands, there is his father's great suffering. It is not clear whether by that he means the suffering he experienced when he was killed or the suffering of the unavenged ghost who is about to be invoked in the exchange. There are also his own poverty and the humiliating circumstance of the conquerors of Troy, i.e., the Argives, being ruled by two women, i.e., Clytemnestra and Aegisthus. The mention of poverty is a fine realistic touch: Orestes has come to Argos to repair his fortunes; the action he is planning is his last hope. The reference to the humiliation of the Argives is less convincing. As a reminder of the false position in which the citizens find themselves, it is useful, and it helps to shape audience sympathy. But in the mouth of Orestes, it rings false.

The personal "desires"—that is the word used—averred by Orestes to complement his obedience to the god are unimpressive. We learn nothing about his feelings concerning the lot of his sister or about his private sentiments about his mother. There is a studiously abstract, official air about these desires. They are, in fact, not desires at all, but formal explanations dragged in to shore up the divine directions with a modicum of personal engagement. Their briefness and lack of conviction make them pale before the fury of the divine threats. For the time being, at least, Orestes is an instrument, perhaps even a reluctant instrument, of the divine will. This is the way Orestes appears before the exchange. At the end of it, the chorus tells him that he has been "straightened out" or "set up" in his heart (512). One may assume, therefore, that in the course of the exchange something has happened that has furnished Orestes with that quality of commitment which was lacking earlier.

But what happens when Clytemnestra points to her breast (899) and Orestes turns to Pylades for advice, as Electra had turned to the chorus earlier, and Pylades cites Apollo's oracles once again? The question addressed to Pylades and his answer do not imply a radical revulsion or self-questioning on the part of Orestes. They are a reminder, via the testimony of a bystander, that Orestes, whatever his personal inclinations, has no choice in the matter before him. But that in itself is of great importance. At the crucial moment, when Clytemnestra is to be killed, the audience is alerted, not to the various personal grounds that may have inclined Orestes to act the way he does, but to the external compulsion, bound up with the legend, which controls his conduct. The causes of his action, we are reminded, lie beyond him, and he is given no chance to make them his own, much less to initiate them. The direction of Orestes's thinking is unchanged. What he says after Pylades's "intervention" is identical—insistently so—with what he has said just before (cf. 904–7 with 894–95):

> You like this man? All right, then, you will lie
> Next to him in death.

The sarcasm is biting, but is it his? In the light of the knowledge that the action is powered by Apollo's threats rather than by personal hatred, it is hard to root the derision in Orestes's feelings. It springs, as it were, from the ritual charge of the action itself. On the whole, therefore, Wilamowitz was right to refer to Orestes as the *corpus vile* of the proceedings. It is not just that he is irresolute, that he lacks the driving force that lends to an avenger his proper credentials. It is that his role is conceived primarily as that of an instrument, as what is left over when the god's emasculating demands have been totalled. Within that narrowed scope, Orestes is capable of some subtlety, and of brotherly gentleness. But above all he is a puppet of the gods, and that is how Aeschylus wants him, in view of what is to happen in *Eumenides*.

For the killing of Clytemnestra, however, Orestes needs firing up. The Great Exchange, which is designed to bring this about, is the most remarkable segment of the play. In form and tone, it is close to the lyric exuberance of *Agamemnon* and *Suppliants*. The prominence of the music, the intricacy of the lyric speech and of the versification, point away from the intrigue, but also from the psychological and emotional demands of the homecoming. The utterances of the exchange are not, for the most part, either formally or in their substance addressed to the partners, but to the ghost of Agamemnon and his fellow creatures underground, including (infernal) Zeus. In the intrigue part of the play, as in all of *Eumenides*, we are asked to believe that, in spite of the isolation of character from character, a certain amount of mutual influencing, of understanding and "contagion," and even conversion, is within the realm of possibility. The exchange resolutely excludes all this. As in *Agamemnon*, the principals operate side by side, without any apparent interest in reaching out for each other or commanding assent.

The conjuration of Agamemnon is prepared long ahead. Before Electra finds the lock and the foot tracks, the chorus addresses Agamemnon in song, with words that amount to: Your hearing is sluggish, so I have to insist (156–58). The length of the exchange is predicated on the assumption that Agamemnon's ghost is asleep, and that he needs to be roused and worked on with more than average persuasion. The exchange is an elaborate piece of necromancy, a petition hymn addressed to a Barbarossa who has been dormant too long. There is little point in comparing it to the invocation of the ghost of Darius in *Pers.* 633 ff., which is a choral hymn rather than an exchange, and openly invocational, calling upon the dead king to appear in much the same way as if he was being asked to interrupt a council session and step out of the house. The appeal in *Libation-Bearers* is truly necromantic in that the techniques chosen for the conjuring are indirect. Each of the three parties involved in the effort concentrates on his own desires and his own sufferings. There is no attempt to coordinate the litany, or even, until almost to the very end, to call directly for the king's appearance. The intention appears to be to interest Agamemnon and to enlist his help by a mixture of recollection, description, and despair. In the end, Agamemnon does not appear. But the audience is supposed to feel that the indirect appeals have been successful and that his help will be forthcoming to guide the intrigue and secure its success. The introductory anapaests of the exchange (306–14), with their address to the Fates and their enunciation of the principle of an eye for an eye, have made the nature of the request clear.

At the risk of burdening the reader with technicalities, a few words should be said about the formal arrangement of the exchange, to indicate the uniqueness of its lyric structure. Some of the ascriptions, especially in the last third of the passage, are not fully secure, and certain doubts have been raised concerning the arrangement of some of the lines. But the general scheme is clear, and accepting the arrangement as it has come down to us will not, I think, pose a threat to our understanding. The exchange consists of three diminishing sections: a sequence of four triads each of which is introduced by anapaests, a sequence of two triads not so introduced, and finally a brief sequence of two dyads. In the following tabulation, a letter and the same letter with superscript[1] stand, as usual, for stanza and responding stanza.

| | | |
|---|---|---|
| 306 ff. | Chorus | anapaests |
| 315 ff. | Orestes | a |
| 324 ff. | Chorus | b |
| 332 ff. | Electra | a[1] |
| 340 ff. | Chorus | anapaests |
| 345 ff. | Orestes | c |
| 354 ff. | Chorus | b[1] |
| 363 ff. | Electra | c[1] |
| 372 ff. | Chorus | anapaests |
| 380 ff. | Orestes | d |
| 386 ff. | Chorus | e |
| 394 ff. | Electra | d[1] |

| 400 ff. | Chorus | anapaests |
| 405 ff. | Orestes | f |
| 410 ff. | Chorus | e$^1$ |
| 418 ff. | Electra | f$^1$ |
| 423 ff. | Chorus | g |
| 429 ff. | Electra | h |
| 434 ff. | Orestes | i |
| 439 ff. | Chorus | i$^1$ |
| 444 ff. | Electra | g$^1$ |
| 451 ff. | Chorus | h$^1$ |
| 456 ff. | Or. El. Chor. | j |
| 461 ff. | Or. El. Chor. | j$^1$ |
| 466 ff. | Chorus | k |
| 471 ff. | Chorus | k$^1$ |
| 476 ff. | Chorus | anapaests |

The tabulation should make clear that only toward the end do we have the succession of stanza and responding stanza that we associate with lyric song in Greek drama. Through the bulk of the exchange, Aeschylus gives us a pattern of postponements and dovetailings, set off further, in the first part, by anapaestic chanting, which distinguishes the sequence from all else in the history of Greek dramatic literature.[32] But given its special character, the construction of the exchange is, in its own way, severely regular. In the first and longest section, the distribution of parts follows the same principles throughout: a chanted introduction is followed by a stanza sung by Orestes, a stanza sung by the chorus, and a stanza sung by Electra which responds to that sung by Orestes. What is more, the choral stanzas are themselves responsive; the second responds to the first, and the fourth to the third. The distribution of parts thereafter is a matter for the editor to decide.[33] The assignments given above, though not as symmetrical as those of the first part, seem to account best for what we have in the text. At the conclusion of the terminal anapaests, the dramatic action is continued with Orestes and Electra supporting one another with evenly divided brief speeches and calling upon Agamemnon to help them if he does not want to see the house die out. In this section, the last of the first movement of the play before the start of the intrigue proper, Orestes proves to be the driving

32. Note also that the usual avoidance of reponsive alternation between voices, commented on above, p. 39, is here set aside.
33. I accept the arrangement worked out by Robortello.

spirit, the leader of the argument, with Electra following behind and acting upon the cues offered by him.

In the exchange itself, however, the driving spirit is, strangely, the chorus. They are the ones who, principally in their anapaests, more geared to the demands of action than are the lyric measures, argue the law of retribution and point to the imminence of danger. Crimes are requited, they warn, and bloodshed generates a Fury (312, 400 ff.); let us forget pious wishes, the foe is upon us (372 ff.); the god willing, we shall have a paean instead of a lament (340 ff.). Their warnings contrast with the self-questioning, the elegiac recollections, and the complaints of the two principals. The choral warner is brought in to hammer away at the theme of retribution and to call the princes back to the need for action. It is important that we understand how different Orestes's utterances here, especially in the first part of the exchange, are from what he says in the iambic section that follows. Though we cannot study his stanzas in detail, a summary of his contributions to the exchange is easy enough. Orestes wonders how best to reach his father (315 ff.); he wonders whether it would not have been better for Agamemnon to have been killed at Troy (345 ff.); he calls on Zeus to send up *atē* (Devastation) against the "parents" (382 ff.); and he invokes the powers of the underworld to behold the weakness and the indignity of what is left of the house (405 ff.). Only with his last continuous contribution to the exchange (434 ff.) does Orestes find the strength to make a statement about the future: she, i.e., Clytemnestra whom Electra had just been apostrophizing, will pay the penalty, "the gods willing, and my hands willing." Even after this, Electra and the chorus continue to press their claims, as if Orestes needed further strengthening. But by the time he arrives at the interpretation of Clytemnestra's dream and his determination that he is the snake that sucks her blood, the energies emanating from the chorus and from Electra have dissipated themselves.

What I am trying to say is that the attempts of others to influence Orestes and the taking shape of his resolution have no apparent link between them. Nor is it possible to trace a gradual hardening or resolving toward the necessary act in what Orestes says and sings in the course of the first half of the play. On a number of occasions, he appears ready, only to turn around in the next scene and show himself, if not irresolute, at least unpoised. Unlike Kleist's Homburg, whose successive display of courage, cowardice, and resignation is designed as an interesting character study—one man's response to a forbidding code of conduct, Aeschylus's Orestes answers dramatic needs that pull in a different direction. The lyric nature of the exchange confirms this. Traditionally, lyric song raises less of a presumption of the approximation of psychological truth than does iambic dialogue. By granting as much scope as he does to the lyrics in this part of the play, and by structuring the lyrics as severely as he does, Aeschylus seems to be giving notice that he is not interested in showing us an Orestes who is being won over and who is slowly finding the strength and the motivation for his dreadful deed. Rather, he is showing us the several attitudes available to a person in the position of Orestes: commitment, on the one hand, and the varying kinds of apathy, anxiety, or disorientation which precede a commitment, but which in this presentation vie with it, block it, and threaten to engulf it at every step.

One might have thought that the die was cast after Orestes's long enunciation of Apollo's oracular threats, with its codicil on his own desires. But the exchange does everything over once more. Until Orestes finally performs the terrible deed his role continues to be that of one who oscillates between several options and stances, and thereby drives home their equal power. He is committed from the start; but the impossible alternative is never quite done away with and continues to be part of the world of the play. Orestes is, thus, less a character than a vehicle for the exploration of the courses of action available to one in his (mythological) position and shaping the dramatic language. That is both the strength and the weakness of his role. Weakness, because it is impossible to extend sympathy, much less identification, to a dramatic agent whose agency appears to lack a discoverable self; strength, because under the label of "Orestes," Aeschylus brings together a wealth of alternatives and possibilities, and because the action when it does come has been removed from the orbit of human whim or human initiative, and is chalked up to the impersonal workings of that Devastation, that Fury, whose power the chorus has hymned.

But if there is no psychological development, no overcoming of scruples and wrestling through to a decision, is not the length of the exchange excessive? The answer to this question is that the exchange serves another function. The deed toward which everything points, the killing of the mother, is a heinous act; all civilized thinking shrinks from the contemplation of it. The terms of the trilogy require that it be carried out, and that the doer escape punishment. The exchange, with its musical and choreographic complexity and its hieratic stiffness, is our cushion against revulsion, an instrument to protect Orestes and his helpers against too keen an awareness of the ugliness of the project. As we shall see, it has something in common with certain other ritualizations enacted in *Eumenides*. But this means that it would have been contrary to Aeschylus's interests to construct an interesting or convincing character, for if Orestes were conceived as such he could not be kept immune to the charge of ugliness. As it is, we are not made to feel that Orestes is steering a precarious course attempting to get clear of the shoals of villainy. His voice turns lyric or communal, and his self is dissolved into thematic argument.[34]

Thus the fine psychological insights developed in the meeting between Orestes and Electra do not, in the long run, realize their promise. The exchange disestablishes human particularity. It builds up tension which cries to be relieved through action—any or any one's action. It permits glimpses of Clytemnestra as the intended culprit. It piles up a massive bulwark between our sensibilities and the gruesomeness of the deed. It helps to draw in Zeus and the nether gods, in addition to Agamemnon, as interested parties. But it does not explain Orestes; it does not add anything to our understanding of his role that was not at our disposal before. To use a fashionable term, the exchange unpacks, it does not construct. It unpacks the heavy load of a broadly distributed human commitment; it does not construct a mentality to rise to the challenge of that commitment. Any psychological development that might have been anticipated on the strength of the early scenes is subverted by the ritual stasis. The element of performance, of invocational surrender, confirms this. The only development that can be noticed is the axial shift of Orestes's companions. At first, all parties are turned toward the tomb on the platform, seeking to make themselves heard by the dead King. Toward the end of the exchange, Electra and the chorus have turned to face Orestes. At the very end, the balance is redressed, and Agamemnon and the infernal gods are once more the addressees. But the passing change of orientation on the part of the chorus and Electra is of some importance. It enhances for us, visually, the coming significance of the man, and their increasing reliance on him. Electra will be dropped as the intrigue gets underway. Her phasing out is begun here with a dramatic activation of her dependence upon her brother.

What interested Aeschylus most in the legend of the revenge taken upon Clytemnestra, and what he dramatizes above all in the exchange, is not the shifting or developing attitude of Orestes or Electra toward the deed, but the various factors—religious, social, personal, factual—which should be understood as necessarily involved in such a deed, and in the preparations for it. The "debate" of the exchange does not move toward a personal resolution, or even to the revoicing of a decision made earlier, but toward an ever more oppressive unfolding of the conflicting elements that a fifth-century realization of the ancient legend must take into account. The chorus's constant stress on the rule of blood guilt and on the fullness of grief is the orchestration that accompanies the more sharply fluctuating analysis of

---

34. My interpretation of the Great Exchange has more in common with the reading of W. Schadewaldt, "Der Kommos in Aischylos' *Choephoren*," *Hermes* 67 (1932): 312–54, than with the other classical treatment of the topic, that of A. Lesky, *Der Kommos der Choephoren* (Vienna, 1943).

Orestes and Electra. Of the two, Orestes is the more labile personality. That is to say, the various positions and formulations associated with him cover, between them, a great range of options. That is only natural; Orestes is the one who will perform the action, and the prospect of its perils attaches itself to him. But the need for resolution is dramatized three times—in Orestes's first speech, in the exchange, and again in the murder scene. The resolution is, in fact, never complete, because it is not rooted in a deciding self.

Only with this in mind can we come to appreciate the peculiar emptiness of the Orestes of *Eumenides*. After the deed is done, there is no further need for reflection or for the rhetorical elaboration of the rights and wrongs of the matricide. The Orestes of the last play shows neither repentance nor fear; Wilamowitz concluded that he is not a person at all. In a legal sense, he is, of course, but not as the carrier of the dramatic action. He is not a sufferer, a doer, or a claimant insisting on rights due to him. He relies on Apollo to argue his case for him; in fact, he has no case over and above the orders of the god. If at least we were given to feel that he *knows* that he has no case; if, that is, his humanity could be conveyed by negation, by an admission that he does not himself know how to defend his action, and that this incapacity weighs upon his soul, we might be ready to sympathize. But no such awareness is offered. Cassandra, Xerxes, even the Danaids demonstrate that Aeschylus is quite capable, if he wishes, of suggesting suffering in terms which resemble human needs. Orestes is not beyond suffering; suffering is simply not relevant to the dramatic conception of which he is a part. In *Eumenides*, instrumentalities are prepared to allow men, or rather the Athenians, to function as law-abiding but free individuals. Orestes is not yet such an individual; he is an etiological myth, a founding father. The memory of a founding father must not be disturbed with intimations of self-doubt. This is as it should be. As we shall see later, *Eumenides* is not a problem play, but a masque. Hard facts are revealed, positions solidly demonstrated, and a resolution is imported against the grain of that solidity. In such a masque, there is no room for the persistently human. As Electra is dropped in *Libation-Bearers* so that the plot may unfold with a minimum of distraction, so Orestes is dropped in *Eumenides* so that the squaring-off between Athena and the Furies may be undisturbed. Once the acquittal which the play celebrates has been pronounced, Orestes will not be missed.

If I have spent what looks like an inordinate amount of time on Orestes, that is because the trilogy is named after him, and one might expect that Aeschylus would have taken special pains to bring out the intricacies and refinements of the character of his hero. The difficulty of looking at Aeschylus with anticipations stimulated by Ibsen or Flaubert are most clearly shown in this figure. Barring the gargoyles and the stock types prepared by earlier traditions, Aeschylus's major personae tend to be of the mold exemplified by Orestes. They are characters whose various moves toward internal consistency or complexity are skewed by other dramatic needs. Clytemnestra and Prometheus are two notable exceptions. Of Clytemnestra we have spoken. About Prometheus I have said little because of the doubts that attach to the authorship of the play. But even if it is genuinely Aeschylean in most of its parts, the character of the fallen god cannot compare with Clytemnestra for subtlety or plasticity. As we watch his various moods, changing from desperation to pride, disdain, and choler, we are tempted to read into this succession of tempers a sustained psychology of spiritual rebellion. But then we remember that the bulk of the play consists of lectures—about the history of culture, about travels and monsters and human inventions—delivered with the detachment that befits a teacher. The pride and the anger are functions of the role of the rebel in which Aeschylus has recast the old Hesiodic figure of the malicious Titan. The disdain is a necessary adjunct of the self-absorption with which this author, like Sophocles, equips his fighter for a cause. Together, they strike us with the force of an unremitting commitment; but that commitment is the issue of the play, and the personality of the principal is, on the whole, adequate to it and little more. That later generations should have recognized in the Aeschylean Prometheus a personage upon which to model their own grand aspirations is important, but immaterial. The portrait of Prometheus is compelling; but it is compelling precisely because it is too large to accommodate the minute particulars, or the surprising consistency, that we associate with a convincingly drawn individual.

Plato's warnings against tragedy derive from his fear that the tragic actor, in assuming a part, endangers his own identity by creating in and around himself another. Whatever may be thought of the justice of Plato's analysis, it is clear from his remarks that he is thinking of types: the lamenter, the coward, the arrogant king, the headstrong hero. What is more, he is probably thinking of the theater of his own time. Paradoxically, I suggest, Plato's fears are stimulated by his experience of reading plays rather than by watching them in performance, in spite of what he says about the music and the psychagogic effect of staged drama. The actual dramatic experience, with its masks, its ritual forms, and its other conventions, exercises a powerful alienation effect, pulling the imagination and the sensibilities away from the audience identification which classical criticism, from Plato to Castelvetro, takes for granted. Many centuries after Plato, Lucian was to emphasize the Platonic perspective in his essay *On Dancing*, but with approval. With the value-free indifference of the Sophistic essayist, he expresses admiration for the mimes who could, in spite of the lumbering paraphernalia of their art, communicate the nuances of suffering souls to a public ready to weep with them.

Aeschylus's characters are rather more like the adulterers of Tourneur's
*The Revenger's Tragedy* (1.3.65–68):

> and in the morning
> When they are up and dressed, and their mask on,
> Who can perceive this? Save that eternal eye
> That sees through flesh and all?

No such X-ray vision for Orestes; *his* eternal eye, the Sun who sees all, looks
on actions (*Lib.* 986), not into souls. The notion of a figurative mask has no
standing on the Aeschylean stage. With one or two exceptions, his characters have no dimension of depth; acts do. As Roland Barthes has remarked,
summarizing beautifully what I have been trying to say in this chapter:

> Psychological writing is above all an art of the secret, of a thing both concealed
> and confessed. . . . Hence the traditional drama which makes us see an inner life
> ravaged without the character admitting this to us; this sort of *jeu* . . . provides
> for a drama of nuance, it makes for a disjunction between the letter and the spirit
> of the character, between what he says and what he suffers. But tragedy, on the
> contrary, is based on the notion of complete literalness; passion has no inner
> thickness, it is entirely extraverted, turned toward its civic context.[35]

For "tragedy," let us say "Aeschylus." His public drama, at the beginning of
the line, is still the purest realization of a tragedy that turns on actions, and
that frames passions and suffering without recourse to the construction of
heroes or heroines who interest us for themselves and move us by themselves. That the Aeschylean heroes and heroines, including the multiple
heroines of his active choruses, should loom large in our memories is a
testimony to his skill as a dramatist. But, with the possible exception of the
murderous Queen, we remember them as presences, and as agents, and not
as persons.

35. R. Barthes, *Essais critiques* (Paris, 1964), p. 75.

# Responsibility

# — 9 —

# Gods

The gods of Aeschylus: a subject bedevilled with difficulties. In the eyes of Aristophanes, Aeschylus was a true believer; his tragedy was wholesome, more wholesome than that of Euripides, because there was in it no doubting of the old-fashioned truths of the ancestral faith. This is patent nonsense; a tragedy of Aeschylus is not a mystery play, or a profession of faith. That the gods are essential to Aeschylus's art cannot be doubted. An Aeschylus without gods is no more conceivable than a Shaw or a Bond with them. But just as in Schnitzler or Ionesco we have to ask ourselves what is missing that causes the vast sense of emptiness in their plays, so in Aeschylus we must ask what would be missing if he had not built the gods into his.

The gods form the frame. First and last words are addressed to the gods. In *Agamemnon*, the watchman begs the gods to release him from his labors; at the end of the trilogy we hear the chorus of escorts sing that "Zeus the all-seeing has come down and Moira with him." Both at the end of *Agamemnon* and at the end of *Libation-Bearers*, the intention, if not the standing, of the gods is in doubt. Clytemnestra says that she will rule in the house and put it right; the chorus of *Libation-Bearers* raises a question about the competence of divine power. But with the prayer of Orestes to the infernal Hermes at the beginning of *Libation-Bearers*, and with the priestess's invocation of Earth, Themis and Phoebe at the beginning of *Eumenides*, the pantheon of the pious is once more firmly embraced, and the whole trilogy ends in divine harmony. The same is true of the other plays, all except *Prometheus*, which occupies a special position in the canon.

The protective authority of the frame is deceptive. Electra's prayer and sacrifice (*Lib.* 124 ff.) addressed to the divinities underground, especially to Earth herself, show her to be seeking the shelter of the very powers on whom the Furies, daughters of Earth, rely to prosecute Orestes. It is tempting to chalk this up to some form of irony, but that would be a mistake. Electra's prayer to the chthonic forces is mimetic rather than symbolic; it is in imitation of comparable situations in the religious life of contemporary Athenians. That she should be addressing herself to underground divinities in preference to one of the celestial powers is in conformity with the comparative standing of the two classes of gods in the religious universe. In desperate situations, one is more likely to turn to the patrons who are secretly felt to be more powerful, and certainly more visibly effective, in matters of daily existence.

If drama is, as Aristotle says it is, an imitation of men acting or of the actions of men, religious activity, which occupied a large part of the life of the ordinary men and women, cannot be omitted from the representation. It is, as it were, part of the matrix, the very stuff of life that is caught in the literary artifact, and which as such resists sublimation or re-analysis. At one point in *Persians*, the messenger (497–98) reports that when the troops of Xerxes, retreating from Greece, reached the river Strymon and found it frozen over and seemingly favorable to their salvation,

> even those
> Who once had slighted the gods now prayed to them
> And fell prostrate in awe of Earth and Heaven.

The precise words used make it unlikely that the reference here is only to religious practice. Aeschylus is, it seems, talking as much about religious belief. The Persian army is said to have contained some men who had never thought much about the workings of the gods and who were now, in the light of what looked like a miraculous salvation, willing to acknowledge a higher power. The cruelty of the irony—the ice will break and the saviors will turn into destroyers—is massive. It helps to enhance the impression of human error, of man as the plaything of the gods. It tells us something about the psychology of the Persian court; but it tells us nothing about the Greeks, for, in spite of the near-identification of Themistocles with a demon, the battle of Salamis is narrated by the messenger as a human achievement, planned and carried out by men in the full confidence of their own abilities. Nor is there any intimation that the Greeks need fear the punishment of the gods for this self-reliance.

Mimesis is in force also in the speech of Orestes immediately after the recognition scene at the beginning of *Libation-Bearers* (246–63). Orestes calls on Zeus for assistance. His argument is: Zeus owes something to Agamemnon because Agamemnon furnished Zeus with good sacrifices; he, Orestes, is willing to continue these sacrifices; surely Zeus would not be happy without them. The quid pro quo argument, solidly based on many precedents in the epic and in the ritual formulas of religious practice, strikes some moderns as unworthy. We have to be careful not to read post-classical assumptions about non-profit relationships into the link between a fifth-century worshipper and his god. And yet it is, I think, legitimate to argue that even from the point of view of Aeschylus's audience, the sentiment pronounced here falls short of the occasion offered. This happens to be the lowest point in Orestes's dramatic career, the point at which he must start in order to work his way up to the culmination of what the plot asks of him. It looks as if Aeschylus decided to begin with a Homeric motif, with a move snatched from the blunt realities of a mundane world, to launch the campaign of Orestes toward his god-sanctioned victory.

The mimesis of worship is one of the ways in which the language of religion may enter the texture of tragedy. Mimesis is at the furthest remove from authorial confession. That a work of Aeschylus should acquaint us with the playwright's views of the workings of the gods more or less as Augustine's *Confessions* or Nietzsche's *Zarathustra* does is an unreasonable expectation. The expectation has, one assumes, been generated and lent credence by the convention of the chorus. Without the chorus, the conflicts on the stage would have made it more difficult to associate any one statement about the gods with the author. But with the supposition that the chorus speaks for the playwright in some measure at least, Aeschylus's religion has become an intriguing, though always elusive, quarry. Compare *Suppl.* 524–27, where Zeus is the lord of lords, the most blessed of the blessed, the most complete and perfect power, with *Prom.* 515–18, where the power and permanence of Zeus are limited, and he is subject to Fate. Such a comparison immediately highlights the shifting contours of divine power in Aeschylus.[1] It may be relevant that one of the two is a prayer, addressed directly by the chorus to the god, and that the other is a statement made about Zeus by a person himself interested in celestial power plays. The fact remains that Prometheus's statement can be made without an immediate rebuttal (or, for that matter, without any kind of rebuttal; we do not know what happened in the rest of the trilogy).

Of all of Aeschylus's plays, *Persians* is probably, in the matter of the gods, the simplest. From the very beginning, the suffering imposed upon Xerxes and his troops is defined as a punishment. Yet even here, the variety of formulation is impressive. When one of the Persians wishes to explain a sudden disaster, he talks about "a god" or "a demon," which is the continuation of a tradition known already in Homer. That is to say, men or women attempting to convey a feeling that events are due to the agency of a higher power are content to leave the identity of that power unspecified. After all, it is part of the wonder of divine action that it cannot be narrowed

1. J. Jones, *On Aristotle and Greek Tragedy* (Oxford, 1962), p. 128. The topic of the gods and religion in Aeschylus has attracted innumerable critics. Among the more valuable contributions are: K. Reinhardt, *Aischylos als Regisseur und Theologe* (Bern, 1949); F. Solmsen, "Strata of Greek Religion in Aeschylus," *Harvard Theological Review* 40 (1947): 211–26; idem, *Hesiod and Aeschylus* (Ithaca, N.Y., 1949); H. D. F. Kitto, "The Idea of God in Aeschylus and Sophocles," *Entretiens Fondation Hardt* 1 (Vandoeuvres, 1954): 169–89; W. Kiefner, *Der religiöse Allbegriff des Aischylos* (*Spudasmata* 5; Hildesheim, 1966). H. Lloyd-Jones's "Zeus in Aeschylus," *JHS* 76 (1956): 55–67, and the same author's pertinent remarks in *The Justice of Zeus* (Berkeley and Los Angeles, 1971) argue that Aeschylus can be shown to have religious beliefs, and that these are conservative.

down to accord with the comfortable norms of mythological narrative. Where gods are the movers, their identity usually remains hidden. Conversely, where men take the initiative, gods *are* named, in prayers, and in complaints which are also prayers of a sort. The chorus calls on Zeus the King (532); on Earth, Hermes, and Aidoneus, the king of the lower gods (628 ff.), and on others yet. Darius blames Zeus (739–40, 827) and names Poseidon (750); Xerxes lodges a complaint with Zeus (915). That the Persians can call on Greek divinities is not surprising. Herodotus has acquainted us with the Greek capacity for regarding all foreign gods as if they were Greeks with foreign names attached to them, who can, therefore, be invoked or talked about as if they were Greeks. Side by side, then, with the unfocused references to "some god," we encounter specifically named divinities, both celestial and chthonian. Some of the identifications are narrowly regional; we are told, for instance, that Pan dwells on the island of Psyttaleia (448–49). All this is quite conventional, and occasions few problems.

A jarring note, rupturing the simplicity of the religious picture, is introduced when not only Darius but also Xerxes are stated to be gods, or godlike. That they should be both is itself confusing. By the rules of our own logic, a person cannot be at one and the same time a god and like a god. But worse than this apparent fault in logic is the notion that Xerxes, who is, if not the chief sinner, then the chief victim of the drama, can also be a god. One way of resolving the difficulty is to suggest that the chorus, in predicating divine status of their Emperor, are simply wrong; that, in fact, the destruction of the army and the suffering of the nation have something to do with their readiness to permit Xerxes to occupy a divine place in their imagination. But that cannot be entirely right, for in his account of Salamis, the messenger talks about Themistocles, or whoever it was who spoke to Xerxes and misled him, as if he were not only a man but also an evil demon (353–55), and we know that the Greeks were easily given to looking upon their outstanding leaders as if they were gods incarnate. The most that can be said about the chorus's habit of reading divinity into Xerxes is that when his downfall comes, it is the more disastrous because the fall is from a greater height. Nevertheless, the divinity of Xerxes or his godlikeness shows that even in this relatively uncomplicated play, the religious coordinates are not straightforward.

Let us be clear what the gods do and what they do not do in an ancient tragedy, and specifically in Aeschylus. As the cast of characters in a flexible mythological tradition, they can do just about anything. As counters in the strategy of actions and responses which informs a play, they are at the discretion of the author. This point cannot be stressed too much. We need to remind ourselves again and again that the choice between formulating an event as divinely inspired or divinely guided, on the one hand, and investing it with purely human qualities, on the other, is the author's. The reminder is needed to guard against the misunderstanding represented by a remark such as this: "The Gods, by their hatreds and protective preferences, brought about all the extraordinary happenings in the theatre of the ancients. . . . Men undertook nothing without the Gods' advice, and achieved nothing without their aid."[2] This astonishing statement, which is only more extreme than many others that might have been cited, is unsatisfactory on many accounts, but especially on two: it disregards the variety and the internal inconsistency of the religious fictions available to the playwright; and it forgets about the author. It subscribes to what has been called the documentary fallacy, the assumption that the play we witness is the record of a slice of experience independent of the controlling invention of the playwright.

"The gods," as a collective phrase, is virtually meaningless. It can mean the gods of the legends and of the Homeric pantheon. Though many of them are also the recipients of worship, they are, above all, the heroes and heroines of tales told about the past. Their usefulness to the tragedians was enormous. Because the stories told about them were full of color and human interest, and because their transactions touched upon the abiding issues of a purposeful life, mythology furnished much of the plot material on which the tragedians drew. But besides the gods of the myths, or only indirectly associated with them, there were the divinities to whom men and women turned for satisfaction of their religious instincts: the gods of the clan, the gods of the city, the divinities of the household, and the gods presiding over a craft or an occupation. Each of these exacted a measure of worship. Collisions between the loyalties due to them were by no means uncommon.

Dramatic conflicts are easily reinforced by the fiction that the gods to whom the antagonists pray form opposing camps. Zeus in *Suppliants* is not only a clan god, and thereby in a natural state of conflict with the gods of the Egyptians (921–23); he is also the hero in a tale in which he was the lover of Io and the husband of a jealous wife. The two functions cannot be neatly separated, but each has its particular contribution to make to the quality of the dramatic experience. Finally, there are also certain gods—and again Zeus must be counted among them—that function as organizational tropes rather than as objects of storytelling or objects of worship. They are respected as the forces at work in the material and psychological universe, but their appeal is to the understanding, rather than to fear or love or the luxury of amusement. These are the gods in whom Hesiod was interested, and out

2. Ch. de Saint-Évremond, *Réflexions sur la tragédie ancienne et moderne*, ed. R. de Planhol (Paris, 1927), vol. 1, p. 174.

of whom he generated the cosmogony which was a first step on the road to natural history. Again, there is overlap. Earth can be experienced as the dark goddess to whom the farmer prays on behalf of his crops; she can also be regarded as the equivalent of matter, a primary constituent of the natural universe. Zeus can be little more than a name for the force which a scientist fails to explain after he has explained everything else. Much depends on the rubric under which a particular deity is felt to be cited in the dramatic text.

One would think that the regional use, i.e., the naming of a god in connection with an area over which he is said to preside, should not present difficulties. One might expect Aeschylus to avail himself of the presence of certain divinities for the purposes of local color. Here again, however, we are sometimes surprised. Hera, the patron goddess of Argos, is mentioned only a few times in *Suppliants*, and then usually as part of the myth in which she plays the jealous pursuer of Io. It seems that Aeschylus's aims in this play dictated a sparing recourse to the goddess as a provider of local color. Perhaps Aeschylus's decision to make prominent use of the tale of Hera's punishment of Io—contrast the remarkable underplaying of Hera's role in the version of the tale in *Prometheus* 561–686—stood in the way of exploiting Hera's sovereignty in Argos. The reciprocal limitations imposed by their different functions within a drama are of great interest in analyzing Aeschylus's use of the gods. It has often been pointed out that after Apollo's role in the restoration of Orestes and the punishment of Clytemnestra has been duly stressed, the god is not mentioned even once in the Great Exchange between Orestes, Electra, and the chorus (*Lib.* 306 ff.). The exchange also exhibits another peculiarity: Zeus's name appears only in association with the nether world. The explanation in this case is fairly obvious. The chief addressee of the encounter is Agamemnon, and through him the realm of the underworld where Agamemnon's ghost is at home. Divine assistance can come from a variety of quarters. The dramatic situation requires that, at this juncture in the drama, Agamemnon and his associates be the source of succor. Apollo has to be eliminated temporarily from consideration, and Zeus has to be recast in a role which mythology makes available: that of the Zeus of the underworld, scarcely distinguishable from Aidoneus, or Hades, the principal divinity in the realm of the dead. But whereas Hades is normally a god of legend or a cosmogonic power, here Aeschylus refashions him, or rather his avatar as Zeus, in the image of a cult divinity.

Within the psychology of the drama, the gods are sometimes little more than a pretext. When Orestes and Electra call on Hermes Chthonios, the Hermes who corresponds to the Zeus of the nether world (*Lib.* 1 and 124), the invocation is merely a trigger for what turns out to be the exposition— an exposition vastly more natural and easy flowing, than the ponderous, allusive exposition offered in the preceding play of the trilogy.[3] The fact that there are two expository prayers—that, in other words, both Orestes and Electra can be said to inaugurate the action of *Libation-Bearers*—has its own value in establishing the sibling relationship.

This might be called the near-zero grade of divine significance in prayer. The god's name is invoked because a formal addressee is needed to launch the explanations which cannot subsist by themselves. From the point of view of verisimilitude, a criterion which it would be a mistake to rule out entirely in assessing the strategies of Aeschylean drama, addressing a god for the purposes of exposition is certainly preferable to addressing a friend or a companion or the chorus. As we have seen earlier, the address to the god stamps a speech as a kind of meditation about the past. At the opposite pole, we must put the occasions when a character, or a chorus, calls upon the god to help, and bolsters the invocation with a threat. In the entrance ode of *Suppliants*, the women put Zeus on probation. Though initially they admit (86–95) that Zeus's plans are dark and mysterious, they envisage a situation in which Zeus will be liable to the charge of unjust conduct (168 ff.). By raising this unlikely spectre—unlikely within the confines of this play, though not of others—they put themselves in the position of exerting moral pressure on the god. Between these extremes—the use of the god's name for aims that have nothing to do with religion or mythology, and putting pressure on the god as if he were a member of the petitioner's moral universe—the invocations of a divinity cover a broad spectrum of significance and weight.

Sometimes the invocation is in the second person; equally often, perhaps more often, the god is named in the third person, with the verb in the third person imperative or an equivalent form. This is especially true in cases in which the appeal is formal rather than substantive. But no firm distinction can be made. In the Great Exchange of *Libation-Bearers*, for instance, Orestes favors the vocative, while Electra prefers the third person. It would be rash to infer that Orestes's link with the gods is more direct or more intimate than that of Electra; much less can we base elaborate psychological conclusions on the formal difference. In some cases, we cannot be certain whether the text has the vocative or the nominative.[4] Now and then, it may be possible to tie this or that variation to a special need in the dramatic constellation. But our misgivings about the appropriateness of the fine-toothed comb in gleaning what is meaningful in these texts and what is not still stand.

3. A. F. Garvie, "The Opening of the *Choephori*," *Bulletin Inst. Class. Studies* 17 (London, 1970): 79–91, speculates on the significance of Hermes in this passage.

4. For example, *Suppl.* 1062, where M has the vocative but Robortello rightly, I think, prints the nominative.

The possibility of a relatively easy relationship to the god, including the opportunity for moral influence and indignation, says something about the status of the men and women whose stories are put on the stage. These are, after all, the giants who walked with the gods, the heroes and heroines of a legendary past, whose own being hung precariously in the balance between humanity and divinity. In the eyes of the audience, a Heracles, a Helen, or a Theseus is more than human. There were places in the Greek world where these figures were the recipients of divine honors. The language used of Xerxes on which we commented earlier is more easily intelligible because of the difficulty many Greeks had in deciding for themselves what distinguished a great hero of the past from a god. In addition, according to one theory, tragic drama is in its origins closely associated with the worship of the deceased hero, the "dangerous" individual whose life was too exacting for social comfort and whose death was a source of wonder and solicitation.[5] The tombs of the great ancestors—Agamemnon, Darius, and others— were prominent on the stage. The ghosts that lived in them, and might be called forth, had many of the attributes of the gods. They were felt to have the power of protecting or punishing their descendants and their fellow men. Their epiphany was expected to produce a feeling of awe.

Aeschylus's extant plays give us only two ghosts, those of Darius and Clytemnestra.[6] The differences between them are marked. In *Persians*, Darius engages in conversation with his widow. Perhaps Aeschylus ventured upon this course because Darius is a Persian, and may therefore be counted on to conduct himself in unusual ways. But when he appears, he is respectable, in an elegiac rather than a plaintive mood, and in no way given to exotic habits. He might well be a god except that, to begin with, a ghost must drink blood, or otherwise refresh his touch, before he can know. Otherwise he has, or claims he has, no knowledge of events. As for Clytemnestra, her ghost is querulous, as befits the ghost of a person with a grievance. She makes much of her hideous wounds (a matter of rhetoric, I should think, rather than of costuming) and she has a great deal to say, but she leaves, as a good ghost should, without engaging in significant dialogue. She mentions ghostly sacrifices; she, the ghost, has made ritual offerings to the divinities that rule over ghostdom, i.e., the Furies (*Eum.* 106 ff.):

> So many times I have fed your lapping tongues,
> With wineless offerings, sober palliatives,
> And grave nocturnal meals burnt on the hearth!

5. The theory is that of W. Ridgeway, *The Origin of Tragedy* (Cambridge, 1910). See also H. Patzer, *Die Anfänge der griechischen Tragödie* (Wiesbaden, 1962), pp. 39 ff.

6. On ghosts in Aeschylus, see E. Bickel, "Geistererscheinungen bei Aischylos," *Rheinisches Museum* 91 (1942): 123–64.

The humor of the conception is a grim subspecies of the playfulness which we associate with the frivolous or callous intercourse between the gods in Homer's *Iliad*. The only truly compelling ghost in Aeschylus is one who does not make an appearance, whose power is felt precisely because he is not given a malicious opportunity to appear: Agamemnon, the punishing power in the tomb, directing vengeance from behind the scene. In Thomas Heywood's *The Second Part of the Iron Age*, Agamemnon's ghost does appear, "poynting unto his wounds," with great loss to our sense of horror.

Greek has no word exactly corresponding to our "ghost." Agamemnon, Darius, and Clytemnestra in their graves would be called *daimones*: demons. These are the forces, the vital presences that, according to Thales, Hesiod, and others, could be encountered in almost any realm of experience, if only one's sensibilities were open to the stimulus. In the experience of ordinary men and women, especially where the initiative was thought to reside with the external powers, demons and gods were identical. That is to say, the ordinary man did not interest himself in the question of whether a divine being had once been human or was still in some aspects human. Nor did he make a distinction between divine persons and abstractions, i.e., between divinities that are primarily persons, and that can be made to symbolize specific segments of reality only by a wrenching of the personal contours, and divinities that serve chiefly to pinpoint a realm of experience, and can be made into persons only by an additional act of the imagination. The last divinities mentioned in *Eumenides* (1045–46) are Athena, Zeus, and Moira. It is difficult for us to reconstruct the mentality which puts Athena and Zeus, two eminent celestial personalities with characters and biographies of an exceptional amplitude, in the same series as Moira, the pale personification of the principle of allotment and doom. But the distinction would have meant little to the audience; and, as we have already noted, even the figure of Zeus can be cited for purposes which effectively block a consideration of his mythological and cultic links.

We can go further and say that drama is the literary genre most conducive to effacing the various lines of differentiation which a critic might wish to establish between divine types. As we have indicated, tragedy does not encourage worship. It encourages a kind of thinking which seeks to understand, or at least to get a feeling for, the meaning of human lives, and which does this by adducing principles of organization and interpretation which converge upon religious belief. The major distinction between a drama referring to a curse on a house and a drama introducing a god cursing is that the concreteness of the latter, with its suggestions of familiarity and fallibility, tends to blunt the sharpness of the horror. The famous passages which put the emphasis on the inscrutability of Zeus are designed to strip Zeus of his mythographical and ritual extensions, of his traditional character, and to approximate his being to that of a demon or an abstraction. The central position occupied by the curse in Clytemnestra's speech after she has been told of the death of Orestes (*Lib.* 691–99) is significant. If we have a choice between believing that she is genuinely aggrieved and believing that she is shamming grief, the stress upon the curse, rather than upon a personal divinity chosen by a process of theological refinement, appears to speak for the former.

But what does it mean when Aeschylus has somebody tell us that a god practices deceit, or that a god causes something to happen out of a sense of pique; or, as we read in one fragment, that a god does not refrain from, or dissociate himself from, "just" deception; or, finally, that the god

> breeds a warrant for men
> When he wants to crush the lineage root and branch.?[7]

Given the popularity of the fiction of the jealousy of the gods in Herodotus and other Greek writers, Aeschylus makes but sparing use of the notion. Perhaps he felt that in many instances the anthropomorphism implied in such thinking about the gods was too facile for what he wanted. Divine anthropomorphism is acceptable in situations where gods face one another, as in the divine masques of *Prometheus* and *Eumenides*. It is less useful and requires modification where the focus is on the doings and sufferings of particular men and women. A jealous god or a spiteful goddess might make for too much clarity and would serve to deflect attention from the larger concerns.

Nevertheless, the motif of divine hostility is very much alive in Aeschylean drama. Gods and demons are thought to be at their most powerful when they block or punish, rather than when they advance the course of human happiness. The hostility can be variously formulated as the authority of a god that brooks nothing in its way or as the minor shrugs and jolts of an impersonal resistance. It is fascinating to watch how delicately Aeschylus balances the need for precise definition with the equally pressing need for indeterminacy. Mythology supports the former. *Pers.* 345–46 evokes a brief echo of the *psychostasia*, the mythological conceit of the weighing of lives on the scale, an image which reduces a wealth of irrational factors to the definable terms of a mercantile transaction. But at the next moment, the old fear of the avenging demon, now adjusted to that of the jealousy of the gods (353, 362), broadens our sense of the scope of the action and of the nexus of causation. To suppose that the Aeschylean gods must always be thought to be acting for the best is an impoverishment of the contribution

---

7. For pique, see *Pers.* 362; for deception, see frs. 162, 163 Smyth; the last passage is from fr. 277, lines 15–16 Lloyd-Jones.

the gods make to tragedy. Tragedy differs from comedy, and from Dr. Pangloss's comfort station, in refusing to absorb the bad into the good, and the worse into the better. The gods—even in a play which, like *Eumenides*, is supposedly intended to furnish a resolution—take their places within this refusal.

Occasionally an individual or a chorus makes a pronouncement against heresy or agnosticism. At *Agam.* 369–72, the chorus refers disapprovingly to an unnamed man who said that the gods do not care: "That man was wicked." From the point of view of the respectable elders, gods can do no wrong. But, as we have tried to show earlier, the choral understanding is not without its limitations. In this instance, we might be tempted to say that the members of the chorus have not had the advantage of reading Aeschylus. The whole burden of the trilogy, and of all Aeschylean drama, proves them mistaken. Gods not only can do wrong, they must do wrong; or at least they must not be limited to doing only right, for that would make their function within the tissue of social experience and human suffering superfluous. Orestes does not exercise a moral resistance to Apollo's orders; but Aeschylus's drama does. When Euripides's eloquent questioners raise the issue of divine justice, the challenge is merely a dialectical development of what in Aeschylus is more deeply imbedded in the dramatic experience. Curiously, Euripides often appears to use the resources of drama to convict the questions of irrelevance, or at least of narrowness. Euripidean gods, in the final scenes of many of his plays, come close to suggesting that because mortals cannot understand the reasons for divine action, we have no recourse but to believe that the gods act rightly. In Aeschylus, there is no such propensity toward the construction of a credo, because the gods are not separated from the interplay of forces which constitutes the drama.

One might argue that Cassandra is a forerunner of Euripides's theological questioners. But Cassandra's challenge is not a challenge to the gods, or of divine action as such. It is a challenge cast in the teeth of a particular god, and the burden of the challenge bears on the data of mythology, which in Euripides are only part of what is felt to be objectionable in divine irresponsibility. She complains about Apollo's love for her, and about his revenge. Because of the magnitude of Cassandra's presence, because of her dignity and her pathos, we are inclined to see things as she sees them, and from that angle Apollo's behavior is quite improper. Altogether Apollo's standing in the *Oresteia* is the most marked example in Aeschylus of a god who defies deification. He punishes Cassandra for what appear to be grossly inadequate reasons, he deals with Orestes in an unconscionable manner, and he handles the speech for the defense of Orestes with a degree of casuistry which an Athenian juryman might find gratifying, but hardly elevating. All this can only mean that Aeschylus has no interest whatever in making us like or respect Apollo for himself. He uses Apollo, as he uses most of his gods, to construct a web of impulses and motivations designed to hint at the moral confusion, and often perversity, of human affairs.

It would be a serious mistake to judge the success of the trilogy by whether Aeschylus succeeds in conveying a sense of the rightness and the exclusiveness of divine power. Plato saw this well. In his *Republic* (2.383B), he cites nine and a half lines from a play that may or may not be by Aeschylus, but which on the point at issue accords with Aeschylean practice. In the quotation, Thetis complains about the inconsistency and the caddishness of Apollo. Plato's point is that the dramatist breaks with the principle that the gods can do no wrong. No amount of subtle reasoning or special pleading will lead to the conclusion that Plato has failed to understand what Aeschylus is about. The present objection is merely one of Plato's many criticisms of tragedy, all of them ultimately issuing in the charge that the definition of man in tragedy is irrational. This is, of course, quite correct, and it is exactly for this reason that Aeschylus builds the tradition of divine jealousy and irresponsibility into a human context that cries out for such enrichment.

To say this comes close to saying that Aeschylus's gods are symbols. The many instances of contending divinities in his scheme might lend further credence to this conclusion. In the fragmentary play *Champions at Isthmia*, much of the action appears to have been based on the contention between Athena, protectress of Athens, and Poseidon, lord of Isthmia. *Champions* is a satyr play, and concreteness of conflict is one of the features of that genre. Still, comparable simplicities are observable in tragedy. Toward the end of *Suppliants* (1030 ff.), the fundamental clash between Artemis and Aphrodite, chastity and sex, is opened up. The dialectic of the argument is not far removed from the programmatic opposition of the same two divinities in Euripides's *Hippolytus* and many other works, including documents of Christian piety. But it is noteworthy that this simple contrast is introduced at the very end of the play. It would not do to apply the same conflict to the heart of the drama, and in fact many critics have been puzzled by the seemingly unmediated suddenness with which the issue is imported.

If we look elsewhere in the work of Aeschylus, things are a little more complicated. The relation between the Furies and the Olympians is not entirely one of opposition, but should be regarded as a distribution of labor, with a shifting intelligence of what falls within the domain of the one or the other. Orestes makes things difficult for the gods because he is living proof of the impossibility of a tidy distribution. Aeschylus does not have his characters or the chorus speak of a conflict between divine wills. The disharmony between Artemis and Apollo (*Agam.* 146 ff.) is as important to our understanding of *Agamemnon* as is the peculiar authority of Zeus. But the two divinities are not related logically. They operate independently, and when they appear to run afoul of each other, the disturbance is more like an incidental and unforeseen friction than like a systematic confrontation. We learn that Artemis won out, but we are not left with the impression that the victory entailed a defeat for Apollo. Even in the third play, where Apollo and the Furies lock in battle, the deflections arranged for by the rhetoric of the masque refashion what might have been a battle of wills into a serial exposition of independent voices. For the two divine powers are, dramatically speaking, of entirely different kinds. Apollo orders the killing of Clytemnestra; the Furies externalize Orestes's malaise after the fact. To say that both Apollo and the Furies are symbols may be correct but is not very helpful, for the symbolism is not the same. Apollo is a person, and acts on behalf of another person, Zeus. That he stands for the integrity of the house, against usurpation by an outsider, is a circumstance which cannot be derived logically from the person he is. The Furies are more like abstractions. To the extent that they have a personality, it is a direct consequence of the idea incorporated in them: the righting of the balance after its violent internal upsetting. In essence, they are emblems rather than persons. They owe their personal force in Aeschylus only, or largely, to the dramatic preference of the author. There is little in the religious tradition that could have guided his hand. As emblems, they have a certain affinity with Athena, the emblem of the city of Athens. We can understand why Aeschylus was moved to compose an explicit contention between these two, rather than between Apollo and the Furies. But Athena is a newcomer in the dramatic scheme; this new conflict tells us nothing about the issues on which the earlier parts of the trilogy turn.

Orestes requires the help of Zeus; he requires the help of Apollo; he also looks for assistance from Agamemnon and the nether divinities; finally, he must rely on his own abilities as a planner and fighter. Themistocles works with the aid of a demon, or in his capacity as a demon, which means that the Greeks are also self-reliant. The chorus in *Agamemnon*, within the brief space of one passage (1481–96) speculates that an old demon has been at work; that Zeus is responsible; and that an armed hand has done the deed. Are we to regard these varied formulations as alternatives, or are they meant to work cumulatively? Does Aeschylus attempt to sound the mystery of the causal nexus by shifting the burden around from men to gods and back? Or does he intend us to believe that the various factors cited operate simultaneously? As we have already seen in looking at the figure of Orestes, and as we shall see again, it is probably impossible to make a tidy distinction between the alternative and the cumulative in the formulation of shaping forces. Aeschylus brings together a variety of divine and human factors where, under the auspices of economy, fewer might have been sufficient. Drama—or any literature—is not logic; dramatic figures have other functions beside that of furnishing sufficient reasons.

In *Agamemnon*, Artemis and Zeus appear to be the divinities most frequently appealed to as the powers active in the human universe. In *Libation-Bearers*, Hermes and Apollo take their place; and in *Eumenides*, Apollo is joined by Athena for the purposes of divine direction. One suspects that the nature of this direction changes from play to play, and that that has something to do with the shifting of the personnel. Still, the whole trilogy is full of reminders of the over-arching potency of Zeus. There is the further question whether the *Oresteia* celebrates a progress, a displacement of transcendent control in favor of what amounts to secular power: human institutions taking over from an order defined by the fear of the gods. We cannot be sure of this. The alleged progress may be a mirage; literary fiction being what it is, we must allow for the possibility that the developmental dimension of the drama is a façade gracing what should be savored as a timeless truth. In any case, both the old and the new in the *Oresteia* are formulated in divine *and* human terms. In the old order, the compulsiveness of blood feud materializes as divine constraint; in the new order, the mechanization of justice emerges as divine manipulation. The nature and use of the divine trope vary, but always the ultimate focus is man and human society. Both gods and men are part of a larger rhythm, which the playwright activates to revive the old myths and to exploit the lessons of recent history.

A number of modern critics have underscored the importance of "the demonic" in Aeschylus. It is certainly correct that again and again demons are held responsible for human afflictions. What this means is that the playwright, wishing to dwell on what is painful and unaccountable in such suffering, is at liberty to charge it to unnamed, or named, demons, often from among the chthonic powers. On a continuous scale of ostensible accountability, stretching wide from the individual human volition to the individual divine trap or act of malice, the demonic cause occupies a conveniently ill-defined and mysterious mediate range. The messenger reports (*Pers.* 361 ff.) that Xerxes, "not recognizing the guile of the Greek man or the malice of the gods," communicated the fatal battle plan to his commanders. The double formulation is typical. Just as it is difficult to tell whether Themistocles (or his servant Sicinnus) was himself a demon or whether he worked under the influence of a demon, so a satisfactory tragic account of responsibility must be comprehensive. Any formulation that singles out the human component or the divine is either incomplete or aims at a special effect. The advantage of putting the accent on the demonic is that the ill-defined nature of that concept invites the supposition that the divine and the human are included in it also. To say that the Curse, or the

Demon, or Fate is at the heart of an action or a mishap suggests an unspoken imputation of human error or human crime, as well as the active participation of forces beyond man.

Once this is fully understood, it is no longer possible to say that talk about divine or demonic management is merely that, talk, and that Aeschylus is really asking us to convert his language into propositions concerning the human contribution. In the case of the sacrifice of Iphigenia, for instance, we are told by some that it is Agamemnon and no one else who initiates the action and is therefore accountable and guilty. As a consequence, the devastation of the war at Troy is also to be blamed on him: "He has already resolved that he will avenge a personal wrong through indiscriminate bloodshed. . . . He is indeed helpless because he now finds it too late to draw back; but he is not innocent."[8] Of course he is not innocent. But the psychological formulation rings false because it narrows down the fated act of the sacrifice to the nervous obsession of a lone man. If we accept everything that is in the text, Agamemnon's action arises out of a continuum of agencies, in which the king takes his place side by side with Artemis and with the curse upon his house. To put it differently: in Aeschylean drama, the metaphysical and the natural, the physical and the spiritual, necessity and chance, compulsion and the criminal will are in close proximity.

This is precisely why the demons are so important to Aeschylus. Atē, for instance, awkwardly translated as "delusion" but much closer in force to the potential for destruction and self-destruction, is cited twice within a brief span in *Agamemnon* (730 and 735).[9] In the first mention, the term is relatively uncharged; the reference is to the lion cub that, growing up and recovering the fierceness of its kind, gluts its fury in acts of destruction, murdering sheep. In the second instance, *atē* comes to be hypostatized, and the lion cub turns into a priest of Destruction, the natural agent of an irresistible demonic force. The sliding back and forth between the low-charged and the highly-charged is once again characteristic of the continuum, and of the comprehensive vision before which all narrowing down of liability becomes perilous. We shall have more to say about this in the next chapter.

To repeat, an event or an action can be defined as due to human authorship, or as caused by a demon or demons, or inspired by a specific traditional god, or by two or all of these agencies. In the latter case, what Aeschylus provides is not a double or triple formulation, much less a case of "over-determination," as some have termed it, but rather a full exposition

---

8. H. D. F. Kitto in *Gnomon* 30 (1958): 168.

9. For *Atē*, see R. E. Doyle, "The Objective Concept of *Atē* in Aeschylean Tragedy," *Traditio* 28 (1972): 1–28.

of what is felt always to be the truth, even where the formulation is short-hand.[10] For the Aeschylean universe is a profusion of agents and causes, in which no one statement is ever more than a singling out of what, under the circumstances, will serve as an adequate pointer. The poet works by ab-straction, but he manages to convey the feeling that he could say more, and that the thirty thousand demons which Hesiod tells us are active in the world are still to be reckoned with. This means, of course, that a neat theological accounting of moral issues is not only not possible, but would work to the detriment of the opacity which the tragedy must affirm, even while assigning particular shares of blame or praise.[11]

About Aeschylus's use of the gods, it has been said that "there is much that is crude, and much that is confused, in these conceptions; there is no possibility of deducing a coherent theology, let alone philosophy, from the diversity of demons revealed in only seven plays." Against this false disjunc-tion—either a clear, consistent theology, or a crude one—it has been ar-gued that Aeschylus's theology may not be consistent, but that it is tradi-tional, and that it is not crude but adequate to its purpose.[12] But this argument, like the polemic against which it is directed, runs the risk of shortchanging what matters most: the power and the freshness of the poetic vision, and the sense of fullness and energy which it communicates. Eu-ripides has an interest in theological argumentation. He can use his charac-ters and his choruses to voice conflicting assumptions about the gods, each of them claiming to be a complete statement of what it purports to cover. Aeschylus is a different kind of playwright. He is primarily interested, not in how the universe is run, but in what happens among men, and how these happenings can be presented dramatically without falsifying their larger filiations. No more and no less than most serious twentieth-century play-wrights, Aeschylus tries to say something about man as a planner and doer, while also stressing that the planning and the doing do not happen in a vacuum.

Apollo functions as a cause of action; the Furies function as an emblem or a formal restatement of an issue or an action. A like distinction is made at *Agam.* 810 ff. The gods are said to be *metaitioi*, jointly responsible, with men, for certain events. In Agamemnon's mouth, the statement has a cer-tain arrogance about it, but that does not diminish its dramatic truth. But this way of talking about the gods is immediately modified by the remark-able image which follows, of the gods putting their votes in the urn for

10. The term was most prominently used by E. R. Dodds in *The Greeks and the Irrational* (Berkeley and Los Angeles, 1951) pp. 7 ff.

11. For a fuller treatment of this issue, see below, chap. 10.

12. "Crude": Page in J. D. Denniston and D. L. Page, *Aeschylus: Agamemnon* (Oxford, 1956), p. xv; "traditional": Lloyd-Jones, in the publications cited above, note 1.

destruction. This is a developed picture, and one that will be, by a process the formalists have called "symbolic realization," fully dramatized in the last play of the trilogy.[13] Here it replaces the succinct formula of attribution with a broadly fashioned emblem; the concept of cause is dropped in favor of the pictorial duplication of fact. In this latter use, the citing of the gods is much like the citing of a mythical paradigm. The gods putting their voting pebbles in the ballot urn is roughly on the same level of iconographic elaboration and poetic function as the legendary doings of Tereus and Metis and Aedone brought in to invest the visible lament of the daughters of Danaus with added resonance and meaning.

According to a recent suggestion, the extant plays of Aeschylus may be divided into two groups, on the basis of two different ways of featuring the role of the gods in the world.[14] On the one hand, in *Persians* and *Seven*, the rule of the gods is much like that in Sophocles, Herodotus, and other writers with an interest in the question of divine government. In these two plays, the gods are said to watch closely over man, in case he makes a false step, and to pounce on him as soon as he does so. In the remaining four plays (not counting *Prometheus*), on the other hand, the gods are divided within their own ranks, in conformity with the divisions among men. This makes for tangles and afflictions far beyond anything dreamed of in the other scheme. The suggestion has a certain appeal, if only for its implication that Aeschylus's thinking about the gods underwent a development which can be traced in the course of his writing career. One may wonder, however, whether the distinction is not too simple. Even in *Persians*, the friction between various uses, between trope and commitment, between the gods on stage and the gods off stage, between the god as cause and the god as emblem, is of importance. If it is true that the divine apparatus in the earlier two plays shows fewer of the internal divisions that are, after all, a Homeric legacy, this may have something to do with the fact that those plays, unlike the others, dramatize the sufferings of one nation or city-state fighting a war against another.

In the matter of the gods, it is, above all, important that we do not confuse two distinct things: the avowed beliefs of the characters and the integral effect of the play as it advances from scene to scene and enlists our participating responses. There is a subtle way in which what for the character is an experienced reality becomes for us a succession of constantly modified perceptions. A character may regard himself as controlled by the gods; the same is true of the chorus. But the audience does not accept this commitment unchanged. In its growing understanding of the dramatic con-

---

13. See also my remarks about "anticipation" and Lebeck, above, chap. 5, pp. 136f.
14. C. J. Herington, *The Author of the Prometheus Bound* (Austin, Tex., 1970), chap. 3.

struct, characters and gods collaborate so as to commute the external constraints cited in the play into a fusion of conceptual perspectives and poetic energies. In the end, all statements about the gods, whether about personal gods operating as causes or movers or about personified emblems serving as reformulations, merge with all other statements of motivation to produce the sense of a world, a whole, composed of forces difficult to track, but felt to make up an organic aggregate.

The chorus sings (*Agam.* 184 ff.):

> So too the elder chief of the Achaean ships,
> Holding no prophet in disrespect,
> Breathing in tune with the clash of events,
> When the host was oppressed with depleting calm,
> At Aulis, off Chalcis, where the flow surges back and forth;
>
> And blasts coming from Strymon,
> Producing ill leisure and fasts and tortured anchorage,
> Convulsers of men, wasters of tackle,
> Vast protractors of time,
> Carded the nap of the Greeks, ground down their bloom.

The winds which swirl around man and obstruct him or favor him are an atmospheric realization of the forces which determine his life. Even the figure of Agamemnon "breathing in tune with the clash of events" exploits that same imagery.[15] Each man is alone, exposed to the blasts among which his actions must be coordinated. The appositions personify the winds—which is to say, they elevate them to the status of demons. Aeschylus's plays are full of such wind imagery. It has a hoary ancestry, going back all the way to Homer, who likes to mark the stubbornness of a hero by likening him, in a simile, to a rock or a headland battered by a storm. But if we compare the heros of the *Iliad* with those of Aeschylus, the former appear to be moving in a vacuum. Their massive silhouettes are bounded by a doom, a kind of alarm clock which is set to the time of their death; for the rest, they are free to fashion their lives as they wish. In Aeschylus, on the other hand, men are aware of always moving within a field crisscrossed with contrary forces. The forces are by no means all hostile; note, for instance, the gentleness of the language used of the mistress of the animals (*Agam.* 140 ff.), she who is kind to young whelps and nursing beasts. Usually, however, the tensions are experienced as dangers; men must constantly be on their guard. There is little of the Stoic perception which defines Senecan and later European drama, the feeling that the tensions in the world are merely extensions of the conflicts and the sicknesses in the hero's own heart. The occasional

15. See W. C. Scott, "Wind Imagery in the *Oresteia*," *TAPA* 97 (1966):459–71.

simile, now and then a choral metaphor, might suggest that perspective, but it is a minor theme. Primarily, the world is an obstacle; it is a man's task to find a way for himself through a trackless waste.

Human impotence in the face of divine inscrutability is a common enough choral topic. The idea, and some of the images in which it is rendered, are legacies from the tradition of the lyric, from the poetry of Archilochus, Mimnermus, and Pindar. But once again it is improper to generalize and apply the timid choral perspective to the tragic experience as a whole. Those who think that Aeschylean tragedy shows "the human insect, debating with himself in the night, confronting indifferent gods whom he does not understand," are likely to be better theologians than they are critics of drama.[16] The language of impotence and blindness does not touch the characters, who are aware of the power of the gods, but refuse to cringe before them. Aeschylean tragedy is, in a manner of speaking, a dialogue or, better, a many-sided colloquy between a number of languages, of which the language of the human insect is merely one. The Aeschylean hero acknowledges the power, or rather the presence, of the gods. But when he talks about them, it is almost as equals, as fellow beings, and not as an overwhelming faraway authority confounding his own freedom of action. Traditionally, the pressure on man can be formulated as the workings of fate or the actions of gods. The *Oresteia*, and Aeschylus's tragedies in general, make less of fate and of cognate concepts than of the gods. Gods can be thought of as acting from motives, and offering a semblance of intelligibility. This raises the hope of solutions and salvations. But it must be understood that any solutions that come to be suggested, either by a character or by a chorus, are as much part of the dramatic texture, and hence subject to variation and revocation, as the divine tropes themselves.

Aeschylus's most powerful symbol for the matrix of forces within which the dramatic agent is placed is that of Zeus. It is no exaggeration to say that the mythological and literary notion of the unlimited authority of Zeus owes more to the poetic vision of Aeschylus than to the thinking of Homer or Hesiod, where Zeus works with important, and occasionally curious, limitations. The main function of Zeus in Aeschylean tragedy is to remind us, again and again, usually through choral statements, of the limitations of what a man can do. To invoke Zeus is to remind other characters and the audience of the vastness and complexity of the larger world. The emphasis is on our ignorance, but also on our appreciation. We can know nothing about Zeus, but the prospect is, in the last analysis, challenging rather than frightening. Zeus is never a dramatic character, not even in *Prometheus*; he is a poetic way of talking about the context of human action. All other gods

16. A. J. Festugière, *De l'essence de la tragédie grecque* (Paris, 1969), p. 12.

and demons and curses and dooms are partial ways of expressing limiting circumstance; Zeus comprises them all. Mythologically speaking, they are his ministers.

But as we get closer to Zeus, the relevance of mythology is diminished. It is true that Zeus has his own legends, and that this mythology, with its specific terms and its slippery tales, is not left unexploited. But where it is found, it is bound to be mildly misleading. The stories about Zeus turn out to be rudimentary, mere starting points in the dramatic construct of causes and contentions. That Zeus slept with Io and produced Epaphus, or that he punished rivals, is part of the traditional language which the poet must use to develop his tropes. But the language is sufficiently rich and varied to permit the poet many different choices and modifications. Again, to say that the Zeus of the *Oresteia* or the Zeus of the *Prometheus* plays changes, and that this change determines the resolution of the trilogy, is to put the cart before the horse, and to adopt the shortsightedness of the chorus. Zeus is a divinity prayed to, a god pondered and remembered, and above all a pregnant imaging of the limitations imposed upon man. He is not an agent, much less a cause. Where limiting circumstance emerges in the dramatic forms of responsibility and authorship, it is Zeus's agents, Apollo and Athena and Hermes and Artemis, who are recruited. In *Agamemnon*, to be sure, Zeus is repeatedly said to be a participant in the action, and in *Eumenides* he is prominently associated with the acquittal. But the participation and the association are functions of the symbolic language; the name of Zeus is invoked to lend grandeur to the dimensions of what is being discussed. And so, if the daughters of Danaus at the beginning of *Suppliants* call on Zeus to help them, and threaten him with a loss of prestige if he refuses, the pathos of the gesture is in direct proportion to its abortiveness. The endeavor of Prometheus to set limits to Zeus's competence is of the same order of futility, though pathos is replaced by truculence, and the scope of the attack raises a real problem.

Typically, Zeus's principal epithet is *teleios*, "completer," a term that is already found in this use in Homer, but which gains immeasurably in importance in Aeschylus. It designates Zeus in his universality and his omnipotence, and in his stewardship over the whole of the dramatic action. In other writers, especially Euripides, Zeus the Completer becomes, as it were, the divine symbol for the future-directedness of the drama. But Aeschylean dramaturgy does not exhibit the same straining for completion or resolution. The rhythm of an Aeschylean play is more like a process of exhaustion; as it unfolds, it reveals what has been there from the beginning. The Aeschylean Zeus *teleios*, then, presides over the completeness of the revelation. As the defeat of the Persians is made fully apparent, or as the necessity of Eteocles's fratricidal destruction is assured, or the house of

Agamemnon is saved or restructured, we witness an unpacking of implications and of commitments which document the meaning of Zeus *teleios*.
In a fragment we read that

> Zeus is the air, Zeus is the earth, the sky,
> Zeus is all things and greater than all things.[17]

The lines are spoken; we do not know who speaks them, or for what purpose. In all probability, they are spoken by the chorus leader. Zeus is all there is, and he is therefore the norm against which all should be measured. *Should*; the phrase "greater than all things" makes the measurement problematic. We are reminded of the Platonic conviction that the Forms are knowable, but that our perception of them is at best approximate. The assumption that Zeus is, theoretically, a standard of measurement makes for an association of his name with the principle of insight or learning variously enunciated in choral song. "Learning through experience," the maxim stated in the essay on Zeus in *Agamemnon* (160 ff.), is coupled with Zeus's mythological standing as the third in a series of divine beginnings. The utility of the motto is immediately gainsaid by an emphasis on the inscrutability of the god, until it means little more than: dare to imagine you have a say in things, and you will get slapped down. The "resolution" of *Persians* and *Seven* and even of *Eumenides* shows us that "insight" or "learning" within the dramatic context is a mirage. Orestes does not add appreciably to his perceptions, and the apparent emphasis on cleverness and intelligibility which stands godfather to the reconciliation between Athena and the Furies produces no intellectual or moral gain. Zeus remains unknown.

In the light of this, it matters little, except to the passing mood of a scene, whether Zeus is spoken about in the third person or whether he is addressed in the second, through prayer or supplication. In either case, Aeschylus combines with the naming of the god a sense of power but also an intimation of futility: the power is so large, and our knowledge of its nature and extent so small, that a direct appeal is bound to tilt against hope. The position of the essay on Zeus is characteristic. It comes immediately after the suggestion, closing the reported speech of Calchas, that there will be revenge within the house for the sacrifice of the (unnamed) child. According to one recent critic, this is the wrong position for it; it should rather come after Agamemnon has made his agonizing speech bowing to the prophet's announcement of the will of Artemis.[18] But it would be strange if Zeus were thus drawn into specific complicity with his daughter's wrath. In any case, a

17. Fr. 34 Smyth, from *The Daughters of Helios*.
18. R. D. Dawe, "The Place of the Hymn to Zeus in Aeschylus' *Agamemnon*," *Eranos* 64 (1966): 1–21.

cushion is needed between the moral obscurity of Calchas's first speech and the introduction of Artemis's blockade and Agamemnon's troubled response. The essay on Zeus is such a cushion. It stamps both what precedes and what follows as morally indeterminate, but also as unavoidably, inextricably part of the total order of things. The formal summoning of Zeus converts what is fearful into what is acceptable. The divine trope broadens the scope; Aeschylean drama shuns the specific irrationalities which distinguish divine rule in Sophoclean and, especially, Euripidean drama. In spite of the obscurity attending his governance, the Aeschylean Zeus has a therapeutic function, analogous to, though obviously quite different from, that of the Pauline God. Zeus extends through all, and beyond it; he safeguards some form of meaning, though not necessarily of deliverance.

The availability of Zeus to signal all, or the norm, or the fullness of complete revelation, permits the deployment of other divine figures for more restricted objectives. To make clear the advantages of this kind of distribution, it will be useful to say a few more words about the Furies, a set of demons carrying out their special function within the domain of Zeus. All the various traits we discussed earlier are combined to furnish an unusually concrete picture of demonic activity. For one thing, the word *erinys*, to give the demon her Greek name, can be thought of as spelled either with a capital or with a minuscule initial. The word does not occur at all in the text of *Persians* and *Suppliants*, and only once in *Prometheus*, for the obvious reason that these plays do not envisage a curse on a house or bloody dissension within a family. *Seven* is the play with the most occurrences; it is the final piece in a trilogy which traces the workings of a curse. In the *Oresteia*, *Agamemnon* has the word more often than the two succeeding plays. In *Libation-Bearers*, the engineering of a plot replaces the near-automatic operation of the curse; in *Eumenides*, the concrete appearance of the Furies obviates talk about them. *Eumenides* is, of course, our play for testing the function of the personified *Erinys*, in her capacity as a specialized minister within the system of extrahuman forces culminating in Zeus.

It has been suggested that Aeschylus's Furies are a substitute for psychological realism. That is, where Euripides finds the rhetorical means for expressing the pangs of conscience plaguing a human being, Aeschylus falls back upon the visible presence of mythological figures signifying contrition and retribution.[19] This offers part of the truth, but it is not enough. In the introduction of their binding song (*Eum.* 305), the Furies, through their leaders, say to Orestes:

> You'll feed me alive; no need of ritual slaughter.

---

19. See also above, chap. 8; and M. Class, *Gewissensregungen in der griechischen Tragödie* (*Spudasmata* 3; Hildesheim, 1964), pp. 48 ff.

We are very close here to the kind of language whereby abstract notions are given bodily shape in parable and allegory. Ordinarily, this straight transfer from the abstract to the concrete—often, as in our political cartoons, through the use of animal imagery—is encountered in comedy more than in tragedy. Aristophanic comedy is full of cartoon figures, from the two hostile Arguments in *Clouds*, fitted out, if we may believe the scholiast, as fighting cocks, to Wealth in the comedy of the same name: figures that are transparent allegories of non-physical entities. In *Eumenides*, this would not be inappropriate; as we have had occasion to remark before, the play comes closest of all of Aeschylus's dramas, in tone and in structure, to the patterns of Old Comedy. But the vitality of the Furies is not, as such, comic. In any case, they are the Furies of Clytemnestra. They have come into being, mythologically speaking, only with the murder of the Queen. Or are we to think of them as the permanent representatives of the principle of retribution? Perhaps the distinction would be meaningless to the Greek audience. But the fact that the question can be raised suggests that we may have to be on the lookout for complications. The Furies themselves, in fact, appear to favor an interpretation of their role in more general terms, if we can trust the formulation in the binding song (333 ff.):

> This is the lot that Fate,
> Pervasive, has spun for us to hold:
> When clan murder, sterile, touches a man,
> To wait on him until he perishes.

Clytemnestra feels that she has a claim on them because the Furies attend to a function with which she now identifies herself (135–36):

> Contract your guts with the pain of rightful censure,
> The goad that stays the honest on their track.

From Heraclitus and others, we know that the Furies interest themselves in all irregularities; the philosopher reflects that the Sun cannot overstep his bounds, i.e., deviate from his course, because if he did the Furies, the ministers of Regularity, would find him out and, one suspects, punish him.[20] The meteoric irregularities cited in a beautiful account of monstrosities (*Lib.* 590 ff.) are presumably checked by the Furies. Without the watchfulness of the Furies, the physical world, as much as the social and moral world, would kick over its traces. Indeed, in the first two plays of the *Oresteia*, the Furies are always on the side of justice and normalcy—and that means on the side of the Olympians and Zeus. It is only in the final play that, temporarily, because of the needs of the plot, they are converted into adversaries of the celestial legislators, and that is because the Olympians

---

20. Heraclitus fr. 94 Diels.

are, at that point, given a new function in addition to their role as patrons of domestic and clan stability: the guardianship of a rule of equity which supersedes the familiar lines of justice. The Furies, in their role as upholders of the old institutions, are thus brought into opposition with the innovators, the younger, freer, unconventional gods: a position not unlike the one in which Prometheus finds himself in *Prometheus*. Like him, the Furies are associated with the Earth (*Eum.* 711) and the subterranean powers. They call themselves children of Night. In that capacity, they are removed from human iconography and take on animal shape. Apollo, speaking of the Furies, uses language that recalls the most bizarre formulations of archaic art (*Eum.* 186 ff.). Cassandra also (*Agam.* 1186 ff.) refers to them as an irksome throng, drinking human blood, cacophonous, brash. Their song, if that is the word for the baying Cassandra has in mind, concerns the crime of Thyestes, who slept with his brother's wife. The terrifying visions of the afflicted prophetess support the movement toward concreteness and near-parody of the divine masque, in which gods confront gods in order to give shape to simple antinomies, and in which the losing party suffers the indignity of animalization.

But Aeschylus's art sees to it that the Furies are not merely beasts, bogeywomen calculated to frighten enlightened mortals, but not quite managing to do so. They are, after all, the assistants of Right, and Right is at the center of all three plays of the trilogy. Right, *dikē*, is closer to retribution than to mere justice, especially in the pronouncements of the chorus. In reflecting upon the needs of retribution, the chorus tends to disregard Zeus as well as the chthonian gods; blood works autonomously. The Furies themselves acknowledge, in stately dactyls contrasting pointedly with the skewed rhythms before and after, that they have no intercourse with the rest of the gods (*Eum.* 350). They avow that their business is a bloody one; they adopt a civilized tone of revulsion before it. It is important to appreciate the implication of this alleged independence of action; the Furies seek out and punish offenders without reference to the commands of Zeus. This is an ad hoc contrivance. As we have seen before, they are, in fact, on the side of the Olympians for the most part; generally speaking nothing is exempt from participation in the total order of Zeus. But as the Furies champion the causes that are endangered by the new institutions, and particularly as they defend the cause of women, whose rights the new arrangements are going to restrict, they burn with a spirit of freedom and moral purpose which gains for them an authority far more respectable than that of the argumentative Apollo. Aeschylus's ambitious attempt to present a body of divinities who are both disgusting and noble, both reactionary and profound, both limited and free, may not be fully persuasive. But Gilbert Murray's notion that Apollo expels the Furies from his temple because they are un-Hellenic is not borne out in the text, which says merely that their nature does not fit the Delphic cult.[21] On the contrary, as the Furies, in that frenetic ode with which they initiate their action, charge Apollo that by protecting Orestes he has polluted his holy of holies (*Eum.* 168–70), the judgment is, on its face, convincing.

The shifting nature of the Furies in the *Oresteia* gives us a full measure of the many uses to which Aeschylus can put his divinities. They are ghosts or demons, the crude materializations of a simple terrified faith.[22] But they are also symbols, of varying degrees of concreteness and condensation, cited with an increasing momentum whenever Aeschylus wishes to say something about the conflicting claims of competing and successive social and moral orders. What can be said about them can also, with some small allowances, be said about Zeus and about any of the lesser divinities whom Aeschylus assembles in his plays. In their partnership with men, the gods and demons seem to share in the responsibility for what men do and for the guilt they feel. At the same time, they step forward to punish the guilt that happens to fall within their province. The combination makes for a dramatic language that is extraordinarily rich, richer than anything dreamed of in the humanistic and post-humanistic drama that followed. The Judaeo-Christian God was at once too powerful and too remote, or too narrowly defined, to permit a successful absorption into tragic drama. The Freudian dream world and atavistic memories of a savage past have about them an air of preciousness that makes them largely incompetent to rival the ancient pantheon. What distinguishes the Aeschylean gods is their ease of association, the naturalness with which they inhabit the drama and mesh their purposes with those of men. That naturalness is now irrecoverable, as is the richness of the harmony which their presence provided. In Sophocles, the accent is on divine mystery; in Euripides, the gods are posted on a grid of Sophistic antinomies. Only in Aeschylus are the gods living presences, flesh-and-blood creatures who walk with men or stand in their way or shape the issues over which men fight. With men, they share a fluidity of design; they live in the text, and the text defines their being. For a critic to construct an Aeschylean theology would be as quixotic as designing a typology of Aeschylean man. The needs of the drama prevail.

21. G. Murray, *Aeschylus* (Oxford, 1940), p. 199.
22. The kind of drama which puts Furies on the stage is more plausible today than it was in the enlightened days of Charles Lamb: "Spirits and fairies cannot be represented; they cannot even be painted,—they can only be believed" (*The Works of Charles Lamb*, ed. W. McDonald [London, 1914], p. 36).

# 10

# Guilt; Curse; Choice

Because of the prominence of talk about the gods and demons, it might be thought that Aeschylus can play the role of Sophist—a Gorgias who relieves men of the burden of accountability by charging higher powers. "Paris was *compelled* by the demon 'Persuasion', the *intolerable* daughter of another demon, 'Ruin' . . . the episode was *planned beforehand* by her, and there was *no remedy*."[1] According to this interpretation, Paris's sins are god-conditioned and god-inspired, and man's competence is narrowly circumscribed. But it is only fair to remember that Gorgias himself did not mean his very similar language about Helen to be taken literally. Aeschylus chooses this language, not because he means to absolve men, or because he has a theological interest in the fixing of guilt, but because crimes and misdeeds are connected by a nexus which is often more easily traced by means of cosmic emblems. He does not pinpoint blame, he locates energies and associations. He is, as it were, primarily a statistician, a graphic artist, and only secondarily a judge. His divine emblems are like the curves in a sociological table. And because he does not deal in exclusive judgments, the moral impenetrability of serious action comes through.

The certainty of human responsibility becomes evident only where the action is insignificant. Add to this that there is no word in Greek that precisely corresponds to our "guilt"—i.e., to the combination of *being* guilty before the law and *feeling* guilty before one's own conscience, the conclusive state which, institutionally and psychologically, brands a person a wrongdoer. The Greek *aitia*, which is often translated "guilt," means a number of related things: accountability, authorship, authority, the status of being a defendant on trial. It is a legal and political term. There is in it no reference to feeling, but only to a public standing, the condition of being pointed to, in a relatively closed society, as the suspected author of an action. *Aitia* is subject to revision; with new data in, it may be shifted from one head to another. It designates the standing prior to a judgment, not the findings of the judgment. There is, thus, nothing absolute or definitive about the reference of the term. In Aeschylus's plays, only *Agamemnon* appears to admit a more profound perception of guilt. This has to do with the "lyrical," "prehistorical" quality of the play, by which the trial metaphor is diluted and older, more obsessive ways of thinking make themselves felt.

---

1. J. D. Denniston and D. L. Page, *Aeschylus: Agamemnon* (Oxford, 1957), p. xxix.

But even in this play, or rather, especially in this play, it is virtually impossible to find a definitive statement that isolates human guilt from other causes.

The chorus undertakes to pin the label of *aitia* on specific characters. Both Agamemnon and Paris are said to have desired some thing greatly: Agamemnon the conquest of Troy, Paris the acquisition of Helen. To obtain their desires, they do things, we are told, which they know are wrong: Agamemnon kills his daughter, and Paris destroys Troy. The chorus formulates a pattern of moral failure which is explicitly demonstrated for Paris but is understood to apply also to Agamemnon.

But these are pronouncements and ponderings, limited in time, and potentially reversible. The difficulty is that a tension exists between (at least) two Agamemnons, the tragic father and the light-headed, cruel conqueror. The tension makes it difficult for us to play the game of moral accountants. And so we come back to the recognition that, in spite of the various *pro tem* acknowledgments of wrong-doing, the question remains whether a conclusion that a character *is guilty* can be safely drawn, and whether such a conclusion, if possible, helps us to understand the tragedy better.[2]

To stay with *Agamemnon*, where the question of guilt and punishment has caused the most difficulty: the famous simile of the hawks and the fledglings with which the chorus opens its introductory chant (49–59) would seem to point to an affixing of the blame as the chorus sees it. The progress of the troops under the leadership of the sons of Atreus is illustrated by means of a bird simile; the terms of the simile should help us to appreciate the light in which that progress is to be viewed. But if that is the expectation, it is disappointed. Apollo, Pan, and Zeus in the simile match Zeus in the event; the Fury matches Agamemnon and Menelaus; and the fledglings match Helen. But the two most striking images in the complex, the circling hawks in the simile and the fighting armies of the comparand, are by no means easily matched. In fact, there is a displacement. The playwright had a ready-made comparison available: the hawks match the sons of Atreus. Something like this will be used later (114 ff.). But there, as here, the chorus thinks of the kings as punishers rather than sufferers. Hence the aggrieved hawks, distraught over their young, can be matched here only with the party which, in this play at least, is the only group more suffering than causing suffering to others: the people, both of Argos and of Troy.

In the first instance, their suffering is the consequence, not of the rape of Helen, but of the punishment visited by Zeus. But the syntax, especially the heaping of present participles, produces the effect of simultaneity. In the

---

2. For some fine comments on the topic of guilt and accountability, see K. J. Dover, "Some Neglected Aspects of Agamemnon's Dilemma," *JHS* 93 (1973): pp. 58–69.

statement which precedes the simile, the army serves as an instrument of chastisement, and the sons of Atreus are heard to shriek, like the suffering hawks. But the simile and the statement that follows upon it proceed to alter the relations radically, and the clear lines of guilt and retribution anticipated from the preliminary remarks are frustrated. In the subsequent bird-omen (111 ff.), the group picture of the two birds of prey feasting on the pregnant hare combines the wasting of life's riches with the sense of the unnatural. The moral of the whole sequence appears to cast a shadow over the standing of the sons of Atreus. It becomes difficult to discover the exact terms of reference between image and Argive reality. The curse on the house is obviously involved, but the immediate language presses for a recognition of the power of Artemis. When everything is said and done, and we have listened carefully to the varied strains of the exposition, it is impossible to aver either that Artemis made Agamemnon do something, or that Agamemnon is guilty. Once again, we are reduced to speculating that the network of outrages associated with the house is too engrossing to leave room for mere personal villainies.[3] One is reminded of Goethe's remark that ancient tragedy had become "durch das Sollen . . . gross und stark," as against modern tragedy which had proved itself "durch das Wollen schwach und klein."[4]

The moral opacities of *Agamemnon* are duplicated, to a greater or lesser degree, elsewhere in the Aeschylean canon. Aristotle's *hamartia*, the failing which causes the hero's downfall, is, if taken narrowly, inapplicable to the Aeschylean scene, but in a more general sense, Aristotle's analysis is highly relevant. For *hamartia* is an instrument that helps Aristotle to analyse action as such rather than the human motivation or responsibility that may be regarded as causing the action.[5] The philosophers who were the first to introduce guilt and punishment into tragedy were the Stoics.[6] They looked upon tragedy as an illustration of what happens when the slightest aberration from the ideal of the self-possessed spirit produces infinite guilt. The notion of the tainted spirituality of man, compounded by St. Augustine and the modern theologians, has for its model a relationship between man and god, which simply will not help us with our study of Aeschylus. Pure evil, salvation, the fall, guilt and the feeling of guilt: these are concepts that may be useful in understanding Seneca, and perhaps even certain things in Euripides and Sophocles. But the extant work of Aeschylus does not re-

---

3. See also J. Jones, *On Aristotle and Greek Tragedy* (Oxford, 1962), p. 125.
4. "Shakespeare und kein Ende" (1815), in *Gesamtausgabe*, vol. 15: *Schriften zu Literatur und Theater*, ed. W. Rehm (Stuttgart, n.d.), p. 999.
5. Jones, *Aristotle and Greek Tragedy*, pp. 46 ff.
6. K. von Fritz, *Antike und Moderne Tragödie* (Berlin, 1962), chap. 1 is a magisterial history of the treatment of moral issues in ancient tragedy and European dramatic theory.

spond to them. Scheler's "guiltless guilt," itself derived from the profound reflections of Hebbel on the substance of heroic guilt, also transcends the grid of facile accountability.[7] But it is weighed down with the burden of selfconsciousness, and it owes to the Stoics a preoccupation with the character's inclination to manufacture his own guilt. Aeschylean "sin" is neither pure nor permanent, but it is strong and simple when it is cited, without the self-compounding quality of its modern counterpart. Macbeth's cumulative solidity of sin has no equal on the Greek stage.

Not even fallibility is, in Aeschylus's drama, a clearly attachable property. Euripides's epilogues dwell on the fallibility of man; Sophocles emphasizes the blindness, or at least short-sightedness, of men as they try to make sense of divine counsels. There is little of that in Aeschylus. True, Zeus's power is said to be unlimited and fathomless; men cannot fully understand, much less measure his schemes. But this broad insight remains unexploited for the specifics of the dramatic action. Ignorance, which in Sophocles and Euripides takes on a significant shaping role, and which in the later European tradition continues to loom large, with comedy reinforcing its power, has little functional importance in Aeschylus, with the possible exception of Xerxes. But Xerxes is not so much ignorant as foolish; his attack on Greece is a matter of *hubris*, of animal energy, rather than of misinformation. Certainly "guilt" is inappropriate in his case. It glances off the factors which make his disastrous course the powerful exemplum that it is. He is, after all, a god in his own right, deluded by gods, breaking through natural boundaries, but also intending to fulfill a mission sanctified by Greek popular thought: the victorious advance of a strong ruler who seeks to rectify a slight and to subject the weaker to his law.

In Lope de Vega's *Los Comendadores de Cordoba*, the two principals are, early in the play, tempted to get on two show horses and ride in triumph through the town. After modestly refusing for a while, they accept, and the ensuing hubristic caper serves as an omen for their subsequent downfall. In Lope, the sequence is inevitable; lust for power, temptation, and arrogance are all measured against the Christian convention of humility, and make for a predictable outcome. In Greek tragedy, and especially in Aeschylus, matters are not equally foreseeable. What the playwright does with Agamemnon and his crimson materials is shocking precisely because little in the tradition prepares us for the conclusion that there is something wrong with a conqueror being accorded near-divine honors. True, many choral statements combine to warn about the breaking of barriers; the barrier between humanity and divinity is one such line that must not be transgressed. Hubris, the term conventionally associated with the infringement of divine

7. M. Scheler, "On the Tragic," reprinted in L. Michel and R. B. Sewall, eds., *Tragedy: Modern Essays in Criticism* (Englewood Cliffs, N.J., 1963).

privilege, would appear to qualify what we have said earlier about men and gods not being in conflict. But, as usual, a distinction has to be made between the thinking of the chorus and the larger effect of the play. Within the minds of the chorus, men are indeed limited by divine constraint. Moreover, Agamemnon's act is felt to be sacrilegious principally because, in the economy of the *Oresteia*, it is the culmination of a series of images of trampling and stepping. When Agamemnon places his foot on the dyed materials, the act takes on meaning because no divine compulsion is, for once, involved or invoked, and because Agamemnon himself feels the stepping to be something of an outrage, an illegitimate pendant to other more glorious steppings he has performed. For the moment, the precious materials turn *abebēla*, quite literally "things that must not be stepped on."[8] The man who treads them becomes the transgressor of a boundary just as surely as Xerxes does in crossing the natural boundary between continents. But it is important that we recognize that the act is invested with hubris largely in an ad hoc manner. It is the artist's formulation which compels us to acknowledge the hubris, not the essence of the act in association with other things said about Agamemnon. The choral emphasis on guilt in this case, as on other occasions, works like a musical *obbligato* rather than a thematic emphasis. It makes itself felt as (uncertain) commentary, as accompaniment, rather than as primary intelligence.

Usually, in tragedy and elsewhere, hubris designates the quality or the action of the villain, and the actions so designated are more often than not transgressions which have no major bearing on the central core of the tragedy. Typically it is Polynices, and the sons of Egypt pursuing the Danaids, and Zeus in *Prometheus*, who are charged with hubris. Likewise in Sophocles, "hubris" is applied to the actions of the unheroic enemies of the central character, to Creon, Clytemnestra, and Odysseus. In the eyes of the hero, hubris seems to be the petty trespass of the ordinary man who hits back at the hero because he does not understand him. And in the eyes of the opponent, the hero is hubristic because he does not observe certain rules established for the sake of peace and quiet and mutual safekeeping. This understanding of hubris, as an offence against social and political safeguards, is pervasive in Greek literature. In public life, the conception of hubris was even narrower. As Plato puts it in his *Phaedrus* (238A ff.): the three most common kinds of hubris are gluttony, alcoholism, and lust.[9] The range of meaning associated with "hubris" is so variable, and its link with hoodlum misdemeanor so common, that the critic is left to bemoan the

---

8. A. Lebeck, *The Oresteia* (Cambridge, Mass., 1971), pp. 74–79.

9. See also D. M. MacDowell, "*Hybris* in Athens," *Greece and Rome* 23 (1976): 14–31; and M. Gagarin, "The Athenian Law against *Hybris*," in *Arktouros: Hellenic Studies Presented to B. M. W. Knox* (Berlin and New York, 1979), pp. 229–36.

unhelpfulness of the term. In any case, Aeschylus's language suggests that the workings of hubris have little to do with significant personal guilt:

> Ancient hubris breeds, again and again,
> Another hubris, young and stout. . . .
>
> *Agam.* 763 ff.

Hubris, then, turns out to be fully as elusive as evil or sin or guilt in establishing the lines of responsibility in drama. In the peculiar complex of divine planning and human action in which the two are two ways of talking about the same thing, the best we can do is to watch for the color and the images in which the actions take shape, and worry less about the assigning of blame, though some larger moral judgment is, of course, inevitable. Often Aeschylus teases our moral imagination by proffering plausible explanations of conduct which in the end disintegrate as explanations because they partake in the same shifting process of poetic elaborations as the rest. Wealth is one such misleading cue. Darius accuses Xerxes of having let wealth go to his head. For a time, it is easy to accede to the popular tale, often argued by the chorus, that wealth is the root of much evil, and that the wrong-doings of the King are to be chalked up in part to the temptations that go with wealth. But Darius himself, the stalwart ghost, is, it seems, caught up in the delusions and inconsistencies that go with the popular myth. At the end of his scene, he advises the old councillors to enjoy themselves while there is time, even in adversity, since they cannot take their wealth with them when they die.

Earlier in *Persians* there is a remarkable passage (163–64), possibly corrupt, in which the Empress Mother, immediately after her entrance, expresses her fear that the great god Wealth may come racing up in a big flurry of dust and kick and overturn the prosperity which Darius has established "not without one of the gods." The richness of the imagery defies any analysis into the god-given and the man-acquired, or even into conflicting divinities. Perhaps a contrast is envisaged between material wealth and a prosperity which is spiritual as well as material. But the contrast is not insisted on, and it is clear from other passages that the moral standing of all wealth is in the eye of the beholder or in the purpose of the literary craftsman.

When the Empress Mother first enters, she comes in a carriage and wears full regalia. Then, after bad news, and to propitiate the gods, she divests herself of her rich clothing and reappears on foot, simply clad (607–9). Later, Darius tells her to get ready Xerxes's regalia for his arrival (833–34). That the Empress does not get a chance to act on the recommendation does not undo the effect of Darius's counsel. Let us assume that Darius's own sumptuous clothing (660–62), is not considered a demonstration of wealth. Or does he not wear what the chorus expects him to wear? The ritual tradition perpetuated in the costuming of Greek drama favors costliness. What we have here is a playing with the theme and the opportunities of wealth which answers to momentary impulses rather than a larger understanding. This is the pattern to be found in all the plays. In spite of the popular animus against an affluence which happens to accrue rarely to the kind of people for whom the chorus speaks, no lasting identification of wealth with crime, or of good fortune with disaster, is permissible. In a notorious qualification in *Agamemnon* (750 ff.), the chorus itself criticizes the popular prejudice and points to human purpose. More typically, the thinking about wealth is indefinite and sombre. To cite one example, there is the dark (and possibly corrupt) message of the entrance ode of *Libation-Bearers*: the pendulum of justice is quick for those in the light; for those who live in the no-man's-land of darkness, troubles lie in wait; others again are held in endless night. The division appears to be between the rich, the poor, and the dead (61–65). But whatever the precise explanation of the passage, the pessimism expressed leaves no room for the facile thought that wealth is sin and poverty is virtue. Aeschylus is not a puritan or a Franciscan, in spite of the effectiveness of the occasional lurid suggestion of where wealth may lead.

The difficulty of assigning blame and praise emerges further in a device that is found in all three tragedians, especially in Sophocles, where it has succeeded in confusing generations of interpreters. I am referring to the belated explanation. When Sophocles's Ajax has left the stage to kill himself, the messenger who comes with news from Calchas completely upsets our assumptions of what may be at the root of the hero's suffering and madness. For the first time, without prior warning, we are told that on two earlier occasions Ajax has committed indiscretions against Athena (764 ff.). The new information comes very late—too late to affect our feelings concerning the hero and his moral standing. Perhaps the moralizers in the audience needed an etiology for Ajax's misery just prior to its completion in death. At the same time, it seems hardly likely that Sophocles means to have the revelations understood as touching on the heart of the tragedy. They are mentioned only, as it were, in passing, and forgotten immediately thereafter.

Belated explanations in Aeschylus are to be treated with the same careful skepticism. Having learnt of the great disaster, Darius remembers a prophecy, a pronouncement by Zeus (*Pers.* 739–40): it has been fulfilled more quickly than he had anticipated. This is the underscoring use of the oracle, as against the anticipatory use. In both its functions, the oracle has confirmatory power. Its evocation endows the action or event with a brilliance and a density that it might not otherwise have. But it explains nothing; and in its guise as a belated explanation, it is deceptive. In the present case, the citing of the divine voice goes hand in hand with what appears to be a deliberate move to blacken the standing of Xerxes, ex post facto: after the description of the defeat at Salamis, the language becomes more violent and the terms used of Xerxes more disrespectful. The messenger reports that the Greeks "butchered" the Persians (463) and that Xerxes gave himself over "to disorderly flight" (470). What had started out as an extraordinarily delicate aesthetic and moral equilibrium between Greeks and Persians degenerates into a game with the dice loaded.

But this change of language halfway through the play cannot be taken as a *truer* account, as if the earlier treatment of the relation between Greeks and Persians were delusory, and only the later point of view were to be accepted at face value. It is not a case of the earlier formulation serving as a kind of veil through which the truth has gradually to be revealed, with some difficulty. On the contrary, a fair argument can be made for claiming that Aeschylus changes his language in order to secure, with the logically specious means of an unprincipled rhetoric, the acceptance of an outcome which it would be difficult to derive by itself from the dramatic situation as originally posed. Later, when Xerxes's failure is explained as the consequence of bad advice acquired in bad company (753–58), the explanation is ludicrously out of step with the massive intimations of divine delusion and Oriental turbulence suggested earlier in the play. The intelligence happens to fit in with the popular picture of the tyrant who can never count on honest advice, and whose disorderly mind prefers its own impetuous desires to the reasoned counsel of friends. Such explanations make the horror more palatable to an audience that wants to see poetic justice done. But their lateness casts doubt on their sufficiency.

What is said about Xerxes is of the same order of adequacy as Darius's allegations about the Persian garrison left in Greece. Its defeat at Plataea is stated to have been a punishment for the soldiers' crimes against Greek gods (807 ff.). By the standards of some Greek historians this is, without a doubt, correct. But within the argument of the drama, the plea sits awkwardly. Aeschylus is turning from tragedy to theodicy. What started out as bad generalship and incautious behavior on the part of Xerxes is reformulated as punishment for cumulative sacrilege. With a view to Xerxes's imminent appearance on stage, the development has its risks. And so, when he enters, within a hundred lines of the comments about Plataea, we can no longer regard him with the modicum of respect due to a tragic figure. The play is converted into the representation of a fall from nobility into criminality and from pride to abjectness, from which not even the laments of the accused can rescue it. The hubris which is first mentioned at 808 (cf. 821) stamps Xerxes a petty criminal. The message with which we appear to be left (823–26) is clear: do not lust after what other people have. But it is hard to credit that this is what Aeschylus wanted to impart. It is more charitable to believe that, in *Persians*, Aeschylus attempted the belated explanation to provide a minimum of moral footing for those who do not like their tragedy subtle; but that he went too far with it, until it virtually undid the moral balance of the earlier part of the play. In this respect, *Persians* is a failure.

For a better, more mature, use of the same procedure, we may look at *Agamemnon*. After the murder of the king, when the chorus levels its accusations, Clytemnestra cites the death of Iphigenia as a sufficient reason for what she has done (1412 ff.). The charge is by way of a rebuttal or deflection: Why accuse *me*? Why do you not accuse Agamemnon, who . . . ? But the maneuver is transitory; the burden of the tragedy quite simply proscribes any suggestion of Clytemnestra having done what she did in order to avenge her daughter. The timing of the "explanation," the narrow scope granted to it, and the almost throwaway quality of the announcement combine to reduce its importance within the larger scheme. Similarly, at *Agam.* 799–804, we discover that popular opinion in Argos had opposed the war. Does this tardy intelligence help to shape our view of Agamemnon's responsibility in Iphigenia's death? I think not. The whole idea of retroactive shaping, which underlies the concept of an effective belated explanation, is fraught with difficulty. In the case of a play like *Agamemnon*, which may be said to owe its power to the withholding of precise information and to the ultimate breakthrough of a purpose long, but not altogether, hidden from sight, the difference between a belated explanation and a significant revelation may be difficult to spot. But most critics have agreed that Clytemnestra's reference to Iphigenia is no more calculated to correct our understanding of the significance of the drama than is Aegisthus's argument that all the violence is in payment for the crime of Atreus. In its way, it is comparable to Iago's remarkable

> I hate the Moor;
> And it is thought abroad, that 'twixt my sheets
> He has done my office.
>
> *Othello* 1.3.392–94

From the vast range of possible causes and occasions, now this and now that is brought out and polished off as if it alone sufficed to make the events of the drama intelligible. But the actions and the pathos are too big for many of the explanations.

If this is so, what are we to make of the appeals to Right, *Dikē*, made by the chorus and many of the characters? "However 'positive' a style, or moral injunction, may contrive to be in its wording, behind it always lurks the Basic Negative, The Great, Tragic, Feudlike *Lex Talionis*, itself a universal principle of Justice, and one without which the art of an Aeschylus would be meaningless." The words are those of Kenneth Burke.[10] If I understand them correctly, they say that action in Aeschylus tends to be reaction, a retribution for ills previously enacted, and that moral imperatives in Aeschylus border upon the punitive. It is true that there is much of this in the *Oresteia*, which Burke principally has in mind. But Aeschylus's *Dikē* is too broad in its coverage to be narrowed down to retribution. It designates the state of normalcy, and the spirit and the institutions required to maintain or restore that normalcy. *Dikē* is a social metaphor for the whole, and for the health of that whole. I shall deal with the subject at greater length under the heading of "solution," especially as it relates to the trial in *Eumenides* (below, chapter 12).

Here we must concern ourselves briefly with how individuals in Aeschylus see their own actions and those of others in the light of what they conceive to be the state of normalcy and Right. Aegisthus, like Polynices, says that Right led him back (*Agam.* 1607; cf. *Seven* 647). Clytemnestra, in defending her action, summons Right along with *Atē* and the Fury (*Agam.* 1432–33). In *Libation-Bearers* (639 ff.), the chorus disagrees and invokes Right with her two helpers against the Queen. In what amounts to an expansive iconography of Right, coming at the end of a comparison of the crimes of legendary heroines with those of Clytemnestra, they sing (I paraphrase): *Dikē*'s sword pierces the breast of the villain; her foot kicks him on the ground; her anvil is deeply embedded; *Aisa* (Decree) is her smith and furnishes the sword; the Fury restores the son of the house to exact vengeance. The retrogressive order—the thrust of the sword coming before the return of the avenger—is part of the economy of the final dyad of the ode, which returns us from reflection and philosophy to the concrete event.

Thus each party, including the chorus, has its own perception of what is justified by Right. It would not be surprising if the tragedian were to arrange the conflict as a clash of *Dikai*, a battle of Rights. It is perhaps significant that this does not happen. In *Seven*, Eteocles does not go beyond demolishing Polynices's claim to *Dikē*; he does not set up his own Right to combat his brother's vaunt. The only passage that has been interpreted to refer to a clash of *Dikai* (*Lib.* 461) probably means something quite different. Close to the end of the Great Exchange—in fact, this is his last utterance in that unique sequence—Orestes sings:

Ares will meet with Ares, Dikē with Dikē.

10. K. Burke, *Language as Symbolic Action* (Berkeley and Los Angeles, 1966), p. 453.

What does this mean? It is probable that the figure of Ares here has a function analogous to that of *Atē* and the Fury and Decree in the earlier passages: Ares is to be thought of as the mechanism, the cutting efficiency, with which *Dikē* maintains her rule. The previous utterances by Orestes, Electra, and the chorus emphasize the need for cooperation, not only between the members of the conspiracy, but also between them and Agamemnon in his tomb. This renders it implausible that "meet" in Orestes's last statement signifies a discord. The sense is rather: Ares will work with Ares, and Right with Right.[11] They are the *Dikai* of Orestes, Electra, and Agamemnon, each recognized as valid and closely related to the others. Orestes ends his participation in the exchange with an assurance that their various claims will combine to create a mighty power of purging and adjustment.

The assertion of *Dikē*, especially in the sense stressed by Burke, gets us close to revenge tragedy. Revenge tragedy superficially articulates moral balance and justice. In fact, however, it proceeds to leave justice far behind, because retribution travels far in excess of the hurt, and turns tyrant. Justice, in a revenge tragedy, provides few answers, and fewer satisfactions. The frivolities of *Measure for Measure* are a cruel index of the moral morass in which an exclusive emphasis on justice can be mired. In the *Oresteia*, the competing claims of blood revenge and Athenian jury justice make for a clash not unlike the antinomy featured in the Elizabethan or Jacobean revenge play. The Renaissance playwright puts God and religion on the side of the state and condemns the private revenger to a hellish punishment. The Aeschylean treatment has no such easy substructure of heaven and hell at its disposal. This is a gain for the Greek tragedy. The unceasing calamities resulting from the chain of private retaliation are invested with a morality of their own. The Furies, demanding the continuation of the retributive series, defend a position which is by no means inferior to that of Athena, who demands an end to it. Under the active sponsorship of Right, the murder of Agamemnon will lead to further sufferings, as the chorus assures us (*Agam.* 1535–36):

> Now one, now another whetstone of Doom
> Helps sharpen Right for a work of hurt.

There is reason to believe that this insistence on the near-automatic perpetuation of guilt and punishment is a poetic construction. The social and legal realities had conditioned people, long before Aeschylus, to accept financial recompense and other surrogates in the place of the life which blood guilt would seem to demand. Precisely because "a life for a life" was

---

11. For *symballein* as convergence, see, e.g., Sophocles *Oedipus in Colonus* 901.

an atavistic fantasy, a literary sanctification of what could no longer be enacted without suicidal harm to society, it gripped the imagination in a way that everyday reality could not. At the same time, the absence of a religious veto on striking back prevented revenge drama from sliding into melodrama, as it usually did in the later European tradition, except in the most skillful hands.

The principal poetic shorthand for the conception we have discussed is the curse on a house. As we know from a number of plays, especially from *Oedipus in Colonus*, and from the mythographers, the curse is a self-perpetuating power, a blight virtually impossible to extinguish, and one that gains added force from being invoked anew in each generation. The curse on the house of Oedipus works upon Eteocles and Polynices as fiercely as it works on Oedipus himself. But the might of the curse is refurbished before our eyes by Oedipus's malediction of his sons. The principle of a suffering that is not reserved for an individual, but attaches to a larger grouping, and especially to the vertical lineage, has an intriguingly modern quality about it. As Oscar Wilde puts it: "The scientific principle of heredity is Nemesis without her mask. It is the last of the Fates, and the most terrible. It is the only one of the gods whose real name we know."[12] Today we are no longer certain we know the name, what with mutation, organic or induced. But the science which has enabled us to recognize or trigger mutations is bringing with it its own discovery of the tragic.

The unit within which the irrational continuities of punishment are explored is the house. The limited focus is best suited to a genre which enjoins contraction. In the *Odyssey*, the scout whom Aegisthus has detailed to watch for Agamemnon's return is stationed on the coast; in the *Oresteia*, the watchman is part of the house, and muses about the house: "If the house could talk. . . ." The house is the dominant reality in the first two plays of the trilogy, until the Areopagus takes over. Within the confines of the house, each generation not only revoices the curse, but contributes its share to its endurance by concrete action. Drama requires this constant refurbishing of ill, and the dramatist gains from it: he has a substructure of wrong upon which to play off interesting events, without having to motivate each and every suffering.

It follows that this tragic vision is not necessarily geared to the social experience of archaic Greece.[13] The house, as a principal unit of suffering and as the identifiable vessel of wrong, is a poetic fiction, a literary compounding of the diffuse experiences of wrong traced in contemporary social

12. Oscar Wilde, *The Critic as Artist*, cited in T. R. Henn, *The Harvest of Tragedy* (London, 1956), p. 71.
13. *Pace* Vernant in J. P. Vernant and P. Vidal-Naquet, *Mythe et tragédie en grèce ancienne* (Paris, 1972), pp. 28–29, passim.

experience. To be sure, blood guilt is not unknown in the legal discussions of the archaic period, and the concept remains sufficiently alive for Plato to come back to it in his *Laws*. But it looks as if its importance is propagandistic, or at best psychological, rather than legal or moral. Religious propaganda, political slogans, dramatic poetry: they are closely related, as significant fictions. There is no immediate link between them and the perceptions of ordinary citizens in the ordered community that Athens had come to be long before Aeschylus took pen to hand. What the notion of the curse on the house does is to enlarge the vision until all suffering is subsumed under the rubric of punishment for a crime.

The grimmest definition of the fixity of blood guilt is given by the chorus at *Lib.* 66 ff.:

> And the blood drunk by Mother Earth
> Stops running, clots, a rigid death.
> A piercing *Atē* racks the culprit
> With sickness spilling through his limbs.
>
> No cure for one who assaults the virgin
> Sanctuaries; all streams flow strong
> And join but fail to cleanse
> Foul-handed blood.

The language opens up a vision of barbarism, echoes of a world when men and beasts were one, and when congealed gore was an inevitable companion of living. But there is also the reminder of sickness, as if the violence and the suffering were not normal but a deviation from civilized existence. The most elaborate poetic treatment of the curse occurs in the Cassandra scene. Cassandra's coverage of the crimes within the house includes Thyestes's feasting on his children (*Agam.* 1095–97) and the killing of Clytemnestra by Orestes (1280 ff.). Concerning the latter, she predicts that "another punisher" will come to avenge his father and to put the coping stone upon the family's house of crimes. Orestes is not named, as if the solidarity of the house obviated the naming of individuals.

The architectural formula shows what is involved. But the curse is expansive beyond the structure of the family. Cassandra herself is, as she appears to imply, embraced in the workings of it, and devoured by it. That is the only way in which we can explain her death, if an explanation is desired. Perhaps the question "why?" should not be asked.[14] She herself says very little about Apollo, although that little is likely to suggest that it is supposed to give some kind of accounting for her predicament. But Cassandra's

---

14. H. D. F. Kitto, *Poiesis* (Berkeley and Los Angeles, 1966), p. 24. Kitto suggests that asking why Apollo punishes Cassandra is much like asking a spearless warrior in a pediment

willingness to have Apollo regarded as somehow involved in her suffering is better regarded along the lines of the belated explanations cited above (the belatedness is only in relation to the play, not in regard to Cassandra's own utterance, where it comes immediately at the start: *Agam.* 1072–87; also 1202–10). Compared with the overwhelming presence of the curse, Apollo's agency appears minor and fleeting. Perhaps it is even fair to say that Apollo turns into a tool of the expansiveness of the curse. As it flowers and attracts everything into its spell, Cassandra falls a victim to it through her alliance with Agamemnon, and Apollo, the alleged punisher of Cassandra, is by the force of the poetry reshaped into a subaltern of the curse.

The early sections of *Agamemnon* contain very few open references to the curse. The same is true of *Libation-Bearers*; only the final choral ode (935 ff.) concerns itself at length and explicitly with the curse on the house. In *Eumenides*, there is no mention of it at all. When the curse does move out into the open, with Cassandra's visions and the song of the libation-bearers, it is nothing unexpected, but merely the full voicing of an apprehension that had been perceived dimly before. Still, in the plays in which the curse on the house is activated—*Agamemnon*, *Seven*, *Libation-Bearers*—its full revelation comes late, and it is tempting to regard its use by the poet in the same light as belated explanations, to emphasize its function as a trope, a means of reverberating the suffering, rather than as a guiding principle of myth. It is significant that when Orestes voices his fears about the crime which he must undertake, he sees himself less as a member of the clan than as a member of his immediate family, the son of a mother and father—precisely the terms which define the city perspective of Athena, and not the broader, clan-controlled imagination of Cassandra and the Furies.

Where the trope of the curse on the house prevails, the agent thinks that he can somehow put an end to it by compromise, extinction, or some noble or notorious action. Clytemnestra certainly believes (*Agam.* 1568 ff.) that she has cut the chain of the curse. Eteocles similarly hopes against hope that the defeat of Polynices can be brought about without involving the further doom of the house, which includes himself—a fond hope that is given up in the great speech that follows the news that Polynices stands at the seventh gate (*Seven* 653 ff.). In actual fact, the workings of the curse are conceived to be a more abiding current in the structure of the trilogy of which *Seven* forms the last part than they are in the *Oresteia*, where the "nuclear" family—father, mother, and children—constitutes a saving rival of the house as the focus of artistic formulation. The figure of Orestes is humanized, and

---

whether he has forgotten or accidentally lost his spear. A witty acknowledgment of G. Wilson Knight's *spatial* assessment of the dramatic text? Cf. Knight's *The Wheel of Fire* (Oxford, 1930).

touches us with the possibility of conflicting personal motives, precisely because the house is only one of the larger units poetically competing for his allegiance.

It is important to understand that the curse on the house is not something that underlies the very conception of Aeschylean drama. It is a theme that Aeschylus can pick up and use or not, as he chooses—and he does not so choose in four of the plays that have come down to us. Where the curse is introduced, men become aware of it much in the way that Corneille's *Horace* (act 2, scene 3) finds out that he and his brothers have been chosen to oppose the Curiatii. The sudden illumination of Eteocles (*Seven* 653), who in a flash realizes that the curse is his doom, and whose very being is affected by the insight, parallels the discovery of Horace, who is stripped of his humanity and turns into a fighting machine. (Where Eteocles, under the curse, becomes more violent in speech, Horace freezes: "And let me now cut short this useless talk: / Alba names thee, and I no longer know thee." Eteocles perishes; Horace triumphs, and lives, but in his heart he is destroyed also.) The recognition of the curse is tantamount to sudden insight into the inevitability of unlucky constellations. The house, in such a moment, becomes a transparent cypher for the world as a whole, in which tragic clashes between friends and brothers are unavoidable. The tenses in the selection scene in which Eteocles reports on the dispositions he has made, or will make, for the defence of the gates suggest a degree of self-involvement in what is fated which further strengthens the coincidence of necessity and commitment.[15]

That the curse on the house is only one of several such formulas possible within one and the same play or trilogy is clear from *Agamemnon*. In the recriminations between chorus and Clytemnestra (1399 ff.), a scene seemingly well suited to furnish explanations, the chorus first cites the demon of the house, thus essentially agreeing with Clytemnestra's contention that the present troubles derive from an ancient corruption. But then the chorus shifts the responsibility for what is happening to the shoulders of Zeus. Clytemnestra herself, who invokes the demon (1501), had earlier (1432 ff.) talked about justice in terms which narrow accountability down to the relations between individuals. It seems as if talk about the curse or the demon of the house is likely to come in at points when agents, sufferers, or, for that matter, bystanders sense a need for unusually emphatic formulations. It answers psychological needs rather than strictly etiological considerations. There is, of course, no point at which the playwright can tell us unambiguously in his own voice what the "real" explanations are. But the freedom with which formulations are modified, overturned, and switched

15. For the variation of tenses, see E. Wolff, "Die Entscheidung des Eteokles in den *Sieben gegen Theben*," *Harvard Studies in Classical Philology* 63 (1958):89–95.

around argues not for the gradual revelation of a temporarily hidden truth, but for an open-ended fluidity, a constant enrichment of poetic and dramatic perspectives. Because there is no ideological commitment on the part of the plot, no fixed and instructive moral outlook, we can allow ourselves to be constantly surprised and refreshed by the wealth of the available alternatives.

But this is not freedom in the sense of choice. In Sartre's *The Flies*, Argos is for Orestes a foreign land into which he puts himself to document his freedom of choice. In Aeschylus, Argos is a homeland, and Orestes has no choice.[16] We are entering here upon a discussion of issues made problematic by the circumstance that the Greek terminology applied to actions that are subject to litigation differs from ours. In common Greek parlance, but also in juridical contexts, an action was either *hekousios* or *akousios*, words which are usually translated as "voluntary" and "involuntary" or "intentional" and "unintentional." In fact, *hekousios* covers every action that is not imposed by external constraint, whether it is intentional or not, or premeditated or not.[17] By the same token, *akousios* points to the presence of some form of constraint. The finer distinctions to be drawn within this twofold area—to determine whether an act is due to negligence, imprudence, accident, or self-defense, and so forth—are legal concerns, and may be studied in Plato's *Laws* or Aristotle's *Ethics*. The play in which there is the most considerable attention to the "mode" of an action, Sophocles's *Oedipus in Colonus*, where the question of responsibility for an involuntary act is discussed, could not have been written by Aeschylus. Aeschylus does not bear down on legal questions or solutions; the mode of an act is less important in his dramatic vision than the effect of the act upon the group and the individual. Nor does the distinction between *hekousios* and *akousios*, between freedom and constraint, tell us anything about psychological attitudes. The fluidity of the explanatory formulations that we have observed stands in the way of any precise distinction between the voluntary and the imposed. On the contrary, as Goethe and many others have seen, everything in classical tragedy works toward representing action as largely constrained, hence *akousios*.

Scholars who have studied Greek psychological notions as summarized by, and culminating in, Aristotle have noted the difference between them and our own assumptions. The Aristotelian postulate that action follows necessarily from a junction of desire and judgment argues for a kind of

16. "Aus dem Orest der Antike, der schuldig werden muss, macht Sartre einen Orest, der schuldig werden will" (K. Hamburger, *Von Sophokles zu Sartre* [*Sprache und Literatur* 1; Stuttgart, 1962], p. 59).

17. Vernant, in J. P. Vernant and P. Vidal-Naquet, *Mythe et tragédie*, p. 53. See Aristotle's discussion in *Nicomachean Ethics* 3.1.

determinism. The concentration upon determining factors obstructs any perception of spontaneity. There are other differences. Pre-Stoic Greek has no word for "duty," only the vaguest notion of "obligation," and little that corresponds to the modern concept of the will.[18] There is thus ample cause for proceeding with the utmost caution in trying to talk about qualities of action and degrees of freedom of decision. We have already commented on Agamemnon's sacrifice of Iphigenia. In theory there is much to recommend the view that Agamemnon's submission to the will of Artemis was a necessity; it is certainly to be preferred to its converse, that Agamemnon freely chose to kill his daughter. The emphasis on the action, independent of private engagement, is good Aristotelian thinking. But Aeschylean tragedy does not permit us to see matters quite as sharply as that. And when it is said that tragedy "is most moving when the human victim is involved against his will (like Agamemnon) or unawares (like Oedipus) in criminal error for which the penalty must be paid," the ease of the wording and the use of "will" and "unawares" give us pause.[19]

In many ways, Agamemnon's killing of Iphigenia is an anticipation of Orestes's murder of Clytemnestra. It shares with it such elements as the divine command, the personal reluctance on the part of the executor, and the stress on necessity, both logical and circumstantial. Because of the difference in treatment—one is a "report" in the form of a choral ode, the other a dramatic event almost entirely open to our eyes—and because of the differences between the two victims, the two events are not felt to be comparable. But with regard to the questions we are trying to ask here, the comparability is indeed great. It will be useful to take a closer look at the sequence (*Agam.* 198 ff.) in which the killing of Iphigenia is related, and particularly at the "thinking" that goes into it. To begin with, there is the announcement by Calchas that the "bitter storm" calls for "another, heavier remedy." The self-questioning by Agamemnon follows: disobedience weighs heavily, so does killing his child; but how can he think of turning deserter? His allies have a claim on him, and a right to desire the sacrifice. After the questioning, the mental consequences: once Agamemnon has recognized the need, he bends his mind to the unholy deed. And finally the madness: "truculent madness, of ugly design, the seed of suffering, drives men to act." Note the generalization. Because it is a truth that applies to all men, the particular application to Agamemnon is deprived of its worst sting.

18. Vernant, in J. P. Vernant and P. Vidal-Naquet, *Mythe et tragédie*, pp. 48 ff. On the question of "will" see A. Dihle, *The Theory of Will in Classical Antiquity* (Berkeley and Los Angeles, 1982).

19. Denniston and Page, *Agamemnon*, p. xxviii.

This brash summary of one of the densest and least paraphrasable passages in *Agamemnon* will have to do. The total effect is one of constraint, hardening, madness, regret exhausted by fury. The question of responsibility is left outside of the realm of discussion. Aeschylus, or the chorus, does not assemble and analyze the factors that go into Agamemnon's decision, nor does he furnish the description of a psychological sequence that would authorize us to supply such an analysis. The whole tenor of the passage is designed to block such an analysis.[20] In the course of a few lines, Agamemnon proceeds from the anguish of self-questioning to the brutality of the gag (235–36). Clytemnestra's later accusations are certainly based on the allegation that Agamemnon's act could have been avoided, and that it carries the stamp of depravity. But a careful translation of the key phrase which links the divine direction to the human act would roughly be: "and when he had the runner of the yoke of Necessity adjusted to his neck. . . ."[21] It is not that he did his own adjusting or that he could have fought shy of it. The forward impetus of the tragedy hides the moment when the harnessing takes place and the manner of the adjustment from our eyes.

The *hamartia*, if it is legitimate to use that term here, is not a product of the agent's purpose or a consequence of his past actions; it exists autonomously, beyond him, including him in its power. In a sense, this conforms to what has been said to be an older way of looking at crime. But this does not mean that we should necessarily regard the gods or a god as the responsible factor. The fusion set up between the wrath of Artemis and Agamemnon's compulsive deed seems to me too suggestive, too explosive, to favor so simple a reduction.

There is a further difficulty. For several decades now, it has been customary to emphasize the element of decision making and choice in tragedy, and of the mental anguish that precedes the choice.[22] In support of this emphasis, it is argued that the epic does not yet know the anguish of decision making; that the lyric does know it, but only on the sufferer's horizon: since the lyric does not feature actions, choice is stripped of its urgency. Only in drama, with the growing awareness of the moment of decision, do choice, and the freedom of choice, come to be fully realized. Henceforth we can speak of a tragic dilemma, the decision making in the face of contradictory options which defines much of later European drama. An example is the

---

20. R. Lattimore, *Story Patterns in Greek Tragedy* (Ann Arbor, Mich., 1964), p. 40.

21. A. Rivier, "Remarques sur le 'nécessaire' et la 'nécessité' chez Éschyle," *Revue des Études Grecques* 81 (1968): 5–39, is the best discussion of this aspect of Aeschylus's art.

22. The most forceful argument on behalf of this position is found in B. Snell, *Aischylos und das Handeln im Drama* (*Philologus Suppl.* 20.1; Leipzig, 1928).

question, in Racine's *Bérénice*, whether Titus will marry the princess or send her away. The simplicity of the choice, and its minute compass, encourage a full dramatization of the dilemma, as does the delicacy of the sentiments. Most dramatists do not affect Racine's unadorned centripetality. Personal relations proliferate, the sphere of action is broken up, and the manifold commitments of the characters remove the moments of decision from the center of the stage.

Take Goethe's *Egmont*. Alba, after discovering that Orange is not coming, wonders whether to go on with the plot against Egmont alone. He has a real choice, and it is fully dramatized in a monologue, complete with doubt, groping in the dark, and the conjuring up of two pressing evils. But Egmont's appearance solves the doubt for Alba: "For me no choice is left." That is logical nonsense, but psychologically convincing. And, in truth, Racine's ability to generate a sustained period of indecision and preparation, leading up to a final choice, is rather the exception in the history of high tragedy, though the bourgeois *drame* of the eighteenth and nineteenth centuries fixes upon its heroes' hesitations and indecision as its stock in trade. That may be connected with the fact that the heroes and heroines of Diderot, Lessing, and other dramatists of the Enlightenment are fated to act in a world that is both open and empty, unburdened with the standards and the commitments of an earlier faith. Aeschylean drama does not allow the freedom of choice. In the matter of decision making, it has not, in fact, retreated very far from the epic mode of analyzing the factors that enter into a human action. True, it exhibits a new sense of urgency and less reliance on the mythical construct of Necessity or the "sayings" of the gods. Conversely, whereas the epic Odysseus can ponder two alternatives and, with a minimum of divine instruction, choose the one that seems better to him, the Aeschylean character does not dispose of so unencumbered a method for picking a course of action.

Typically, Aeschylean heroes deliberate, and arrive at decisions. But the element of choice, of freely and responsibly selecting a line of action from among stated alternatives, is almost entirely lacking. In its place, the dramatist summons *anankē*, constraint, external pressure, to trigger the decision. Constraint does not make the agent into a robot; it is not a mechanical cause. It compounds variously with other elements to produce an amalgam which appears to leave some scope for initiative. But the principal requirement of a free choice, namely that it be practiced in the virtual absence of all other constraints except the mutual exclusiveness of the options, is not found in Aeschylus. Similarly, the psychological moment, the experience of the choosing endured in the heart of the chooser, and the release afforded by the act of choosing, lies outside the Aeschylean focus. In this respect, Aeschylus resembles Corneille more than Racine.[23] The hero is on the verge of recognizing a choice, but in the next moment admits to himself that he has no choice. The heroic decision in Corneille is a compliance with predetermined constraints; choices can be recognized, but not acted upon. In *Le Cid*, in *Polyeucte*, in *Oedipe*, a character can protest, he can rebel, or he can accommodate himself, but he cannot freely choose. The poetic vision of a heroic universe, with its fluid and counterpoised strains, forbids the enactment of a test-tube choice.

Aristotle's syllogism of constraints underlying his analysis of practical reason leaves little room for a free choice.[24] It is a useful model to remember as we search Aeschylus's language for relevant clues. Loosely, in the abstract, it might be argued that Agamemnon "chooses" to step on the crimson materials. But the text makes no mention of a choice. In its place, we find an initial reluctance and a final compliance—precisely, in other words, what we are also given, by way of a report, for Agamemnon's "decision" to sacrifice his daughter or for Pelasgus's "decision" to admit the suppliants to the city.[25] Nor does Prometheus "choose" to oppose Zeus; his action springs from the center of his being, as much as from the requirements of the legend. Not even retrospectively does Aeschylus provide an anatomy of the moment in which Prometheus declared himself, any more than Shakespeare does this for Coriolanus.

The Aeschylean term *tolma* (truculence) is sometimes cited in this connection as signaling the surmounting of an internal resistance, but does not mean that at all. It tells us nothing about the inner mechanism of an action, and all about the "looks" of the deed in the eyes of man or god. Agamemnon has this quality as he kills his daughter, Clytemnestra has it as she kills Agamemnon, and Orestes has it as he kills his mother; at least so we are told by the chorus, by Cassandra, and by Orestes. *Tolma* suggests a convergence of necessity and crime, of suffering and aggression. But it defines the action itself, not the life of the mind that initiates it. As the term is used by reporters in their comments on actions of which they disapprove, we can appreciate the evaluative color of it. It points to an upsetting of the established order as much as to personal villainy.[26] The *tolma* which is pictorially

23. A. Stegmann, *L'héroisme cornélien* (Paris, 1968), vol. 2, pp. 443–44: "Rodrigue se représente un instant sa situation de cette manière (v. 305), mais il se rend vite compte qu'il n'y pas de choix. Il en sera toujours ainsi chez Corneille dans la décision héroique."

24. See *Nicomachean Ethics* 7.3.1147a24–36; and D. J. Allan, "The Practical Syllogism," in *Autour d'Aristote: Receuil offert à Monseigneur A. Mansion* (Louvain, 1955), pp. 325 ff.

25. On the precariousness of the notion of "choice," see also Lattimore, *Story Patterns*, p. 39.

26. For this and what follows, see Jones, *Aristotle and Greek Tragedy*, pp. 121 ff.

realized in the lion cub circumscribes a complex reality, in which Paris is merely one element. As we look more closely at the terms which have been linked to supposed psychological processes or events in Aeschylus, we are likely to get further and further away from the individual's stake in the action.

The test case for the issue of choice must be the question that Orestes addresses to Pylades before he kills his mother (*Lib.* 899). Those who bear down on the freedom of choice in Aeschylus virtually call it the climax of the play. "What am I to do?" is in their eyes an utterance of despair born from an impasse.[27] I suspect that the Greek audience would have seen in the question only a delay occasioned by considerations of decorum. Orestes briefly shrinks from what is felt to be unavoidable and is immediately reconfirmed to be so. Apollo's threats, the emotional preparation built up in the Great Exchange, and the knowledge that all the divine powers, with the exception of the Furies, command the execution of Clytemnestra, leave little doubt that Orestes knows what he has to do and is ready to do it. The question addressed to Pylades does not indicate uncertainty, but is akin to the questioning in shuttle speech, where the questioner is a prompter rather than an inquirer.[28] Orestes's "Mother!"—here for the first time—and the singular interposition by Pylades bring out the gravity of the moment and characterize Orestes's reluctance. But the decision has already been made, both for Orestes and by him; all Pylades can do is reassure Orestes of what he knows only too well himself.

Pelasgus, the Argive king for whom the coming of the Danaids means a cruel dilemma between war and peace, is a more promising vehicle of decision making and choice. Pelasgus supplies something very much like a fundamental tragic motto when he says (379–80):

> I am at a loss; fear grips me as I think
> To act and not to act and to grasp the chance.

The second line is difficult to construe. Acting and not acting are clearly alternatives; but what is their relation to the third term, "taking the [or 'a'] chance"? Do they jointly form a unit that is to be coordinated with, or contrasted with, the chance taking, or is the latter tied in with only one of the earlier terms? Whatever the answer—and perhaps no precise clarity is intended—the sentence appears to be a satisfactory definition of the problem facing a potential chooser frightened by the prospect. A little later, the king likens the pondering of the options to the descent of a diver into the deep "with unflinching eye."

The choice to be made, or rather the reflection that might lead to the

27. B. Snell, *Aischylos*, pp. 126 ff.
28. Jones, *Aristotle and Greek Tragedy*, p. 102.

choice, is twice called a "saving thought," and this means, apparently, the plotting of a course that will skirt the horns of the dilemma. The materials that must go into such pondering are given in a brief chorus song that is delivered while the king is silent—engaged, one presumes, in the pondering whose need had just been acknowledged. Precisely how this is to be accomplished on stage is difficult to tell; the vase paintings do not help us to guess what might have been the gesturing or the pose of a man pondering a decision. More significant is the fact that Aeschylus prefers not to articulate the process of reflection. There is no reasoned speech in which Pelasgus explores the pros and cons in detail. What we have is the announcement that such exploration is necessary, followed by silence—if the inactivity of the king while the chorus sings may be called silence—and finally an announcement of the decision taken. Choice is not dramatized; it is reported, just as other decisions are reported in Aeschylean drama. The agony of the decision making is hinted at, but largely displaced and in effect neutralized by imagery, silence, and the intrusion of the chorus.[29]

If, in this instance, we come closer to the actual dramatization of choice than anywhere else in the Aeschylean corpus, the instance is unique. There is nothing that even remotely parallels Pelasgus's indecision. Perhaps Aeschylus handled the role of the king in this manner because he wanted to lay a solid foundation for what happens in the later plays of the trilogy, when the fears of the king, the considerations which first prompt him to reject the application of the fugitives, bear full fruit in the fighting which befalls his country and leads to his death. The pondering of alternatives, then, may be as much for the sake of information as in answer to a desire to show a living soul venturing upon a protracted course of choosing. It is also worth noting that the king's final decision is pressured from him, against his better judgment, by the threats of the women, and that even then he seeks a confirmation of his "choice" by going to the citizens for their authorization. In spite of the great difference in mood, Pelasgus may be said to resolve the issue very much along the lines chosen by Athena in *Eum.* 470 ff. There the goddess explains, in a speech superbly assured of its proprieties, that the business she faces is serious; that it is not her job to adjudicate a case of murder; that Orestes appears to have come with clean hands; that the Furies have a case and that they will, if unsuccessful in their suit, bring destruction on the land; that there is disaster in store whichever way the decision goes; and that therefore she will—set up a jury. The paraphrase, with its mock ending, savoring of the presidential habit of appointing a committee whenever there is trouble, fails to do justice to the dignity of the speech. But the

29. For a more detailed analysis of Pelasgus's "choice," and of the role of "choice" in classical tragedy, see T. G. Rosenmeyer, "Wahlakt und Entscheidungsprozess in der antiken Tragödie," *Poetica* 10 (1978): 1–24.

objective coolness of the analysis lets us see the scheme which also underlies the sequence in which Pelasgus copes with his difficulties.

Let us conclude, then, that Aeschylean drama avoids putting on the stage what moderns have come to look for under the name of freedom of choice, and that it deals with action as a compounding of constraints which are variously approximated to divine compulsion and human appetite. The Furies themselves can sing of murderers in a language that makes it seem as if their murders "happened upon them" (*Eum.* 337).[30] Whether in any one unit of the dramatic text the intrinsic is emphasized at the expense of the external or vice versa depends on the part the unit is designed to play in the whole. Generally speaking, tragedy, in the wake of the archaic lyric, extols the power of the divinity and the pathos of man. But where suffering is meant to seem deserved, and where the roots of man's pride are laid bare, the language can become virtually secular, with little recourse to the divine share in things. On the other hand, a greater sounding of the rule of the gods or of demons, or of the curse, or fate, or the demon within man, serves to allay, if only temporarily, the nagging knowledge that a man's stake in his own sufferings and downfall cannot be denied. The oscillation between constraint and initiative, between the psychological and the objective, must be constant enough to prevent the audience from ever settling into an unambiguous understanding of the causes of action. The mythological is not a superstructure, but part of the poetic web stretched over the impenetrabilities of an experienced life. The situations created by Aeschylus are extreme and implausible; the causes cited and the processes sketched are, in their rich profusion, adequate reminders of the asymmetries of social reality, perhaps more so than the geometrical niceties of Racine's tightly organized dilemmas or the thinly disguised moral disquisitions of Ibsen or Shaw. In the fluctuating oxymora of Aeschylus's interweaving of the human and the divine, we detect a spirit akin to that of Shakespeare, especially in his "pagan" works, where he could, at least on the surface, move outside of the circle of a Christian moral fixity.

Let us sum up by saying, perhaps too bluntly, that in spite of the ostensible references to motivation and causes, the dramatic movement compels us to abandon the search for reasons and be satisfied with poetic facts; and that this factuality of the dramatic body stands in the way of the moral need to assign liability and guilt. (We shall return to this below, in chapter 12.) Aeschylus asks us to respond to his drama not as judges of the good and the evil in it, nor as fellow sufferers of the characters, blind like them to the implications of what is happening. The role he forces upon us is that of historians, recorders of actions that are complete in themselves, though

30. Turnebus's emendation of the corrupt text has been generally accepted.

naturally meshed with other actions similarly open to view. We know that Agamemnon will be murdered—or rather, was murdered—before the characters of the drama do. Both as versions of the known legend and as poetic constructs of unusual power, the dramas appeal to us with a force that, in the respects that matter, bars the search for right or wrong. Dreams, prophecies and oracles, to which Aeschylus accords a lesser role than does Sophocles, help to underscore the status of dramatic events as facts—compelling data authenticated by pre-direction. Against so massive an apparatus of factuality and the interrelatedness of facts, the plotting of responsibility and guilt must resign itself to impotence. Each spectator will continue to cling to the fictions of his moral imagination; but he deludes himself if he finds his responses confirmed by clues in the text.

# The Drama

# _ 11 _

## Plot; Tension; Time

> Another thing in which the French differ from us and from the
> Spaniards, is that they do not embarrass, or cumber themselves
> with too much plot. . . . But by pursuing closely one argument,
> which is not cloyed with many turns, the French have gained more
> liberty for verse, in which they write; they have leisure to dwell on a
> subject which deserves it.
>
> <div align="right">Lisideius in Dryden's <i>Essay of Dramatic Poesy</i></div>

If for "the French," we put "the Greeks," or, better, "Aeschylus," the statement leaves nothing to be desired. *Agamemnon* is, even within the Aeschylean corpus, an unusual play. But in one respect, it is not uncharacteristic:
in the apparent inadequacy of anything that might conceivably be called a
plot. As the writer of the *Life of Aeschylus* that appears in the Medicean
manuscript says: he composed his plays with few of the reversals and complications that the more recent playwrights have. Corneille's proud words
about his *Rodogune*, that it contained "an original and unusual action . . . a
logically constructed plot . . . the whole felicitously composed and carried
forward with mounting intensity from act to act," might have puzzled
Aeschylus, who was more likely to fall in with the twentieth-century suspicion that a well-made play is bound to be devoid of serious content.[1] Naturalism, Expressionism, Symbolism and other more recent waves of innovation have consolidated the modern sense that an interesting plot may run
counter to the needs of a tragic vision of life.

For Aeschylus, we may wish to distinguish between plot and action.[2] By
action we mean the sequence of entries and exits and the various ways in
which actors associate with one another on the stage; by plot, the sequence
of changes in the fortunes of the characters, the advancement of an argument, via struggles and confusions, to its deadlock or resolution. The two
go hand in hand. The unusually tensed action of the second half of *Libation-
Bearers* derives its energy from the rallying of the plot: Orestes has returned,
and the health of the house is about to be restored. Usually action and plot
move in some kind of harmony; and sluggishness on the part of the one is an

---

1. Cited by W. G. Clubb, ed. and tr., *Pierre Corneille: Rodogune* (Lincoln, Nebr., 1974),
p. xiii.
2. F. Fergusson, *The Idea of a Theatre* (Princeton, 1949), pp. 229 ff., distinguishes between action and plot, but along somewhat different lines.

indication that the other is grinding to a standstill. But the relationship is not constant. In *Agamemnon*, we have to wait till late in the play for the stage action to rouse itself in earnest. The actor playing the king does not enter until the play is half over. But it can be argued that the fortunes of the man called Agamemnon have already, by that time, undergone a considerable mutation—from domestic peace to disaster to sacred conquest, with its implications of further disaster. Can we say that what we learn about Agamemnon in the choral songs, in the speech of the herald, and in Clytemnestra's dark hints amounts to the makings of a plot?

The action is slow to get underway. After the test of strength, on stage, between Clytemnestra and Agamemnon, we are prepared for an acceleration of the pace. But further development is blocked once again when Clytemnestra reappears, and Cassandra launches into her prophesies. The death of Agamemnon—though off stage, his voice is audible—and the action resulting from that death are squeezed into the last three hundred lines of the play. Even there, after the double cry has been sounded, the gain in momentum turns out to be illusory. The quarrel between Clytemnestra and the Elders, and the entry of Aegisthus, are further retardations, dramatically akin to the speech of the herald and to the confrontation between Clytemnestra and Agamemnon earlier in the play. The action appears to follow its own unhurried pace, seemingly out of step with the perturbations unhinging the personal fortunes.

A similar somnolence of the action is observable elsewhere. Only in *Libation-Bearers* does the intrigue furnish the elements for a fine acceleration and tangling of the tale. But the intrigue is restricted to the second half of the play; the great lyric exchange of the first half appears, for a while, to bring everything to a dead stop. In fact, the exchange sees to it that the dramatic fortunes of Electra and Orestes go through their own shifting inflections. By the time the exchange has run its course, the emotional base on which the intrigue is built has been fully secured. Along with *Eumenides*, *Libation-Bearers* may be said to exemplify Francis Fergusson's pattern of purpose, passion, and perception, and to create the appearance of characters being affected by the plot which they initiate or to which they are exposed. At the other end of the spectrum, *Prometheus* and, to a degree, *Seven* are witness to Aeschylus's gift for constructing an action with a minimum forward movement. *Prometheus* has no plot whatever. When the play comes to its end, we have come to learn a great deal about the past struggle between the hero and Zeus, and we have heard from a number of interested, and some only vaguely interested, persons. But Prometheus's position and attitude are exactly what they were at the start, and there is no moment in the drama that suggests a straying from that fixity. In *Seven* and *Persians*, changes of insight and temper are produced in certain characters on the strength of information gathered in chance meetings and messenger reports. But "plot" is not a convenient concept for reducing these changes to a significant pattern.

The concept of "lyric drama" is occasionally cited to account for the scarcity of dramatic development, as if the prominence of choral or solo singing and the mode of experience which finds a lyric form were Aeschylus's substitutes for interesting forward moves and complications and resolutions. But music is a function of the vehicle, not of the argument. In any case, it so happens that *Prometheus* is, of all the plays in the canon, the least lyrical—a circumstance that has contributed to the doubts expressed about its authenticity. Its choral singing is brief and undistinguished. The principal medium of the play is the sustained use of iambic trimeters, of a plain style quite adequate to the purposes of the great engineer at the center of the drama, but surprising in the author of *Suppliants* and *Agamemnon*.

Perhaps the plotlessness of so much Aeschylean drama has something to do with the genius of mythology. The Greek convention of using the past, especially the legendary past, to supply the materials of drama was in many ways a fortunate thing. Because the dramatic present is invested with the perfectiveness of the past, the temptation toward verisimilitude which much later killed high tragedy was staved off. Where the pathos is that of Troy, or the Argos of the line of Tantalus, and where the main players are heroes and gods, the genre is not easily adjusted to the realities of the council chamber, of suburbia, or of the ghetto. But this same reliance on legendary material helps to blunt the appetite for those inventions which might make for a rousing plot. Because the main events in the tale of Orestes are well known, the construction of an interesting argument becomes less crucial than clothing the legendary data in the flesh and blood of varied utterance. The importance of the communal stipulation of a shared knowledge can hardly be exaggerated. Early in *Agamemnon* (338 ff.), Clytemnestra warns that if the Greek conquerors at Troy injure the rights of the gods by forcing their way into the temple precincts, great trouble will befall them. What is the point of the warning? Many in the audience knew about the lesser Ajax and his crime against Trojan Athena. The warning is, in reality, a kind of prediction. Because the spectators know more than the chorus is, for the purposes of the "plot," assumed to know, a mere speculation can come across with the power of a prognosis. Foreboding, ostensibly vague, shapes the audience's way of looking at the chain of events into a relatively comfortable certainty. Clytemnestra's conditionals are, in their effect upon the audience, closely akin to Cassandra's crabbed assertions. This is an instance of how Aeschylus drew benefit from the audience's familiarity with the significant features of the legend. There could be no getting away from the fact that the Danaids fled Egypt and were given refuge in

Argos, that Eteocles went under fighting against his brother for the rule of Thebes, that Prometheus was fettered by Zeus for disputing his dominance, or that Orestes killed his mother. Similarly, of course, there could be no doubting of the general outlines where the play relied upon recent history rather than distant myth. A tragedy in which Xerxes defeated the Athenians and the Spartans was unthinkable.

*Because* the legend, or the history, is known, the playwright can produce results which a more freewheeling author—and that includes the writer of Old Comedy—cannot. Clytemnestra's warning is effective because it exploits shared knowledge to reach out beyond the fable for new gains. As Gilbert Murray put it: the intent of *Agamemnon* is to make us feel what it is to take a city, to sacrifice a daughter, to hate a husband so much as to kill him. Murray wisely observes that this is not a matter of psychology—"that would give us a play like Zola's *Thérèse Raquin*"—but a way of piercing into the ultimate meaning of these ghastly and incredible disturbances of the cosmos of life.[3] "Ultimate" is perhaps too grand a word. The ancient dramatist does not chase after ineffables. He assimilates the tales of the past to the more familiar thinking and the social sensibilities of his own time. In Lessing's famous phrase, the tragedian—in his case, Euripides—expected to move his audience less with what was to happen than with the manner in which it was to happen.[4] The "was to" is, we should add, one of the critical points of the formulation. The tale of Agamemnon's murder was both past history and a new experience. The uses of the past do not rule out a special function of the present.

The scope left to the poet's recreative and critical powers is considerable. In spite of some reservations,[5] it is now generally believed that the ancestry of Prometheus, i.e., his descent from Themis and Ge, and especially his standing as a Titan, a brother in suffering of Cronus, is due in large measure to Aeschylus's willingness to change the details of the legend for the sake of elevating his hero. In the earlier tradition, for once fully available, Prometheus had been a potter, a craft divinity, and, in Hesiod's account, something of a trickster. Similar revisions can be traced in the treatment of other legends, though it is difficult to be certain; often the Aeschylean version is the first extended rendering of a particular legend. It may be asked, for instance, whether the complex of reasoning—it will hardly do to speak of motives—that the playwright associates with the flight of the Danaids is Aeschylus's own contribution to what was a simple tale of frightened young

3. G. Murray, *Aeschylus* (Oxford, 1940), p. 178.
4. G. E. Lessing, *Hamburgische Dramaturgie* (1769–71), section 48.
5. Notably on the part of M. Pohlenz, *Die griechische Tragödie*[2] (Göttingen, 1954), vol. 2, pp. 30 ff.

women running away from barbarian, or even bestial, pursuers. The answer is, yes, probably. But the extent of the reformulation remains uncertain, except that we can be fairly sure that the changes do not include a revising of the major outlines of the myth. In *Agamemnon*, Aegisthus's spy can be shifted from the seashore, where Homer has him, to the house. Aegisthus himself can be killed in the house, or in the open field where Euripides stages the execution. But Aegisthus cannot become the hero of the tale, nor can he be omitted entirely.

The tales Aeschylus chose—or, more properly, the few tales of his choosing that have come down to us—are of various kinds. The *Oresteia* is the story of a house endangered and brought to the brink of destruction. The same is true of the *Oedipodeia*, the trilogy of which *Seven* forms the last play. The *Oresteia* provides for a last-minute rescue of the house, at a new level of social and political vitality, whereas the *Oedipodeia* completes the undoing of the house. Probably this has little to do with any difference in the tales on which Aeschylus drew. *Eumenides* is exceptional; it is the one play we have in which Aeschylus indulged in a degree of inventiveness otherwise known, in extant fifth-century drama, chiefly in Old Comedy. In the trilogy about the Danaids, if our guesses are near the mark, the dangers and perhaps the final reconciliation concern not a house, but a state and the groupings within the state. *Persians*, as we have seen, is not drawn from the legends; it is also not part of a continuous trilogy. Its argument turns on the downfall of one man, and through him of a proud civilization. The accent on civilization, and the clash of civilizations, is to be found again in *Suppliants* and its trilogy. Finally, *Prometheus*, and perhaps the whole *Prometheia*, was a divine masque, with formal parallels to what we find in *Eumenides*, but alone in the range of its allegorizing and of its talk about social and cultural issues, topics which elsewhere in Aeschylus are found mostly in his satyr plays.

What are some of the organizing principles which Aeschylus brings to bear upon the material he takes up? It is not easy to isolate them, because the more applicable they are, the less significant they may well turn out to be. The old distinction between tradition and originality crumbles before our increasing awareness of the subtle crosscurrents between the fluidity of the tradition, the autonomy of the creative forces latent in it, and the limitations upon authorial freedom. The most promising lead takes us to a pattern of thinking which the fifth-century dramatists shared with some of their contemporaries. Aeschylus lived at a time when Athenian social and political institutions were changing, and when the men who thought about public issues—the orators, the statesmen, the historians—tried to make sense of what was happening by analyzing the changes as a seesaw between opposites. Unfortunately, our evidence of this dialectic comes mostly from the second half of the century, from such writers as Thucydides, Antiphon, and the political pamphleteer known as the Old Oligarch. It is our misfortune that most of the external evidence that ought to throw light on the forms of ancient tragedy—including, as we have seen, its costumes and masks—comes from a period subsequent to its great flowering. But what we know of the party struggles during Aeschylus's own lifetime, and what has come down by way of indirect information about arguments used by some of the earlier Sophists, suggests that antithetical thinking and arguing was in use long before the middle of the century. The emphasis on the clash, in *Suppliants*, between the powerless just and the powerful unjust reflects a thinking which Herodotus and Thucydides mirrored in their treatment of the wars.

We have to be careful here. Greek tragedy, more than most kinds of poetry, is vulnerable to an extreme literary reductionism. It is depressingly easy to pare down the thought pattern of a play to the predictable rhythms of a United Nations debate. The question "What is Justice?" and the slow march past contrasting positions recur in many plays. In Euripides, the progress of the argument is often indistinguishable from the flourishes of a philosophical or a juridical tug-of-war. One might instance the debate between the Argive herald and Theseus in Euripides's *Suppliants*. Like the play as a whole, which pits the spirit of Athens against the spirit of Sparta, the debate contrasts the spirit of democracy with its opposite. The fate of Medea, Phaedra, or Helen is brutally bound up with the cheerless clarity with which opposing premises or pleas are spelled out. The tragedy proper is often, as Aristophanes saw very clearly, imperilled by the contentiousness, alternately clarifying and distracting, of the central characters.

In Aeschylus, the lines are, as a rule, less sharply drawn, and the antinomies are more artfully embedded in the stuff of living encounters and the ferment of musical action. Take the opposition between love and freedom, a clash which is explored, or lived through, in Aeschylus's *Suppliants*. The play could have been organized like Euripides's drama of the same name; it could have exhibited the emotional and intellectual equilibrium of a *Bérénice*. But Aeschylus does not work like a mathematician; he does not exhaust antinomies. He has them emerge, as it were incidentally, from a dramatic situation which takes its cue from the anomalies of the past. Racine constructs an elaborate network of the possible functions of ideal opposites in conflict, mixing in just sufficient life by way of the psychology of small motions to make the severe dialectic barely believable. Aeschylus marshals ancient tales, with a view to bringing out their implications for human suffering and triumph. And as he does so, he has his agents, including the chorus, hit upon certain moral and social components which conveniently resolve into sets of opposites. Only in *Prometheus* is the discussion conducted at a high enough level of abstraction to isolate the dialectic as a key element in the dramatic experience. At the same time, *Prometheus* makes it harder than ever to locate the characters, present and absent, on the grid of antinomies which serves as their tilting ground.

The opposites, and the problems on which they turn, can be defined as "themes." But the notion of "themes" in Aeschylus is as precarious as any other ordering of the dramatic tissue. There are agents, and actions, and a language in which they are presented, a language in which key terms and key maneuvers can be analyzed. But it is doubtful whether, beyond this, themes are sufficiently independent or circumscribed to register tellingly upon the imagination of the spectators. Only in the *Oresteia*, where we can follow the action over an extended curve, does it seem possible with some assurance to trace a few of them—largely, once again, by way of antinomies, such as the male and the female, the Greek and the barbarian, life and death, triumph and defeat. But just as soon as these are baldly stated, their illusoriness is apparent. We have had occasion to observe earlier (above, chapter 10) that the supposed contrast between freedom and necessity, a set which has been thought to reside at the very heart of the tragic experience, turns out to be inadequate as an index of the subtle fluctuations of Aeschylean drama. In spite of these cautions, we shall proceed with a gingerly step to look at some of the pairs of contrasts which Aeschylus appears to favor.

*Prometheus* provides us with the first set: the contrast between the old and the new. It is a contrast which the Athenian political experience, the conflict between the old rule of the landed gentry and the new popular dispensation, readily offered, though there was enough shifting of positions, enough crossing of lines, to make the moral accents on the opposites a matter of some uncertainty. In *Prometheus*, Zeus is the new man; Prometheus is a member of the older generation. What this means in terms of political philosophy, much less in the terms of a philosophy of life, is not easy to say. In some important respects Prometheus, the older, is more "modern," more forward-looking than the tyrannical Zeus, who appears to stand for little but the darker aspects of the rule of the common man (I am not here concerned with the more formal functions of the divine figures, discussed in chapter 9). Some have argued that the moral highlights distributed between the two argue for an Aeschylus who opposes the proposals of the more radical democratic leaders. That may or may not be true. It is certainly true that in several plays, the old is given an edge in wisdom and in sheer humanity over the new. The old Darius clearly establishes his authority over Xerxes (*Pers.* 783; also 744). The Elders of *Agamemnon* contrast favorably with the viciousness or the vanity of the younger principal characters. Even in *Eumenides*, the centenarian Furies in the end show themselves to be the upholders of lasting principles, while the Olympians, the upstart gods, are made to scramble and improvise. This is, in fact, one of the concerns in which Sophocles turns against Aeschylus. In Aeschylus, old men tend to be endowed with maturity and respectability, while young men are given to imprudence. Perhaps this is an accident of the transmission; perhaps some of the lost plays, including those featuring Achilles, would disclose a different tendency. In any case, Sophocles seems to be the first dramatist to throw systematic doubt on this equation.[6] Some of his young men and women have a fresh, brave honesty which is superior to the tired thinking of their elders. Chronological age comes to be dissociated from expectations of maturity and immaturity. The set of opposites continues to hold, but it is crossed with new, compounding antinomies, different from those with which Aeschylus matches youth and age.

Another natural contrast is that between barbarians and Greeks. Once again, political experience, and especially Aeschylus's own experience as a soldier in the wars, help to shape the thinking. In two of his plays, *Persians* and *Suppliants*, he sets Easterners against Westerners. But the contrast is not allowed to stand unmodified. In *Suppliants*, the refugees are both Greek and barbarian. Their identification as descendants of Io and their claim to their ancient Argive heritage are as prominent as the constant reminders of their Egyptian upbringing and their open nostalgia for the Nile (854–57, 879–81). Their costuming will have conveyed this doubleness; the text suggests that their skin is dark (785), and yet their bearing is indistinguishable from that of the Greek girls of other choruses. Perhaps it is because their singing and dancing are so obviously Greek that Pelasgus, upon meeting them and listening to their tale of Argive origin, harps on their barbarian identity, in a curiously footloose speech touching on Libya, the Nile, Cyprian sculpture, Indian camels, Ethiopia, and the Amazons (279 ff.). Conversely, in *Persians*, the emphasis on the barbarian status of Xerxes is muted. The old Homeric habit of regarding Easterners as if they were cultural cousins of the Greeks is as alive as ever. The play is thoroughly committed to the *interpretatio Graeca*, the lexical sleight of hand which sanctioned Herodotus's talk of the Persians as worshippers of Zeus. Finally, the struggle between Thebans and Argives in *Seven* is made to look as if the Thebans were the Greeks and the Argives the barbarians (72 and 170), a bit of outrageous trickery which proves how useful Aeschylus found the set for the structuring of conflict, and how far he was willing to depart from the "truth" in the interests of the drama.

The simplicity of *Persians* makes it, as always, a convenient laboratory for the study of Aeschylean techniques. One passage in particular, a part of the

6. J. de Romilly, *Time in Greek Tragedy* (Ithaca, N.Y., 1968), pp. 150 ff.

speech of Darius, and thus a kind of demonic revelation, manages to tie together and virtually identify the potencies of a number of sets: freedom and slavery, land and sea, mortality and divinity, wealth and poverty, nature and convention (743–52):

> The source of these ills, all of us see it clearly.
> But my son did not see. Young as he is, he stormed ahead.
> He thought he could block the Hellespont, the sacred stream,
> The current of God, Bosporos, with the chains of a slave.
> He warped the straits. With hammered irons he yoked it
> And made it a mighty freeway for thousands of marching men.
> A mortal, he thought to dictate to the gods, above all, Poseidon.
> A foolish thought. Some sickness, surely, controlled the mind
> Of my son. And now I fear that the vast hard-won wealth
> Will fall a prey to others, whoever is first to arrive.

Other passages point in the same direction. The antithesis between Greeks and barbarians is sustained by a whole subsidiary set of (symbolic) antitheses: spears versus arrows, democracy versus kingship, logicality versus the unforeseen and the monstrous. The tidiness of the referential system is, of course, deceptive. The Persian scene is invested with refractory properties which help to distort the symmetry. But it would hardly do to deny that, at a basic level of poetic organization, the contrasts are sufficiently well coordinated to give body to the tragic fall.

In the introduction, the choral singing is full of reminders of the people serving under the Emperor. Because drama has a use for kings whose claim to rule absolutely is challenged, tragedians of the seventeenth and eighteenth centuries liked to go to the East—to Turkey, Persia, Byzantium—to find such kings. The later practice corresponds to Aeschylus's choice of Xerxes, but with an added dimension of the exotic and the marvellous. The forces of Xerxes are less outlandish, but they are not a free citizen army. The bridge across the Hellespont (65–72) is an extension of the yoke of servitude imposed on all living things Xerxes happens upon. The barbarian insistence on despotic rule emerges startlingly in the surprise conclusion of a remark of the Empress Mother's (211–14) about Xerxes. As she ponders his fate, she observes that if he is doing well, he merits admiration; but if he has run into misfortune, he owes the city (!) no accounts, and should, if he returns safely, continue to rule the country. The surprise ending, skewing the anticipated correspondence of fortune and position, puts a harsh light on Xerxes's need to be master. The mother's reluctance to draw the balance of a disjunctive proposition is a pendant to the irresponsibility that goes with kingship. The significant thing about this passage is its language. The mention of accounts and of the city furnishes a Hellenizing touch. More important, Aeschylus manages to convey the importance of the dialectic of freedom and slavery without quite saying so. The Greek word for liberty occurs only twice in the Aeschylean corpus (typically in quick succession: *Lib.* 809, 863; cf. above, chapter 4). The adjective occurs in all seven plays, but the total of eleven incidences seems unusually low, considering the importance of the set. Aeschylus is a poet, not a pleader; the opposites are suggested rather than stated. They are part of the tissue of imagery and event; they do not assert themselves in isolation.

Early in the play (101–14) the chorus notes that fate destined the Persians to win their successes on land, but that they had learned to "look upon" the sea also, and to rely on precarious pontoons. The distinction between (correct) nature and (slippery) acquisition or invention strikes a properly ominous note. The contrast between the natural and the factitious came to be one of the chief generators of Sophistic debate. In Aeschylean tragedy, the same antinomy, with its suggestion of failure and disaster in the wake of the unnatural, is common enough. The freezing and unfreezing, in preternaturally quick succession, of the river Strymon (*Pers.* 495 ff.) is an analogue to the setting up of the pontoon bridge. It involves a dubious reliance on what goes against nature, and it issues in catastrophe. The yoking together of two dissimilar women which is contemplated in the dream of the Empress Mother (181 ff.) carries the same stamp of the anomalous. Of the three tragedians, Sophocles is the one in whose plots the contrast between nature and convention has the most creative function. But its prominence in *Persians*, and its presence also in the other Aeschylean plays, show its pervasiveness in the ancient tragic scheme.

The song about female monsters (*Lib.* 585 ff.) is strange and powerful. We are told that impassioned men and women are more pernicious than non-human—i.e., biological and meteorological—deviations from the norm. At the end of the ode, we learn that the Fury will set things right, so that natural balance, the norm, *Dikē*, is restored. The body of the song furnishes four illustrations of the excess of passion: Althaea who killed her son, Scylla who betrayed her father, an unnamed figure guilty of crimes (whose exact nature is obscured by textual corruption), and the Lemnian women who slaughtered their men. The unnamed third probably refers to Aegisthus and Clytemnestra. In all four cases, it is not an excessive vitality as such that merits the reproach, but the flouting of natural standards, in the form of a subversion of normal social ties. The paradigms and the rhetoric establish Orestes as an instrument of *dikē*, an agent for the reestablishment of what is natural. As it turns out, Orestes himself becomes yet another representative of unnaturalness, and the Furies reject him, and prepare to punish him. But it is good to be reminded that the dialectic we read into the drama is there largely by implication. Aeschylus's undialectical verse steers clear of the combined use of *nomos* and *physis*, the Greek technical terms used in Sophistic essays and debates.

The relation between imagery and thought, between poetic discourse and structural arrangement, is always fluid. The crossing of the Hellespont in *Persians*, a prize example of breaching nature, recurs in *Suppliants*, but in quite another sense. The text (544–46) is difficult. Literally translated, it says of Io: "cutting through the billowing strait she marks, fitly, the land across in its separateness." The awkwardness of the phrasing, which exceeds the usual limits of lyric extravagance, owes something, perhaps, to the chorus's awareness that Io crossed the sea from west to east, and this does not precisely create the desired precedent for their own crossing in the opposite direction. But "fitly" and "marks" show the language to support the sense that Io's exchange of one land mass for another is within the bounds of the natural. The pressures of the context and the ethos of the argument as a whole have to be considered as specific formulas and images are given their value. In the next chapter, we shall ask whether Aeschylean drama makes for a cancellation or resolution of the antitheses around which the action is built. Our answer will be largely in the negative. The richness of the poetic language absorbing the referential system helps to keep the tension alive.

Before we take our leave from the subject of sets of contrasts, a brief glance at a related matter, on which we have already touched in chapter 10, is in order. Does Aeschylean drama favor two kinds of justice, each valid in its own right, in conflict with one another? Some scholars have proposed to read Hegelian antitheses into the arguments of *Prometheus*, *Seven*, and *Suppliants*: e.g., not only the Danaids, but also their Egyptian pursuers have justice on their side; or, to put it differently, each party is equally burdened with a mixture of justice and injustice. Wilamowitz wondered whether the young women were not legally unjustified in their flight; their cousins' claim that they owed them a marriage contract was perhaps recognized by law.[7] Similar balances between the moral and juridical claims of contending parties have been read into the arguments of *Persians* and *Libation-Bearers*. On this assumption, the equilibrium between the positions would in the end, through learned wisdom and third-play compromise, produce a resolution of the kind announced by Athena in *Eumenides*. The present trend is away from Hegel and Bradley. The more recent commentators have, for the most part, preferred to believe that Aeschylus distinguishes between, well, perhaps not heroes and villains, but at least between commendable men and women, and those whose actions and speeches put them in an untenable position.

---

7. For a good discussion of this issue, see A. F. Garvie, *Aeschylus' Supplices* (Cambridge, 1969), pp. 220–21.

Aeschylus is a skilled dramatist; he does not leave matters at the melo-dramatic level of right struggling and prevailing against wrong. He intro-duces enough modifications and distractions to blunt the edge of what is commendable and of what must be rejected. Clytemnestra has her moments of dignity; Prometheus flares with the hot humor of an uncontrolled animal; the noble Eteocles disintegrates under the impact of the curse and shows the raw man under the veneer of the public figure. Still, there can be little doubt whom Aeschylus wants us to admire and whom to abhor, which position to favor and which to eschew. In this, Aeschylus's way is the op-posite of Racine's. For Racine's purpose, it is necessary to suggest that all loves are equally meritorious, but also that the love of any one character is never answered. The asymmetry of the dramatic treatment is at odds with the symmetry of human deserts. In Aeschylus, the symmetries of the dra-matic treatment deflect our imagination from the unsettling recognition that, logically speaking, the conflict is between right and the wrong, or at least between the better and the worse.

At the same time, Aeschylus shuns ambivalence. "Law" in Sophocles's *Antigone* and "wisdom" and "madness" in Euripides's *Bacchae* are terms that ring with the dissonance of contrary perceptions. Antigone's law is at war with Creon's law; madness, when applied severally to Dionysus and Pen-theus, is felt to signify very different things. This kind of dialectic, exploit-ing divergent meanings of single terms, is not completely lacking in Aes-chylus (see the remarks on *dikē* below, chapter 12). Pelasgus uses the word *kratos* to refer to the legitimate power of the constitutional authority; the Danaids use it to designate the raw violence of the Egyptians. But little is made of the fact that the word looks both ways. Nothing is made of the possibility of a tragic misunderstanding or confusion that has its roots in speech. Aeschylus's language is too closely geared to the vigorous turns of the imagination, too flexible in its simulation of exuberant public speech to harden into the contrived opacity required by multivalence. The staged puzzles of Euripidean controversy and the verbal cruxes of the early Sophists are the hubs of a highly structured intellectual universe. They are the points at which the radii of their manifest designs meet. Aeschylus's freer structur-ing of the drama—some would say his stiffness, the absence of a flexible structure—makes them unnecessary.

Aeschylus's art of antinomies, his handling of the sets of opposites which controlled the social and political thinking of his time, is one of conceal-ment and of refraction. Even so, it has an important function in the way he develops motion and plot. For if we try to draw the balance of his practice, we might say that it serves to slow down or obstruct the motion. Other dramatic poets draw from the flash of contrary positions a furious energy that propels the action and brings it to a climax. From Euripides to Ibsen, and from *The Winter's Tale* to *Rhinoceros*, the dialectic of contrasts makes for complications, peripeties, and explosions. In Aeschylus, the counterpoint generates no such forward force. The meshing locks into place. The action, such as it is, takes place in disregard of the tensions, and conforms largely to the succession of odes and episodes which all Greek drama has in common. Nor is suffering made into a source of dramatic development. Where anguish is voiced, as in the musical contributions of Cassandra and Io, it is a consequence, not a shaper of action.

Even the plotless plot has to have its elements of movement. And so we return to the question of suspense. As we have seen, the audience was not greatly taken up with the question: What is going to happen? The major contours of the story provoked no curiosity. Furthermore, in several of the plays, notably in *Prometheus* and *Persians*, Aeschylus begins more or less at the end, and unloads the antecedents as he goes along—not in the manner of *Oedipus the King*, where the ignorance of the principal is the mainspring of the drama, and of the terror—but by way of reminding the audience, through fully informed characters, of what they broadly speaking know already. The tightly held coils of suspense which characterize Euripidean intrigue and the Sophoclean duels of character are not to be expected. And yet Aeschylus, also, chooses to enliven the action with his own means of anxiety. When the watchman in the prologue of *Agamemnon* says, in his last four lines (36–39),

> The rest is silence. A mighty ox stands on
> My tongue. The house itself, could it find voice,
> Would speak most clearly. My wish is to reach
> Those who understand, and make no sense to others,

or when the chorus, a little later (67–68) falls back on the ominous chanted phrase,

> things stand
> Where they stand; they will end as decreed,

the suspense created is formal rather than substantial. In the one case, a minor personage knows something, but will not talk about it. In the other case, the chorus pleads ignorance and intimates fear. In both cases, the audience, though presumably going along with the spirit of fear and despair, is in a position to fill in the missing outcome. The formulas of suspense do not touch upon the certainty of knowledge. What they do is to permit the spectators a momentary thrill of complicity. They are invited to take pleasure in a small effort at mystification, and to enter into a pact with the author to observe a quantum of bewilderment. The doubt helps to dull the transparency of the argument. A fund of common understanding freely shared is, by mutual agreement, darkened by slender exercises in silence and professions of uncertainty.

The watchman's phrase, circumscribing a piece of information not readily shared, is rare in Aeschylus. The only important parallel is the refusal of Prometheus to reveal his foreknowledge concerning Zeus's marriage problems—and there, for once, the audience itself is in the dark, because of the remoteness of the subsidiary legend used. More common, and indeed strongly characteristic of Aeschylus's art, is the choral admission of perplexity (see above, chapter 6). It would be amiss to regard such avowals of ignorance as cases of dramatic irony. Dramatic irony forms a cushion against empathy and elevates the audience to a position of superior judgment. An audience that from a vantage point of full information watches the vain contortions of witless sufferers runs the risk of not being able to look upon their sufferings without experiencing the specific pleasure that comes from knowing more. The great cleavage between knowing and ignorance which makes dramatic irony possible leaves little room for simple human sympathy. Dramatic irony is greatly reduced in scope in Aeschylus, because the principal characters are conceived of as knowing, or as sharing the limitations upon their knowledge with the audience.

Even so, Aeschylus's way hardly encourages the kind of identification between spectators and characters that Aristotle had in mind. Once again, the stiffness of much of the action, the prominence of lyric reinterpretation, and the ceremonial qualities of the art cut down on the chances for compassion or fear. But at least Aeschylus does not insist on the incongruity between what the audience perceives and what the chorus and the characters do not. Even the chorus's blindness, the anxiety which is exploited for the surface tension which we are now discussing, is not, after all, a true ignorance, but the useful convention of a knowledge momentarily unrealized. In Sophocles and Euripides, where intrigue and plotting assume an expanded role, ignorance is endemic, and sharply separated from knowledge. Without this separation, Aristotle thinks, good tragedy is difficult to achieve. In Aeschylus, incomprehension is a way of proceeding poetically. Behind the bewilderment we sense, at each step, a readiness to intuit the truth.

Like Sophocles, Aeschylus has scenes of premature joy and of unnecessary or revocable fear. He knows how to deflect and complicate the lines of the action by means of responses that seem to run in the wrong direction. But the momentary sprint on a new course lacks the energy of Sophoclean departures. Aeschylus has nothing quite analogous to Oedipus's delight at the message that Polybus of Corinth has died (*Oedipus Tyrannus* 964 ff.), or to the chorus's happiness when they believe that Ajax has come round to their way of thinking (*Ajax* 693 ff.). The threat of the women that they will hang

themselves in response to Pelasgus's initial decision not to take them in
(*Suppl.* 438–54) is swathed in layers of protective phrasing. Everything in
the scene is calculated to suggest to us that the King's decision will be
rescinded. His speech of explanation is larded with proverbs, prudential
reflections, and imaged wisdom. These formulas should be introductory, or
by way of annotation or transition (see above, chapter 6). But they overrun
the body of the speech, retarding the announcement of the decision, which,
in fact, never materializes. With equal deliberation, via the slow steps of
shuttle speech, the refugees then acquaint the King with their counter-
measure. In the eleventh line of a thirteen-line shuttle structure, the threat
is finally defined. The King immediately capitulates from a position that
had never been made entirely clear. The shadow-boxing of Pelasgus and the
muted response of the young women are hardly the most efficient means of
the rousing of "false fear."

A potentially more serious and sustained piece of deliberate miscueing is
the speech made by Orestes just before the onset of his madness (*Lib.* 1021
ff.). With seeming calm, he goes about making a series of dispositions. The
"arrangements" character of the oration is of the kind which in later tragedy
comes to be associated with the deus ex machina. As on earlier occasions, he
runs over the threats whereby Apollo had forced him into his action. But
now he contemplates a religious undertaking: he is about to become a suppliant in the temple at Delphi. For good measure, he calls on the Argives to
testify on his behalf when Menelaus returns home and occupies the throne.
This last touch is, in view of what happens in the rest of the trilogy, quite
misleading.[8] Altogether the speech leaves us with the impression that
Orestes is tying up all the loose threads before the action comes to an end. It
generates a specious sense of security, which is shattered when his madness
takes over. But note how the economy of the scene differs from what Sophocles would have done with a like occasion for false hope. At the start of his
speech, Orestes informs us himself that he feels the madness coming on.
The speech is, from the outset, advertised as a hopeless attempt to eke a
saving portion of sanity out of the crash into which he is moving. The
procedure is similar to what happens in the speech of Aegisthus at the end of
*Agamemnon*. Aegisthus, too, begins on a self-confident note, which is belied
by the manner of his introduction and finally reduced to a shambles by the
opposition of the chorus and Clytemnestra's barely concealed indifference.

In Aeschylus's scheme, moments of joy quickly decline into foreboding
and sorrow. Joy and fear, confidence and worry, are not neatly held asunder,
as they are in Aeschylus's successors, to be played off against each other in a

---

8. But note that the satyr play *Proteus* dealt with the experiences of Menelaus reported in
*Odyssey* 4.351 ff.

tragic see-saw; they embrace and color one another. Each expression of a sentiment is felt to be only a momentary detachment from a common pool of mingled emotion. In this respect, the art of Aeschylus is less stylized than that of the early Sophocles, and closer to the complexities of a psychological naturalism. Let us say that in Aeschylean drama, joy and assurance are only fleetingly isolated from the common ground of fear which determines much of the action. Joy cannot deceive, for in the compact between author and audience it is assumed to be short-lived or fictive. The watchman of *Agamemnon* hopes for release and, like the Danaids and the Persian Elders, prays to the gods that they will grant it. The chorus of *Agamemnon* starts out by looking to Clytemnestra for the wished-for deliverance (98–99). The force of the prayer is to elevate her to divine standing, which is tantamount to an admission that the hope may be unreasonable. The terror voiced by this chorus is at its simplest merely a worry about the war and the fate of the armies. But even after the news of the victory has come through, the worry persists and changes into a malaise which, to trust the chorus, is more easily expressed than accounted for. It helps to animate the drama; but it should be noted that the animation proceeds from a source that is alien to the specifics of the dramatic argument. The release prayed for is never granted. The resolution that closes the trilogy is of quite another order. By the time it is introduced, a different chorus has taken over, one whose station makes it insensible to the anxieties suffered by the choruses of the first two plays.

The chorus's fear, we saw earlier, is not something that can be relieved. It is the common man's intelligence that happiness perches crazily on a wave of trouble. The messenger's report of *Agamemnon* exhibits the pattern exemplarily. As the messenger comes to the end of his speech, triumph has turned into dejection, praise into complaint, conquest into doom. At first, Agamemnon is the fortunate victor, and Paris the guilty victim. But the distribution of moral accents shifts, along with the mood. It transpires that Agamemnon, too, is guilty and punishable. The widening stain of guilt and crime is exploited for her own purposes by a woman who shows, in her own person, how tightly triumph and disaster are linked. Clytemnestra's Parmenidean experiment (320 ff.) with the conquered city is instructive.[9] To begin with, she argues that oil and vinegar do not mix; the distance between conqueror and conquered is unbridgeable. But the swift vignettes that follow—the families of the vanquished comforting each other; the conquerors prostrate in exhausted sleep—issue in the warning we have noted before: to reach home, the victors must mind their step and not tamper with the Trojan divinities. In the end, that is, oil and vinegar *do* mix. Parmenides is refuted by implication, suffering is shown to be un-

---

9. Parmenides fr. 8.15–18 Diels: Being and Not-Being do not mix.

avoidable, and foreboding resumes its wonted function. Clytemnestra's ad-
monition is of the same monumental and open abortiveness as Calchas's call
to Apollo (146 ff.) not to block the Greek ships. The desperate prayer, the
apotropaic gesture, are not meant to mislead. They are understood to be the
small ripple of grace authenticating the larger movement of despair. [10]

Aeschylus has one exceptional case of radical miscueing. Darius asks the
Empress Mother to get decent clothing ready for the arrival of Xerxes. The
Empress Mother leaves the stage with the understanding that she will return to bring the garments; but she does not come back. Whatever may
have been in Aeschylus's mind as he holds out the promise of sartorial
rehabilitation but then fails to carry it through, the announcement appears
to be a truly false lead, much like the proposal in Molière's L'Avare that the
old man might become interested in another nuptial catch: an idea once
entertained and then abandoned without an appropriate modification of the
text. There have been attempts to explain the matter by showing that every
time a character decides to do something in Persians, another character
moves the action around to a different end. The chorus wants to deliberate;
the Empress Mother interrupts. The Empress Mother wants to sacrifice; the
messenger arrives. [11] The disaster manifests its irruptive force by dislodging
the agents from their course of action. But one may wonder whether the
implied model is adequate. Does it not assume that the plot demands a
natural sequence of planning and action and results? More properly, I think,
it might be said that the abortiveness of the actions is not dramatically
apparent, because there are no pressing expectations to respond to. The
Aeschylean stage does not tolerate council sessions or sacrifices. The decla-
ration that somebody is going to deliberate or conduct a sacrifice is sufficient. The word becomes a stand-in for the action. But the providing of new
clothes is just the kind of spectacle which Aeschylean drama craves. There is
some reason to believe that Seven contained an arming scene prior to the
final exchange between Eteocles and the chorus after 685; [12] and Athena's
words at Eum. 1028 suggest that the Furies exchange their black robes for
crimson. To be dramatically alive, the announcement of the Empress
Mother cannot remain a mere promise. The absence of an investiture from
the finished version of the play suggests that Aeschylus preferred not to

10. K. Reinhardt, Aischylos als Regisseur und Theologe (Bern, 1949), pp. 79 ff., is especially good on what he calls "Bild und Gegenbild," Aeschylus's creation of a sense of doom
along with a sense of victory. See also B. Snell, Aischylos und das Handeln im Drama (Philologus
Suppl. 20.1; Leipzig, 1928), pp. 113 ff.

11. D. Korzeniewski, "Studien zu den Persern des Aischylos," Helikon 6 (1966): 548–
96; also W. G. Thalmann, "Xerxes' Rags: Some Problems in Aeschylus' Persians," AJP 101
(1980): 260–82.

12. W. Schadewaldt, "Die Wappnung des Eteokles," Eranion: Festschrift für H. Hommel
(Tübingen, 1961), pp. 105–16.

provide the action with even a modicum of terminal relief. The disjunction between promise and delivery intensifies the feeling of frustration. At the same time, the burden of the promise cannot be entirely denied. The audience knew that Persia would go on, and flourish, with Xerxes securely at the helm, as indeed the Empress Mother had predicted (213–14; 290–95).

Where characters and audience share a common understanding, and where the broad developments of the action are known ahead of time, the outcome is not, as in other kinds of drama, something that needs to be discovered, or strained, from its natural antecedents. It is a dimension that is already available. The play moves toward it only in the sense that it is distilled from the present. Suspense and foreboding are not the signposts of a courageous and fatal march from a certain past to an uncertain future. They are the modalities which define the links between a known outcome and the varied experience leading to such an outcome. The eventual harvest of the action is a datum which is uncertain only in the sense that the way to it lies through mediate actions and divine fictions. This would almost seem to endow Aeschylean drama with some of the qualities we associate with a Proustian search. The audience proceed from a bastion of knowledge and rejoice in the exploration of the manifold world in which their experience is rooted. But Proust, and the genre he founded, move openly back into the past, discarding all suspense in the luxuriousness of surprise, whereas Aeschylus reshapes the tale as if it were not known, and gives to suspense a role that is entirely natural, sanctioned as it is by the indeterminacy of the moral world.[13]

Within the slow motion of a plot whose end is already in sight, there is some limited room for the unexpected, and even for the shocking. The climax of the selection sequence in *Seven*, the moment when Eteocles perhaps puts on his armor, is of this nature. With his dispatching of the defenders to the gates, Eteocles has increasingly narrowed the options. Hence, when the scout announces that the seventh gate is under siege by Polynices, and Eteocles is the only leader left to counter his brother, we should have been prepared for the blow. But the wealth of names and functions paraded in the selection sequence has left us with the feeling that the pool of defenders is inexhaustible. As Eteocles has it brought home to him that he will have to fight with his brother, the surprise and the recognition that this is the doing of the Fury are as overwhelming as if the legend had not all along stood surety that exactly this would happen. The surprise, then, is a consequence of Aeschylus's way with the rhetoric of scenes. Absolute surprise, unrelated to the known patterning of the argument, is es-

13. On the role of suspense in drama, see P. Pütz, *Die Zeit im Drama* (Göttingen, 1970).

chewed; there are no *coups de théâtre* to steal a sudden march on the imagination of the audience.

At *Lib.* 565 ff., Orestes reflects that because the house is in a state of frenzy, it may not offer hospitality. Clytemnestra's speech of welcome (668–73) confutes his suspicions. This is to be expected in an intrigue play, where checks upon the calculations of the plotters are needed as obstacles to their design. Psychologically, Clytemnestra's reception is a let-down. Both psychologically and morally, a surly welcome would have strengthened Orestes's hand. It appears that Aeschylus is willing to use surprise to his advantage. If we had more intrigue plays by him, we might be ready to say that he is closer to Euripides in this respect than the bulk of the extant plays suggests. But, once again, we note that the development is not entirely unexpected, and that the surprise is to the character rather than to the spectator. *Agamemnon* had prepared us for a Clytemnestra given to dissimulation. Her present greeting does not indulge in the extravagances that marked her earlier salaams. But the audience is conditioned to suspect that the welcome is of a piece with the grief shown at the message of the death of Orestes; and that that grief is spurious becomes only too evident before the scene is out. In the end, Clytemnestra's dissembling is precisely what was required to give Orestes the temporary moral advantage after all. His plotting is excusable, because his standing as a rescuer of the house depends on the success with which he adapts himself to a world in which intrigue and lying are standard behavior.

There is this important difference between an intrigue play by Euripides and *Libation-Bearers*: in Euripides, most of the agents are caught in a web of incomprehension, and an epilogue spoken by a god is needed to make them see. Aeschylus's conspiracy, though initially prompted by the command of a god, is carried out by men, and all parties involved, including even the victim at the moment of crisis, have the same benefit of clear-sightedness. Euripidean intrigue tends to conclude with a recognition of what had been hidden, of what had become obscured in the imperfect human search for truth. In Aeschylus, there is no need for such an enlightenment. Neither Orestes nor Clytemnestra can be said to gain insight or knowledge. All she learns is that she has been mistaken about a particular identity. We are reminded of Gerald F. Else's finding that Aristotle's *anagnōrisis* is a recognition of kinship.[14] The pithy briefness of Clytemnestra's exclamation that "by craft we killed; by craft we are undone" (888) argues a ready adjustment of perspective, not a significant wrench.

---

14. G. F. Else, *Aristotle's Poetics: The Argument* (Cambridge, Mass., 1957), pp. 383, 437 ff.

It is conceivable that *Agamemnon* could have been composed as a play of intrigue. The Homeric versions of the tale encouraged such a treatment. Aeschylus chose not to adopt that mode. Perhaps he felt that the theme and the needs of the trilogy made the hustle and bustle of an overt conspiracy inappropriate in a first play. What is needed to lay a base for the dramatic progression (no implication of a historical evolution here) from the world of the clan jungle to the world of the law court is the exposition of antecedents, lyric legato, the measured rhythm of "primitive" thought, and as little city politics as possible. The opportunities for plotting are realized only in retrospect, as Clytemnestra refers to "suitable words" (1372), the lies with which she entertained and caught her husband. In *Libation-Bearers*, the language of conspiracy prevails in the body of the play, as when Orestes tells the chorus to play its part in the plotting (582):

> Silence where needful, and words where suitable.

*Agamemnon* contains no complicating mechanism, no confidences, no arrangements for deceiving the opponents. The towering figure of Clytemnestra quashes all such externals by absorbing them into her secretive presence. The excitement of overt action is reserved for the second play, and there only after the Great Exchange has reaffirmed the inwardness of the earlier play.

I have suggested that the typical Aeschylean action, as evidenced in *Persians*, *Seven*, *Suppliants*, and *Agamemnon*, is one of near stasis. By absorbing the future, along with the past, into the present, the playwright blocks the sense of movement. Does this mean that the Aeschylean theater, in choking off change and development, is less dramatic than other kinds of theater, and perhaps not drama at all? As a genre, drama is thought to rely more heavily than other literary genres on the perception of time and change. "Tragedy is best understood . . . by remembering always that it is designed to resolve *temporal* tensions."[15] Both terms in this statement, "temporal" and "tensions," are key terms. "The phenomena that fill time are tensions—physical, emotional, or intellectual."[16] In turning to the issue of time, I am not concerned with Aristotle's "revolution of the sun," which some have explained as a reference to the course of a single day within the dramatic mimesis. Aeschylus shows no anxious concern for a completion of the argument within a day, nor does he track the progress of the day. The normal internal setting is daylight, but little attention is paid to what the daylight means to the activities and sensations of men. The sun is called to witness, it is prayed to, its shining is taken for granted, with some

15. K. Burke, *Language as Symbolic Action* (Berkeley and Los Angeles, 1966), p. 137.
16. S. Langer, *Feeling and Form* (New York, 1953), p. 112.

notable exceptions that confirm the rule. There is no measuring of the sun's distance from the horizon, no complaints about its concealment by clouds, or about its standing in the zenith, except at the beginning of *Prometheus*, where Hephaestus remarks compassionately on what the harsh sun will do to Prometheus through the eons. Dusk and dawn, like clouds or rain, are not temporal realities in Aeschylean drama. At the beginning of *Agamemnon* and of *Seven* and at the end of *Eumenides* (and, perhaps, of *Suppliants*) night is assumed, so that the talk of sacrificial flames and of the beacon signal and torch processions may register properly on the imagination. But these are special situations, called for by needs that have nothing to do with observing the passage of time. The change from night to day, and from day to night, is not calibrated. Only twice is a change specifically mentioned, once when Danaus expresses the hope that the falling dusk will slow the landing operations of the Egyptians (*Suppl.* 769) and again when Orestes relies on it to justify his seeking of shelter in the palace (*Lib.* 660). Night has, in Aeschylus, the same exceptional standing that it has in the *Iliad*. In reports about the past, it is the matrix for frightening dreams or heralds destructive battles. Contrast the greater awareness of the meteorological context in the drama after Aeschylus. It is the *rising* sun, coming upon a night of suffering, whose rays are greeted by the elders of *Antigone*. The chiaroscuros of *Bacchae* are an essential element in the shaping of an equivocal reality; and Aristophanes's hero is discovered fumbling about in the bourgeois ambience of nocturnal implements: mattresses, candles, and a snoring household. The sleep of the Furies, near the beginning of *Eumenides*, is set in broad daylight. Aeschylus gives us men and women; their relationship to the natural environment holds little interest for him. The pathetic fallacy, anticipated by Homer's rains of blood and darkenings of the sun, is not part of his dramatic universe. Neither clock-time nor the "feel" of the day are drawn in to disturb the pure stillness of the dramatic climate in which his agents move.

Nevertheless time is of the essence in Aeschylus.[17] In important respects, Aeschylus is the heir of Solon, in whose reflective verse time is invested with the brightness of a conclusive future.[18] It purges and illuminates; it brings about the punishment of the evildoer and conducts the triumph of truth and justice. This pointing toward an implementation is entirely different from the conception of Homer, where time is empty duration, measurable only on the strength of time-points, particular moments of crisis in a human life. Solon's organic growth model envisages a human life that is meaningfully

17. De Romilly, *Time in Greek Tragedy*. See also J. Duchemin, "Le déroulement du temps et son expression théâtrale dans quelques tragédies d'Éschyle," *Dioniso* 41 (1967): 197–218.

18. H. Fränkel, *Wege und Formen frühgriechischen Denkens*[2] (Munich, 1960), p. 9.

integrated in a larger temporal structure guarded by the gods. This pious emphasis cannot be fully maintained once the gods become in their turn potential victims or villains of a tragic scheme. But the playwright can draw on Solon's vision for purposes of his own. The sustained arc reaching from the past to the present carries with it a tensive energy which is of great benefit to the static plot.

The Aeschylean character is unselfconsciously aware of his dependence on time or his living in time. There is nothing like "the failure of the tragic hero to perceive his place and function in *time*,"[19] such as is notably the case with the Sophoclean Ajax, Antigone, and Hercules, and, for that matter, with some of Ibsen's most impressive characters. Time does not, in Aeschylus, become an object of isolated, much less hostile, contemplation. Suffering is not triggered by a feeling of "time being out of joint." The dramatis personae take it for granted that they are subject to the power of time to disclose, to bear witness, to create, and to destroy. But there is nothing rigid about the conception. Like *atē*, *dikē*, and other such "demons" (see above, chapter 9), time can be conceived of as a property or a function working within the agent and his actions; or it can be writ large, subsuming, as it were, the agent and his actions under its rule; or again, it can be regarded as a companion of the agent, maturing and growing old at his side. The flexibility of the language endorses the freedom with which Aeschylus handles psychological and social realities. That this same freedom should be available to him as he talks about time must mean that time is felt to be an organic constituent of the dramatic vision, not an autonomous dimension or an a priori grid against which to read off movement and events.

Solonic time, the accomplisher of justice and revealer of truth, is not equally at home in all the plays. In *Prometheus*, as I have indicated already, the enormity of the temporal vista faced by the hero and his companions almost gets us back to Homer's empty duration, without his compensatory mechanism of the day of doom to relieve the hopelessness of the waiting. The unceasing rotation of parching days and freezing nights locks everything into place. In *Agamemnon*, especially in the sections in which the prophetic mentality comes into its own—I am thinking of Cassandra and certain choral passages, including the report of Calchas's announcements— the distinction between past, present, and future, between cause and effect, is obscured. The lyric imagination, fired by the prophetic vision, merges the before and the after into a vivid present. The unity of the curse infecting the house of Atreus, crime merging with crime as if they were all part of one and the same central, timeless stain, testifies to the synoptic understanding. Thyestes devouring his children, Helen deserting her husband, the

19. T. R. Henn, *The Harvest of Tragedy* (London, 1956), p. 79.

leaders moving toward Troy, Troy burning: all are refashioned into an engulfing present. Perhaps this means that for Aeschylus, at the height of his poetic power, time is only a construction whereby the internal tensions of human experience are strung out as the dramatic plan demands. In *Agamemnon*, the call is for assimilation and condensation; the tensions are brought into feverish proximity and synthesis. In the other two plays of the trilogy, the tensions of *Agamemnon* are separated and laid open to inspection. *Agamemnon* 168 ff. tersely anticipates the thematic invocation of the triad—the unfolding of the three waves—in what is said about the advent of Zeus. But it is in the following two plays that the sequence of the three generations, of three advents, of two trials and one success, is fully realized. Orestes knocks three times, the slave shouts thrice, the chorus speaks of the third storm; Orestes's relation to his predecessors is paralleled with Zeus's relation to his, and the earlier homogeneity of the corruption of the house is broken up into predecessors and latecomers.

*Suppliants* is, like *Agamemnon*, a first play. In it, as a recent critic has put it, "time is abolished under the pressure of archaic terror."[20] The reasons are, one presumes, roughly the same as those responsible for the prominence of the lyric present in *Agamemnon*. Aeschylus offers a comprehensive fusion, a stockpile of identifications, before the sorting out and development begin. *Seven* is a last play. It calls for a sharper distinction between present and past, and a searching in the past for the sources of the future. This is precisely what we find there, different though the play is in its stiff collocation of tableaux from the relaxed back-and-forth movement across the borders of time in *Eumenides*. Both of these terminal plays cause the spectator to become aware of the logical connection between past and present, and to gear their expectations to the temporal pattern of long preparation and swift fulfillment.[21] Divine justice favors lateness. The hope that justice will be delayed, and the relief when it comes, are the psychological moorings with which Aeschylus secures the final outcome of his trilogies. Here time is experienced as a threat and a gift: a threat to the old and corrupt, but also to the doomed; and a gift to the beneficiaries of a new order.

Crisis threatening and crisis overcome are as crucial in drama as they are in the epic. In the introduction of *Persians*, the chorus pronounces its fears concerning the safe return of the army, without adding that it has been a long time since the army left or since messengers have come back to report. There is no need to furnish this information. The crisis-consciousness of the chorus is intelligible without plausible apologies. It is worth reminding

20. De Romilly, *Time in Greek Tragedy*, p. 28.
21. A. Lebeck, *The Oresteia* (Cambridge, Mass., 1971), pt. 2, chap. 2, "Time and Vengeance."

ourselves that drama is *the* agonal poetry of classical Greece. Everything in its arrangements points to contest and trial. The spirit of the *agōn* is alive in the myths chosen for the argument, and in the way the argument is shaped. Under this aegis, time is structured as coming sharply to a head in a critical conjunction. Not only human characters, but the gods also are affected by the crisis psychology. In Aeschylus, no god appears to be exempt. The Zeus of *Prometheus*, if we can trust what we hear about him, hedges his rule of empty eternity with a fear of sudden defeat. Prometheus engages him in a trial of authority whose outcome is, for once, not evident, and into whose meshes the adversary, Zeus, is thrust by the tightening of the secret. This remains true in spite of the lack of plot, in spite of the stasis. We are made to believe in the struggle of the principal, and this struggle, stirring the whole cosmos into whirlwinds and conflagration, creates a momentum that defies the alleged automatism of day and night.

*Prometheus* does this most startlingly. But in the other plays, too, it must in the end be admitted that several time standards exist side by side or cross each other in productive ways. Crisis-consciousness and empty time, coalescence of present and past, seeming forward movement via a vast arc of tension: these are the shaping forces whose interaction determines, in the absence of a structured plot, the energy and the brilliance of the action. Finally, the special tension between the several parts of a trilogy, each with its own amalgam of time vectors, completes the fullness of the dramatic experience. It also raises a problem relating to character. To what extent is the audience to accept at face value the "earlier" and the "later" in a sequence of three or four plays? [22] If the Apollo of *Eumenides* is successively an august sovereign and a casuistical bully, are we to assume that these impressions— either or both of them—should color, retroactively or by divination, our understanding of his (implied) role in *Agamemnon*? If not, as I think they should not, how far do we go in entertaining the proposition that the theatergoer submits unreflectingly to the disparate stimuli of the succeeding moments of the drama? [23] How far, conversely, may we venture in constructing a natural evolution that would lead, by imperceptible steps, from one impression to the next, and so on to the end? The latter conception is at the bottom of the view that *Prometheus* gives us the first stage in the historical evolution of the gods from barbarism to justice, and from warfare to compromise. My own inclination is to be skeptical. Aeschylean drama does not, in my opinion, any more than Hesiod's theogony, imitate natural evolution

---

22. Cf. above, chap. 8.

23. This was the view of T. von Wilamowitz-Moellendorff, *Die dramatische Technik des Sophokles* (*Philolog. Untersuchungen* 22; Berlin, 1917); see also E. Howald, *Die griechische Trag-ödie* (Munich, 1930). As a corrective to the psychologizing interpretations, Tycho Wilamowitz's position still has much to commend it.

and progress, if only because the rules pertaining to gradual change are beyond the reach, and contrary to the best interests, of high drama.

To revert to an earlier formulation, Aeschylean tragedy is antithetical in its structuring of the material, without giving the antitheses too obvious a place in the language.[24] The first and the second plays of the *Prometheia*, or of the Danaid trilogy, do not, I assume, reflect successive stages in history, but contrasting formulations of conflict, spurred on by a continuing effort to exhaust the fund of all such possible formulations. The several versions of what an Apollo can do, like the various constructions of what men are capable of in their dealings with one another, owe less to the forward thrust of history than to the richness of multiple experience. Aeschylean drama traces the potential patterns of human suffering and restructures them along the lines of contrast and collision, without hardening the positions into fixed identities. The slowness of the action—the plotless plot—is particularly well equipped to underscore the amplitude of the compound.

There is much that remains difficult. For the moment, let us conclude that Aeschylus's slow-moving dramas manage, in their own peculiar way, to create the illusion of motion. They do this without recapitulating the predictable movements of organic life; without straining for the verisimilitude of smooth progress or violent mutation; without building up to quotidian climaxes of fulfillment. What makes them succeed is their virtual disregard of patterns and forms abstracted from daily commerce. Their life is less brisk, but also less prefabricated, than that. It is inspired by the tension of words, of images, of agents clashing and feelings intimated within the frame of familiar tales and settled traditions. Nor is this life tied to the archetype of complication, reversal, catastrophe, and resolution. It was Sophocles who chose to assimilate the dramatic plot to the biographical curve of growth, disenchantment, despair, and salvation. The fractured life of the Sophoclean hero furnishes the model for the dramatic plot. Not so in Aeschylus, who celebrates no heroes, but narrates and analyzes the fates of houses or cities, or whole worlds: embattled universes coming to grips with their destined fate. The men and women who people these universes draw strength from the largeness of the setting. But the structure of the action which defines them answers to no one pattern and resists a shapely organization. Faced by a choice between the virtues of clarity and articulation and the fullness of unremitting conceptualization, Aeschylus preferred the latter.

24. K. Reinhardt, *Aischylos als Regisseur und Theologe*, pp. 68 ff.

# 12

# Trilogy; Trial; Resolution

"The constant occupation of a sane mind is to choose, establish, and maintain frames of reference for the things of its experience; as the high value placed on artistic unity attests, one of the attractions of art is that it offers a degree of holiday from that occupation."[1] And: "A play is 'poetic,' then, when its concrete elements (plot, agency, scene, speech, gesture) continuously exhibit in their internal relationships those qualities of mutual coherence and illumination required of the words of a poem."[2] Here are two recent statements in support of the proposition, first outlined in Plato's *Phaedrus* and in Aristotle's *Poetics* though not particularly adverted to in later antiquity, that literature, including the drama, to be judged good must satisfy a man's craving for integration. Unity, consistency, coherence, logical structure: these are the terms which the postlapsarian mentality, terrified by the thought of an unstructured world, has conjured up for its comfort. Modern psychology, Gestalt and otherwise, has contributed evidence that the expectation is not without substance. And deliberate departure from the artistic principle of unity—aleatory music, the new novel, the happening in art—have in the end come round, or been thought to come round, to satisfy the belief that some kind of coherence can be predicated of everything made by man.

Aeschylean drama furnishes a particularly promising instrument of proof: the dramatic trilogy. Sophocles and Euripides, also, offered their plays in bundles of three. But it appears that the later playwrights normally regarded the bundling as a purely mechanical matter, without the least obligation to the author to make the individual plays hang together.[3] Aeschylus himself offered some "disconnected" trilogies, packages of plays put together only for the sake of institutional convenience. *Persians*, for example, was apparently flanked by two plays whose plots derive from legend, and though it could be argued that all three plays showed an unusual interest in monsters and monstrous behavior, it is quite out of the question that the spectators could have perceived them as constituting a larger whole.

1. W. C. Booth, *The Rhetoric of Fiction* (Chicago, 1961), p. 151.
2. D. Donoghue, *The Third Voice* (Princeton, N.J., 1959), p. 10.
3. But Euripides's trilogy of 415 B.C., consisting of *Alexandros*, *Palamedes*, and *Trojan Women*, seems to have been a connected one. The trilogy of 438, consisting of *Cretan Women*, *Alcmaeon in Psophis*, and *Telephus*, may have possessed certain thematic connections, but nothing definite is known.

Aeschylus's most famous productions, on the other hand, were "connected" trilogies, aggregates of three (or, counting the satyr play, four) dramas linked in plot, cast of characters, and, it is assumed, artistic concept. Only one of them, the *Oresteia*, has survived. It will be useful to take a close look at it, to check out the assumption that in composing a connected trilogy Aeschylus meant to create a coherent structure.

The assumption is, indeed, a plausible one. For those who are interested in a measurable design, it will not be an accident that half way through the Great Exchange of *Libation-Bearers*—and that means roughly in the middle of the play and hence roughly in the center of the trilogy—the chorus chants the following (400–404):

> It is the rule that drops of blood
> Shed on the ground summon another
> Death. Murder invokes the Fury; she
> Brings from those who died before
> Blight to pile on blight.

With some justice, it could be said that this is the central theme of the *Oresteia*. It is a drama, not of men acting, but of a whole world thrusting up representative shapes and voices to reveal its inner life through the interconnectedness of crime and outrage. We begin with a darkness that is illuminated by a war signal, and we end in a darkness, with the torches of peace heralding new possibilities of friction. All three plays open on a note of weariness, shaken off temporarily for illusory gains. The release prayed for by the watchman and promised to Orestes by Apollo (*Eum.* 83) appears to have been granted at the end of the last play. But given the central conviction voiced by the chorus, how much faith are we to put in that release?

Unity is, of course, not just a matter of parallels, but also the function of some kind of development. The expository style of the prologues helps us to trace the stages of one possible development, unless it turns out that the development is nothing more than subtle variations upon a common theme. The prologue of *Agamemnon* begins: "I ask the gods to . . . for. . . ." An avowal of worship addressed to the world at large, including the spectators, is followed by an explanatory phrase which starts the exposition, such as it is. In *Libation-Bearers*, the speaker turns directly to the god: "Hermes . . . help me . . . for. . . ."; the ensuing exposition is now largely lost. In *Eumenides*, the avowal is once again to the world at large: "I pay my respects to Gaia . . . ," but instead of a for-clause, it is a relative clause, ". . . Themis, who . . . ," that leads into the exposition—a historical survey which on the surface has rather little to do with the ostensible plot. (But see above, chapter 5.) Thus the beginning of *Libation-Bearers* is the most dramatic; the beginning of *Eumenides* least so. The watchman of

*Agamemnon* is only lightly involved, Orestes is deeply committed, while the priestess of the last play is little more than a mechanism to get the action moving. The dramatic weight of the trilogy rests within the middle piece. Framed as it is by two plays featuring unstable relations and large masses of people, *Libation-Bearers* settles down to converge upon individuals, on Orestes and his commitment. The trilogy as a whole gets its name from the character who dominates the central section (one may assume that it was Aeschylus himself who was responsible for the title attached to the trilogy).

Thematically, also, there are parallels and variations that appear to support the notion of a developing unity. The clot of blood that Clytemnestra offers along with her milk in the dream narrated by the chorus (*Lib.* 533) inevitably reminds us of the spray of blood in which Clytemnestra reveals herself toward the end of *Agamemnon*. The prayer of the Furies for the good health of the flocks (*Eum.* 938 ff.) and other similar blessings called down upon the commonwealth as a whole seem to be conceived as a reparation for the evil omens pervasive in *Agamemnon*: the healthy lambs make up for the blighted hare's offspring. Read in this fashion, the trilogy traces the difficulties attached to the tempering of a savage humanity that finally learns to live with itself. The meshing of sameness and evolution is maintained to the end when, after the pacification of the Furies, Athena, the seeming embodiment of temperance, can still break out in a flash of fury that recalls the old savagery. There is progress, but also a stubborn retention of the old.

*Agamemnon* and *Libation-Bearers* are full of pictures of children killed and eaten. With the nurse of *Libation-Bearers*, however, we find ourselves in the more homely atmosphere of an arrangement which allows the fondling and cherishing of children. In *Eumenides*, children become an issue for a medical debate, and it may well be asked whether the pseudo-scientific objectivity with which Apollo and Athena conduct their argument is more humane than the waste of offspring heralded in the first two plays. The speech of the nurse is the realistic heart of the trilogy, and also its greatest unbending from the cruelties of the mythological vision. Beginning with the obsessive lyricism of *Agamemnon*, and ending with the evasive allegories of *Eumenides*, we stop off briefly in the middle to watch, for one fleeting moment, domestic gentleness and warmth, embodied in a woman whose social status is further evidence of the marginality of that warmth. But it is real nonetheless, just as real as is the concentration in *Libation-Bearers* upon the moral fate of one man, a narrowing from the circling seasons, celestial processions and astral principalities advertised in the watchman's speech, and a brief respite before the scene broadens out again, but now into the world of politics, legal regulations, and institutional settlements.

It is understood that the conceptual development of the trilogy is toward a more and more civilized world. The catalogue of divine politics at the beginning of *Eumenides* alerts us to the notion that we are leaving the larger cosmos, with its jealous personal divinities, behind us and are entering upon the canton diplomacy presided over by local gods. Apollo's advent is said (*Eum.* 12–14) to have been facilitated by the "sons of Hephaestus," shadowy culture heroes who built roads and cleared the country. The compacted synthesis of generations in the first play gives way before a willingness to accept the before and the after, the change from barbarism to culture. This at least is the mode in which *Eumenides* presents itself, regardless of whether it means that the whole trilogy is a record of continuous progress and whether the playwright was concerned with the amelioration of man and his institutions. Again, the house, which looms so large in the first two plays and which functions as the principal locus of the clan solidarity whose injury cries out for blood, is dismissed quite unceremoniously in the last play, to be replaced by the nuclear family—the household consisting of father, mother, and children—and the city-state. Zeus and Apollo come to stand for city law, while Moira and the Furies represent clan practice: this neat distinction argued by the Marxist anthropologists, George Thomson among them, has much to be said in its favor, in spite of the purely speculative assertions about the tensions between a matrilineal and a patrilineal world which are usually associated with it.[4]

By the same token, comparing the choral lyrics of *Eumenides* with those of the first two plays suggests a shift toward mimetic immediacy and personal relevance. The Furies have, after all, a role to play and a position to defend, which invests their singing with an authority that is lacking in *Agamemnon* and *Libation-Bearers*, even though the slave women of the latter, in the sequence of the Great Exchange, develop a surprising measure of authority. The movement towards immediacy and greater concreteness is most obviously experienced on the level of imagery. The lyric images of the two earlier plays are translated into tangibles and visible events. The trope of war as a lawsuit becomes the trial scene, that of hunting and the net issues in actual pursuit, the serpent of Clytemnestra's dream emerges in the ghostly costuming (to be imagined only?) of the Furies. Much of what was earlier expressed in the evocative multiplicity of the lyric is, in the last play, channeled into immediate visual impact. Similar progressions from lyric density to openness of action enliven the final portions of *Agamemnon* and *Libation-Bearers*; the poetic movement of the trilogy is mirrored in the movement of each of its parts. This dovetailing increases the effectiveness of the pattern. But it is only in the third play, as barbarism and clan-concrescence are abandoned, that the greater discursiveness of the presentation becomes an

---

4. G. Thomson, *Aeschylus and Athens*[3] (London, 1966), pp. 47 ff., 259 ff.

appropriate vehicle for the meaning. *Eumenides* is, of course, a minor trilogy in its own right: the sequence of Delphi, trial, and conversion repeats, in a fashion, the larger sequence of prophetic lyricism, personal intrigue, and political resolution offered in the total structure. Yet we must remain careful not to interpret the sequence and the gradual loosening of the coil as if they signalled a historical evolution. The recalcitrance of the Furies and their ascendance in the ultimate compromise should be sufficient warning.

　　The trilogic structure may be characteristic of the late Aeschylus. The Danaid trilogy, the *Prometheia*, and the *Oresteia* all come from the last decade of his creative life.[5] Other Aeschylean trilogies, besides the *Oedipodeia* (the trilogy of which *Seven* is the final play), which was performed eleven years before his death, may have been, in an approximately descending order of certainty: a *Lycurgeia*; a trilogy about Achilles; one about Ajax; one about the Argonauts; one about Odysseus; one about Perseus; a Dionysiac trilogy; a trilogy about Memnon; one about Telephus; and one about Adrastus.[6] Most of this is very uncertain speculation. But we can be tolerably sure that Aeschylus's corpus contained at least six or seven connected trilogies, where Sophocles may have produced one, and Euripides two. Thus it appears that Aeschylus's concern with unity, or at least with larger compound structures, was exceptional. We wish we could say more about the plot of the *Prometheia* or the Danaid trilogy; the fact is that we know next to nothing about the lost plays. It has sometimes been argued that *Agamemnon* and *Libation-Bearers* illustrate a structural parallelism which should also be instanced in the case of the first two plays of the *Prometheia*. (It is now generally assumed that our *Prometheus* was the first play of the trilogy, and that *Prometheus Unbound* came second; but this is largely guesswork, and continues to be denied by some.) In actual fact, *Agamemnon* and *Libation-Bearers* are structurally comparable only in the sense that each of them contains a murder. Otherwise the differences vastly outnumber the resemblances. It looks, curiously, as if a hasty inference about the relationship between the first two plays of the conjectural *Prometheia* was, in a curious gambit of arguing from the unknown to the known, responsible for the error of regarding the first two plays of the *Oresteia* as structurally comparable. Later, the origin of the error was forgotten, and the supposed similarity between *Agamemnon* and *Libation-Bearers* was held up as a model for reconstructing the second (?) play of the *Prometheia*: an instructive instance of the perils attending the reconstruction of lost plays.

　　We do not really know the plots of *Laius* and *Oedipus*, the plays which

5. For the *Prometheia* see C. J. Herington, "Aeschylus: The Last Phase," *Arion* 4 (1965): 387–403. The argument is premised on the Aeschylean authorship of our *Prometheus Bound*.

6. H. J. Mette, *Die Fragmente der Tragödien des Aischylos* (Berlin, 1959), pp. 259–60.

preceded *Seven* in the *Oedipodeia*. To be sure, a third play can be relied upon to contain reminders of what occurred in the first and the second, and so certain passages in *Seven* have been mined for information about what the preceding plays may have contained. But though this procedure is eminently respectable, and though its findings may be lucky enough to be verified by subsequent discoveries, it cannot give us certainty or, in most cases, even plausibility. Thus we know roughly which elements of the legend Aeschylus used, but we cannot tell how he used them to achieve what might strike his audience, or a modern audience, as an integrated whole. We are even worse off when it comes to reconstructing the missing two plays of the Danaid trilogy. In this case, we are not even completely certain, though the presumption is overwhelming, that our *Suppliants* was the first play. Those who have speculated that the end of that trilogy featured a trial, and that its resolution celebrated the institution of marriage and its guarantees, have very little to go on. Herodotus (2.171) reports an account that the Danaids taught the rites of the Thesmophoria to the Pelasgian women. This may refer to the institutional *aition* at the end of a drama, but if it does, we cannot be certain that the reference is to an Aeschylean play. In any case, if there was a trial, who was the plaintiff? The various candidates for that position, including Aphrodite, and Hypermestra, or her murderous sisters, do not readily qualify for the task.[7]

In fact, our misgivings should be more categorical. Even scholars who are properly skeptical of our ability to reconstruct the plot or parts of the plot of lost plays are often too willing to believe that a connected trilogy means a consecutive tale and a meaningful conclusion in the terms of the tale. But if we look at *Libation-Bearers* and *Eumenides* without preconception, it is only too apparent that the plays do not really form a single tale so much as scenes from a larger cycle, chosen perhaps for their adequacy to the central idea of the trilogy, but not necessarily because they fit together in an unbroken chain. It is conceivable that the treatment in the Danaid trilogy was even more episodic. To suggest that "from many passages it is certain that the fate of the city of Argos will be of some concern in the following plays" is like guessing that because Argos is important in the first two plays of the *Oresteia*, it must be important in *Eumenides* also, which is only very partly true.[8]

The time has come to recognize that even in the one trilogy that we have, the *Oresteia*, there is much that bids fair to challenge the notion of a unified conception. Those who say that the *Oresteia* records an ideological or institutional transformation, the setting up of a state of law, and the abandon-

---

7. On the subject of reconstruction, see the salutary remarks of A. F. Garvie, *Aeschylus' Supplices* (Cambridge, 1969), chap. 5, "The Trilogy."

8. Garvie, *Aeschylus' Supplices*, p. 181.

ment of the custom of blood guilt have taken their cue solely and unduly from the last play. It is as if one were to argue that Apuleius's *Golden Ass* was a record of the giving up of witchcraft in favor of the worship of Isis, or that Wagner's *Ring* was dedicated to the proposition that the ancient gods are dying. Such formulations have only a small grain of truth in them. Since most ancient trilogies were, as we know, not connected, it is logical to assume that even in a connected trilogy, the forces of unity are not overriding, and that the three plays can be appreciated as relatively independent units. Above all, Aristotle's organicism, formulated to apply to the criticism of a single play, should not be permitted to suggest that in a trilogy, the first play necessarily contains elements that point forward to, and explain, elements in the second and the third. I shall argue directly that *Eumenides* is, in part, an attempt to bring the dramatic business to a close in an artistically and institutionally satisfying way. But that is just about the opposite of claiming that the ending necessarily and logically follows upon the antecedents. The establishment of the state of law is the termination, but not the goal, much less the theme, of the trilogy. It is as unrelated to the major design of the business that precedes it as a Euripidean epilogue, with its neat disposition of awkwardly dangling threads, is a surprise ending to what comes before.

This is, perhaps, overstating the case. But it may be salutary to keep an open mind as we consider in what sense *Eumenides* can be said to furnish a solution, and perhaps a catharsis, of the "problems" developed in the preceding plays. The idea of a catharsis is plausibly suggested at the point (*Eum.* 566 ff.) when the sound of the trumpet is made to usher in the second movement of the play, the court session. We have no stage direction informing us that the trumpet was indeed sounded. But even if we were perverse enough to doubt its reality, the four lines by Athena, conveying the order to the trumpeter, have a liberating effect. Coming as they do immediately upon the completion of that remarkable ode in which the Furies announce the *katastrophai neōn thesmiōn*, the "revulsion of new statutes" and the imminent overthrow of Right, the blast of the trumpet helps to still the echoes of private contention, and prepares us for a meeting of the "host," as Athena calls the people in session.[9] H. D. F. Kitto's common sense interpretation of Aristotle's use of catharsis is relevant here.[10] Upon this interpretation, mimesis achieves its effect by taking sufferings that are likely to work through pity and fear and cleansing them of their haphazard and possibly

9. For the liberating climate associated with the open air court, see O. Weinreich, "Blutgerichte EN HYPAITHROI," *Hermes* 56 (1921): 326–31.

10. H. D. F. Kitto, "Catharsis," in *The Classical Tradition: Literary and Historical Studies in Honor of Harry Caplan* (Ithaca, N.Y., 1966), pp. 133–47. Kitto acknowledges his debt to G. F. Else.

counterproductive elements so they prove suitable for the achievement of the pleasure associated with mimesis. Catharsis thus becomes an element in the ordering and shaping of the material, not in the perceptions of the audience, though the two cannot, of course, be completely separated. In the present case, the conflicts painfully brought home to the audience in the course of the first two plays are said to terminate in a crisis of the new which is also a crisis for the whole trilogy. Everything that precedes it served to harden the *desis*, to snarl the skein of the argument. Now the hole-and-corner killings, the vicious violence of the earlier movements—axing a man in a bathtub, killing a woman in her bedroom—are succeeded by the liberating regimen of the open-air court. The many (and often, as we shall see, superficially confusing) references to purification in this last part of the trilogy lend their own force to the effect of purging and unblocking, of getting a fable that has run off course back on the rails.

Logically speaking, a curse is organic, natural, inescapable; it cannot be made to end, it must proliferate (see above, chapter 10). In that light, the solution offered in *Eumenides* is an abortion. Which is roughly the same thing as saying that a true tragedy, as we understand it, cannot have an ending, but must go on. The Greek playwrights worked out special techniques for subverting this hopelessness, for instituting artistically and even ideologically satisfying endings in defiance of the modern philosophical axiom that the tragedy cannot be untangled. Aristotle's remarks about untangling (*lysis*) pertain to that largely aesthetic disposition rather than to the dialectical "Aufhebung" which modern metaphysicians of the tragic demand. In the *Oresteia*, the resolution is in terms of Right, and it is the coming of Right that is announced by the trumpet call, in the teeth of the Furies, who have their own view of what Right is and want the tragedy continued. The trumpet call is part of the apparatus of deception the playwright needs to bring about an end. The Right toward which the earlier segments of the trilogy had appeared to be heading is about to be buried, and only a compromise, juridical and artistic, will enable Athena to maintain the fiction that the resolution she offers was intended all along.

Those who insist on an ideological explanation of the course of the argument in the *Oresteia* have their difficulties. As Reinhardt saw, if the idea is the replacement of tribal law by political institutions, then it is a pity that the case is so complicated, and that Apollo could not find worthier arguments for the change. If the idea is the replacement of the underworld divinities—demonic, dark, female, hoary, instinctual—with the Olympians—luminous, male, young, reflective—then the final compromise between Athena and the Furies is curious. The drama is too rich, and the lifelines too confounded, to permit an easy casting of the sum. The same caution applies to the standing of Right in the course of the trilogy. Of the matricide, it might be said that it signals a whole complex of activity in which a man is compelled, often with conflicting motives but with no obvious alternative, to commit an unwelcome act. How is society to judge? Aeschylus's partial answer, if we look for an answer, may well be: by not judging at all, but by adjusting the relation of the individual to his society, by utilizing the energy which he has displayed in a new, more constructive channel. In this sense, the moral of the play would not be legal, much less ethical or philosophical, but pragmatic. One might compare the ending of Sophocles's *Philoctetes*, in which the hero surrenders his narrow insistence on his Right, and allows himself to be returned to a position of usefulness within a persistingly hostile society.

It is of some interest that Orestes, after a speech of thanks to Athena, leaves the stage. There is no reconciliation between him and the Furies. In what follows, he is quickly forgotten. *Libation-Bearers* is inconceivable without Orestes; in *Eumenides* he is something of a supernumerary, and in fact need not have been introduced at all. As the Furies and Athena engage in the final argument, the House of Atreus slips from sight; Athens, and an entirely new order of social reality, supervene. Fear retains its power; the same fear which had terrified the chorus of *Agamemnon* and which prompted Orestes to obey the threats of Apollo is now recognized as the special birthright of the Furies, and has its role reaffirmed. The terror of the vendetta is politicized and domesticated for institutionally fruitful ends: the Areopagus, and Athenian justice, will rely on fear, and its near-synonym, respect, to keep the people from irresponsibility and anarchy. The verbal parallels between what the Furies sing (*Eum.* 526–27) and what Athena says (696–97) are almost too obvious. Athena emerges as a latter-day Fury, a role to which her status as veteran goddess and virago suits her well enough.

It has been said of another great work of literature that "like other true poems, it is first and most concerned with being true to itself, and so fails to solve its elected problems except in terms of its own poetic fiction."[11] One of the most striking things in the history of drama is the toughness, not to say cruelty, with which terminal adjustments, including marriages and penalties, are staged by Calderón. In *The Physician of His Own Dishonor*, in which the only attractive character is bled to death for her deserts, the killer is married off to his boyhood love, an arrangement which may not satisfy him personally, but which helps to untangle the disarray. In *Life is a Dream*, Segismondo marries Estrella, and Rosaura is married off to Astolfo, not because they desire or deserve one another, but because these are the proper

---

11. A. Stein, *Heroic Knowledge* (Minneapolis, 1957), p. 77, concerning Milton's *Paradise Regained*.

alliances now that Segismondo has reached the throne. Throughout, apparently, even where Calderón elects to draw characters that attract our sympathy, we are asked to look at them as if they were not men and women with their own ambitions and weaknesses, but temporary stand-ins for hierarchic personages who cannot afford, or will not be permitted, the luxury of private satisfactions. Clarin, Rosaura's servant, and a likeable fellow if there is one in the play, is the only one who gets killed. The outcome is shocking, because the need for killing off the *precioso* is not immediately apparent. In other plays of Calderón, hierarchic constraints are offset by an assertion of human dignity in the face of the demands of public order. *The Mayor of Zalamea* is such a play. But the more representative dramas are those in which public order, the rule of the princes, is the decisive factor, and where the ending unscrambles the human complications by violently adjusting them to the needs of that order.

I have talked about Calderón at some length because his practice seems to me to present an issue not unlike that of Aeschylus's procedure in *Eumenides*. In the face of the vital need for public order, traditional heroism and the desire to live up to one's inner convictions are sacrificed, or at least left unconsummated. The great difference is, of course, the nature of the public order. In the place of royal or princely highhandedness, Athena offers popular agreement. Democracy and parliamentary protocol are singularly ill-equipped, and certainly less effective than royal grace, to help shape a destiny for heroism on trial. Athena, in her final exchange with the Furies, chants that Zeus of the Rostrum has won, and that the competition of the good (a Hesiodic echo), the respectful rivalry between Athena and the Furies, rests victorious. The reference is to persuasion and cooperation, to lobbying and committee work: a resolution that makes decent sense within its own context, but that has little to tell us about the issues of the earlier plays.

The visible symbol of the new spirit is the ballot box, and the law court of which it forms the central implement. Athena's foundation speech, delivered after the closing of the litigants' presentations and before the balloting, is curiously placed. Should it not come earlier, before the start of the "trial," or later, after the court has concluded its session? The answer must be that the central location of the speech, close to the balloting itself, enhances our understanding of the significance of the voting. At the same time, the institutional burden of the address lulls our moral and aesthetic sensibilities. The force of Athena's mythographic flourishes works on behalf of Apollo's establishmentarian pragmatism and against the ethical puzzle worried by the Furies. The institutional arrangement is not completely unprepared. At an inconspicuous place in *Libation-Bearers*, in the second stanza of the choral song between the departure of the Nurse and the arrival of Aegisthus (800–806), the chorus calls on the gods within the house, protectors of the wealth, to

> Resolve the blood of the ancient crimes
> By means of fresh decrees, to stop it
> From teeming within the house.

The sequel shows that they are thinking primarily of Hermes, the god of business transactions and the law court. It is, in fact, surprising that *Eumenides* brings on Apollo, rather than Hermes, to play the role of the lawyer and friend-in-need. The displacement may be a measure of Aeschylus's awareness of the disparity of antecedents and termination. Apollo takes over the task of Hermes because Apollo, not Hermes, is the divinity saddled with the ordeal of the second play. But now Apollo is in disguise; his defense of Orestes's action and of the nuclear family is a performance in fancy dress, a Mardi Gras surprise.

The foundation tale recited by Athena in support of the competence of the Areopagus to sit in judgment on cases of murder is a terminal *aition*, an "explanation" analogous to what is found in Euripidean epilogues. But before the play is over, two further foundations have been celebrated: the institution of the alliance between Athens and Argos, commemorated in the reception on Athenian soil of the Argive Orestes; and the establishment of the cult of the Eumenides which we know from other accounts, including that of Sophocles's *Oedipus at Colonus*, to have been of some importance in Athenian worship. The tripling of foundation tales testifies to Aeschylus's desire to secure an ending that is concrete, familiar, and hallowed in Athenian ritual and contractual experience. In the face of these tangibilities, inapposite though they may seem, an excessive concern with logicality, and with the purport of the trilogy as a whole, would appear to be a piece of pedantry. The romantic expectation that the resolution of a tragedy must bring with it an equal mixture of victory and defeat gives way before an ending that pays little attention to the great issues of freedom and necessity, or even to the inescapable obsessions embodied in the world of Clytemnestra and Cassandra. That is, perhaps, precisely why the *Oresteia*, with its final celebration, has been found so satisfying as drama. As Hebbel put it: "Reconciliation in tragedy—most people mean by that that the contending powers first cudgel each other, and then go off dancing with each other." [12] The solving of social and ethical questions is not a priority business. Ionesco wants to eliminate the voicing of social problems and the simulating of precarious social conditions from serious drama. [13] The *Oresteia* partly bears

---

12. *Hebbels Dramaturgie*, ed. W. von Scholz (Munich and Leipzig, 1907), p. 128.
13. E. Ionesco, *Notes and Counter Notes* (New York, 1964), pp. 89 ff.

out his prescription. For the discontinuity of the social models used in the three plays is so great that we are tempted to conclude that each play uses social formulations only for its own restricted figurative purposes. In the end, deception removes the tragic sting and relaxes the spirit long before the satyr play takes over and substitutes animal energy for the heroic passions of the trilogy.

"Suppressions and sublimations alike are devices by which we endeavour to avoid issues which might bewilder us. The essence of tragedy is that it forces us to live for a moment without them."[14] But only for a moment. Attic drama delights in organizing human needs so enormous and aggressive that they do not fit the usual social and moral nexus. The need of Orestes is one such case. We are not to worry whether Orestes is right or wrong; the question of justice is not as important as the fact of the enormity. After the enormity has been given its full play, the author turns around and shows us how even the special case of Orestes, with due modifications, can be made to fit into a manageable human scheme. The social arrangement, then, is consequent upon the tragedy, not built into it. According to Greek religious thinking, the great destructive heroes, a Heracles or an Oedipus, can be integrated into the social fabric only after their death. The explosive force which in their lives compelled them to maim and kill is later, after they are safely in their sepulchres, thought to be employable for ends beneficial to the society. Similarly in *Eumenides*: the heroic stance and the irreducible conflict are laid aside, and a new order supervenes. In other plays, notably in Sophocles, no institutional arrangement or social fiat clears the air. The heroic fall triumphs over its setting. Perhaps this is tied in with the fact that Sophocles steered clear of the trilogic pattern. In Aeschylus, if we can regard *Eumenides* as a representative last play, accommodation wins out over significance and cunning over profundity.

By Aristotle's standards, Athena is a kind of dea ex machina. Her contribution seems to differ from that of a standard machine divinity only in that she appears within the drama, and not by way of an isolated epilogue. Her foundation speech delights with the concreteness of its stipulations. It contains an outer and an inner *aition*. The principal outer *aition* is the foundation of the court; the inner *aition* is the siege by the Amazons (685 ff.):

> . . . this hill, the encampment of
> The Amazons, whose armed battalions came
> To break a lance with Theseus; here they built
> Their bastion, to rival the older city,
> And sacrificed to Ares, whence the rock
> Derives its name.

14. I. A. Richards, *Principles of Literary Criticism* (New York and London, 1924), chap. 32.

The Amazons are avatars of the Furies. Hostile women whose aggression was, in the event, beneficially incorporated into the national experience, they come into the picture because the logical jump from suffering to celebration is relevant to what Athena is doing for the drama. The vivid colors of the national past in procession enhance the air of unreality imported by Apollo's tortuous observance of legal precedent, while also helping us to forget its less dignified moments. Athena's lecture paves the way for the settling of the Furies and introduces the coda of the torch parade. Such crowning processions are well known from Aristophanic Comedy. Just as the festive mayhem at the end of a comedy is in imitation of popular forms of celebration, so the final procession of *Eumenides* is a simulation of the Panathenaic torch parade. The Furies/Eumenides have been made into *metoikoi*, resident strangers (1011, 1018). We know that these resident strangers were especially favored at the Panathenaic Festival. The familiar patterns of the rejoicing take us out of the dim past and put us in the present, and thus furnish a more vital therapy than the ordinances of Euripidean epilogues, with their academic stiffness and their specious grandeur.

Having said all this, we must turn round and confess that we cannot after all think of Athena as a dea ex machina, for the good reason that the principal agents of *Eumenides* are themselves gods. For a machine god to be effective, he has to be shown breaking in upon a snarl of human confusion. In *Eumenides*, Orestes is a shadowy reminder of his former importance. The action of the play is a *Göttermimus*, a masque staged by contending gods. Homer's scenes on Olympus had accustomed generations of listeners to look upon divine contention as a likely source of humor. It is difficult to believe in the gravity of a quarrel between parties that cannot die, and therefore cannot stake their lives. There are differences. The threats of the Furies are, after all, directed at Orestes rather than at their fellow divinities, and we momentarily quake at the danger to the man. What is more, the Furies are underground divinities, and they constitute a chorus of undifferentiated characters. On neither score do they lend themselves easily to the kind of bourgeois comedy that the *Iliad* had made popular. With the Furies largely exempt from the more frivolous strains of the *Göttermimus*, the comedy gets deflected to the side of Apollo, to the discomposure of his dignity. This is also why Athena has to replace Apollo as the minister of Zeus. Being traditionally exempt from the foolishness of the *Göttermimus*—even in Homer she is not absorbed into its comic scheme—and because of her closer association with the land in which Aeschylus locates the resolution, she is the more credible authority. It is also worth remembering that it is under Athena's aegis that another compromise in a case of blood guilt is achieved—in the last book of the *Odyssey*, when the relatives of the dead suitors are about to overwhelm Odysseus and his small band. Contrary, then, to what the earlier segments of the trilogy may have suggested, the whole terminates not as a defense of Delphi, but in support of a more familiar order. Unlike Delphi, with its commitment to hierarchy and reaction, Athens can offer a tradition of tolerance and reconciliation.

Both the Furies and Apollo recognize the appropriateness of Athena's authority (*Eum.* 229–34). As the two parties announce why they had to act as they did—the Furies stating that it is the mother's blood that drives them, and Apollo responding that the wrath of a rebuffed suppliant cannot be endured—we find that both of them derive the motives for their respective roles from outside themselves: the Furies because they are driven, and Apollo because he fears the consequences of inaction. It is only with Athena that the action proposed becomes self-authenticating; she is not driven or beholden, but ushers in the compromise out of a joy in partnership that takes its inspiration from historical experience. The carefully balanced symmetry between Apollo and the Furies is broken when the former is dropped, rather unceremoniously, along with Orestes, at the end of Orestes's speech of thanks. Thereafter, what remains of the contention is between the Furies and Athena. But Athena's position as reconciler and innovator means that the Furies are merely hanging on to prolong the tensions of the play a little longer, rather than opening another valid round of conflict.

For the purposes of bringing the action to an end, with a display of color calculated to put our questions to sleep, Athena is in many ways a perfect instrument. Her own personality is an adventurous blend of contrasts. She is a woman, with the assurance and the temperament of a man, and a natural inclination to support the rights and activities of men. She presides over the peaceful activities of the household, but her armor associates her with war. Being a daughter of Zeus, she must be ranked with the newer generation of gods, but her championship of the city is immemorial. In the Homeric tradition, she is closely linked with the great heroes; but, as an emblem of Athens, she embodies the ambitions of a community of citizens. None of this is fully spelled out by Aeschylus. But her appearance on stage is bound to convey a deep sense of fairness and of a larger-than-life understanding. The Furies, certainly, acknowledge her qualifications as an arbitrator and consent to the trial. This is their undoing; as Furies they should not have consented to anything that minimizes the immediacy of their vengeance. To accede to an impartial tribunal is to prepare for defeat. Thus the case of Orestes is decided before half the play has run its course, at *Eum.* 435.

An Argive case is decided in Athens, apparently for no reason except that Aeschylus, to reinforce the persuasiveness of this artifice, wishes to link the trial with the establishment of the Areopagus. As a consequence, he adds the further fiction that the Eumenides venerated in Athens were originally Furies—to wit, the particular Furies that grew out of Clytemnestra's death. But the central displacement is the shift from Argos to Athens. How could the Athenian audience have taken to this? The answer is relatively simple: the dramatic tradition—or should we say the Aeschylean tradition?—plays with the identification of cities. The Argos featured in *Suppliants* is, as we can tell from the demarcation of the empire outlined by Pelasgus (254–70), really a stand-in for Athens. So is the Thebes of Oedipus, with its plague and its leader fallen from grace. The city represented on the dramatic stage is invested with the national experience of the audience. Mythological regionalism gives way to a more directly experienced parochialism. By the same token, there is no reason why an Athenian court should not be dramatically equipped to dispose of a case which only by the accident of a distant legend is said to be Argive. But then, wittily, Aeschylus breaks the illusion by reminding his audience of the treaty of friendship between the two cities, Argos and Athens. But that is a marginal reminder. More centrally, Argos is incorporated into Athens by the simple process of having Orestes take refuge in the only place where, in the spectators' view, he can hope to receive a fair trial, and where his lawyers can trust their persuasion to work.

Persuasion is a prominent theme throughout the trilogy. Indeed, no Attic tragedy can do without the awareness that men are easily moved by persuasion, though in some of the plays the power of persuasion is more prominent and more overtly identified than in others. In *Agamemnon*, Persuasion starts out in close company with Crime and *Atē* (385–86):

> Grim Persuasion, galling brood
> Of preemptive *Atē*, forces her way.

By the end of *Eumenides*, she has grown respectable by dint of Athena's pacification of the Furies, though Apollo's handling of her reminds us of her lasting capacity for skulduggery. Clytemnestra's rhetoric, as she soothes Agamemnon into a greedy docility, is seductive Persuasion at her most frightening. The lies of Orestes to Clytemnestra are more pedestrian, though their effect is not dissimilar. Athena's success with the Furies differs from Clytemnestra's success with her husband largely in that persuasion is now practiced for a beneficent purpose. But the technique is not greatly different; "suitable words" are spoken in order to charm a person into dropping his guard or renouncing a principle. The possibility of salutary persuasion is touched on early in the trilogy. In the entering chant of *Agamemnon* (94–95), the chorus remarks on the altars burning brightly,

> Drugged with the gentle artless
> Admonitions of sacred oil;

and when the chorus proceeds to the ode, the choristers ascribe the song to the power of divine persuasion (105–6). But soon thereafter we learn that Truculence, *tolma*, flowers through Persuasion, child of *Atē*; it corrupts man, and brings him to grief, and his city along with him. This passage (374 ff.), deals with the quality commonly called hubris. Its tenor is broad, and the abstract nature of the terminology enables Aeschylus to include within its field such disparate human experiences as war and sex. In both of these, Persuasion reigns supreme; as is implied in the line about the sacrificial fires, words, though commonly used, are not essential to its success. Helen exercises a silent persuasion upon Paris. Persuasion, along with Victory, is one of the auxiliary figures associated with sex in the emblem tradition started by Hesiod.

We may recall that Plato, in several of his dialogues, has Socrates face up to the double dominion of persuasion, for seduction as well as for teaching.[15] In Aeschylus, too, this ambivalence is recognized. In *Suppliants* (615 ff.), Persuasion leads to the success of Pelasgus's argument in the Argive assembly, but Persuasion is also a satellite of Aphrodite (1040). In *Prometheus* (172), the hero says that he will resist the persuasion (tantamount to blackmail and violence) which Zeus is going to practice on him. But he himself is scarcely more successful with his various attempts to persuade others, including his fellow Titans (333). In *Persians* (697), Darius is persuaded to appear, and Xerxes is persuaded by vain hope (804). On balance, only *Prometheus* assigns to Persuasion in its varied aspects as powerful a role in the drama as does the *Oresteia*; and in *Prometheus* persuasion fails. In this, the play resembles a number of Sophoclean dramas in which heroic characters withstand the blandishment of political persuasion, but are incapable of exercising their own more substantial persuasive powers effectively. The *Oresteia*, and especially *Eumenides*, is virtually unique in its terminal strategy of stripping away everything dubious from the successful exercise of persuasion.

Let us look more closely at one particular instance of Athena's skill. She tells the Furies (794 ff.) that there are three good reasons why they should be willing to compromise. First, the votes were equal, hence there is no defeat, no blow to their dignity.[16] Second, it is Zeus whose wishes are being followed; Apollo, Orestes's counsellor, is Zeus's representative. And finally,

15. G. R. Morrow, "Plato's Concept of Persuasion," *Philosophical Review* 62 (1953): 234–50. At *Laws* 722B ff., the instructive function of persuasion is virtually identified with its potential for seduction.

16. I follow the scholiast and Wilamowitz (*Aischylos-Interpretationen* [Berlin, 1914], p. 184) in believing that Athena is the twelfth juror, and that her vote makes for an equal division.

they will have a seat of worship into the bargain. Of these arguments, the first is an appeal to public opinion: the Furies should take comfort from the fact that in the healthy judgment of a politically experienced public, they are not regarded as losers (it is in Athena's interest that her reasoning should gloss over the fact that, not counting her own vote, a majority of the eleven votes went to them; see below). The second argument is an appeal to nature: if Zeus stands for normalcy and Right, his wishes stand for what is natural. Finally, the third argument is a bribe, especially as it is developed a little later (851 ff.): Athena holds out honors and privileges too good to turn down. But there is something else (826 ff.):

> I am close to Zeus; and I alone have access—
> Need I say it?—to the keys of the room
> In which his thunder is safely stored
> We do not need it, do we? I can persuade you . . . ?

This is a threat. But it is voiced only to be withdrawn in the same breath, the merest token of a threat, a delicate hint of mythological possibilities. Here again, the divine masque makes for opportunities that are closed to ordinary human drama. Athena is an adroit politician; but her success is qualified by the thought that, unlike human persuaders, she cannot fail. As the Furies ask her for a guarantee of her promise, her ingenious reply is impossible to translate and almost impossible to interpret unambiguously, though the Athenian audience would have found its general meaning familiar. A full paraphrase might run as follows (the parts in brackets are not in the Greek): [No need for me to give you a guarantee; my word is sufficient] because it is in my power not to say anything which I am [in fact] not going to do [which is tantamount to saying: it is in my power to do what I say I shall do; or better: it is my nature to say only what in fact I shall do]. The phrase between the brackets is by itself akin to the figure *litotes* championed in the rhetorical handbooks. The Furies, clearly anxious to surrender, accept the stratagem with pleasure, while noting (900) that they consider themselves bewitched.

Persuasion, then, is the mechanism which overcomes heroism and heroes and reduces them to the status of socially integrated citizenship. It accompanies love; it is wielded by demagogues, including tyrants. It implies bribery, and instruction; it bewitches, and helps to secure insight. In using Persuasion and appealing to her power, Athena employs the skills of an expert negotiator to break the resistance of the Furies and to apply the coup de grâce to the old order of heroism and clan loyalty. But Athena's reliance on Persuasion is also symptomatic of what Aeschylus does with his trilogy. Just as Athena manages to bend the will of the Furies and deflect them from their purpose, so Aeschylus, with the device of the transfer to Athens and the trial and the allaying of the Furies has practiced his kind of persuasion on an audience that may have expected something rather different—something that would perhaps continue to focus on the House of Atreus or that might terminate with a Delphic ritual. If the Furies are asked to abandon or compromise their expectations, so is the audience invited to accommodate itself to a solution whereby one kind of pleasure will be exchanged for another.

Unlike the philosopher, and unlike the lyric poet, the dramatist is in a position to plant the philosophical discussion of Right in an environment of action. Drama analyzes Right through action; agents expose the power and the obscurities of Right as they announce their intentions. Detached analysis, though not rare, is secondary to the meaning of the acts. Clytemnestra invokes the authority of Right as she persuades Agamemnon to step on the crimson materials. Her agitation, and his submission, are claimed for the rule of Right. The scene carries its own meaning; no reflection, no abstract disquisition, is required to communicate to us what Clytemnestra thinks, or pretends to think, Right to be.

Right (*dikē*) is one of Aeschylus's favorite words. His control of the concept is obvious from the frequency tables. *Eumenides*, one might expect, uses the word eighty times, perhaps a record for any significant noun in the Aeschylean text. Next closest are *Agamemnon*, with forty-nine occurrences, and *Libation-Bearers*, with forty. After that come *Suppliants*, with twenty-five; *Seven*, with nineteen; *Prometheus*, with eight, and *Persians*, with no occurrence at all.[17] It is this last figure that clinches the case: that Aeschylus should have written a play in which Right is not mentioned even once seems astounding, until one begins to realize that the argument of *Persians*, with its reliance on history, its tricky shuffling of the notions of barbarian and Greek, and its radical use of other antinomies, would have been fruitlessly tangled by a further introduction into the moral scheme of the tale of the principle of Right. That does not make *Persians* into an amoral play; it simply means that Right is not the only focus for a contemplation of morality.

Within the *Oresteia*, the meaning of Right shifts subtly. The chorus of *Libation-Bearers* sing of their *anankē amphiptolis* (75), the constraint exercised on them by the fact that they belong to two cities, their own—they are prisoners of war—and Argos. Unlike the chorus of *Agamemnon*, a vigorously indigenous body sure of its roots, the chorus of *Libation-Bearers* is rootless, supernational, hence more attached to individuals and to the ob-

17. I take the figures from H. G. Robertson, "Legal Expressions and Ideas of Justice in Aeschylus," *Classical Philology* 34 (1939): 209–19.

vious separability of right and wrong. "Right and not right" (78) is not part of the same universe of discourse as the Right memorialized at length by the chorus of *Agamemnon*. It is a matter of loyalty and personal identification, rather than of lofty moral principle determined by the welfare of the city or the court. The city justice of Athena in *Eumenides* could be said to revert to the Right of the elders after the temporary deflection witnessed in *Libation-Bearers*. Historically speaking, it would be fair to say that the three plays offer us concepts of Right as they might be expected to dominate in three worlds: the heroic, the tyrants', and the city's. One qualification is in order: in their commitment to revenge on behalf of Clytemnestra, the Furies exhibit the same narrow sense of loyalty as the chorus of *Libation-Bearers*. In the interrogation scene (*Eum.* 605 ff.), the Furies declare that they declined to pursue Clytemnestra because she had killed a man who was not of her own clan, while Orestes killed a blood relative. This puts Orestes in a quandary, and turning to Apollo he asks the same question that has just been asked by the Furies (490 ff., 612): whether killing Clytemnestra was in accord with Right. At this point, Apollo has his great chance to produce a theological case for the act he has demanded of Orestes, an act whose horror stands alongside such other horrors as the sacrifice of Isaac, the incest of Oedipus, and various other causes célèbres enjoined or foreseen by the gods. Apollo answers (614 ff.) that Zeus's power outweighs all else. That is, he uses the argument from the unknowability and irrationality of God. Because such an answer is even less satisfactory to an Athenian audience than, say, to a medieval one, Apollo proceeds to buttress its cogency with other pleas, taken largely from the arsenal about to be publicized by the Sophists. Perhaps Apollo, Zeus's representative turned barrister, is not the most suitable person to answer so difficult a question. Or the special difficulties of Aeschylus's dramatization of the old tale of the sons of Atreus are not easily reconciled with an exclusive fixing of Right. There *is* moral good and moral bad in Aeschylean drama. What is the relation of Right to them?

"It is remarkable that Greece did not have, properly speaking, a philosophy of law, but rather . . . a philosophy of justice; remarkable also that, in Aristotle's theory, the most substantial part of justice . . . is the 'distributive justice' by which the 'parts' are not discovered but constituted." This comes from what is perhaps the finest modern book on Greek social institutions, Louis Gernet's *Droit et société dans la Grèce ancienne* (Paris, 1955).[18] What Gernet is saying is that Athenian justice, unlike Roman law, failed to recognize the notion of individual rights or objectively existing rights needing to be adjusted to each other. Rather, Greek thought recognized an objective notion of justice which is flexibly and subtly applied to individual

18. P. 81.

cases. What the individual may claim for himself and for his actions can be determined to be "right" only in the light of a standard to which his own needs and titles are not readily related. As applied to Orestes, this means that he has no case validated by his position or his moral standing. His case becomes adjudicable only in terms of what society requires and what a very broad sense of equity demands.

Looked at in this light, Apollo's answer is not unintelligible. Right (*to dikaion*), he says, has a certain authority; the resolve of Zeus must be followed; no oath used in support of asserting *to dikaion* is stronger than Zeus (*Eum.* 619–21). At first glance, this looks as if Apollo were out to depreciate *to dikaion*, the principle insisted on by the Furies. More likely, however, he is merely emphasizing the multivalence of the term and its comprehensiveness under the aegis of Zeus. Drama being a dynamic record of actions undertaken by agents, its language registers a constant drift from abstractions and neutral terms toward the interests of the agents. Zeus cannot be kept entirely distinct from Right, even though certain dramatic situations appear to make room for a friction between the two. The absorption of Right into the rule of Zeus is further encouraged by the clearly demonstrable connotation of *dikē* in the sense of "the rule of the stronger" and of its passive equivalent, "not getting into trouble." [19] Above all, however, Apollo appears to be driving home the point that Right is not to be associated with this or that individual or family, but is a universal concept, identifiable primarily with the universal rule embodied in Zeus.

Still, our own habits of thought predispose us to a certain skepticism concerning the moral authority of Zeus. In the debate between the Furies and Apollo, the former, nourished by a strong sense of their own victimization, would appear to answer for some kind of justice, while the credentials cited by Apollo imply a larger human tolerance. But these conceptual extensions are not apparent in the words of the contest, in which Apollo meets the complaints of the Furies with arguments from administrative convenience and institutional arbitrariness. This goes far to enlist our sympathies on behalf of the Furies, and to make us look critically at what Apollo and Orestes have to say: a desirable enough effect at this stage of the dramatic proceedings.

What has happened to the original emphasis on Right by the time the trilogy is complete? For the first time in Western thought, an explicit and significant distinction is made between Right in the sense of what a person may expect as payment for a crime obviously and measurably committed;

19. V. A. Rodgers, "Some Thoughts on DIKĒ," *CQ* 21 (1971): 289–301. The multivalence of the term is noted also by E. A. Havelock, *The Greek Concept of Justice* (Cambridge, Mass., 1978), chap. 16, "The Justice of Aeschylus." For a speech by *Dikē*, perhaps from *The Women of Aetne*, see fr. 282 Lloyd-Jones.

and Right in the sense of an institutional arrangement for the ascertaining of the guilt or innocence of a person.[20] This shifts the dramatic focus from the personal to the legal, from the play of forces in which the agent is automatically caught up to the fiction that a person is to be defined in terms of what he has done. The development heralds a new understanding of personality. If the new insight is taken seriously, it is fated to lead to the death of Attic tragedy. For tragedy is predicated on the assumption that gods and men, divine forces and human ambitions, cooperate in the establishment of a crime. The new Right, with its increasing separation of the human from the divine, and its measurement of motives and opportunities in human terms, is a vital step in the history of jurisprudence, but it leaves drama without the resonance it needs. The conversation between the Furies and Athena (428 ff.) compactly registers the change from one species of litigation to another. The Furies make their appeal to oaths—to the ancient system of compurgation; Athena counters this by proposing an examination of the issues with herself as arbitrator, an offer which the Furies accept. The swearing of oaths secures the gods as guarantors; the newer form of litigation is an exercise in human resources. Because it is the last play of its trilogy, *Eumenides* can live with the new fiction. But its presence once again confirms the difficulty of relating the developments of the final play to its antecedents.

The trial makes it possible to look at the various issues tidily and symmetrically. But the divided vote also argues the larger insolubility of the case. The goddess's decision to support acquittal records society's ability to secure a settlement in a spirit of philosophical laissez-faire. One way of putting it is to say that Equity wins out over Right, and that if it had not, the gods would stand condemned. Recent investigations have shown that the roots of the Golden Rule reach back into the fifth century B.C.[21] Indeed, it is hard to conceive of a civilization that does not recognize humane exceptions to a strict constructionism. But quite apart from the legal issue, too methodical an emphasis on the justification of what the trial has to offer is mistaken. A trial is a performance; if there were doubts about this, the remarks of Socrates in the *Apology* should allay them. At an Athenian trial, especially one of the blue-ribbon variety, the jurors were apparently ready enough to have their sense of justice swayed by their sense of spectacle. How

---

20. Anticipations of this systematic distinction are, of course, found in earlier literature from Hesiod on.

21. A. Dihle, *Die goldene Regel* (*Studienhefte zur Altertumswiss.* 7; Göttingen, 1962). See also G. Murray, *Aeschylus* (Oxford, 1940), pp. 199 ff. R. Schottländer, "Um die moralische Qualität des Freispruchs in den *Eumeniden*," *Das Altertum* 16 (1970): 144–53 argues, unconvincingly I think, that the acquittal is based not on equity or any stretching of the law, but on the legally sanctioned need to secure a provider for the household.

much more likely is this to have been the case in the theater, where no juror's oath and no critical consequences for a human life interfered with an untroubled enjoyment of forbidding issues conveniently settled.

As an outgrowth of the artistic scheme, the trial has its own cogency. In *Agamemnon* and *Libation-Bearers*, the trial is figurative. The *agōn* through which the principal characters have to pass is one of the vital images of the drama. Agamemnon and Menelaus are imagined to be dwellers in the same house, so that together they can become plaintiffs against Paris and Priam. The expedition to Troy is a kind of suit. In *Libation-Bearers* (726–29) the chorus chants:

> The time is ripe for Cunning and Charm
> To join our ranks; for Hermes the god
> Of Night and shades to direct their steps
> In the trial of murderous sword-play.

In *Eumenides*, the trial ceases to be a figure of speech and turns visible and audible. Its standing as a concrete summation of an earlier network of tropes makes for a more compelling persuasiveness. The bloody urn into which the gods had cast their votes against Troy (*Agam.* 813–17) becomes the vessel into which Athena has the jurors place their ballots. It would be going too far to say that the divine jurors have been replaced by human jurors; the jurisdiction of the gods is not easily caught in the terminology of the popular law courts. In any case, the vote of Athena counts. Divine direction and human agency continue to move in step, in spite of the new institutions. Still, the freeing of shapes and concepts from their initial bondage in figurative discourse goes hand in hand with the emancipation of men as practitioners of Right.

To be sure, Athena remarks (*Eum.* 470–72) that the issue is too great for men; but she adds that for herself to be sole judge would not be proper either. As it stands, this double negation is peculiar; we may assume that it is Athena's way of wiping the slate clean for the introduction of the new relationship that is about to be announced (487–88). The momentum is shifting toward what men can do for themselves—and that means toward the institutional. It has been observed that *Eumenides* is the only play in the tragic repertory in which Athens has no king.[22] Dramatically speaking, the presence of a king would have cut into Athena's authority, and imperilled her supposed impartiality towards the litigants. More important, perhaps, Aeschylus eliminated the king as head of state, in defiance of what the conventions and the density of tragedy rightly require, in order to absolve

---

22. E. R. Dodds, "Morals and Politics in the *Oresteia*," *Proc. Cambridge Philol. Soc.* 186 (1960): 20.

the institution celebrated of all possible intimations of arbitrary power and individual fallibility.

The establishment of the court involves some curious circumstances. For one thing, as we have seen, Athena rules herself not competent on her own to judge cases of homicide. For another, she admits that the Furies have a substantial case and that if they do not win it, they will cause much trouble for the country. In this respect, the position of the Furies is analogous to that of Orestes, of whom Apollo has said (*Eum.* 232–34) that a suppliant must be assisted, for if he is not, his wrath is terrible; or like that of the Danaids in *Suppliants*, whose menace Pelasgus found himself unable to resist. The solidity of a case is felt to be a direct function of the power of the litigant to harm. In the political and legal experience of the Athenians, this may often have been the case. But, at this juncture, the formulation is probably due to other considerations, which have something to do with the tradition of myth. In the case of the Danaids, no compromise is contemplated or possible. The threat of the women is too dangerous to tamper with. *Eumenides* permits a compromise. But Athena's nodding reference to the atavistic fear reminds us how far removed we are from an enlightened recognition of the legal claims of those out of power. And the language remains sufficiently obscure to leave it unclear (470 ff.) whether it is she or the jurors who will do the "discerning" of the action. In the end, her announcement of her own vote *prior* to the decision of the jurors completes a sequence of irregularities and deflections well equipped to support the central business of persuasion, or deception, and to remind us that this is not life but play-acting. The argument with which she bolsters her vote, her favoring of the male and paternal principle, is plausible enough in a goddess who is widely recognized as a woman only in the most formal sense of the word. But its relation to the evident issues of the trilogy is, like other relations we have examined, extremely artificial. The mythology and the etiology do little more than confirm the power of Zeus. Athena's contribution, we conclude, is not a verdict, properly speaking, but a first buoyant use, to best advantage, of a novel piece of machinery, with little concern whether that use answers demonstrable moral needs.

The outcome of the trial is fully anticipated. Earlier in the play (179 ff.), Apollo has, in the strongest and most shocking terms, called on the Furies to remove themselves from the scene, when they round on him (198 ff.) and successfully engage him in a discussion of the legal aspects of the case, and he falls in with their wish. The respective arguments advanced—the Furies pushing the demands of the clan, Apollo deliberately misunderstanding them and supporting the sanctions of matrimony—are not gainsaid or bettered by anything that follows. The length of the subsequent proceedings, and the drama of the conflicting positions, is sheer theater. At one point, Athena invites the Furies to become "producers" (583–84):

> The plaintiff, telling his full story first,
> Becomes, I think, a producer of the action.

The word here translated as "producer" is *didaskalos*. It has two principal meanings in Greek: "teacher," and "theatrical producer," i.e., the poet staging his drama. There is no juridical sense attached to the term. Whether the use of the word here is punning or not, its implication of pleasing presentation is obvious. The trial is not only a legal dispute, it is also part of the dramatic contest. It is an *agōn* in both senses.

After Apollo has put forward his arguments against motherhood and on behalf of Argos, Athena cuts off debate. The exchange between the Furies and Apollo is, therefore, rather brief (622–73). Aeschylus provides nothing to compare with Euripides's full analyses of moral and legal positions. Should we blame Athena for her haste, or commend her for her tactfulness? Is she putting the Furies at a disadvantage? Is she saving Apollo from the need to plead a virtually hopeless case? The truth is that no further debate is needed, since the "conversion" of the Furies has already started with their great ode (490 ff.). The main issue now is not an analysis of the opposing views, but a healing of the breach. It would have been difficult to insist on a fair trial, for Apollo has told us that he is going to act as witness, as counsel, and as a defendant in his own right (576–79). Perhaps our understanding of Apollo's words is unduly exact; a later remark by Orestes (609) suggests that "witness" is too technical a translation. Apollo is, more probably, offering himself as an "interpreter" of religious ordinances and traditions. In that case, "witnessing" would have nothing to do with evidence, but with religious thinking which, Apollo and Orestes believe, provides arguments in their support.

But the tergiversations and sophistries which Apollo undertakes in defense of his client-colleague are precisely the kind of courtroom fireworks which the Athenians had come to expect of their best speakers.[23] His "bewitching words" (81) bring to Orestes salvation and success. For once, Apollo is not the purifier (see below) or the oracular champion of truth, but the patron divinity of one man, a peacetime replica of his role in the *Iliad*. He had compelled Orestes to carry out his deed; now he labors to save his man from the consequences. The effort is surely noble; if in practice it necessitates unseemly and distracting pleading, so be it. Supposedly Apollo

---

23. For the sophistries of the god, see K. Reinhardt, *Aischylos als Regisseur und Theologe* (Bern, 1949), pp. 144 ff. He concludes that the trial constitutes an evasion rather than an answer to the ultimate questions.

instructed Orestes in what he was to say in his defense. But, before long, Orestes leaves the speaking to his protector, a decision which could, at a pinch, be reconciled with the Athenian legal requirement that a foreigner cannot speak in his own behalf but must be represented by counsel, though the Furies do not seem to recognize this provision when they express surprise at the fact that Orestes does not respond to their charges (303).

The irrationalities of Apollo's performance are easily punctured by the Furies. At one point (640–43), they convict him of a fallacy. Apollo had argued, in defense of Orestes's deed, that Zeus considers killing a father a graver matter than killing a mother. But is it not true, the Furies ask, that Zeus had shackled (and, the implication is, virtually eliminated) his own father? Though they do not say so, they further imply that the tradition has nothing about Zeus misbehaving toward his mother, or condoning such misbehavior in anyone else. In answer to the demonstration of the blunder, Apollo turns abusive and falls back on the distinction between binding and killing: Zeus can free a man as easily as he has bound him, but even he cannot undo a killing. Apollo's first argument was based on the tacit assumption that the power of Zeus must be the source of all explanations, an assumption which the earlier segments of the trilogy had done much to fortify. The rebuttal of the Furies reduces Apollo to the position of throwing doubt on that power. The "philosophical" theme—with its echo of Xenophanes—that Zeus can do and undo as he wishes, without the slightest effort, is undercut by the reminder, common in tragedy, that death does not bow even to the gods.

Given that the crime of Orestes was carried out on behalf of his father, and that the trial must take this into account, it is curious how little is done to build up Agamemnon's stature during the winding down of the trilogy. Apollo's words (631–32) are remarkably diffident about the man, with a diffidence bordering upon evasion:

> When he came home from the war, having managed
> Most things well, she received him . . .

Because the tragedy has not shown Agamemnon as a person greatly worth avenging, the counsel for the defense might be expected to repair his image. What Apollo furnishes instead is something quite different. He argues that a mother is not a parent but a temporary shelter for the fetus, and one that is sometimes not even required for the birth of the child, as the legends concerning Zeus and Dionysus and others indicate. A modern audience is likely to find little humor in this, unless it has fallen under the spell of recent psychoanalytic speculations concerning the void of parenthood; ancient audiences, more conditioned by the defensive machismo of the culture, may have found the conceit tolerably amusing. The silliness is merely part of a larger complex of frivolities. The chorus has asked (652–56) how Orestes, now that he has committed matricide, can once more become a full member of the religious and political community. The argument against mother-hood that follows is not exactly attuned to the chorus's signal. It is, more-over, coupled with an announcement that strays even further from the con-text: Apollo says that he has sent Orestes to Athens to create a bond between Athens and Argos. One would think that Apollo would have to provide better reasons for the ritual admissibility of Orestes before appointing him to his ambassadorship. Instead, Apollo acts the aggressive lawyer: he im-plies, with his reference to the mission of Orestes, that it would be foolish to ask about the man's qualifications. Since he is already an ambassador, how could he not be admissible?

Critics have ransacked the ancient records for traces of the theory of male superiority which Apollo advances. Pythagoreans, Egyptians, Hippocrat-ics, and others have been put under obligation as the source.[24] But, as George Thomson has rightly seen, the emphasis on the role of the male and on the authority of the father is one of the buttresses of the new democracy. By comparison with oligarchic Sparta, or with the heroic world of Homer, democratic Athens allowed its women but a negligible social role. What Apollo gives us is a forensic ad hoc argument, emphasizing the physical or natural, rather than the ethical—a gross exaggeration of an emphasis which the Athenians valued, and which it was relatively easy to adjust to the Hesiodic tradition of Zeus the Ruler. The extravagance of the reasoning is intentional; its cleverness will have registered easily enough with the male chauvinists in the audience.

Apollo has little need, in this scene, to be attractive; attractiveness is being reserved for Athena. Apollo acts as a lightning rod for the undesirable impressions that might conceivably be attached to her stand. In the end, in spite of momentary transmogrification, Apollo can always be rescued by the reminder that he is merely carrying out the will of Zeus. If, in the process, he uses lines of argument that get Zeus himself embroiled, the gambit is amusing, but without lasting effect upon his credibility. It is not, I think, correct to conclude that the portrait of Apollo in *Eumenides* is intended to be critical of the god or of Delphi. In the light of Apollo's standing elsewhere in the trilogy, and in the light of what all Athenians would recognize to be the legitimate pressures of the courtroom, there is little blackening.

There is, in fact, no character to be blackened. Quite apart from what we have said about the ascendancy of action over character in Aeschylus, gods must always behave in mysterious ways, even in a drama as close to comic opera as *Eumenides* in parts is. The sophistry could, at worst, be considered a

24. For Pythagoreans and Egyptians, see A. Peretti, "La teoria della generazione pa-trilinea in Eschilo," *Parola del Passato* 11 (1956): 241–62.

light-hearted commentary on known courtroom practices; its association with the god is, as it were, accidental. We must be careful not to turn solemn about the exaggerations expounded by the lawyer god. Let us leave them what they are, clever distortions devised to cope with an embarrassing situation and to help move the tragic complex to its "solution."

It is true, however, that the theme at the heart of the rhetoric is by no means new. The contrasting of women and men (along with the occasional blotting out of the contrast) forms one of the lasting preoccupations of the trilogy.[25] And there may just be a grain of truth in Kenneth Burke's suggestion that guilt surfaces specifically as guilt towards women as a class: "Women, socially submerged . . . may thus come to stand for nearly all submerged motives. . . . And in this trilogy, problems of social conscience, as reflected in the individual conscience, are finally resolved by an astounding intellectual . . . feat whereby women's *biological* function of childbearing is in effect denied, through being interpreted in purely social terms."[26] Does this mean that Aeschylus, the progressive, is assisting women out of their purdah by giving us, in the end, a male chauvinist in all his priggishness to laugh at? Hardly. Still, the honors paid to the Furies turned Eumenides, and the standing of Athena, half male as she is, suggest that we take Apollo's special pleading to be little more than a trifling version of Agamemnon's insistence on male prerogative.

The *Oresteia* is not the only drama in which the tension between men and women is enacted. The stage contrast between the immobilized, purposeful Prometheus and the agitated, alienated Io; the opposition in *Suppliants* between the Danaids and the Egyptians; the difficulties that Eteocles in *Seven* has with the women of Thebes: all these bear down on the same conflict between temperaments and between allegiances.[27] This is, in fact, one of the differences between the epic and the drama. In Homer, the great tensions exist between men. Even in the *Odyssey*, the relations between men and women are not the fuel that fires the tale. But in Attic drama, the great tensions are often enacted between the opposite sexes, even where—as in the extant plays of Aeschylus and Sophocles—love is played down. It is as if, in the severely repressive social climate of Athens, hobbled rights were allowed to reassert themselves through the protest medium of popular drama. But where Sophocles and Euripides are willing to put on stage women who are both feminine and heroic, Aeschylus plays on the percep-

25. M. Gagarin, *Aeschylean Drama* (Berkeley and Los Angeles, 1976), chap. 4, "Sexual and Political Conflict in the *Oresteia*."

26. K. Burke, *Language as Symbolic Action* (Berkeley and Los Angeles, 1966), pp. 129–30.

27. G. J. M. J. te Riele, *Les femmes chez Éschyle* (Paris, 1956). See also R. P. Winnington-Ingram, "Clytemnestra and the Vote of Athena," *JHS* 68 (1948): 130–47.

tion that the natural woman is not of heroic dimensions. Hence the emphasis on unnatural masculine elements in Clytemnestra's constitution. The
natural woman is afraid, and to be pitied. Even an Electra, in Aeschylus's
conception, can enter into effective action only if led by a man. Women who
want to leave their imprint on society must be denatured, which may explain the song about female monsters (*Lib.* 585 ff.). Aegisthus is called a
woman because he does nothing on his own (*Agam.* 1625) except in the
secrecy of the bedchamber. He is a woman-man to complement Clytemnestra's man-woman. Athena, the divine man-woman, points up, e con-
trario, the weakness and insignificance of a mere woman. The distance
between men and women is narrowed as the trilogy proceeds; Apollo's pa-
ternalistic fireworks are a last flaring up of a perspective which the progress
of the trilogy is about to render irrelevant or illusory.

Deceptive persuasion is carried out on one further level. In *Libation-
Bearers* we had been told, by the chorus as well as by Orestes, that Orestes,
as the next step after the murder of Clytemnestra, would seek purification at
the hand of Apollo. When Orestes enters the precinct of Athena, he says
that he is *not* coming as a suppliant, and that his journey has brought him
into many homes; he is, or his pollution is,

> Blunted down, and scoured, from contact with
> The houses of men, and goings back and forth.
> (*Eum.* 238–39)

The meaning must be that Orestes regards his reception into many homes as
part of the mechanism, if not the major mechanism, of his cleansing. His
words leave us with the impression that the visits were not only a proof of
his increasing purity—the implication is that his hosts came to no harm
from associating with him—but also a significant means towards achieving
the cleansing. The pig's blood mentioned a little later (283), as Orestes
harks back to the instructions of Apollo, is the more conventional, not to say
primitive, detergent. Now we happen to know that purificatory rites by the
use of animal blood were foreign to Delphi and those institutions, like
the Delphinion in Athens, associated with Delphi.[28] The idea points in the
direction of Eleusis, rather than to the worship of Apollo. So for Orestes to
say (281–83) that the pollution has been washed off with pig's blood at the
altar of Phoebus is both strange in itself and conflicts with the gradualism
and the more cultivated spirit of the reference to travel and hospitality. The
Furies, for their part, cannot accept his words; their binding song (321 ff.)

---

28. This and the following point are made by R. R. Dyer in *Gnomon* 39 (1967): 189–
90, and in "The Evidence for Apolline Purification Rituals at Delphi and Athens," *JHS* 89
(1969): 38–56.

testifies to their continuing belief that Orestes is polluted, and that he is theirs to snatch—but perhaps also to their fear that he is managing to escape their claim on him. The gulf between that claim and the dramatic and psychological realities is widening. Athena, who had not been present when Orestes talked about his status, supposes (441) that he is a suppliant in the manner of Ixion. Now we know, from this very play (717–18) that Ixion was the first to shed blood; we also know that he was purified by Zeus after getting nowhere with his pleas to other gods. A fragment of Aeschylus speaks of Zeus undertaking a purification by pig's blood.[29] Athena, one presumes, meets Orestes with certain traditional assumptions about his status and his need. Orestes replies that he is in no need of purification; his purification with blood and water has already been accomplished in other homes.

The upshot of all this appears to be that Aeschylus wanted Orestes cleansed before he entered Athena's precinct and the law court, but that at the same time he did not want Apollo prominently involved in the cleansing, in spite of what had been suggested at the end of *Libation-Bearers*, when Apollo was, for all practical purposes, the only authority for good or ill. And yet, a little later again, at 578, Apollo says of himself that he has cleansed this man of murder. What are we to make of this hide-and-seek play with the motif of purification by blood? What is the precise relation between ritual cleansing and abatement of the shame by educational travel and time, all of which are put in the past so that Orestes may now appear on stage and ask for nothing but justice? Is there a suggestion of the incompleteness or even irrelevance of physical purification? In spite of our comparative ignorance about the details of Athenian homicide law in the fifth century B.C., this much seems certain: it paid little attention to the issue of clarifying its relation to the fact of pollution.[30] We have many texts that show that penalties were applied to secure vengeance, or deterrence, but only one that appears to say that the object of a penalty was to get rid of pollution. Considering the emphasis placed on a juridical resolution of the trilogy, it is understandable that Aeschylus would find himself embarrassed by the competing claims of the judicial and the ritual. What he is apparently trying to do is to bring in the ritual without encumbering the significance of the court proceedings. To omit the ritual aspects entirely would have been unthinkable, given the strength of the ritual constraints upon the

29. Fr. 182 Smyth.

30. D. M. MacDowell, *Athenian Homicide Law in the Age of the Orators* (Manchester, 1963), p. 150: "It is unwise to take for granted a belief in pollution was fundamental to Athenian homicide law. It is possible that it was no more than the subject of an appendix." The solitary text referred to is Demosthenes 23.72.

tradition, and of the conservative attitudes prevalent in the audience. So purification, and pig's blood, are introduced at the risk of confusing the issue, but the pertinent data are jumbled so as to leave us with no clear picture of how they fit in. It is enough that, in their confusion, they assure us that Orestes has done, and suffered, everything he must, to serve his new function as ambassador.

Finally, the "conversion" of the Furies is a piece of inventive theatricality that crowns the persuasive contrivance of the drama. One recent critic has some harsh words about the conclusion of *Eumenides*. I cite his words at length because, in their own articulate way, they pose an important question:

> In the *Eumenides* . . . the problem of what to do with the arbitrary, vengeful, bloody-minded deities of tribal primitivism is all-absorbing, and the solutions highly significant. Blood-guilt, symbolized by the obscene pursuing Furies, is to be exorcised by way of the statute-book. Athena herself will intervene to modernise Athenian justice and cast a democratic vote in favour of acquittal. . . . The moral presumption of this programme is only matched by its stupidity. . . . Far more dangerous [than Aeschylus's and Pericles's attempt to transform Zeus into an abstract idea], certainly in psychological terms, was their naive attempt to neutralize dark irrational daemons such as the Furies, together with the whole bloody, ghost-haunted legacy of Athens' pre-rational past. The attempt not only failed; it had effects which could not be undone. . . . [The Furies] sat demurely while a civic committee put fancy costumes on them, changed their name (that old crypto-magical standby so dear to all rationalists) and offered them a niche under the Acropolis. Then, the moment it was dark, they winged their way back to the place from which it had taken aeons to remove them—the inner recesses of the human mind—and there they have remained ever since, defying all efforts to remove them. In a broader sense, they went underground, along with various other chthonian creepy-crawlies, and began to pop up again, in disturbing places, as the Peloponnesian War dragged on.[31]

Thus Aeschylus is held partly responsible for the spectres which Sigmund Freud attempted to exorcise more recently. It is an intriguing conceit, but to go along with it one has to believe that Aeschylus wants to be accepted as a philosopher, a physician, or a therapist. Much better to take a leaf from Aeschylus's cat-and-mouse play with the theme of purification, accept the deception for what it does and is, and go along with the preposterous idea that Furies can be gentle. But we need not go very far to do that. In actual fact, there is little about the metamorphosis of the Furies that goes against the ancient grain. The abode which Athena assigns to

31. P. Green, *The Shadow of the Parthenon* (Berkeley and Los Angeles, 1972), pp. 41–43.

them at the end is really not so very different from the god-given, respected abode in the earth in which they have always lived (389–96). As the Furies sing the song of blessings, whose length shows that it is the finale to the whole trilogy and not just to *Eumenides* (916 ff.), Athena vigorously reminds us of their great power to punish the sins of the fathers (930–37, 954–55, 990). Long before (698), Athena had counselled the citizens not to banish fear. The terror for which the Furies stand continues to be recognized as an important element in all public life. The temptation is to translate the pertinent terms as "awe" or "respect" or "discipline"—just as Aristotle was to intellectualize and civilize the understanding of "fear" in his analysis of tragedy. The fear which is at issue in the continued rule of the Furies is radical and elemental: the fear of the gods, the fear of the law, the fear that is felt at the dead of night. It is the same fear that Orestes felt both before the murder, when he was exposed to the threats of Apollo, and after. The fear now recommended by Athena and the Furies is more productive, socially and politically; it is, as often as not, a shrinking from an action, rather than being terrorized into action. But the experience of the terror is the same.

The continuing talk of fear hints that, in the new dispensation, the Furies continue to exercise their ancient rights. Their admission (902) that they have been converted has an improbable air about it. The only song they know is the song of vengeance; what are they to sing about now? So Athena has to instruct them in a new song. She does so by giving them a beautiful sample of the kind of ode that the Danaids had known how to sing spontaneously: about the blessings of fertility. The Furies prove adequate students, throwing themselves whole-heartedly into what Horace more than four hundred years later would have branded a ludicrous specimen of lack of decorum. The exchange and the reconciliation of the Furies are, structurally, an afterthought. They are very exposed, not part of the body of the drama, but a special epilogue, outdoing the rationalizations, the *aitia*, of Athena and Orestes with a super-*aition*. But with all this, the darker side of the Furies is preserved so that the transformation becomes almost acceptable. Even now that they are settled in Athens and are granting good as well as ill, their old name of Furies remains with them (950). "Eumenides" does not occur in our text, though it is conceivable that the name may have occurred in a line now dropped out. And in calling up the blessings, the Furies turn to the Fates (961–67), as if the task were too much for them unaided. The conversion of the Furies turns out to be both more and less than it promises: less, because they remain the dark, fear-inspiring spirits they had always been; more, because the festive comedy at the end of the trilogy lifts what happens to the Furies, to Orestes, and to all who cooperate in the masque, well above the level of intent with which the earlier drama had acquainted us. In the end, the trilogy bursts its bounds, the need for solutions and consequences is forgotten, and we participate in the liberation *from* tragedy that the final moments secure.

There is, then, much to perplex those who regard the form of the trilogy as a convenient vehicle of resolution. The Aristotelian principles of unity, wholeness, coherence, and economy have been subjected to much criticism, also in relation to more recent dramatic traditions. But Georg Lukács was probably correct in saying about classical tragedy that from the point of view of the agents and of its conception of the world it is a posteriori, and that therefore it does not insist on thinking its issues through to the end, while modern—i.e., nineteenth-century—drama is used to illumine and give meaning to the phenomena of life.[32] Our trilogy confirms Lukács's perception. It is an instrument designed in the end to make light of the points in which life and thought fail to measure up to one another, and to strike capital from their incongruence. It is, in its way, a certification of the autonomy of art. Aeschylus the persuader, the master of nourishing deception, produces a satisfactory progression from the demonic vastness of *Agamemnon* to the sophistries and the celebration of *Eumenides*. We, the audience, perceive the daring of the route; we also feel that we have reached a saving terminus. Other trilogies, we must assume, furnished different "solutions." In writing and producing his trilogies, Aeschylus created his own brand of dramatic continuity. Unlike some later playwrights who composed plays in multiples and who insisted on the conceptual cogency of their patterns—Goethe, Grillparzer, and Claudel come to mind—Aeschylus devised his trilogy to succeed at one sitting, and to provide his audience with at least the appearance of a progression from chaos to order. In this, he gave considerably more than was thought proper or probable by Hebbel, who wrote: "It is foolish to demand from the poet what God himself cannot offer, reconciliation and a tempering of dissonances. But we can at least demand that he give us the dissonances, rather than taking a position half way between the accidental and the necessary."[33] It is the greatness of Aeschylean drama that, in its accurate conception of what makes for power-

---

32. G. Lukács, *Schriften zur Literatursoziologie*[2], ed. P. Ludz (Neuwied, 1963), p. 293: "[Die alte] Tragödie ist vom Gesichtspunkt der handelnden Personen und der Stilisierung der Welt aposteriorisch. Daher ist auch das theoretische zu Ende Gedachtsein des Problems weniger notwendig. Die Neuen hingegen nehmen als erstes die Tragödie wahr und sehen in dessen Beleuchtung die einzelnen Erscheinungen des Lebens, die Menschen und Geschehnisse des Dramas; die Tragödie ist hier dem Leben gegenüber apriorisch." The essay dates from 1909.

33. *Hebbels Dramaturgie*, p. 116.

ful theater, it can overcome the shortcomings of both of Hebbel's options. The dissonances are by no means suppressed. But in the festive clamor of the final scenes they are set aside as if they no longer mattered. The tragedy is completed, and transcended; the festival carries the day.

# APPENDIX

## THE LIFE AND TIMES OF AESCHYLUS

Readers of this book will have been disappointed to find that I have made very little effort to connect Aeschylus's drama with the events and the developments of the time in which the playwright lived, and especially that I have not explored the possible links between the institutional arrangements staged in *Eumenides* and the reconstitution of the Areopagus, the most honored court in Athens, in 462 B.C. The reason for this omission is my sense that the pleas offered in support of such links have been speculative and the results uncertain. Even the most persuasive arguments, such as those of E. R. Dodds and K. J. Dover, have added more to our understanding of the social and political circumstances in which the playwright worked than to our appreciation of the plays themselves.[1] Still, Aeschylus lived at a time and in a city whose fortunes favored a broad spectrum of shared experience. To be a citizen of Athens meant to share in a well-defined, clearly articulated corporate life. What is more, the momentum of social and political change during Aeschylus's lifetime is bound to have left its imprint on his productions. When he was born, the city was under the rule of a family of tyrants, who had broken the power of the nobles and favored small peasants and merchants; its political influence abroad was limited, in spite of its increasingly strong position in trade and commerce. When Aeschylus died, the tyrants had long been expelled; the city had become the most radical democracy the world has ever seen; it had defeated the Persians, and had built up a maritime empire that stretched across the Aegean and dominated large parts of mainland Greece.[2]

The expansion of the Persian kingdom and its repeated checks by Greek fighting men were the most significant factors shaping the life of which Aeschylus was a part. Through their contacts with the Persian king and his

1. K. J. Dover, "The Political Aspect of Aeschylus' *Eumenides,*" *JHS* 77.2 (1957): 230– 37; E. R. Dodds, "Morals and Politics in the *Oresteia,*" *Proc. Cambridge Philol. Soc.* 186 (1960): 19–31. See also A. J. Podlecki, *The Political Background of Aeschylean Tragedy* (Ann Arbor, Mich., 1966).
2. For a convenient discussion of the relevant historical developments, see N. G. L. Hammond, *A History of Greece* [2] (Oxford, 1967).

provincial administrators, and through their travels, the Athenians had acquired a knowledge of the Eastern world, including Egypt and Mesopotamia and the country northeast of the Crimea, which greatly enlarged their cultural horizon. In the west, Aeschylus's younger and middle years coincided with the consolidation of Greek settlements in Sicily under a group of tyrants, notably Gelon and Hieron, who became strong enough to repel the advances of the Carthaginians and of the Etruscans. The tradition appears to know of two occasions on which Aeschylus responded to an invitation from Sicily, once when Hieron was at the height of his power and wished Aeschylus to honor his reign with a performance, and later when the tyranny had been abolished and the citizens of Gela exercised their free choice in asking the playwright to live among them. It may be that Sicily in the middle of the fifth century B.C. had for the mainland Greeks some of the attractions of modernity and adventurous living that America once had for European artists and intellectuals. In any case, Aeschylus spent the last two years of his life in Sicily, and died there, in Gela.[3]

Within Greece, the greatest power during Aeschylus's youth was the Peloponnesian League, under the leadership of Sparta and her kings. As Athens gained in strength and influence, her relations with Sparta became sometimes difficult, although the Persian threat compelled them to cooperate on many occasions, a cooperation which lasted intermittently until about five years before Aeschylus's death. Throughout the latter half of the sixth century and the first half of the fifth, Athens often found herself at war on more than one front. Her relations with other city-states and regional bodies were regulated by a complex, and often changing, set of treaties. Some students of the period have found reflections of these relationships within the plays. It is said, for instance, that the setting of *Suppliants* and the details of what is said in the play about Argos can be explained in terms of the compact then in force between Athens and that state, and that the choice of the legend was perhaps in the first instance dictated by the prominence of Argos in the political thinking of the day.[4] But even if this is true—and we should remember that Sophocles's *Oedipus King* was performed at a time when Athens was at war with Thebes—the gain for our understanding of the drama would be minimal.

Internally, Athens went through a remarkable development. Ten or

3. For the visits to Sicily, see C. J. Herington, "Aeschylus in Sicily," *JHS* 87 (1967): 74–85. M. Griffith, "Aeschylus, Sicily and *Prometheus*," *Dionysiaca by Former Pupils of Denys Page* (Cambridge, 1978), pp. 105–39, finds no evidence for Aeschylus's Sicilian periods in the plays themselves.

4. Ch. Gülke, *Mythos und Zeitgeschichte bei Aischylos* (*Beiträge z. klass. Philologie* 31; Meisenheim, 1969), pp. 61 ff.

eleven years after Aeschylus was born, Hipparchus, the more brilliant of the brothers who occupied the tyranny of the city, was murdered; four years later, his brother Hippias was expelled and the tyranny came to an end. From then on, beginning with the reforms of Clisthenes in 508, when Aeschylus was probably getting his military training, the city-state embarked on a program of democratization, which reached its climax two years before Aeschylus's death with the bill that empowered the *zeugitai*, the men of the second-lowest property ranking, to serve as magistrates. Four years earlier, Ephialtes, the patron and predecessor of Pericles in the position of acknowledged popular leader, had deprived the last stronghold of the old landed gentry, the Areopagus, of its remaining political power, and had reassigned most of its legal functions to broadly based citizens' courts. The progressive democratization of the city coincided with the start of an ambitious building program, making municipal Athens into one of the architectural jewels of Greece, and with the construction of a navy that came to dominate the high seas from Sicily to Syria and from the Dardanelles to Africa. In the end, the Delian maritime confederacy which Athens established and led for defensive purposes turned into an empire, stamped with all the marks of a cruel and exploitative tyranny. But Aeschylus had died by the time the members of the confederacy came to regard Athens as their brutal mistress rather than their principal ally.

A word is in order about the intellectual revolution we associate with fifth-century Athens. The sixth century had witnessed the rise of the pre-Socratic philosopher-scientists, from the grand cosmological speculations of Thales to the dark sayings of Heraclitus. In the fifth century, their successors, including Empedocles and Anaxagoras, continued to refine the insights of the philosophers.[5] In the popular mind their efforts were linked with those who were later called "Sophists," itinerant teachers who offered instruction in a number of disciplines geared to an improved management of the lives of cities and of individuals. Gorgias and Protagoras, the earliest of the Sophists, were born about a generation before Aeschylus's death; Socrates was their younger contemporary. The intellectual currents broadcast by these teachers were not yet fully available during Aeschylus's time. But it is no exaggeration to say that his own plays, and those of Sophocles, are in many ways dramatic anticipations of some of the issues—questions of justice, of good government, of personal integrity and of man's challenge to divine ambivalence—which were to exercise the ingenuities of the next generation (for some details, see above, chapter 11). Aeschylus's own satyr plays, not discussed in this book, often turn upon themes of invention and

5. See the literature cited in W. Rösler, *Reflexe vorsokratischen Denkens bei Aischylos (Beiträge z. klass. Philologie* 37; Meisenheim, 1970).

discovery, a *topos* which the Sophists found useful in their lectures and publications.[6]

One of our difficulties in correlating the evidence of the plays with the world into which Aeschylus was born is that the extant plays date from the last sixteen years of Aeschylus's life. If, in the course of his career as a dramatist, he allowed his material and his approaches to be shaped by the fast-changing events taking place around him, we lack much of the evidence that would confirm this. His response to the increasing radicalization of institutions—he was close to forty when the chief magistracies ceased being elective and became assigned by lot—is variously interpreted. Some have called him a conservative, others a progressive. Throughout his life, he performed his duties as a citizen. Aeschylus, our sources tell us, fought at Marathon, where his brother gave his life, at Thermopylae, at Salamis, and at Plataea; we may assume that he was engaged in other battles as well. The funeral inscription that is said to have marked his tomb refers to him as a citizen and a soldier, and makes no mention of his role as a playwright, an omission which speaks for the genuineness of the tradition.[7] It is altogether likely that Aeschylus was well acquainted not only with prominent citizens and politicians, but with artists and philosophers and writers, who, especially beginning in the second quarter of the fifth century, began to visit Athens or even make their homes in an environment hospitable to innovation and change. Attempts to associate this or that character in his plays with prominent figures of his day have failed to enlist a consensus. Again, attempts to link certain passages in his oeuvre with the writings of Pindar, Xenophanes, or Protagoras have proved unavailing, and even if they were successful they would tell us little that we did not already know about the function of the passages within the larger work.

The best we can do, for the purposes of the present book, is to lay out the ancient evidence bearing on Aeschylus's life, confining ourselves to infor-

6. For the fragments of the lost plays, see A. Nauck, ed., *Tragicorum Graecorum Fragmenta*[2] (Leipzig, 1889), and the forthcoming third volume of B. Snell, ed., *Tragicorum Graecorum Fragmenta* (Göttingen). Translations of the more important fragments are to be found in H. W. Smyth, ed. and tr., *Aeschylus* (Cambridge, Mass., 1922, 1926; 2nd volume rev. by H. Lloyd-Jones, 1957), and in H. J. Mette, tr. and comm., *Der Verlorene Aischylos* (Berlin, 1963), a work based on Mette's own collection of the fragments: *Die Fragmente der Tragödien des Aischylos* (Berlin, 1959). For a succinct discussion of the satyr plays see R. G. Ussher, "The Other Aeschylus," *Phoenix* 31 (1977): 297–99.

7. The epitaph may be translated as follows:

> Aeschylus, son of Euphorion, of Athens, lies beneath
> this marker, at wheat-rich Gela, where he died.
> For his manhood and fame, ask the plain of Marathon,
> and the long-haired Persians, who found out.

mation that is either reliable or highly plausible, and leaving out, with one exception (the tale of Aeschylus's death), the many embellishments with which a later tradition, stimulated by the wondrous world of the plays, saw fit to garnish the little they knew.[8] The skeletal biography that has come down is given in one column; in the other I cite a selection of dates and events which may help to give some indication of the political and social setting of Aeschylus's career. The ancient sources are primarily a *Life* that appears in the Medicean manuscript, and which apparently goes back to the researches of Chamaeleon, a Peripatetic scholar of ca. 300 B.C.; the *Hypotheseis* attached to some of the plays in several manuscripts (for the *Life* and the *Hypotheseis*, see above, chapter 1); the *Marmor Parium*, a Hellenistic marble chronicle registering important dates from the time of Cecrops and the founding fathers of Athens down to the third century B.C.; the *Suda* (formerly named Suidas), a Byzantine encyclopedia of the tenth century A.D. incorporating much valuable information from earlier collections; a papyrus of ca. 200 A.D. reporting on Aeschylus's victory with the tetralogy containing *Suppliants*;[9] and several other papyrus scraps with pertinent entries. Between them, these documents provide us with the data whose authority is generally accepted.

It will be useful to quote a few brief excerpts from the *Life*: "An Athenian by birth, of the borough of Eleusis, of noble lineage. Started composing tragedies as a young man . . . a contemporary of Pindar. Born in the sixtyfourth Olympiad . . . participated in the battles of Marathon, Salamis, and Plataea. . . . He visited Hieron . . . because he felt the Athenians did not value him and because the young Sophocles had defeated him. . . . In Aetne, just established by Hieron, he staged *Women of Aetne*. . . . Highly honored by the tyrant Hieron and the citizens of Gela, he lived there for some two years. . . . He died an old man, when an eagle snatched up a

---

8. The fullest collection of the evidence bearing on Aeschylus's life is by F. Schoell, ed. *De Aeschyli vita et poesi testimonia veterum*, in F. Ritschl, ed., *Aeschylus: Septem adversus Thebas* (Leipzig, 1875), pp. 3–52. Notable interpretations of the evidence are found in U. von Wilamowitz-Moellendorff, *Aischylos-Interpretationen* (Berlin, 1914), pp. 231–52; W. Schmid, *Geschichte der griechischen Literatur*, vol. 2 (Munich, 1934), pp. 184–93; and A. Lesky, *History of Greek Literature* (London, 1966), pp. 242–43. The ancient *Life* and the ancient lists of Aeschylean titles are studied by W. Steffen, *Studia Aeschylea praecipue ad deperditarum fabularum fragmenta pertinentia* (Wroclaw, 1958); also by A. Wartelle, *Histoire du texte d'Éschyle dans l'antiquité* (Paris, 1971), pp. 19–38. It should finally be mentioned that not all scholars accept the dates that we have for Aeschylus's life. For a recent systematic attack on Hellenistic methods of computing biographical dates, see A. A. Mosshammer, "Geometrical Proportion and the Chronological Method of Apollodorus," *TAPA* 106 (1976): 291–306.

9. E. G. Turner reviews *Oxyrhynchus papyrus* no. 2256, fr. 3 in *Classical Review* 4 (1954): 20–24.

# COMPARATIVE TABLE OF DATES AND EVENTS

| 525 | Birth of A. |
|---|---|
| ca. 522 | Execution of Polycrates, tyrant of Samos |
| 522 | Accession of Darius; consolidation of the Persian Empire |
| 518 | Birth of Pindar |
| ca. 515 | Birth of Parmenides |
| 514 | Murder of Hipparchus, tyrant of Athens |
| ca. 513 | Darius invades Scythia |
| ca. 510 | Croton destroys Sybaris |
| 510 | Expulsion of Hippias, tyrant of Athens |
| 508 | Clisthenes begins his constitutional reforms |
| ca. 500 | Ionians revolt against Persia |
| ca. 500 | Birth of Phidias; birth of Anaxagoras |
| 499–96 | A.'s first dramatic competition |
| ca. 493 | Birth of Empedocles |
| 493 | Themistocles chief magistrate in Athens |
| 490 | Battle of Marathon |
| 486 | Death of Darius; Xerxes king of Persia |
| ca. 485 | Birth of Protagoras |

| | |
|---|---|
| 484 | A.'s first dramatic victory |
| 472 | A. victorious with *Persians*; expenses borne by Pericles |
| 468 | A. defeated by Sophocles |
| 468 | A.'s first journey to Sicily: performance of *Women of Aetne*; perhaps revival of *Persians* |
| 467 | A. victorious with *Seven* |
| 463 (?) | A. victorious with *Suppliants*; Sophocles comes in second |
| 458 | A. victorious with the *Oresteia* |
| 458 | A.'s second journey to Sicily |
| 456 | A. dies at Gela in Sicily |

| | |
|---|---|
| 483 | Athens embarks on shipbuilding program |
| 481–61 | Intermittent cooperation between Athens and Sparta |
| 480 | Battles of Thermopylae and Salamis |
| 479 | Battle of Plataea |
| 478 | Hieron becomes tyrant of Syracuse |
| 478 | Foundation of Delian Maritime League |
| 475 ff. | Cimon and others begin a building program in Athens |
| 474 | Hieron defeats the Etruscans at Cumae |
| ca. 471 | Themistocles ostracised |
| ca. 470 | Birth of Socrates |
| ca. 469 | Athenian defeat of Persians at Eurymedon |
| 468 | Death of Simonides |
| 465 | Xerxes murdered; Artaxerxes king of Persia |
| ca. 465 | Sparta struck by earthquake; uprising of Helots |
| 462 | Cimon leads Athenian relief force to Sparta; rebuffed |
| 462 | Ephialtes strips Areopagus of its powers |
| 461 | Cimon ostracised; Ephialtes murdered |
| 461 | Sicilian tyranny abolished |
| 460 | Athenian expedition to defeat Persians in Egypt |
| 457 | Zeugitae empowered to serve as magistrates |
| 456 | Aegina placed under Athenian control |

tortoise and, unable to control its prey, dropped it on the rocks to crack its shell, but the tortoise hit the poet and killed him.[10] . . . He lived for sixty-eight years. . . . It is said that Hieron asked him to revive *Persians* in Sicily. . . ." The *Life* also has much about Aeschylus's accomplishments as a creator of drama and especially as an inventor of new dramatic conventions and forms. There are references in it to scenes in plays of which we have only fragments, and to revivals of his plays after his death.

Aeschylus was over forty years old before he achieved his first victory. Unlike Sophocles, who began winning competitions early in his career, Aeschylus had to wait fifteen years before a jury awarded him his first prize. But, in all, Aeschylus is reported to have won victories with thirteen tetralogies—that is, on an average, every other year after he started winning. The total number of plays ascribed to him, including satyr plays, varies between seventy-three and ninety. We know the titles of eighty-three, and possess fragments of many of them, but in most cases we are unable to determine which are the titles that together make up the trilogies and tetralogies. We have no reliable portrait; Aeschylus died two generations before Socrates, the inspirer of the first authentic portrait sculpture in Greece.

10. See also Spenser's *The Shepheards Calender* (1579), "May," lines 213–28, where the same tale is told of the death of Algrin, a possible mask for Bishop Grindal.

# SELECT BIBLIOGRAPHY

The Bibliography is arranged by rubrics rather than alphabetically. Within each rubric the order is chronological. The standard of selection is severe but varied; I have chosen items on grounds of quality, or of coverage, or because the recent date of the publication and the references to earlier treatments found in it make it representative. In many cases I have had to omit a plausible listing in favor of one that seemed to me to provide a more convenient introduction to the topic at issue. I have included both highly specialized discussions and works of competent popularization, in the belief that it would not do to omit triumphs of classical scholarship even from a book that primarily addresses non-specialists. Some of the items cited in the footnotes do not appear in the Bibliography. Conversely the Bibliography contains titles that do not occur in the notes. I trust that the discrepancy, prompted by my desire for economy, will not cause surprise or inconvenience.

## GREEK DRAMA

*General Discussion*

U. von Wilamowitz-Moellendorff, *Einleitung in die griechische Tragödie* (Berlin, 1906).

P. Friedländer, "Die griechische Tragödie und das Tragische," *Die Antike* 1 (1925): 5 ff., 295 ff.

H. D. F. Kitto, *Greek Tragedy: A Literary Study* (London, 1939).

R. Lattimore, *The Poetry of Greek Tragedy* (Baltimore, 1958).

J. de Romilly, *L'évolution du pathétique d'Éschyle à Euripide* (Paris, 1961).

K. von Fritz, *Antike und moderne Tragödie* (Berlin, 1962).

A. Lesky, tr. H. A. Frankfort, *Greek Tragedy* (London, 1965).

W. Steidle, *Studien zum antiken Drama* (Studia et Testimonia antiqua 4; Munich, 1968).

J. de Romilly, *La tragédie grecque* (Paris, 1970).

J. Ferguson, *A Companion to Greek Tragedy* (Austin, Tex., 1972).

A. Lesky, *Die tragische Dichtung der Hellenen*[3] (Göttingen, 1972).

G. A. Seeck, ed., *Das griechische Drama* (Darmstadt, 1979).

B. M. W. Knox, *Word and Action: Essays on the Ancient Theater* (Baltimore, 1979).

*Stage Antiquities*

L. Séchan, *Études sur la tragédie grecque* (Paris, 1926).

R. Löhrer, *Mienenspiel und Maske in der griechischen Tragödie* (Studien zur Geschichte und Kultur des Altertums 14.4–5; Paderborn, 1927).

M. Bieber, *The History of the Greek and Roman Theater* (Princeton, 1939).

A. W. Pickard-Cambridge, *The Theatre of Dionysus in Athens* (Oxford, 1946).
P. Arnott, *Greek Scenic Conventions in the Fifth Century B.C.* (Oxford, 1962).
I. Brooke, *Costume in Greek Classic Drama* (London, 1962).
A. D. Trendall and T. B. L. Webster, *Illustrations of Greek Drama* (London, 1971).
E. Simon, *Das antike Theater* (Heidelberg, 1972).
S. Melchinger, *Das Theater der Tragödie: Aischylos, Sophokles, Euripides auf der Bühne ihrer Zeit* (Munich, 1974).

*Origins and History*

A. Peretti, *Epirrema e tragedia* (Florence, 1939).
A. D. Ure, "Threshing-Floor or Vineyard," *Classical Quarterly* 5 (1955): 225–30.
H. Schreckenberg, *Drama: Vom Werden der griechischen Tragödie aus dem Tanz* (Würzburg, 1960).
H. Patzer, *Die Anfänge der griechischen Tragödie* (Wiesbaden, 1962).
A. W. Pickard-Cambridge, rev. T. B. L. Webster, *Dithyramb, Tragedy and Comedy*[2] (Oxford, 1962).
G. F. Else, *The Origin and Early Form of Greek Tragedy* (Cambridge, Mass., 1965).
A. W. Pickard-Cambridge, rev. J. Gould and D. M. Lewis, *The Dramatic Festivals of Athens*[2] (Oxford, 1968).
H. J. Mette, *Urkunden dramatischer Aufführungen in Griechenland* (*Texte und Kommentare* 8; Berlin, 1977).

*Actors and Chorus*

W. Kranz, *Stasimon: Untersuchungen zu Form und Gestalt der griechischen Tragödie* (Berlin, 1933).
H. D. F. Kitto, "The Dance in Greek Tragedy," *Journal of Hellenic Studies* 75 (1955): 36–41.
A. M. Dale, "The Chorus in the Action of Greek Tragedy," in *Classical Drama and Its Influence: Essays Presented to H. D. F. Kitto* (London, 1965).
G. Prudhommeau, *La danse grecque antique* (Paris, 1965).
M. Alexiou, *The Ritual Lament in Greek Tradition* (Cambridge, 1974).
P. Ghiron-Bistaque, *Recherches sur les acteurs dans la Grèce antique* (Paris, 1976).
D. Bain, *Actors and Audience: Study of Asides and Related Conventions in Greek Drama* (Oxford, 1977).
O. Taplin, *Greek Tragedy in Action* (Berkeley and Los Angeles, 1978).
G. M. Sifakis, "Children in Greek Tragedy," *Bulletin of the Institute of Classical Studies* 26 (London, 1979): 67–80.

*Structure*

W. Schadewaldt, *Monolog und Selbstgespräch* (Berlin, 1926).
J. Duchemin, L'AGŌN *dans la tragédie grecque* (Paris, 1945).
W. Jens, *Die Stichomythie in der frühen griechischen Tragödie* (*Zetemata* 11; Munich, 1953).
R. Lattimore, *Story Patterns in Greek Tragedy* (Ann Arbor, Mich., 1964).
L. di Gregorio, *Le scene d'annunzio nella tragedia greca* (Milan, 1967).
W. Jens, ed., *Die Bauformen der griechischen Tragödie* (Munich, 1971).
R. Hamilton, "Announced Entrances in Greek Tragedy," *Harvard Studies in Classical Philology* 82 (1978): 63–82.

*Language and Thought*

L. Bergson, *L'épithète ornamental, dans Éschyle, Sophocle et Euripide* (Uppsala, 1956).
H. F. Johansen, *General Reflection in Greek Tragic Rhesis* (Copenhagen, 1959).

B. M. W. Knox, "Second Thoughts in Greek Tragedy," *Greek, Roman, and Byzantine Studies* 7 (1966): 213–32.

J. de Romilly, *Time in Greek Tragedy* (Ithaca, N.Y., 1968).

H. Parry, *The Lyric Poems of Greek Tragedy* (Toronto, 1978).

J. Gould, "Dramatic Character and 'Human Intelligibility' in Greek Tragedy," *Proceedings of the Cambridge Philological Society* 204 (1978): 43–67.

S. Said, *La faute tragique* (Paris, 1978).

### Aristotle and Tragedy

H. House, *Aristotle's Poetics* (London, 1956; rev. 1964).

G. F. Else, *Aristotle's Poetics: The Argument* (Cambridge, Mass., 1957).

J. Jones, *On Aristotle and Greek Tragedy* (Oxford, 1962).

A. W. H. Adkins, "Aristotle and the Best Kind of Tragedy," *Classical Quarterly* 16 (1966): 78–102.

H. D. F. Kitto, "Catharsis," in *The Classical Tradition: Literary and Historical Studies in Honor of Harry Caplan* (Ithaca, N.Y., 1966), pp. 133–47.

D. W. Lucas, ed. and comm., *Aristotle: Poetics* (Oxford, 1968).

E. Schütrumpf, *Die Bedeutung des Wortes ēthos in der Poetik des Aristoteles* (*Zetemata* 49; Munich, 1970).

S. Radt, "Aristoteles und die Tragödie," *Mnemosyne* 24 (1971): 189–205.

H. Flashar, "Aristoteles und Brecht," *Poetica* 6 (1974): 17–37.

T. C. W. Stinton, "*Hamartia* in Aristotle and Greek Tragedy," *Classical Quarterly* 25 (1975): 221–54.

D. Keesey, "On Some Recent Interpretations of Katharsis," *Classical World* 72 (1978/9): 193–207.

A. B. Neschke, *Die Poetik des Aristoteles* (Frankfurt, 1980).

### Versification and Music

A. M. Dale, *The Lyric Metres of Greek Drama* (Cambridge, 1948; rev. 1968).

K. H. Lee, "The Influence of Metre on Tragic Vocabulary," *Glotta* 46 (1968): 54–56.

C. Prato, *Ricerche sul trimetro dei tragici greci* (*Studi di metrica classica* 6; Rome, 1975).

E. Pöhlmann, "Die Notenschrift in der Überlieferung der griechischen Bühnenmusik," *Würzburger Jahrbücher* 2 (1976): 53–73.

## AESCHYLUS

### Bibliographies

A. G. McKay, "A Survey of Recent Work on Aeschylus," *Classical World* 48 (1955): 145–50, 153–59; 59 (1965): 40–48, 65–75.

A. Wartelle, *Bibliographie historique et critique d'Éschyle* (Paris, 1978).

### Dictionary

G. Italie, *Lexicon Aeschyleum* (Leiden, 1955; 2nd ed. 1964); addenda and corrigenda in H. J. Mette 1959 (see below, *Fragments*), pp. 291–307.

### Modern Editions and Translations

U. von Wilamowitz-Moellendorff, ed. *Aeschyli Tragoediae* (Berlin, 1914).

H. W. Smyth, ed. and tr., *Aeschylus* (Cambridge, Mass., 1922, 1926; 2nd volume rev. 1957 by H. Lloyd-Jones).

P. Mazon, ed. and tr., *Éschyle*⁵ (Paris, 1949–52).

O. Werner, ed. and tr., *Aischylos: Tragödien und Fragmente* (Munich, 1959).
D. Page, ed., *Aeschyli Tragoediae* (Oxford, 1972).
D. Grene and R. Lattimore, eds. and trs. *Complete Greek Tragedies* I (Chicago, 1959).

*Transmission*

A. Turyn, *The Manuscript Tradition of the Tragedies of Aeschylus* (New York, 1943).
R. D. Dawe, *The Collation and Investigation of Manuscripts of Aeschylus* (Cambridge, 1964).
G. Thomson, "The Intrusive Gloss," *Classical Quarterly* 17 (1967): 232–43.
A. Wartelle, *Histoire du texte d'Éschyle dans l'antiquité* (Paris, 1971).
W. Spoerri, "Die Edition der Aischylosscholien," *Museum Helveticum* 37 (1980): 1–24.

*Fragments*

A. Nauck, *Tragicorum graecorum fragmenta*[2] (Leipzig, 1889; 2nd enlarged ed. Hildesheim, 1964).
H. W. Smyth and H. Lloyd-Jones (see above, *Modern Editions and Translations*).
W. Steffen, *Studia Aeschylea* (Wroclaw, 1958).
F. Solmsen, *Hesiod and Aeschylus* (Ithaca, N.Y., 1949).
D. Kaufmann-Bühler, *Begriff und Funktion der Dike in den Tragödien des Aischylos* (Bonn, 1955).
W. Kiefner, *Der religiöse Allbegriff des Aischylos* (*Spudasmata* 5; Hildesheim, 1966).
A. Rivier, "Remarques sur le 'nécessaire' et la 'nécessité' chez Éschyle," *Revue des études grecques* 81 (1968): 5–39.
W. Rösler, *Reflexe vorsokratischen Denkens bei Aischylos* (*Beiträge zur klassischen Philologie* 37; Meisenheim, 1970).
G. M. A. Grube, "Zeus in Aeschylus," *American Journal of Philology* 91 (1970): 43–51.

*Special Topics*

S. Srebrny, *Wort und Gedanke bei Aischylos* (Wroclaw, 1964).
A. J. Podlecki, *The Political Background of Aeschylean Tragedy* (Ann Arbor, Mich., 1966).
A. Lesky, "Decision and Responsibility in the Tragedy of Aeschylus," *Journal of Hellenic Studies* 86 (1966): 78–85.
O. Taplin, "Aeschylean Silences and Silences in Aeschylus," *Harvard Studies in Classical Philology* 76 (1972): 57–97.
P. E. Easterling, "Presentation of Character in Aeschylus," *Greece and Rome* 20 (1973): 3–19.

*Diction and Style*

C. F. Kumaniecki, *De elocutionis Aeschyleae natura* (Cracow, 1935).
J. Seewald, *Untersuchungen zu Stil und Komposition der aischyleischen Tragödie* (*Greifswalder Beiträge* 14; Greifswald, 1936).
W. B. Stanford, *Aeschylus in his Style* (Dublin, 1942).
F. R. Earp, *The Style of Aeschylus* (Cambridge, 1948).
O. Hiltbrunner, *Wiederholungs- und Motivtechnik bei Aischylos* (Bern, 1950).
A. Sideras, *Aeschylus Homericus: Untersuchungen zu den Homerismen der aieschyleischen Sprache* (*Hypomnemata* 31; Göttingen, 1971).
S. Ireland, "Stichomythia in Aeschylus," *Hermes* 102 (1974): 509–24.
D. Sansone, *Aeschylean Metaphors for Intellectual Activity* (*Hermes Einzelschriften* 35; Berlin, 1975).

H. J. Mette, ed., *Die Fragmente der Tragödien des Aischylos* (Berlin, 1959); addenda in *Lustrum* 13 (1968): 513–34; 18 (1975): 338–44.

H. J. Mette, tr. and comm., *Der Verlorene Aischylos* (Berlin, 1963).

R. G. Ussher, "The Other Aeschylus," *Phoenix* 31 (1977): 287–99.

*The Life of Aeschylus*

F. Schoell, ed., *De Aeschyli Vita et Poesi Testimonia Veterum*, in F. Ritschl, ed., *Aeschylus: Septem adversus Thebas* (Leipzig, 1875), pp. 3–52.

W. Steffen (see above, *Fragments*).

M. Griffith, "Aeschylus, Sicily and *Prometheus*," in *Dionysiaca by Former Pupils of Denys Page* (Cambridge, 1978), pp. 105–39.

*General Discussion*

U. von Wilamowitz-Moellendorff, *Aischylos-Interpretationen* (Berlin, 1914).

H. W. Smyth, *Aeschylean Tragedy* (Berkeley and Los Angeles, 1924).

W. Porzig, *Die attische Tragödie des Aischylos* (Leipzig, 1926).

B. Snell, *Aischylos und das Handeln im Drama* (*Philologus Suppl.* 20.1; Leipzig, 1928).

M. Croiset, *Éschyle: Études sur l'invention dramatique dans son théâtre* (Paris, 1928).

G. Murray, *Aeschylus* (Oxford, 1940).

G. D. Thomson, *Aeschylus and Athens* (London, 1941).

K. Reinhardt, *Aischylos als Regisseur und Theologe* (Bern, 1949).

J. de Romilly, *La crainte et l'angoisse dans le théâtre d'Éschyle* (Paris, 1958).

H. D. F. Kitto, *Poiesis* (Berkeley and Los Angeles, 1966), pp. 33–115.

E. Hommel, ed., *Wege zu Aischylos* (Darmstadt, 1974).

M. Gagarin, *Aeschylean Drama* (Berkeley and Los Angeles, 1976).

O. Taplin, *The Stagecraft of Aeschylus* (Oxford, 1977).

V. di Benedetto, *L'ideologia del potere e la tragedia greca: Ricerche su Eschilo* (Turin, 1978).

*Aeschylus as Religious Thinker*

F. Solmsen, "Strata of Greek Religion in Aeschylus," *Harvard Theological Review* 40 (1947): 211–26.

*Imagery*

J. Dumortier, *Les images dans la poésie d'Éschyle* (Paris, 1935).

D. van Nes, *Die maritime Bildersprache des Aischylos* (Groningen, 1963).

W. C. Scott, "Wind Imagery in the *Oresteia*," *Transactions of the American Philological Association* 97 (1966): 459–71.

A. Lebeck, *The Oresteia: A Study in Language and Structure* (Cambridge, Mass., 1971).

## THE TRAGEDIES

*Persians*

P. Groeneboom, ed. and comm., *Aeschylus: Persae* (Groningen, 1930).

L. Roussel, ed. and comm., *Éschyle: Les Perses* (Montpellier, 1960).

H. D. Broadhead, ed. and comm., *The Persae of Aeschylus* (Cambridge, 1960).

A. J. Podlecki, tr. and comm., *Aeschylus: The Persians* (Englewood Cliffs, N.J., 1970).

H. D. F. Kitto, "Political Thought in Aeschylus," *Dioniso* 43 (1969): 159–67.

E. B. Holtsmark, "Ring Composition and the *Persae* of Aeschylus," *Symbolae Osloenses* 45 (1970): 5–23.

M. Anderson, "The Imagery of the *Persians*," *Greece and Rome* 19 (1972): 166–74.

J. Vogt, "Die Hellenisierung der Perser in der Tragödie des Aischylos," in *Festschrift H. E. Stier* (Muenster, 1972), pp. 131–45.

R. P. Winnington-Ingram, "Zeus in the *Persae*," *Journal of Hellenic Studies* 93 (1973): 210–19.

D. J. Conacher, "Aeschylus' *Persae*: A Literary Commentary," in *Serta Turyniana* (Urbana, Ill., 1974), pp. 143–68.

## Seven Against Thebes

T. G. Tucker, ed., tr. and comm., *The Seven Against Thebes of Aeschylus* (Cambridge, 1908).

C. M.Dawson, tr. and comm., *Aeschylus: The Seven Against Thebes* (Englewood Cliffs, N.J., 1970).

A. Hecht and H. H. Bacon, trs., *Aeschylus: Seven Against Thebes* (New York, 1973).

F. Solmsen, "The Erinys in Aischylos' *Septem*," *Transactions of the American Philological Association* 68 (1937): 197–211.

E. Wolff, "Die Entscheidung des Eteokles in den *Sieben gegen Theben*," *Harvard Studies in Classical Philology* 63 (1958): 89–95.

B. Otis, "The Unity of the *Seven Against Thebes*," *Greek, Roman and Byzantine Studies* 3 (1960): 153–74.

W. Schadewaldt, "Die Wappnung des Eteokles," in *Eranion H. Hommel* (Tübingen, 1961), pp. 105–116.

T. G. Rosenmeyer, "*Seven Against Thebes*: The Tragedy of War," *Arion* 1.1 (1962): 48–78; repr. in Rosenmeyer, *The Masks of Tragedy* (Austin, Tex., 1963): 5–48.

A. P. Burnett, "Curse and Dream in Aeschylus' *Septem*," *Greek, Roman and Byzantine Studies* 14 (1973): 343–68.

R. P. Winnington-Ingram, "*Septem Contra Thebas*," in T. F. Gould and C. J. Herington, eds., *Greek Tragedy* (*Yale Classical Studies* 25; New Haven, Conn., 1977), pp. 1–48.

A. L. Brown, "Eteocles and the Chorus in the *Seven Against Thebes*," *Phoenix* 31 (1977): 300–318.

W. G. Thalmann, *Dramatic Art in Aeschylus: Seven Against Thebes* (*Yale Classical Monographs* 1; New Haven, Conn., 1978).

R. D. Dawe, "The End of *Seven Against Thebes* Yet Again," in *Dionysiaca by Former Pupils of Denys Page* (Cambridge, 1978), pp. 87–103.

## Suppliants

H. F. Johansen and O. Smith, eds. and trs., *Aeschylus: The Suppliants* (Copenhagen, 1970).

J. Lembke, tr., *Aeschylus: The Suppliants* (New York, 1975).

R. D. Murray, *The Motif of Io in Aeschylus' Suppliants* (Princeton, N.J., 1958).

A. E. Garvie, *Aeschylus' Supplices: Play and Trilogy* (Cambridge, 1969).

C. Gülke, *Mythos und Zeitgeschichte bei Aischylos* (*Beiträge zur klassischen Philologie* 31; Meisenheim, 1969).

John Gould, "HIKETEIA," *Journal of Hellenic Studies* 93 (1973): 74–103.

P. Burian, "Pelasgus and Politics in Aeschylus' Danaid Trilogy," *Wiener Studien* 8 (1974): 5–14.

R. S. Caldwell, "The Psychology of Aeschylus' *Supplices*," *Arethusa* 7 (1974): 45–70.

M. McCall, "The Secondary Choruses in Aeschylus' *Supplices*," *California Studies in Classical Antiquity* 9 (1977): 117–31.

*The Oresteia*

G. Thomson, tr., *Aeschylus: The Oresteia*, in W. H. Auden, ed., *The Portable Greek Reader* (New York, 1948): 249–373.

R. Lattimore, tr., *Aeschylus: Oresteia*, in D. Grene and R. Lattimore, eds., *The Complete Greek Tragedies* I (Chicago, 1953).

R. Fagles, tr., and W. B. Stanford, comm., *The Oresteia* (New York, 1975).

R. Lowell, tr., *The Oresteia of Aeschylus* (New York, 1978).

K. Burke, "Form and Persecution in the *Oresteia*," *Sewanee Review* 60 (1952): 377–96.

E. T. Owen, *The Harmony of Aeschylus* (Toronto, 1952).

R. Kuhns, *The House, The City and The Judge* (Indianapolis, 1962).

F. I. Zeitlin, "The Motif of the Corrupted Sacrifice in Aeschylus' *Oresteia*," *Transactions of the American Philological Association* 96 (1965): 463–508.

H. J. Dirksen, *Die aischyleische Gestalt des Orest* (*Erlanger Beiträge* 22; Nuremberg, 1965).

D. S. Carne-Ross, "Aeschylus in Translation," *Arion* 5.1 (1966): 73–88.

E. Vermeule, "The Boston *Oresteia* Krater," *American Journal of Archaeology* 70 (1966): 1–22.

A. Lebeck (see above, *Imagery*).

D. J. Conacher, "Interaction Between Chorus and Characters in the *Oresteia*," *American Journal of Philology* 95 (1974): 323–43.

P. Vellacott, "Has Good Prevailed? A Further Study of the *Oresteia*," *Harvard Studies in Classical Philology* 81 (1977): 113–22.

F. I. Zeitlin, "The Dynamics of Misogyny: Myth and Mythmaking in the *Oresteia*," *Arethusa* 11 (1978): 149–84.

W. E. Higgins, "Double-Dealing Ares in the *Oresteia*," *Classical Philology* 73 (1978): 24–35.

*Agamemnon*

E. Fraenkel, ed., tr., and comm., *Aeschylus: Agamemnon* (Oxford, 1950).

J. D. Denniston and D. Page, eds. and comms., *Agamemnon* (Oxford, 1956).

L. MacNeice, tr., *The Agamemnon of Aeschylus* (London, 1936).

H. Lloyd-Jones, tr. and comm., *Aeschylus: Agamemnon* (Englewood Cliffs, N.J., 1970).

J. H. Quincey, "The Beacon-Sites in the *Agamemnon*," *Journal of Hellenic Studies* 83 (1963): 118–32.

A. Lesky, "Die Schuld der Klytaimnestra," *Wiener Studien* 1 (1967): 5–21.

J. J. Peradotto, "The Omen of the Eagles and the ETHOS of Agamemnon," *Phoenix* 23 (1969): 237–63.

M. Simpson, "Why Does Agamemnon Yield?" *Parola del Passato* 137 (1971): 94–101.

K. J. Dover, "Some Neglected Aspects of Agamemnon's Dilemma," *Journal of Hellenic Studies* 93 (1973): 58–69.

D. M. Leahy, "The Representation of the Trojan War in Aeschylus' *Agamemnon*," *American Journal of Philology* 95 (1974): 1–23.

M. W. M. Pope, "Merciful Heavens? A Question in Aeschylus' *Agamemnon*," *Journal of Hellenic Studies* 94 (1974): 100–113.

H. Neitzel, "Funktion und Bedeutung des Zeus-Hymnos im *Agamemnon* des Aischylos," *Hermes* 106 (1978): 406–25.

*Libation-Bearers*

U. von Wilamowitz-Moellendorff, ed., tr., and comm., *Aischylos: Orestie II: Das Opfer am Grabe* (Berlin, 1896).

T. G. Tucker, ed., tr., and comm., *The Libation Bearers of Aeschylus* (Cambridge, 1901).

H. Lloyd-Jones, tr. and comm., *Aeschylus: The Libation Bearers* (Englewood Cliffs, N.J., 1970).

W. Schadewaldt, "Der Kommos in Aischylos' *Choephoren*," *Hermes* 67 (1932): 312–54.

F. Solmsen, *Electra and Orestes: Three Recognitions in Greek Tragedy* (*Med. Nederl. Akad., Afd. Letterk.*, n.s. 30.2; Amsterdam, 1967).

A. F. Garvie, "The Opening of the *Choephori*," *Bulletin of the Institute of Classical Studies* 17 (London, 1970): 79–91.

J. Carrière, "Sur deux chants lyriques des *Choéphores*," in *Festschrift für Konstantinos J. Merentitis* (Athens, 1972), pp. 67–74.

*Eumenides*

F. Blass, ed. and comm., *Die Eumeniden des Aischylos* (Berlin, 1907).

P. Groeneboom, ed. and comm., *Aeschylus' Eumeniden* (Groningen, 1952).

H. Lloyd-Jones, tr. and comm., *Aeschylus: The Eumenides* (Englewood Cliffs, N.J., 1970).

K. J. Dover, "The Political Aspects of Aeschylus' *Eumenides*," *Journal of Hellenic Studies* 77.2 (1957): 230–37.

H. J. Dirksen (see above, *The Oresteia*).

R. Dyer, "The Evidence for Apolline Purification Rituals at Delphi and Athens," *Journal of Hellenic Studies* 89 (1969): 38–56.

R. Schottländer, "Um die moralische Qualität des Freispruchs in den *Eumeniden*," *Das Altertum* 16 (1970): 144–53.

*Prometheus*

G. Thomson, ed., tr., and comm., *The Prometheus Bound* (Cambridge, 1932).

W. Buchwald, ed. and comm., *Prometheus* (Bamberg, 1962).

E. A. Havelock, tr. and comm., *The Crucifixion of Intellectual Man* (Boston, 1951).

J. Scully and C. J. Herington, trs., *Prometheus Bound* (New York, 1975).

F. Solmsen 1949 (see above, *Aeschylus as Religious Thinker*).

L. Séchan, *Le mythe de Prométhée* (Paris, 1951).

L. Eckhart, "Prometheus," *Realencyclopädie der classischen Altertumswissenschaft* 23.1 (1957): 653–730.

C. J. Herington, "A Study in the *Prometheia*," *Phoenix* 17 (1963): 180–97; 236–43.

R. Unterberger, *Der Gefesselte Prometheus* (*Tübinger Beiträge* 45; Stuttgart, 1968).

A. Burns, "The Meaning of the *Prometheus Vinctus*," *Classica et Mediaevalia* 27 (1966): 65–78.

C. J. Herington, *The Older Scholia on the Prometheus Bound* (*Mnemosyne Suppl.* 19; Leiden, 1972).

M. Griffith, *The Authenticity of Prometheus Bound* (Cambridge, 1976).

M. L. West, "The Prometheus Trilogy," *Journal of Hellenic Studies* 99 (1979): 130–48.

# INDEX OF PASSAGES CITED

Page references in bold-face signal passages quoted in English or analyzed at some length.

# SUBJECT INDEX

The Index does not cover material cited in the Notes and in the Bibliography. Human and divine characters and mythological data in the plays are also, with a few exceptions, omitted.

action, 311ff; miscueing, 324ff; suspense, 164, 198, 323ff
actors, 48; interpolations of, 11f; male, 51
Aeschylus
  *argumenta*. see Aeschylus, *hypotheseis*
  catalogue of plays, 17
  editions, 12ff
  *hypotheseis* of plays, 17, 373
  *Libation-Bearers*, beginning of, 23
  life, 369ff
  *Life*, 17, 373
  lost plays: *Cabiri*, 219; *Champions at Isthmia*, 32, 270; *Edonians*, 33; *Myrmidonians*, 190; *Niobe*, 74, 190f; *Orithyia*, 105; *Women at Aetne*, 59, 373
  *Prometheus Bound*, authenticity of, 5f
  satyr plays, 19
  text: dislocations of, 24f; emendations of, 26f; intrusive glosses in, 26; lacunae in, 23f; manuscripts, 14; papyri, 19, 373; readings of, 15ff; scholia, 16f, 46, 69; stage directions, 20, 64; transmission of, 11ff
Agatharchus, 58
*agōn*, 334, 357, 359. *See also* trial
*aition*, 284f, 346ff
Alcaeus, 36
Alcman, 188f
Alexandrians, 220
allegory, 132
Amazons, 120, 348
*amoibaion*. *See* encounter
Anacreon, 80
*anankē*. *See* constraint
anapaests. *See* speech, chanted; verse

Anaxagoras, 371
Anderson, Maxwell, 30
answerer, 41
anticipation, 136f
antinomies. *See* opposites
Antiphon, 316
antitheses. *See* opposites
Apuleius, 342
Archilochus, 80, 277
Aristides, 200
Aristophanes, passim
Aristophanes of Byzantium, 20
Aristotle, passim
Artaud, A., 138, 223
*Atē*, 273, 294
Athena, 347ff
Athenaeus, 219
Athens, 369ff; and Argos, 349f, 370; democracy in, 371
Auden, W. H., 30
Augustine, 261, 286
*aulos*, 50
authorial voice, 166ff, 261

Bacchylides, 188
Barthes, R., 15, 255
Beckett, S., 41, 83, 176, 192, 223
Bond, E., 259
Bradley, A. C., 5, 211, 321
Brecht, B., 168, 214
Büchner, G., 84
Burke, K., 129, 293f, 362
buskin, 52
Byron, G. G., 84

Calderón de la Barca, P., 344f
catalogue. *See* inventory

389

Designer:    Barbara Llewellyn
Compositor:  G&S Typesetters, Inc.
Printer:     Braun-Brumfield, Inc.
Binder:      Braun-Brumfield, Inc.
Text:        11/13 Garamond
Display:     Garamond